Brief contents

CONTENTS

GARY HUNTER, TERRY TINTON and CLARE MANNALL

Hospitality Supervision

Level 3 S/NVQ

DELMAR
CENGAGE Learning

Australia • Brazil • Japan • Korea • Mexico • Singapore • Spain • United Kingdom • United States

DELMAR
CENGAGE Learning

Hospitality Supervision, Level 3 S/NVQ
Gary Hunter, Terry Tinton and
Clare Mannall

FE Publisher: Melody Dawes

Development Editor: Rebecca Hussey

Content Project Editor: Lucy Arthy

Head of Manufacturing: Jane Glendening

Production Controller: Paul Herbert

Marketing Manager: Jason Bennett

Typesetter: Macmillan Publishing
Solutions, India

Cover design: HCT Creative, Bramley, UK

Text design: Design Deluxe, Bath, UK

For product information and technology assistance,
contact **emea.info@cengage.com.**

For permission to use material from this text or product,
and for permission queries,
email **clsuk.permissions@cengage.com.**

British Library Cataloguing-in-Publication Data

A catalogue record for this book is available from the British Library.

ISBN: 978-1-4080-0925-3

Cengage Learning EMEA
Cheriton House, North Way, Andover, Hampshire. SP10 5BE.
United Kingdom,

Cengage Learning products are represented in Canada by Nelson Education Ltd.

For your lifelong learning solutions, visit **www.cengage.co.uk**

Purchase your next print book, e-book or e-chapter at **www.ichapters.co.uk**

Printed by Seng Lee Press, Singapore
1 2 3 4 5 6 7 8 9 10 – 12 11 10

Author introductions

GARY HUNTER Gary is the Head of Department for Culinary Arts at Westminster Kingsway College. An award-winning author with extensive experience of the hospitality industry sector, Gary is the chairperson for the London branch of the Professional Association for Catering Education and is an active member of the Academy of Culinary Arts and Craft Guild of Chefs. Travelling the world as a consultant, Gary is also an experienced culinary competition competitor and international judge.

TERRY TINTON is a senior lecturer and course co-ordinator for hospitality and the foundation degree at Westminster Kingsway College. He has spent over twenty years in the hospitality industry, working across Europe and in UK in five-star hotels and Michelin-starred restaurants and is an accomplished author with textbooks used throughout the industry and catering colleges both in the UK and abroad. Terry is responsible for sharing best practice with other colleges and establishments which are being used to raise the standards in hospitality.

CLARE MANNALL Clare is a Curriculum Team Leader for Hospitality Higher Education at Westminster Kingsway College. Clare has a Masters in Hospitality Management and had previously trained in the industry, opting to specialise in finance. Since joining the college in 2000 Clare has become an advocate for employer engagement in the classroom and in assessment. She also maintains the belief that to meet the needs of modern day students, 'anywhere, anytime learning' is now part of their culture and that colleges need to be innovative in the way they present their resources. She is a keen developer of the online resources, piloting online assessment and marking for students in the college and sharing good practice in the wider field of hospitality.

Acknowledgements

The authors and publishers would like to thank the following:

Personal Acknowledgements
For Gary:

Sarah Jane Hunter   Charlotte Hunter   Estelle Hunter
Bev Puxley – for his vision and continued inspiration I am truly indebted
Melody and Lucy – for their enduring and thoughtful support

For Terry:

Margaret Tinton   Lewis Tinton   Ava-Grace Tinton

For Clare:

Ann Mannall   Michael Mannall   Mungo Mannall   Clare Rowland
Rachel Sansom   Bev Boughen

Reviewers

Kerry Davidson
Briege McRory
Adrian Martin
Christophe Baffos

Industry profile contributors

Anneliese K.J. Hainz   Ben Purton   Sirieix Fred   Gerry Clinton
John Williams   Phil Broad   Robyn Jones   Philip E. Corrick

For providing the image for the cover
William 'Bill' Hull, Professional Photography www.billhullphotography.com

For providing images for the book
www.canstockphoto.com   www.istockphoto.com   www.livebookings.co.uk

Every effort has been made to trace the copyright holders, but if any have been inadvertently overlooked the publisher will be pleased to make the necessary arrangements at the first opportunity. Please contact the publisher directly.

Introduction

Hospitality, leisure, travel and tourism is a large and growing sector currently employing nearly 1.4 million people in England. The sector is made up of 14 industries which vary in size with the largest industry – restaurants – employing over 430,000 people.

These figures could be even more successful. The hospitality industry's performance is being undermined by a poor skills record and a review of this by the Sector Skills Council (People 1st) highlighted the following points:

- 54 per cent of managers do not possess the minimum level of qualification required for their position
- 63 per cent of employers believe their staff's customer service skills are not sufficient to meet their needs
- High labour turnover is resulting in a chronic recruitment crisis with 70 per cent of recruitment being undertaken to replace existing staff
- Approximately 50 per cent of sector business start-ups fail within their first three years

It seems that poor management is at the heart of the problem, with independent sector research firmly highlighting poor management and a lack of recognition of the problems as the key reasons why staff are not prepared to stay in the industry.

This book will lead you through a journey with its authors on a discovery of how to supervise and lead a team effectively in a variety of hospitality functions. Its design and industry-relevant information will give you the opportunity to uncover the aspects of leadership you need to succeed in this qualification and influence the wider development of your own career, thus increasing your value to your employer or business.

This book aims to ensure that current and future managers have the appropriate skills and knowledge to manage and develop their workforce and businesses. In order to underpin this it is important that you follow a planned route to this qualification so that your skills are developed and appropriately exploited to meet the increasing needs of clients and business requirements that provide flexibility and initiative for you to use in this industry.

Without sounding too melodramatic, the future of this industry relies on good managers such as you!

Gary Hunter

A quick reference guide to the qualification

NVQs (National Vocational Qualifications) are nationally recognised and follow a common structure and design across all vocational subjects. To be awarded an NVQ/SVQ demonstrates that you have the competence (having sufficient skill and knowledge) to perform a job at a certain level. **Assessment** will take place once you and your assessor consider you to be competent.

Each NVQ/SVQ is divided into **units**. The unit relates to a specific task or skill area of work. The **element/s** that make up a unit describe in detail the **skill and knowledge** components of the unit. To pass a particular unit you will need to accomplish various tasks.

- *What you must do* – gives information on the actions to be undertaken to pass each element within a unit.
- *What you must cover* – gives a range of situations and tasks for you to cover.
- *What you have to know* – this is the underpinning knowledge or theory section that proves you understand the subject covered in the element.
- *Evidence requirement* – this addresses how much you need to cover by assessment using observation and alternative methods of assessment.

To achieve an NVQ/SVQ there will be a set of specific tasks and processes to go through.

1 At the commencement of any programme of study you should receive an **induction**. This will give you a detailed explanation of the qualification and the support that is available for you to use.

2 An **initial assessment** should be undertaken to assess your current degree of understanding and skills level for the qualification and to set out an action plan of the particular units you will undertake to complete the NVQ/SVQ. This assessment system will also identify specific areas of training and teaching that you will require.

3 Your competence and ability to carry out a task will be **assessed** by your assessor when you both consider you to be ready. Your assessor will regularly observe the tasks that you are carrying out, the outcomes of which will be recorded into your **portfolio of evidence**.

4   Your understanding and the background knowledge of the unit subject is also measured through questions asked by your assessor. The questions are usually required to be answered in a written format or verbally and then recorded in your portfolio of evidence. This is known as **underpinning knowledge**. The activities and theory covered in this book will provide you with plenty of examples, knowledge and practice to help with these.

5   The portfolio of evidence will be eventually completed by you and your assessor. It is designed to help you demonstrate your competence at a particular level. At this stage and usually during the process of training and assessment an **internal verifier** will check the consistency of the assessor's work.

6   Finally the **awarding body** (the body responsible for checking the qualification and awarding you the certificate) will appoint an **external moderator** to carry out final checks before certification.

This book will cover the breadth of knowledge and skills necessary to meet the qualification requirements at NVQ/SVQ Level 3. Moreover it will give you the opportunity to enhance your knowledge of the industry with modern up-to-date hospitality skills, supervision and leadership techniques alongside classical skills that are the fundamentals of a good leader.

Technical certificate

Level 3 Award in Hospitality Supervision and Leadership Principles

Structure of the Qualification

To achieve the Level 3 Award in Hospitality Supervision and Leadership Principles, you must pass a total of **two** units.

1 Principles of Leading a Team in the Hospitality Industry.
2 Supervision of Operations in the Hospitality Industry.

Principles of leading a team in the hospitality industry

Level: 3

Credit value: 3

The aim of this unit is to provide the learner with the knowledge and skills to work effectively safely and legally within the complementary and integrated healthcare sector.

The skills developed by the learner include: communication skills, written skills, research skills and accountability. The knowledge acquired by the learner will enable them to understand and explain the key legislation that applies to professional practice within complementary therapy.

Learning outcomes

There are **four** learning outcome to this unit. The candidate will:

1 Know the different types of hospitality organisations.
2 Understand the need for effective communication.
3 Understand how to lead a team effectively.
4 Understand factors that impact on the hospitality industry.

Supervision of operations in the hospitality industry

Level: 3

Credit value: 3

The aim of this unit is to provide the learner with the knowledge and skills to work effectively safely and legally within the complementary and integrated healthcare sector.

The skills developed by the learner include: communication skills, written skills, research skills and accountability. The knowledge acquired by the learner will enable them to understand and explain the key legislation that applies to professional practice within complementary therapy.

Learning outcomes

There are **three** learning outcomes to this unit. The candidate will:

1 Understand customer service supervision.

2 Understand the principles of stock control.

3 Understand how to use resources effectively.

You will be able to find reference to these associated technical skills within the book as you work through it which will help you to identify the skills required to conclude these units.

Wherever you see the symbol (right) in the book, it indicates the relevant information for this part of the qualification.

What you must do

The performance criteria of an NVQ/SVQ will list the required actions that you must achieve to complete a task in a competent manner. This means demonstrating the practical skill in an acceptable, professional and safe way to your assessor. In all NVQ/SVQ portfolios this is now stated in the form of 'what you have to do'.

As an example the what you must do the criteria for unit HS10 Supervise the food service states that to achieve the national standard the candidate must be able to achieve some of the following statements:

1 Make sure you have relevant up-to-date information about food safety procedures.
2 Carry out your own responsibilities for the implementation of food safety procedures.
3 Make sure that good hygiene practices are in place in your area of responsibility and that all work complies with organisational procedures, food safety guidelines and legal requirements.
4 Ensure staff have the required skills, knowledge and resources to carry out their work.
5 Check service equipment is ready for use and correctly located and that service areas are stocked in preparation for service.
6 Make sure staff follows the procedures for clearing, cleaning and stocking service areas.

All of these criteria must be adequately assessed against the next stage called 'behaviours which underpin effective performance'.

Behaviours which underpin effective performance

This next section states clearly exactly what skills should be covered on a range of different types of behaviour required to maximise your performance in the supervision of the food service operation. The unit covers the following as an example:

1 You identify people's information needs.

2 You comply with, and ensure others comply with, legal requirements, industry regulations, organisational policies and professional codes.

3 You are vigilant for possible risks and hazards.

4 You clearly agree what is expected of others and hold them to account.

It is important to understand that all of the features have to be assessed in order to pass the unit. The NVQ/SVQ portfolio will normally state the minimum requirements that are needed to pass the unit through observation of the physical task and how the rest of the assessments can be covered, usually by professional witness statements or questioning.

What you have to know

Further assessment of a candidate's knowledge and understanding of the skills relating to the unit may be assessed through theoretical tasks such as questions or assignments. This stage is known as the 'what you have to know' section. Any questioning should be performed under certain test conditions that have been set by the Sector Skills Council (People 1st);

■ In an environment that the candidate feels comfortable to take the assessment

■ That it supervised to ensure the assessment is authentic

■ That it is conducted in line with the appropriate Awarding Body guidelines

Assignments can also be used under the assessment strategy. The strategy allows centres to use materials that have been developed, and the use of assignments is an option within this.

A centre wishing to use an assignment will need to get the Awarding Body's prior approval before using the assignment. Assignments will also need to be administered within controlled conditions by the centre or college.

Witness testimony

Testimonies are used as a type of supplementary evidence whereby they can confirm performance evidence in two ways:

1 *Witness testimony*, for example from a customer, supplier or colleague that provides evidence towards a candidate's assessment, or

2 *Expert witness testimony* that provides authoritative evidence of competence, which maybe sufficient for an assessor to consider that competence has been proved.

Expert witnesses may be other approved assessors who are recognised to assess the relevant occupational area and level, or line managers, who may not be approved assessors but whom the awarding body agrees has sufficient occupational qualifications or experience to make a judgement on the competence of a candidate. Expert witness testimony must be used in line with all awarding body requirements.

Mapped to the qualification
Each chapter addresses a specific unit of the Level 3 Hospitality Supervision S/NVQ qualification.

Glossary

24-hour service Round the clock continual service for consumers.

Accommodation services Can also be referred to as 'room division'. This refers to individual departments who are responsible for the upkeep and selling of rooms within the establishment.

Active documentation This term is used to describe the paperwork or files being used at the present time in relation to a function, e.g. the booking sheets, menus.

Advanced deposit This term refers to a set amount of money paid to secure the event. This will ensure the room is not double-booked.

Allergy An acquired, abnormal immune response to a substance that can cause a broad range of inflammatory reactions.

Ambience The mix of background noise and other reflected sounds that make up a room's character.

Appellation A geographical indication used to identify where the grapes for a wine were grown.

Appraisal A judgment or assessment of the professional performance of someone, especially a subordinate.

Assessment This is when a person is given a task to carry out and a judgement will be made on how they performed.

Audit A review, check or inspection of something, such as a process or goods.

Auditory To do with the sense of hearing.

Bill of fare Menu: a list of dishes available at a restaurant.

Blacklisted This term refers to guests who have been systematically barred from the establishment for non-payment of the bill or unacceptable behaviour.

Bulk checkout This refers to groups of guests whose accommodation and any other authorised services are charged back to the tour operator.

Carbon footprint A measure of the impact that human activities have on the environment in terms of the amount of emitted carbon dioxide.

Cask-conditioned beer The cask is a barrel made of aluminium, stainless steel or oak, used to store beer.

Cellar A room used to store beer and drinks, sometimes found in the basement, underground.

Cheques These are carried by the customer and filled in to pay for goods, they are usually backed up with a guarantee card issued by the bank.

Chip and PIN The system used by the customer to input a PIN code when paying for goods or services.

Cleaning frequencies The amount of time an area or item needs cleaning and how often.

Cleaning schedule A permanent list of all the cleaning task to be completed and the frequency of those cleans.

Colleagues An associate that one works with – a workplace team member.

Communication This term refers to the transfer of information, verbally, physically or via another means such as email.

Communication barrier Poor communication skills such as poor language, listening, noise, prejudice or verbal skills.

Competence The level at which an individual is able to carry out a skill effectively without supervision.

Concierge This name refers to the person or persons who are in charge of the portering.

Conference groups This refers to groups of guests who are attending a conference, this can be internal or external.

Confidential information Information that you should only share with certain people, for example your manager or personnel officer.

Consensus General agreement.

Contingency plans Plans that allow you to identify and plan for things that may go wrong. Back-up plans.

Control points In reference to the HACCP system these are the steps at which food safety could be compromised and therefore action need to be taken.

Controlling This refers to the information made available to the management team for decision-making purposes.

CPD Continuing professional development.

Credit check This check is occasionally used to ensure the organiser has sufficient funds to pay for the event.

Criteria This is the measurement by which an assessment takes place.

CRM Customer relation management.

Cross-contamination The transfer of pathogens from a contaminated food or surface to another food either directly or indirectly.

CRS Central reservation system.

Customer requirements Understanding and determining what the customer expectations and needs are on an individual basis.

Customers These include individual clients, plus other departments within your organisation and external organisations to whom you may provide a service.

Glossary
A relevant, easy-to-use glossary at the back of the book explains specialist industry terms in an approachable way.

Assessment of knowledge and understanding
at the end of each chapter contains questions, so you can test your learning.

1
Provide leadership for your team

HS1 Provide leadership for your team
LEARNING OBJECTIVES
This unit is about providing direction to hospitality staff and motivating and supporting them so that they can achieve the objectives of the team as well as their personal work objectives.

After reading this chapter you will be able to:

- Set out and positively communicate the purpose and objectives of the team to all members.
- Involve members in planning how the team will achieve its objectives.
- Ensure that each member of the team has personal work objectives and understands how achieving these contributes to achievement of the team's objectives.
- Encourage and support team members to achieve their personal work objectives and those of the team and provide recognition when objectives have been achieved.
- Win, through your performance, the trust and support of the team for your leadership.
- Steer the team successfully through difficulties and challenges, including conflict within the team.
- Encourage and recognise creativity and innovation within the team.
- Give team members support and advice when they need it, especially during periods of setback and change.
- Motivate team members to present their own ideas and listen to what they say.

Cycle for purchasing goods

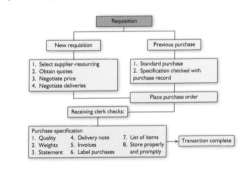

473

Learning objectives
at the start of each chapter explain the skills and knowledge you need to be proficient in and understand by the end of the chapter.

Helpful features
Informative diagrams, a concise glossary and industry case studies all help to deepen understanding of key topics.

Assessment of knowledge and understanding

You have now learnt about some key elements involved in the use of technological equipment in the hospitality industry.

As you have worked through the chapter you have already discussed some elements of technology, but to test your level of knowledge and understanding further, answer the following short questions. These will help to prepare you for your summative (final) assessment.

1. What are peripherals?

2. Name at least three input devices used in hospitality.

3. What are the main operations of spreadsheet application?

4. What is difference between POS and EPOS?

5. What operations and tasks can be supported with computer technology in the front of house?

6. What are the main characteristics of reservation systems?

Industry profiles provide advice from leading industry figures, and an insight into what has motivated them throughout their training and career.

INDUSTRY PROFILE

Name: ROBYN JONES

Position: Co-founder and Chief Executive

Establishment: Charlton House Catering Services Ltd

Current job role and main responsibilities: I am responsible for the strategic growth of the company and for driving innovations to ensure that our food and service standards remain at the cutting edge of the contract catering sector.

Can you describe how you present a strong leadership example for your team at Charlton House?
I work tirelessly to get things right. In this business you are only as good as your last meal so I feel very passionate about keeping standards high. There is a great sense of pride within Charlton House, which in turn leads to a motivated, passionate team and a happy customer base.

When did you realise that you wanted to pursue a career in the hospitality industry?
From a very early age. I have always loved cooking and knew that I wanted to work in hospitality on leaving school.

Training: (detailing any college training/apprenticeship and where you started out)
I completed an OND in Hotel Catering and Institutional Management at High Peak College in Buxton, Derbyshire, followed by a HCIMA in Hotel Catering and Institutional Management at Norwich City College.

What do you find rewarding about your job?
I get a great buzz when clients are delighted with what we provide and when someone in the company comes to me with a new idea or innovation. The business is evolving all of the time and it's great when other people share our passion and interest. We are known for our cutting edge approach to food in the workplace so it's important that we seek out new ways of exciting and satisfying our customers.

What advice would you give to students just beginning their career?
Follow your dreams and never give up. If you really feel that you want to do something, then just do it. Put all of your efforts into making it successful. If you work hard now, you can play hard in years to come.

Who is your mentor or main inspiration?
I have a quote on my wall by Sir Winston Churchill: 'Never, never, never give up'. That says it all.

What traits do you consider essential for anyone entering a career in the hospitality sector?
Attention to detail and a sense of pride. Food and service standards have to be impeccable. People are so discerning these days and second best will never be acceptable. I think it's important to give it your all, whether you work back of house or front of house.

A brief personal profile: (explain your interests and achievements to date)
I am a trustee of the PM Trust and a patron of the Association of Catering Excellence. I am also a guardian member of Hospitality In Action, a benevolent organisation for people within the hospitality industry. I was named the Credit Suisse Outstanding Woman in Business at the National Business Awards 2006 and appeared in 29th place in the CatererSearch 100 league table of the UK's 100 most influential people in hospitality.

Charlton House now has a current annual turnover of £75 million and we employ 1,900 people nationwide. One of our recent highlights was to win a Cateys award, the hospitality industry's equivalent to an Oscar. In 2006 we were named Cost Sector Caterer of the Year and last year we were listed fourth in an industry poll of Britain's top 50 companies within the hospitality sector. We won our second Cost Sector Catering Award this year for a company-wide marketing initiative.

Juggling work with the needs of our two young children keeps me busy, but in my spare time I love to cook, swim and travel.

Can you give one essential management tip or piece of industry advice?
Always deliver your promises.

Key words at the beginning of each chapter define key terms relating to the unit.

KEY WORDS

Brainstorming
A group creativity technique designed to generate a large number of ideas for the solution to a problem. The method was first popularised in the late 1930s by Alex Faickney Osborn in a book called *Applied Imagination*.

Carbon footprint
A 'measure of the impact that human activities have on the environment in terms of the amount of greenhouse gases produced, measured in units of carbon dioxide'. These gases are produced by the burning of fossil fuels for our everyday living. For example, heating and electricity: its purpose is for individuals, nations and organisations to conceptualise their personal (or organisational) carbon dioxide contribution.

Demographics
Refers to selected population characteristics including race, age, income, disabilities, educational attainment, home ownership, employment status and even location.

Economy
The social system of a country's revenue based on their ability to produce, exchange, distribute and consume goods and services. An economy is the result of a process that involves the uses of the country's technology, history, geography and natural resources among other factors.

Social responsibility
An ethical or ideological theory that a government, corporation, organisation or individual has a responsibility to behave appropriately towards the rest of society

Sociology
The scientific study of individual behaviour in society.

Sustainable
The ability to maintain a certain process or state, i.e. to sustain the existing environment.

Activity boxes help you explore and research the industry and put your knowledge into practice.

ACTIVITY

Create a departmental induction booklet which covers all of the above induction training. To interest all staff make sure that it is easy to read, and includes colour and pictures.

Remember boxes draw your attention to important and relevant information.

! REMEMBER

A registration card must be completed on arrival for several reasons:

- By the Immigration (Hotel Records) Order 1972 it is a legal requirement that everyone over the age of 16 who books sleeping accommodation in return for payment, completes a registration form giving full name and nationality
- Customers who are not British have to give additional information such as passport number, place of issue, next destination and full address
- Customer accounts can be accurately made up
- Helps internal audit processes
- Information can be gained for the sales department
- In an emergency, an exact record of customers is required

Tip boxes share the authors' experiences of the industry, with helpful suggestions for how you can improve your skills.

 TIP

People that write down their goals in a SMART format are more likely to achieve them.

Just imagine what you could achieve if you put your mind to it!

1

Provide leadership for your team

Provide leadership for your team

LEARNING OBJECTIVES

This unit is about providing direction to hospitality staff and motivating and supporting them so that they can achieve the objectives of the team as well as their personal work objectives.

After reading this chapter you will be able to:

- Set out and positively communicate the purpose and objectives of the team to all members.
- Involve members in planning how the team will achieve its objectives.
- Ensure that each member of the team has personal work objectives and understands how achieving these contributes to achievement of the team's objectives.
- Encourage and support team members to achieve their personal work objectives and those of the team and provide recognition when objectives have been achieved.
- Win, through your performance, the trust and support of the team for your leadership.
- Steer the team successfully through difficulties and challenges, including conflict within the team.
- Encourage and recognise creativity and innovation within the team.
- Give team members support and advice when they need it, especially during periods of setback and change.
- Motivate team members to present their own ideas and listen to what they say.

■ Encourage team members to take the lead when they have the knowledge and expertise and show willingness to follow this lead.

■ Monitor activities and progress across the team without interfering.

KEY WORDS

Communication
This term refers to the transfer of information, verbally, physically or via another means such as email.

Controlling
This refers to the information made available to the management team for decision-making purposes.

Decision making
This refers to the point at which a person chooses an option from the list of suitable choices.

Effectiveness
Ensuring that all tasks are executed with optimum efficiency to ensure the targets are met and if possible exceeded.

Efficiency
When a task is completed to its optimum level by using the minimum amount of resources possible; thus ensuring optimum efficiency.

Leadership
This refers to a person who influences another person; using positive reinforcement to motivate and train.

Management
The process associated with organising work, people and events to run in a controlled efficient manner.

Motivating
The way in which a person steers his or her colleagues and staff to achieve their goals to the best of their ability. Motivation is all about behaviour.

Organising
The effective organised way in which predetermined goals are achieved, ensuring that all jobs are accounted for, tracked and completed to the best of the establishment's ability.

Planning
The process used to ascertain what goals are required, what is needed and how they will be achieved.

INTRODUCTION

Leadership can be defined as: *'the position or function of a leader'. For example, he managed to maintain his leadership of the party despite heavy opposition.*

Within the hospitality industry no one individual works alone: each and every person is both responsible to others within their team.

The diverse nature of the hospitality industry ensures that it is very unlikely that a task is carried out by a single person; there is usually at least one other helping to prepare, serve, clear or manage.

This gives a leader the opportunity to help steer the group towards achieving their goal.

THE ESSENTIALS OF GOOD LEADERSHIP

Some say that leaders are born and leadership cannot be learnt. A good leader should have experienced working from the bottom up, because a sound understanding of the hospitality industry will assist you in delivering the highest possible service.

Within the hospitality industry the one singular leadership trait is excellent interpersonal skills. These include listening, questioning, negotiating and interaction with both guests and employees.

As leaders grow within an organisation they use their technical skills less and less as these are replaced by other more conceptual and cognitive skills.

When identifying a good leader or assessing your own performance there are numerous key points worth considering:

© ISTOCKPHOTO.COM/JACOB WACKERHAUSEN

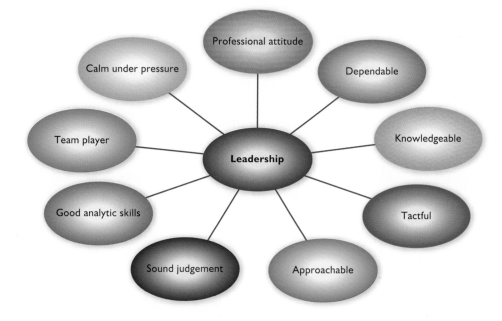

Leadership is a skill that requires practice and dedication; enthusing staff and ensuring the team stays focused on the common goal are major factors.

A leader should be:

- ■ Challenging – ensuring that you look for opportunities to improve, taking calculated risks to expand and develop the business
- ■ Inspirational – motivating staff, sharing your vision for the business and future, empowering them at all levels
- ■ Leading by example – set guidelines, work in a professional inspirational way
- ■ Open to discussion – share best practice, discuss improvements in a controlled professional manner

Leadership is often defined in two ways as either transactional and transformational leadership: this definition was developed over years of research and evaluation. A leader meets certain criteria which are then assigned either way.

A transactional leader

This refers to the way in which a leader achieves their goals; by using behaviour, incentives and rewards to motivate staff. The term transaction is the same as in a business transaction where one person receives an exchange or payment for goods or services offered. The diagram, shown left is an example of how the transactional cycle works.

An example of this in the current industry would be when waiters in restaurants work on a commission basis based on the quantity of items that they sell. Restaurants such as T.G.I. Friday's use this as a tool to both motivate and retain their waiting and bar staff.

A transactional cycle

A transformational leader

A transformational leader has the ability to assess, develop and eventually change the behaviour and mindset of the team over a long period of time. This type of leadership is highly sought after, as it enables the business to achieve a common goal amongst all staff members: to exceed their own expectations and deliver a first class package.

A successful leader will work with staff to ensure motivation and encouragement and to make the staff feel respected in their day-to-day work.

Three factors which are essential in becoming a transformational leader:

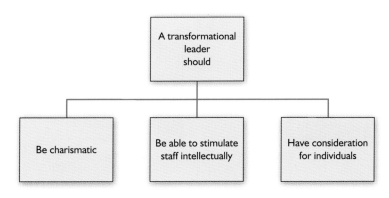

A leader who can achieve a balance between both transactional and transformational will ensure not only that the business prospers but that they will too.

A motivated team

LEADERSHIP AND ITS DEMANDS

A leader has to be able to cope with pressure from all directions and ensure that they maintain a cool façade. There are two aspects of a leader's job which they must come to terms with very quickly:

- Meeting set targets and achieving goals
- Maintaining and developing positive working relationships

Unfortunately the two are not always easy to achieve together, and a target may require increasing a person's workload.

In the hospitality industry there are many intrinsic and extrinsic factors that a leader must manage, such as:

- The owner's requirements
- Guests
- Employees
- Competitors
- The head office
- Market fluctuations, e.g. costs

For a leader the traits that should be acquired over time are:

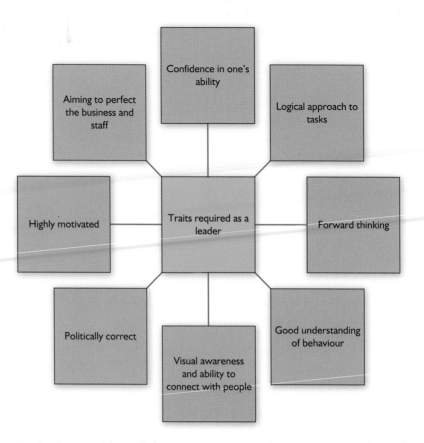

Every leader has an idea of the correct approach to management and will have stronger values in one particular area than others.

As a leader it is imperative that you ensure positive working relationships are developed and nurtured; an enthused workforce will increase productivity and improve customer service. Staff members are essential within the business and a leader can only function when there is staff to work with!

Management

The role of a manager is diverse and varies from establishment to establishment; it may include:

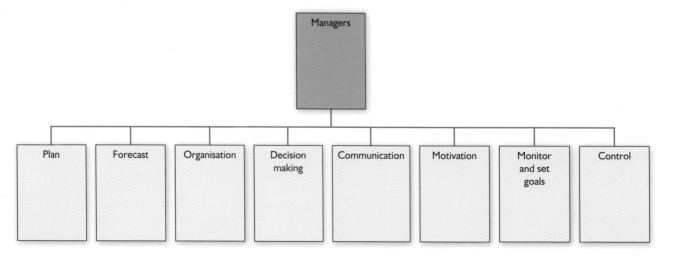

A manager will determine in the direction in which the establishment is heading: this is achieved with experience, staff and external consultation. There are many different styles of management, some of which will now examine.

Autocratic. This is when the single manager or management team make all the decisions and the workforce are expected to do exactly as required. This method can decrease motivation as the employees have no say in their working environment. The advantage to this approach is that the business will remain constant.

Paternalistic. This is when decisions are made more in the interests of the employees rather than to meet the needs of the business. Resulting motivation amongst employees may be high but productivity can be low.

Democratic. This style encourages employees to be part of the decision-making process. It can help complex changes occur in a business as the employees have already bought into the change. However, this style can be long-winded and does not always achieve the best outcomes for the business.

Laissez-faire. This style is more common in businesses which are scattered across individual units. It leaves individuals responsible for their own areas of the business. This style is great for high-performing groups but can also be a sign of bad management.

© ISTOCKPHOTO.COM/JACOB WACKERHAUSEN

No one style is better than the others, and a good manager should be able to identify the different styles and how best to use them across their teams.

Assessment of knowledge and understanding

The following projects, activities and assessments are directly linked to the essential knowledge and understanding for unit HS1.

Make sure that you keep this for easier referencing along with your work for future inclusion in your portfolio.

Leadership

■ There are three factors that are associated with a transformational leader: describe them.

■ List five examples of leadership qualities.

■ Can you describe four of the demands placed on leaders?

■ Can you give a brief explanation of a leader?

Research task

Using a leading industry figure, give two examples of decisions that they have had to make within their company. How you would imagine the style of leader that they are has impacted on these decisions?

2

Develop productive working relationships with colleagues

HS2 Develop productive working relationships with colleagues

LEARNING OBJECTIVES

This unit is about developing working relationships with colleagues within both your own organisation and other organisations, which are productive in terms of supporting and delivering your work and that of the overall organisation. 'Colleagues' are any people you are expected to work with, whether they are at a similar position or in other positions.

After reading this chapter you will be able to:

■ Establish working relationships with all colleagues who are relevant to the work being carried out.

■ Recognise, agree and respect the roles and responsibilities of colleagues.

■ Understand and take account of the priorities, expectations, and authority of colleagues in decisions and actions.

■ Fulfil agreements made with colleagues and communicate.

■ Advise colleagues promptly of any difficulties or where it will be impossible to fulfil agreements.

■ Identify and sort out conflicts of interest and disagreements with colleagues in ways that minimise damage to the work being carried out.

■ Exchange information and resources with colleagues to make sure that all parties can work effectively.

■ Provide feedback to colleagues on their performance and seek feedback from colleagues on your own performance in order to identify areas for improvement.

KEY WORDS

Colleagues
An associate that one works with – a workplace team member.

Communication
This term refers to the transfer of information, verbally, physically or via another means such as email.

Confidential information
Information that you should only share with certain people, for example your manager or personnel officer.

Customers
These include individual clients, plus other departments within your organisation and external organisations to whom you may provide a service (internal and external users of your service).

Diversity
When there are people you work with who belong to different races, cultures, religions or who have specific needs.

Empathising
Understanding and having compassion in a particular situation.

Feedback
The process of sharing observations, concerns and suggestions between persons or divisions of the organisation with the intention of improving both personal and organisational performance.

Information management
Present information clearly, accurately and in ways that promote understanding.

Limits of your authority
What you can and cannot do according to your organisation's standard procedures.

Motivate
Help staff to feel enthusiastic about their jobs and keen to achieve high standards.

People from outside your organisation
This could include delivery people, contractors, clients, investors or inspectors

Positive image
This covers personal appearance, behaviour and the way you communicate with customers.

Prioritising
Placing the main concerns or more important matters for their first attention before others.

INTRODUCTION

Hospitality is a people industry. Positive working relationships between colleagues and between staff and customers are an essential element of making the organisation work effectively. Anything that does not reflect a positive working relationship in your area of work will inevitably create discontent within the team, resulting in customer dissatisfaction and poor teamwork.

These issues can damage your organisation's efficiency and the vital relationship with the client. As a supervisor or manager you will be in the front line of this process every day, acting as a decisive link between the business and other employees. You will also be the first point of contact between the client and your manager.

To work in the hospitality industry, you have to be capable of developing effective relationships with people. These are the people you work for, the people you work with, and the people you provide services for. These skills can be taught; but they require a measure of endeavour and motivation to succeed. An enthusiastic person with a lower skill level is superior to a highly trained person with an indifferent attitude.

The main aim of a business is to satisfy or exceed the customer's expectations, which will help to build the organisation. This can only be done by the individuals in the group working as a coherent team.

WHAT IS AN EFFECTIVE RELATIONSHIP?

In an effective working relationship groups listen to and understand others' positions and opinions. The easy way to understand what is important to another colleague or to a group is to ask and then *listen* to the answer. We understand when someone else is really interested in our opinion. The other person is attentive, does not interrupt, does not fidget and does not speak about themselves. This makes us feel accepted, rather than judged. Listening leads to understanding; if you understand someone else fully, then you distinguish what needs to be done to work better together.

In effective relationships, colleagues can openly express their positions and beliefs. To make our relationships more effective, we should treat ourselves and each other with respect. Respect is the hub of any accomplished relationship. We show respect by listening to the other person and by trying to understand how they view things. Quickly forming judgements based on prejudice is the complete opposite of respect. You can respect people (even if you find their behaviour difficult to understand) by acknowledging that they are doing the best they can when their circumstances and history are taken into account.

Respect is the key foundation for a strong working relationship, and self-respect will enhance your views on your colleagues and the organisation. It will be much easier to see positive aspects in colleagues and treat them with due respect.

Another means of forming effective relationships is to confront differences directly. Differences between colleagues create a diverse environment. In a meeting where each person pays full attention to the other colleagues, they may discover a new fact that integrates two opposing perspectives. This is more rewarding than the alternatives – for example, withdrawing, becoming rebellious, or complaining to someone else. Learning to understand differences takes time and can be uncomfortable, but confronting and attempting to understand them is a good learning exercise.

What can help to build effective working relationships?

1 *At least one colleague should decide the relationship is important.* If we decide a relationship is important, then we will invest time and energy in trying to understand the needs of the relationship and to work around any barriers to the association.

2 *Learn to listen effectively, and without judgement.* Effective and non-judgemental listening will help us to understand the other person or team. When someone listens to you, both your own sense of worth and the worth of the listener increases. Judging another person almost always creates distance and defensiveness.

Building an effective working relationship is an important piece of the jigsaw of team building

3 *Meet people informally, so they feel comfortable raising issues that are important to them.* Most colleagues will feel more comfortable in informal settings. If you are intending to meet with someone with the specific purpose of developing your relationship with that person, think about holding the meeting in a setting in which they will feel comfortable. When people are relaxed they are more able to speak about what is important to them.

4 *Develop a culture whereby people can express their feelings.* We create relationships by sharing thoughts and feelings. When we express happiness, joy, contentment, anger, irritation, sadness or fear we feel more vulnerable, but we can also feel more connected. Unexpressed feelings can get in the way of building closeness. Organisational cultures that encourage people to connect can generate an ardent commitment to achieve the organisation's objectives together.

ESTABLISHING WORKING AND ROLE RELATIONSHIPS

In order that your organisation can achieve its aims and objectives, the work of the individual must be linked into coherent patterns of activities and relationships. This can be achieved through the 'role' structure of the organisation.

The concept of a role is important to the function of groups or teams. A role is the expected behaviour pattern associated with individual members who occupy a specific position within the structure of the organisation. It is through this role differentiation that the structure of the group and relationships of its members are established.

Some form of structure is necessary for good examples of teamwork to thrive and for co-operation to exist within the team. The concept of roles helps to define the pattern of complex relationships within the group and to clarify its structure. The role that the individual plays within the group is often influenced by a combination of:

PHOTOGRAPHY: REBECCA HUSSEY

- *Situational factors*; such as the requirements of a task, the style of leadership and the needs of the organisation
- *Personal factors*; such as values, attitudes, ability, personality and motivation

In any organisational team or group certain formal relationships between individual positions will occur from the defined responsibilities. Mullins (2001) has described these as *individual authority relationships* and they are defined as:

- Line
- Functional
- Staff
- Lateral

The design of the structure of the team or group in an organisation in terms of these principles will determine the pattern of working relationships and interactions with other roles.

Line relationships are created with an authority line that flows vertically down through the team or group structure. This is sometimes referred to as the 'chain of command', for example from the managing director to the managers, section leaders, supervisors and other staff. There is a direct relationship between superior and subordinate, with each subordinate responsible to only one person. Line relationship structures are generally associated with a kitchen brigade in a hotel or the front of house team in a restaurant.

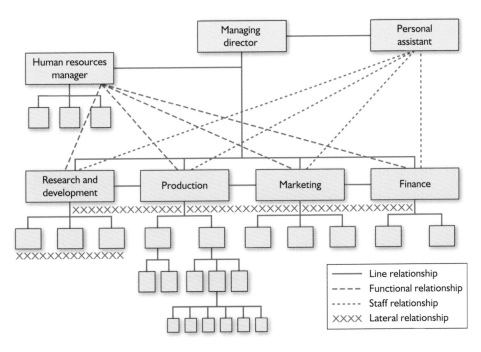

A diagram of formal organisational relationships

Functional relationships are those between people in specialist or consultant positions. The specialist offers a common service throughout all departments of the organisation, but has no direct authority over staff in other departments. An example is the position of the human resources manager, who is usually sanctioned by the managing director, so in this case other staff might be expected to accept advice which is given. It is also important to note that specialists in a functional relationship with other managers will still have a line relationship with both their own superior and their own departmental team.

Staff relationships arise from the appointment of personal assistants to senior members of staff. People in a staff position normally have little direct authority in their own right but act as an extension of their superior and can exercise representative authority. There is no formal relationship between the personal assistant and other staff except where delegated responsibility has been given for a specific duty or task.

Lateral relationships exist between individuals in different departments or sections and especially individuals on the same level. These lateral relationships are based on contact and consultation is necessary to maintain effective organisational performance. Lateral relationships may be formal, but they depend upon the co-operation of staff and in effect are a type of informal relationship.

THE IMPORTANCE OF TEAMWORK

How people behave and perform as members of a group or team is as important as their behaviour or performance as individuals. Harmonious working relationships and good teamwork help to create a high level of staff morale and work performance. Effective teamwork is an essential element of management practice, for example in the use of empowerment. Teamwork is important in any organisation but may be especially significant in the hospitality industry where there is a direct impact on customer satisfaction.

Effective teamwork will improve organisational competitiveness by:

- ■ Improving productivity
- ■ Improving quality and encouraging innovation
- ■ Taking advantage of the opportunities provided by technological advances
- ■ Improving employee motivation and commitment

> **! REFLECTION**
>
> How do you think that managers in a hospitality organisation might best achieve a high group performance? What would you do to improve teamwork?

Recent studies from some of Europe's top companies have shown that there is a need for new managers and new methods of management to meet the demands of a dramatically changed business environment, and that making teamwork effective is a new and indispensable skill.

Groups and teamworking are an essential and integral part of the organisation. People will always value their individuality and their own identity, but the real skill of management is to use people's individuality for the mutual benefit of the group as a whole.

DEVELOPING POSITIVE WORKING RELATIONSHIPS

Just as the organisation's managers must retain, develop and look to continuously improve the quality of its physical resources, marketing performance, financial health and business capabilities, so they must also take the same approach to developing working relationships between themselves and all other internal and external partners in the organisation. For the organisation to achieve its operational targets and strategic objectives, it is essential that all working relationships are healthy and productive and continuously improving. The leaders of the organisation must ensure that this is the case.

© ISTOCKPHOTO.COM/JACOB WACKERHAUSEN

To develop positive working relationships there are essentially five areas that need to be addressed, and these will now be examined.

Maintaining high standards of personal behaviour

The reasoning is that by:

- ■ Maintaining high standards of personal beliefs
- ■ Behaving with integrity and fairness

■ Behaving ethically, and

■ Showing respect and sensitivity for the views of others

the leader aspires to be a role model for high standards of personal behaviour, so that they are ultimately trusted by colleagues and stakeholders.

Establishing effective communication systems

Effective communication systems are the essential foundation blocks on which positive relationships can be built so that consultative and participative decisions can be made at all levels. By establishing a structure that supports communication and collaboration between internal and external individuals and groups, managers can successfully ensure that key information reaches appropriate people in a timely manner. Without this underlying framework in place, information will be dissipated and misinterpreted, decisions will be based on inadequate information, and relationships will invariably deteriorate.

Promoting values and standards

Ensuring that all working relationships are assembled and developed against a background of shared values and standards and that all parties are aware that the value of internal and external relationships is important. Leaders will also identify and establish a set of appropriate values and standards for the organisation. Taking prompt and visible action when established values and standards have not been maintained is critical to the maintenance of standardisation.

Gaining the trust of colleagues

This is vital in enabling the leader to draw the best performance from colleagues, and for those colleagues to achieve their personal performance targets. Managers should work with colleagues in a way which demonstrates the leader's commitment to the values and standards of the organisation, and in a manner which demonstrates to colleagues that they have the respect and support of their leader.

Gaining the trust of external stakeholders can be just as important, by consulting with stakeholders and keeping them appropriately informed about the organisation's progress. The aim is to behave with stakeholder in an honest, open and positive manner. For the relationship between the organisation and the stakeholder to be successful, there must be mutual understanding, mutual respect and a desire to develop a relationship that is beneficial to both parties. This is essential in all external relationships and particularly critical when the relationship is intended to be long term.

> **! REMEMBER**
>
> **Employment Policy Institute:**
> 'Changes in working methods and technology have had a profound effect on work. People who work well in groups, are well organised and can solve their problems are the people who get on best at work and get promoted.'

Evaluation of relationship performance

Regular and thorough assessments of the condition of relationships are vital. Without these evaluations and suitable corrective action, many relationships will deteriorate. Some will remain in a poor condition, causing a constant flow of minor business difficulties: some will implode and cause major problems. These problems can be avoided by a regular health-check on each set of relationships followed by appropriate action. This can be done by setting clear quality criteria for the assessment of the condition of relationships, establishing monitoring procedures which include scheduled evaluation review points and insisting that evaluation reviews are carried out even though the relationship appears to be healthy.

COMMUNICATION

Communication is an elementary building block with which the organisation can succeed and grow. It can be as simple as a conversation between chefs, waiters, food and beverage managers or customers; but each is as fundamental as the next.

Good communication is essential

Organisational communication generally is people working together to achieve individual or shared goals.

Effective organisational communication is an essential requirement of successful management. Without effective communication, management and supervision becomes difficult or impossible. Organisations with more than one level of management may experience communication problems that can interfere with almost any aspect of the organisation.

The purpose of communications management is to ensure that managers, supervisors and employees have access to strategic and practical information. Hypothetically, all parties will be able to agree on the tasks to improve the organisation, and everyone will work together in a corresponding fashion. In practice, the same objectives must apply to all managers, supervisors and employees, otherwise groups with differing overall objectives will develop different goals, negating the effect of the shared information.

The communication roles of supervisors and managers

The role and concept of communication for supervisors and managers is pivotal. Each aspect is clearly defined below:

■ Define communications philosophy and standards within the remit of the supervisor/manager

■ Plan the communication goals of the department

■ Manage and monitor information flow

- Organise crisis communications
- Implement an effective communication strategy
- Organise communications training for staff
- Provide presentations to the team, the public, media and for the Internet

The weekly reporting method

One simple and popular communication approach is the weekly reporting method: every employee composes a report, once a week, including information on their activities in the preceding week, their plans for the following week, and any other information deemed relevant to the larger group. Reports are sent to managers, who summarise and report to their own managers, eventually leading to an overall summary led by the chief executive officer (CEO), which may be sent to the board of directors. The CEO then sends the board's summary back down the ladder, where each manager can append an additional summary or note before referring it to their employees.

Weekly reporting

Eventually, each employee will receive feedback, containing many or all of the mentioned summaries, from every level of management.

Types of communication flow

- **Downward communication**. This is communication that moves down a chain of command, where people at the top of an organisational hierarchy send messages to those at the bottom
- **Upward communication**. This moves up a chain of command: people at the bottom of an organisational hierarchy send messages to those at the top
- **Horizontal communication**. Occurs when people on the same level of the hierarchy are engaged in interactions with each other. These people can be from different departments but on a similar level

Organisational communication can include:

1 **Flow of communication**
   - formal, informal
   - internal, external
   - upward, downward, horizontal
   - use of communication networks

2 **Induction**
   - the induction of new employees
   - introduction of organisational policies and procedures
   - communicating employee benefits

3 **Channels of communication**

- electronic media such as email, intranet and Internet
- teleconferencing
- printed media such as memos, bulletin boards and newsletters
- face-to-face meetings

4 **Meetings**

- briefings
- staff meetings
- project meetings
- team meetings
- appraisals

Breakfast meetings can be a daily, quick and informal way of communication with the team

Recently, organisational communication has moved from the acceptance of mechanical models (e.g. information moving from a sender to a receiver) to a study of the persistent and 'taken-for-granted' ways in which we not only use communication to achieve certain tasks within organisational settings but also how the organisations in which we participate affect us on a daily basis.

These approaches include 'critical', 'participatory', and 'organic' communication. Thus the management and supervisory field have studied occurrences such as:

■ How communicative behaviours modify organising work processes or overall products

■ How the organisations within which we interact affect our communicative behaviours

The use of an intranet system within the organisation which delivers a constant flow of information on a computer screen is an example of an organic approach which may become participatory if the opportunity to add to the communication is given.

The issues surrounding perception and communication are complex and varied. What we see and hear are often reconciled by a range of cultural and individual factors which can misrepresent our understanding of what is happening and will in turn affect our reactions to it. The way in which people in organisations communicate and how those communications are perceived and acted upon can have a major impact on individual success and team performance.

The use of body language

Body language is a technique which allows a professional to express themselves without words. The techniques can be used in conjunction with verbal communication to great effect.

Body language can take many forms, as shown in the illustration.

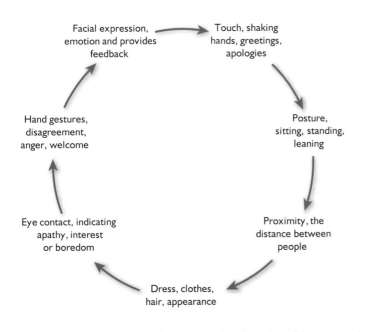

Facial expression, emotion and provides feedback

Touch, shaking hands, greetings, apologies

Posture, sitting, standing, leaning

Hand gestures, disagreement, anger, welcome

Proximity, the distance between people

Eye contact, indicating apathy, interest or boredom

Dress, clothes, hair, appearance

An essential element of communication is asking questions or making a point; this takes confidence and practice. Questions should be asked to achieve the best possible informative answer; by using incorrect questioning or body language there may be a risk of a poor end result.

Key points to remember:

■ Once a speaker has finished express your appreciation

■ Use a brief summary of the speaker's points to show you have listened and grasped the concept of the discussion

■ Ensure you have your say but in a controlled professional manner; if necessary write the question down and read it using a calm clear voice; always avoid aggression as this stops any worthwhile feedback

Listening skills are of paramount importance in communication and teamwork. They help us to understand what information or support other people need and ensure we can work cohesively as a group.

> **! REMEMBER**
>
> Body language is used by everyone on a daily basis. The skill lies in using body language to your advantage and create the atmosphere/ environment which suits you.

PROVIDE FEEDBACK TO COLLEAGUES ON PERFORMANCE

Performance appraisal is an important part of performance management.

The performance appraisal or review is essentially an opportunity for the individual and those concerned with their performance – most usually their line manager – to get together to engage in a dialogue about the individual's performance, development and the support required from the manager. It should not be a top-down process or an opportunity for one person to ask questions and the other to reply. It should be a free-flowing conversation in which a range of views are exchanged.

Performance appraisals usually review past behaviour and so provide an opportunity to reflect on past performance. However, to be successful they should also be used as a basis for making development and improvement plans and reaching agreement about what should be done in the future.

How to conduct a performance appraisal

The five key elements of the performance appraisal are:

1 **Measurement** – assessing performance against agreed targets and objectives.

2 **Feedback** – providing information to the individual on their performance and progress.

3 **Positive reinforcement** – emphasising what has been done well and making only constructive criticism about what might be improved.

4 **Exchange of views** – a frank exchange of views about what has happened, how appraisees can improve their performance, the support they need from their managers to achieve this and their aspirations for their future career.

5 **Agreement** – coming jointly to an understanding by all parties about what needs to be done to improve performance generally and overcome any issues raised in the course of the discussion.

Some businesses develop an appraisal form with space for appraisers to rate appraisees on aspects of their work such as their contribution to the team, role development and effectiveness. The approach will depend on the nature of the business and the people involved. However, as a minimum it is helpful to have a structure used to collect consistent information on the appraisal. This may be in the form of a free dialogue from appraisers with the opportunity for appraisees to reply and comment.

As a general rule it is helpful to have some information on the following:

1 **Objectives** – whether they were achieved and if not the reasons why.

2 **Competence** – whether individual's performance is below, within or above the requirements of the role.

3 **Training** – what training the individual has received in the review period and what training or development they would like to receive in the future.

4 **Actions** – a note of any actions that need to be carried out by the individual or the appraiser.

Increasingly organisations are putting more emphasis on the kind of behaviour they want their employees to exhibit. Behaviour, particularly management behaviour, has been identified as a significant source of value.

> **! REMEMBER**
>
> The performance appraisal is frequently the central post of performance management. A performance management survey carried out in 2004 found that 65 per cent of organisations used an individual annual appraisal, 27 per cent used twice-yearly appraisals and 10 per cent used rolling appraisals.

Therefore they are not solely concerned with the achievement of objectives but *how* these were achieved. Some businesses are identifying a set of *positive management behaviours,* for example, and then rating against them. Others are identifying the behaviours associated with outstanding service and rating against these in the appraisal process. Again the design of the process will depend on what is important to the particular business and will therefore be influenced by the wider performance management process.

> **! REMEMBER**
>
> It is important that people do not achieve their objectives at the expense of their colleague's morale.

Self-assessment

In some instances it may be helpful to guide appraisees through a self-assessment process, encouraging them to assess and analyse their own performance as a basis for discussion and action. This can improve the quality of the appraisal discussion because an individual feels actively involved in the process which encourages them to work through the points beforehand. This can be particularly useful with more junior staff or those who may not be used to the appraisal system.

However, self-assessment can only work if individuals have clear targets and standards against which to assess them. It can also only be effective in a climate of trust where individuals believe their appraisers will not take advantage of an open self-assessment.

What a good appraisal looks like

A good and constructive appraisal meeting is one in which:

■ Appraisees do most of the talking

■ Appraisers listen actively to what they say

■ There is scope for reflection and analysis

■ Performance is analysed, not personality

■ The whole period is reviewed and not just recent or isolated events

■ Achievement is recognised and reinforced

■ Ends positively with agreed action plans

A bad appraisal meeting:

■ Focuses on a catalogue of failures and omissions

■ Is controlled by the appraiser

■ Ends with disagreement between appraiser and appraisee

Asking the right questions

The two main issues are to ensure that appraisers ask open and probing questions.

Open questions are general rather than specific; they enable people to decide how they should be answered and encourage them to talk freely. Examples include:

■ How do you feel things have been going?

■ How do you see the job developing?

■ How do you feel about that?

■ Tell me, why do you think that happened?

Probing questions dig deeper for more specific information on what happened or why. They can seek support for the individual's answer and encourage them to provide more information about their feelings and attitudes. They can also be used to reflect back to the individual and check information. Examples would be:

■ That's very interesting. Tell me more about . . .?

■ To what extent do you think that . . .?

■ Have I got the right impression? Do you mean that . . .?

© ISTOCKPHOTO.COM/MARTIN PURMENSKY

Appraisals should be professional but relaxed

Listening

Good listeners:

■ Concentrate on the speaker and are aware of behaviour, body language and nuances that supplement what is being said

■ Respond quickly when necessary but don't interrupt

■ Ask relevant questions to clarify meaning

■ Comment on points to demonstrate understanding but keep them short and do not inhibit the flow of the speaker

Giving feedback

Feedback should be based on facts, not subjective opinion, and should always be backed up with evidence and examples. The aim of feedback should be to promote the understanding of the individual so that they are aware of the impact of their actions and behaviour. It may require corrective action where the feedback indicates that something has gone wrong. However, wherever possible feedback should be used positively to reinforce the good and identify opportunities for further positive action. Giving feedback is a skill and those with no training should be discouraged from giving feedback.

Feedback will work best when the following conditions are met:

■ Feedback is built in with individuals being given access to readily available information on their performance and progress

- Feedback is related to actual events, observed behaviours or actions
- Feedback describes events without judging them
- Feedback is accompanied by questions soliciting the individual's opinion on why certain things happened
- People are encouraged to come to their own conclusions about what happened and why
- There is understanding about what things went wrong and an emphasis on putting them right rather than censuring past behaviour

EQUAL OPPORTUNITIES

The first step in building better work relationships is to become aware of the differences among people and to be willing to accept these differences as a positive force within an organisation. It is the right of every person to be able to apply for and seek employment regardless of their race, creed, disability, sex or any other distinguishing feature. The law has enforced this to allow people to work and prevent them from being segregated or victimised.

Everyone comes into the workplace with a different skill and it is the job of senior personnel to utilise this and help to develop them into well-rounded staff.

Staff should not be chosen because they are black, Asian, white, small or tall, but because they have what it takes to succeed both individually and for the company.

What are equal opportunities?

Equal opportunities seek to influence behaviour through legislation so that discrimination is prevented. They are based on moral and ethical arguments and are concerned with promoting the rights of all members in society.

Equal opportunities focus on securing the equality of groups, particularly minority groups, and seek to alleviate the disadvantages that are experienced by them. Legislation is, therefore, supported by practical procedures such as positive action to assist under-represented groups in a particular area of work or in the workforce generally. Programmes can address such an imbalance by ensuring that training opportunities and funded projects are opened up to the wider community and those groups who have been traditionally under-represented.

What is diversity?

In contrast to equal opportunities which focuses on groups and potential discrimination within those groups, diversity concentrates on the difference of individuals. Managing diversity is based on the economic and business case for recognising and valuing difference, rather than the moral case for treating people equally. Equal treatment offers benefits and advantages to employers if they invest in ensuring that everyone in the organisation is valued and given the opportunity to develop their potential.

By integrating equal opportunities into your programme structure and embracing diversity at an organisational level you will add value to the work you do and meet community needs. You can demonstrate your commitment to equality in a number of ways including:

■ An equal opportunities policy
■ Policy statement
■ Implementation
■ Monitoring and evaluation

By ensuring these points are understood and made available to all staff the equal opportunities/diversity topic will be recognised and acted upon.

As chefs we embrace diversity: food has no boundaries and the larger the ethnic background the more information, techniques and products we can source and learn from.

Equal opportunities and related legislation in the UK

■ Disability Discrimination Act 1995
■ Employment Act 1989
■ Employment Relations Act 1999
■ Employment Rights Act 1996
■ The Equal Pay Act 1970
■ Health and Safety at Work etc. Act 1974
■ Human Rights Act 1998
■ Management of Health and Safety at Work Regulations 1999
■ Maternity and Parental Leave etc. Regulations 1999
■ National Minimum Wage Regulations 1999
■ Part-time Workers Regulations 2000
■ Protection from Harassment Act 1997
■ Race Relations Act 1976
■ Rehabilitation of Offenders Act 1974
■ Sex Discrimination Act
■ Working Time Regulations 1998

This list covers the law/legislation associated with the hospitality industry but is by no means exhaustive. It must be followed and adhered to at all times; the information is usually collated and enforced by a team of trained personnel (usually the human resources department). For further information you should consult the government website detailed in the further reading section at the end of this chapter.

TEAM ROLES

How people behave and perform as members of a group is as important as their behaviour or performance as individuals. We have seen in this chapter that the main focus of establishing positive working relationships, and therefore being able to perform effectively, is a spirit of unity and co-operation. Communication plays a strong part in this and colleagues should communicate in a fair, supportive and clear manner.

The influence of a team will also be directed by the actions and behaviour of individual members, patterns of interaction and the roles that people play. Belbin (1993) developed an analysis of individual roles within a work group which concluded that groups composed entirely of clever people or of people with similar personalities can lack creativity and display a number of negative areas. The most consistently successful groups comprise a range of roles undertaken by various members.

Belbin has identified nine useful types of team roles. A team role is described as a pattern of behaviour characteristic of the way in which one team member interacts with another. Their performance should serve to facilitate the progress of the whole team. The strength of the contribution is always balanced by 'allowable weaknesses'. This is because colleagues are seldom strong in all areas. A description of the team roles is stated in the diagram below.

BELBIN'S NINE TEAM ROLES

ROLE AND DESCRIPTION	ROLE CONTRIBUTION	ALLOWABLE WEAKNESSES
Co-ordinator	Confident, a good chairperson, clarifies objectives, promotes decision making and delegates effectively.	Can be perceived as manipulative. Offloads personal work.
Completer	Meticulous, conscientious, anxious, seeks out errors and omissions. Delivers on time.	Inclined to worry disproportionately. Reluctant to delegate.
Implementer	Disciplined, reliable, measured, conservative and efficient. Transforms ideas into practical actions.	Rather inflexible. Slow to respond to new possibilities.

BELBIN'S NINE TEAM ROLES (*CONTINUED*)

ROLE AND DESCRIPTION	ROLE CONTRIBUTION	ALLOWABLE WEAKNESSES
Monitor–evaluator	Thoughtful, strategic and discerning. Sees all options and judges accurately.	Lacks drive and ability to inspire others.
Plant	Creative, imaginative, unconventional. Solves difficult problems.	Ignores details. Too preoccupied to communicate clearly.
Resource investigator	Extrovert, enthusiastic, communicative, develops contacts and explores opportunities.	Over-optimistic. Loses interest once initial enthusiasm has passed.
Shaper	Challenging, dynamic, thrives on pressure, has the drive to overcome obstacles.	Can provoke others. Upsets people's feelings.
Specialist	Single-minded, dedicated, provides knowledge and skills in rare supply.	Contributes only on a narrow front. Dwells on technicalities.
Teamworker	Co-operative, mild, perceptive and diplomatic. Listens, builds and prevents friction.	Indecisive in crisis situations.

TASK

Looking at Belbin's model decide which role you are within your team. Also try to decide on the roles of your immediate team and conclude whether a role is missing from the team.

The most consistently successful teams were assorted with a balance of these nine team roles. However, the role that a person undertakes in a group is not fixed and may change according to circumstances.

This inventory can be used as a means of examining and comparing team roles. In recent years many layers of management have been removed and the gap in people to lead and motivate has increasingly been filled by the creation of teams. By using this model it is possible to create data about teams and individuals to inform managers about the effectiveness of a team to complete objectives. It may be possible also to consider what additional role is required to complete a team and make it more effective.

Further reading and research

Belbin, M. R. (1993) *Team Roles at Work*. Butterworth Heinemann.

Drucker, P. F. (2007) *The Practice of Management*. Revised ed. Elsevier.

Drummond, H. (2000) *Introduction to Organisational Behaviour*. Oxford University Press.

Dutton, J. *et al*. (2006) *Exploring Positive Relationships at Work. Building a Theoretical and Research Foundation*. Lawrence Erlbaum Associates

Gillen, T. (2007) *Performance Management and Appraisal*. 2nd ed. CIPD toolkit. Chartered Institute of Personnel and Development.

Mintzberg, H. (1990) *The Nature of Managerial Work*. Prentice Hall.

Mullins, L. J. (2001) *Hospitality Management and Organisational Behaviour*. 4th ed. Longman.

Team roles in work http://www.belbin.com

Advice on workplace conduct http://www.worketiquette.co.uk/

Equal opportunities legislation http://www.gos.gov.uk/gol/European_funding/
    Objective3/Equalopps/

Investors in People http://www.investorsinpeople.co.uk/Pages/Home.aspx

Assessment of knowledge and understanding

You have now learned about the responsibilities of working effectively as a team member and the importance of communication and improving yourself. This will enable you to ensure your own positive actions contribute effectively towards the whole team.

To test your level of knowledge and understanding, answer the following short questions. These will help to prepare you for your summative (final) assessment.

1 State three reasons why communication is important within the workplace.

2 Explain clearly what you understand by the meaning of leadership and how you would make a distinction of leadership from management.

3 Describe the difference between verbal and physical communication.

4 List five Acts relating to equal opportunities and state how you think they bear relation to a busy kitchen environment.

5 State how diversity within a team can be of benefit to the organisation's objectives.

6 Describe briefly how diversity can be achieved within the hospitality industry.

7 Describe what is meant by the phrase 'exceeding customer expectations'.

8 State why understanding the needs of customers is important.

9 Using Belbin's team roles inventory select what you think would be your five most important roles to manage a hospitality-based project. Justify your ideas for this.

10 Debate how the realities of organisational behaviour influence organisation structure.

11 Prepare your own diagram to explain the line and staff organisation in your area of work.

Research task

Communication is important when working in a busy environment.

State five considerations you would make as a supervisor to ensure that your team as part of the organisation worked smoothly on a daily basis.

3

Contribute to the control of resources

HS3 Contribute to the control of resources

LEARNING OBJECTIVES

This chapter is about ensuring that you and the staff you are responsible for using resources effectively and efficiently, without undue waste. It covers obtaining supplies, checking equipment, monitoring the use of resources and keeping records.

After reading this chapter you will be able to:

■ Identify the resources available to you.

■ Identify the resources you need for your work and follow the correct procedures for obtaining them.

■ Deal with any problems in obtaining resources, following agreed procedures and keeping the relevant people informed.

■ Check the quality, quantity and suitability of resources before you need to use them.

■ Make sure equipment and materials are correctly stored and maintained.

■ Encourage your colleagues to make efficient use of resources and to minimise waste.

■ Monitor the use of resources in your area of responsibility.

■ Make sure that resources are used effectively, efficiently and in line with organisational and legal requirements.

■ Identify ways of making better use of resources and action or pass on the information according to your organisational requirements.

■ Keep your records about resources up to date, accurate and in the specified place.

KEY WORDS

Appraisal
A judgement or assessment of the professional performance of someone, especially a subordinate.

Colleagues
An associate that one works with – a workplace team member.

Gross profit
The profits before overhead (fixed operating expenses) have been deducted.

Labour
The workers or employed body of staff of a company.

Monitor
To check, track or observe processes and procedures.

Ordering
The action of requesting a tradesman to supply goods or services under certain terms of delivery.

Overheads
Operating expense: the expense of maintaining property.

Reliability
A measure of consistency – giving the same results over a period of time.

Resources
The machines, workers, money, land, raw materials and other things that a business uses to produce goods and services and to make its economy grow.

> **! REMEMBER**
>
> Resources come in a variety of forms; it is important to remember they all have their own roles in the business operation and are equally important.

INTRODUCTION

Equipment, colleagues and suppliers as an important resource

The importance of structured departments within a business is relevant and tangible. However, making sure that each department and all colleagues are fully aware of business issues will help ensure the establishment operates to its maximum potential.

It is imperative that all department members and all suppliers used to resource the relevant areas should try to establish a solid working relationship. Communication skills are the key to being able to achieve this.

EQUIPMENT AS AN IMPORTANT RESOURCE

Without the correct equipment in place the smooth running and professional service required would not be possible and cost-effectiveness would be greatly reduced. Generally speaking, good-quality equipment items – whether this be ovens, trolleys, linen, glasses, computers – will last longer and perform the required job much better than their cheaper counterparts, so long as regular maintenance is carried out.

Although the word equipment encompasses all tools used within an organisation, typically these fall under three different categories; **large equipment** such as tables, chairs, sinks and oven ranges, **mechanical equipment** such as coffee machines, food blenders, electric mixers and micros ordering systems, and **utensils and small equipment** such as bowls, cutlery, linen, ice buckets, telephone and pans.

In advance of opening or altering an existing establishment's role, it should be ensured that all equipment required produces a professional service; each department should be aware of its role and responsibilities. Assuming that this is done in plenty of time, especially where any specialist equipment may be required, if any items are missing or need to be purchased then this can be done without causing any problems.

Regular stock checks should be carried out to ensure that sufficient equipment is available to use. The person in charge of ordering should be notified if any equipment is missing, damaged, broken or needs to be ordered so that they are able to take the necessary action.

It is useful to have an equipment order sheet that all the team are aware of and can add details to of any missing, damaged, broken or newly required equipment, which can be passed to the supervisors/managers at regular intervals.

In January 1995 British Standards combined with European Standards to create a legal requirement that all equipment must carry the **CE mark,** which indicates that the required safety standards are met. Therefore, all equipment within a workplace must conform to the EU Safety Directive. CE marking is a declaration by a manufacturer that the product meets all the appropriate provisions of the relevant legislation implementing certain European Directives: it also gives companies easier access into the European market to sell their products without adaptation or rechecking. The initials 'CE' do not stand for any specific words but are a declaration by the manufacturer that his product meets the requirements of the applicable European Directive(s).

Not all equipment will have a CE mark especially if it is from the US and non-EU countries, which means that apart from the equipment being unmodified to work on AC current, necessitating the use of an electric transformer, it will not usually have a comprehensive warranty. This may require any breakdowns or maintenance be dealt with by the company at the country of origin (unless they have an office in the country of purchase). They will have their own safety standards but they may not be to the same standard as the CE mark.

All staff should be fully trained and competent in the use of all equipment in the workplace. Everyone must be aware of the safety measures that are in place and the correct course of action to take in the event of any accidents. Further, it is advisable that all staff are aware of how to properly clean and maintain all equipment. If equipment is not properly cleaned and stored hygienically, the risk of contaminating foods and implications of food poisoning are significantly increased.

Electrical equipment should be checked and maintained on a regular basis. This will ensure that the safety of staff is paramount, and also that well-maintained and looked after equipment will last longer and therefore not have to be replaced regularly, helping to keep equipment costs low. The *Electricity at Work Regulations (1989)* state that every item of electrical equipment in the workplace must be tested every 12 months by a qualified electrician.

In addition to this annual testing, a trained member of staff or qualified electrician should regularly check all electrical equipment for safety. This is recommended every 3 months but generally most employers undertake this annually. A quick visual inspection by the chef before using an electrical item on a daily basis is a good method of reducing potential accidents or breakdowns. Records must be kept of the check and will include:

- Electrician's name/contact details
- Itemised list of electrical equipment complete with serial number for identification purposes
- Date of purchase or disposal
- Date of last inspection
- Date of next inspection

General checks should be undertaken and reported for potential hazards such as exposed wires in flexes, cracked plugs or broken sockets, worn cables and overloaded sockets. Although it is the responsibility of the employer to ensure all equipment is safe to use, it is also the responsibility of the employee to always check that the equipment is safe to use and to never use it if it is faulty.

Any electrical equipment that appears faulty must be immediately checked and repaired before use. It should also be labelled or have the plug removed to ensure that it is not used by accident before repairing.

If any equipment items break or do not work properly, check the warranty of the product as you do not want to pay for maintenance or replacement costs if any problems will be covered.

The ongoing maintenance costs for all types of equipment are much lower than having to replace items regularly due to poor maintenance or staff not using equipment properly because they may not have been trained.

Taking simple measures to look after items will hopefully mean that they will last longer, such as ensuring that table legs are secure and making sure items are stored safely and securely, not just to protect yourself and others but to also prevent them from getting damaged.

© ISTOCKPHOTO.COM/JOE GOUGH

When purchasing larger equipment items such as desks, sinks and computer terminals, the overall dimensions of the working space must be carefully considered. The layout of an area has to be carefully assessed and planned, taking into consideration details such as the number of staff who will be working in it, how much room people will have to move about, fuel supply, noise, drainage, water supply, maintenance requirements and the turnover of the establishment.

With regard to the storage of equipment items, a good rule is to ensure as far as possible that the most commonly used items are easily at hand. Any heavy items should ideally be placed at a height whereby minimum strain is required to move them and try to make sure that cupboards do not become cluttered or over-full as this will waste time having to search for items and presents a health and safety risk whereby items could fall onto someone.

TECH SKILLS
✔

COLLEAGUES AS AN IMPORTANT RESOURCE

The importance of staff and your work colleagues within the establishment is principal. Generally, good communication skills, understanding, flexibility, adaptability, teamwork and patience will allow colleagues to work well and function as a team.

If you are able to achieve a flexible team with a good morale this will make staff more productive, achieving a lower staff turnover and saving on recruitment costs. Creating a contented environment for colleagues to work in will hopefully decrease time taken off ill or those that leave and should help prevent staff shortages.

Ensuring that regular training and staff development schemes are in place will give employees the opportunity to perfect existing skills and learn new skills and is viewed positively as a company/workplace investing in its members. Also, it is a break from the working day and refreshing to do something a little different from the normal routine. Make sure that all staff are aware of any new or ongoing training schemes in place and sufficient cover is available if they will be away from their working environment.

Appraisal or progress reviews are an important method of communication, where one member of staff looks at the way another employee/member of staff is performing in their job role. It is usual for an employee to receive an appraisal from their line manager.

Appraisals will provide an opportunity to review individuals' performance against targets set. Each team member will have their own strengths and weaknesses and it is important to utilise those strengths and action plan to build upon and improve the weaknesses with appropriate personal goals.

Performance appraisal will identify:

■ Results achieved against preset targets

■ Any additional accomplishments and contributions

This may seem overwhelming, but it is an important and useful process. It can also be used to one's own advantage.

■ Identify with your line manager the tasks you see that need to be accomplished, and how these will be met

■ Identify training needs, this will provide you with a greater range of skills and expertise. This will ultimately improve your opportunities for promotion, giving you increased responsibilities

■ Identify obstructions which are affecting your progress

■ Identify and amend any changes to your current job role

■ Identify what additional responsibilities you would like

■ Identify and focus on your achievements to date against the targets set

■ Update your action plan, which will help you achieve your targets

An appraisal form

Appraisal for	
Date	
Key strengths	Professional attitude with excellent commitment, communication, teamwork and flexibility skills. Good communication within team and kept well motivated. Greatly improved discussion between departments. Improved standardisation of work and feedback to team.
Areas for improvement	Review costings and set new profit margins. Review new staff interview process and investigate structuring a pre-order for successful candidates. Organise the team to utilise other employer contacts to create a work-based forum.
Personal development	Visit other establishments to share best practice.
Professional development	Identify areas for improvement from the training plan, develop new skills and then share best practice within the team and other departments.
Appraisal done by	

If personal targets are not being met it is important to identify the problem. Following this, new performance targets should be put in place to resolve any difficulties. At the next appraisal the agreed objectives and targets set for the previous period will be reviewed.

In order to develop personally and to improve your skills professionally, it is important to have personal targets against which you can measure your achievement. If these are confidential, the workplace policy on confidentiality should be observed. All targets set should be SMART.

Specific	Outlining exactly what the group aims to do, rather than expressing vague general aims.
Measurable	Outlining how the group will know it has met the targets and what evidence will show this.
Achievable	Challenging for the group, but not too difficult.
Realistic	The opportunities and resources should be available.
Time-bound	There should be both interim and final deadlines.

Targets can be even SMARTER. They can be

Enjoyable

Rewarding

To an employer it is important that you are consistent. You must always perform your skills to the highest standard and present and promote a positive image of the industry and the business you represent.

The development of skills by entering into periods of work experience keeps employees in touch with other establishments, builds links and helps develop staff confidence. This is an immense learning strategy on a personal basis and will also give a positive reputation to both yourself and your place of work.

Developing a network of associates, friends and peers is very important for business and learning. Employers, suppliers, training providers and managers are able to exchange ideas and to discuss ways to help meet industry targets such as training, profitability and links to other industries across the world.

The continuation of learning is essential to succeed in this industry and the prospect of continuing to acquire knowledge and further develop skills to advance one's career is a very real incentive. Colleges have diverse courses of study to help match your development plan and they assess the future skills that the industry requires in order for your job to be carried out effectively and for your progress in your profession.

ORDERING: SUPPLIERS AS AN IMPORTANT RESOURCE

Finding a suitable supplier to provide a quality service can be a very challenging and lengthy process, so once this has been established it is vital for the running of a company that a solid working relationship is established.

Finding a supplier that can provide a good quality service on a regular basis at a reasonable price is a difficult task. Most businesses will source their products from wholesalers, with those that supply specialist commodities usually being recommended by word of mouth from other companies or colleagues. A good reputation can surpass a supplier and is invaluable in obtaining your required produce.

There are two main types of buying methods: 'informal' buying which means that an agreement between supplier and purchaser will be verbal, or 'formal' buying which means that a written agreement will be put in place and is usually undertaken by means of a computerised system of ordering.

When considering which supplier to employ, you should examine the following factors:

Quality. You should never instruct a supplier before sampling the produce that they have to offer, even more so with a large wholesaler as you may have to sign a contract agreeing to purchase their goods for a minimum period of time or with a minimum delivery cost. You should always establish work principles and delivery times with the supplier.

Equipment items should be suitably and well packaged and have any relevant instruction manuals present with warranties present. It is a standard practice to request a visit to a supplier's establishment and assess their workplace and code of work. Remember that the food items that are sourced and created into dishes which will be presented to customers are a reflection on the chef and the restaurant.

Quantity. Especially with smaller and local suppliers, you will need to establish the volume of goods that they regularly have available. If this is not determined first, then you run the risk of not having enough stock when specifically required. With equipment items you run the risk of a supplier not being able to replace goods within a reasonable timescale if they do not have a good stock.

Variety. A good variety of produce should be easily made available and speciality items may well require a separate supplier for each. With technology advancing rapidly, as far as possible it should be ensured that a supplier has a wide variety of equipment available and is aware of technological advances and new products. For any specialist supplier, they should have a good supply of general products as well as specialist items.

Cost. Supplier costs must be calculated carefully prior to instruction/agreement. Ensure that any carriage charges are made clear, whether VAT is included in the prices or if this needs to be added, if any ordering charge or minimum order amount applies and if there are any other additional costs that you may be unaware of.

Reliability. Of great importance: any supplier utilised *must* be reliable. Without them being able to deliver the produce to you, as regularly as you require and in a correct state, an establishment will not be able to run smoothly and you could be left without goods and unable to offer the service required to customers. When purchasing any electrical items it is advisable to ask about customer aftercare as there may be additional maintenance/servicing/repairs costs that need to be taken into consideration, as well as timescales for emergency call-outs, i.e. how long would it take to have a piece of equipment repaired if it broke?

If using a supplier on a regular basis, especially for non-specialist items, it is a good idea to negotiate prices, especially on large orders. If you will be using a supplier regularly and can establish special rates for common items or large quantities of items, you will both benefit from saving money and cost-efficiency.

It is imperative that a supplier is given any order requests as soon as practicable so that they have as much time as possible to source produce. By communicating regularly with a supplier you can be kept up to date with details of any special offers and/or specialist goods available and discuss any other matters, for example if a staff member is absent who the next point of contact will be.

MATCHING SUITABLE RESOURCES TO WORK TARGETS

Work targets will be set and each individual will have a personal and team obligation to meet these.

When defining the customer service requirements it is essential to plan the equipment, staff and resources that are required.

It is bad practice to fall behind with targets due to poor preparation, lack of foresight or a negative attitude towards the workplace.

When presented with work targets, it is a good idea to go through this thoroughly, establishing any points that you may have queries on or not be happy with. Once you are happy with what is required and when it is required by, knowing your team and their strengths, the required tasks should be chosen and then briefed accordingly to individuals and the team in a brief meeting.

Time management is an important skill for professional staff working in the hospitality industry. In order to manage your time more effectively, you must have a realistic assessment of all the tasks required and then plan the workload accordingly.

The ability to set shared targets and make plans is decisive to successful teamwork. If staff do not know what they are aiming to achieve, they cannot determine what has been achieved. Summarily, if there is no real planning, progression cannot be properly monitored to review how well things are going and to be able to learn from the experience. It is during these stages that team members can support each other and provide help where necessary to achieve the end result.

The key to matching suitable resources to work targets is:

- **Ascertain** – look and listen at what is being required of you or your team
- **Ask** – if you are uncertain of any points, do not be afraid to ask otherwise errors could occur that you will be responsible for
- **Assess** – establish everything that will be required to carry out the task, such as equipment, staff and whether anyone will need to be briefed with any specialist information
- **Action** – order anything that is required, brief yourself and your colleagues before beginning the task
- **Monitor** – once everything is in place ensure that it is monitored continually. It cannot be assumed that everything will run according to plan
- **Review** – it is only by reviewing how a task has been carried out or whether a target has been successfully achieved that you can receive constructive criticism. Doing this enables you to improve on your skills in order to achieve targets

Setting personal targets enables you to monitor your own progression and understanding in this area and may highlight any areas in which you require further training.

TIME MANAGEMENT

Within all hospitality areas it is important not only to have a good comprehension of personal time management, but the time management of your colleagues also. By establishing this you will be able to work well as a team and ensure that each process is carried out in as much time as possible and will fall in line with the role that each member of staff performs to create a smooth running and efficient workplace.

As in any workplace, prioritising is an important skill. By establishing which processes take longest, which require the most attention and by keeping to deadlines you should be able to complete tasks in plenty of time and to a high standard.

Starting the working shift with a team meeting will enable colleagues to discuss with one another the schedule of events and any issues or concerns that they may have with regard to pre-planning, communication, time setting and special arrangements.

Also, it is good practice to have a daily table of events, detailing what each member of the team is doing and an approximate time that they may complete their task by. Any special events, changes to customer requirements or products to be worked with that require extra attention should be discussed thoroughly with individuals well in advance.

Foresight is key to the smooth running of any workplace and it cannot be assumed that things will run smoothly and to a strict timetable. Therefore it is wise to take into consideration any possible faults, errors or mishaps that could occur and try to allocate sufficient time to prevent these if possible or solve them in the worst case.

© ISTOCKPHOTO.COM/PERTUSINAS

Besides being provided with either a verbal or a written timetable of events, it is advisable that each individual member of staff monitors their own time-management skills. It cannot be assumed that everyone is good at managing their time and there are now a variety of courses available for employees to attend which can help provide individuals with positive methods and tips on how to achieve this. Each member of the team provides a valuable role in the workplace and others will rely on each other being alert and punctual so that colleagues are not left at a disadvantage due to someone else's poor time keeping, time allocation or not being alert and awake.

COST CONTROL

Cost control is essential in the running and maintaining of any business, the aim being to obtain and retain as much money as possible, whilst paying out as little as possible in costs.

The cost of employing staff, produce purchased, equipment repaired, replaced or new items bought in and even the rent on a building must be closely monitored at all times.

First and foremost, any business will need to devise a budget which will allow approximate guidelines of how much money can be allocated (usually on a company financial year basis) to each contributory sector in the running of the business, such as how much money can be spent on staff wages, supplies and equipment.

Based around this budget, a target profit figure will be set which will take into consideration costs and will usually consist of a gross figure (all monies received) and a net figure (minus any expenses paid out).

Knowing the exact cost of each process and every item that is produced allows you to monitor profits made by each division. Further, it is possible to see where any necessary changes may need to be made such as over-ordering (wastage of goods), any economising strategies that could be put into place and also allows you to gain an approximate costing knowledge so that you can quote for catering for any special functions such as weddings or corporate events.

Any cost that is paid for will fall under one of three headings:

1 **Produce or material costs.** The cost of buying these items is variable as several contributory factors will affect this, such as the volume of business, ordering of speciality goods, catering for any functions, any temporary staff that may be required and worst case scenario spoiled goods.

2 **Labour.** Labour costs are split into two subelements, with the first being *direct labour* cost which will encompass payment of wages for staff directly including managers, supervisors, chefs, housekeepers, waiters, bar staff and porters. *Indirect labour* cost will pay wages to all other staff involved indirectly in the running of the establishment, such as maintenance persons and general office staff.

3 **Overheads.** These costs include expenses such as utility bills, any equipment that may be required and rental of premises.

Further to the above, it must not be forgotten that cleaning materials have to be accounted for and these will be considered an overhead. It is easy to forget that everything within an organisation will need to be cleaned regularly and there must be sufficient equipment at all times to be able to do this. Therefore a costing will need to ensure enough monies are allocated for cleaning items such as dishcloths, towels, brooms, cleaning fluids, linen etc.

Profit

Gross profit: The monetary difference between the cost of the produce used to create a service and the selling price purchased by a customer is referred to as gross or profit.

$$\text{sales} - \text{produce cost} = \text{gross profit}$$

Net profit: The monetary difference between the selling price to a customer and the total cost incurred including labour, produce and overheads is referred to as net profit.

$$sales - total\ cost = net\ profit$$

The costing of each item is calculated then worked out per day, per week, per month, per year.

Any profit made is always shown or referred to as a percentage of the selling price and this is calculated as follows

Gross profit

$$gross\ profit \times 100 \div selling\ price = sales$$

Net profit

$$net\ profit \times 100 \div selling\ price = sales$$

When calculating the cost of produce/service, the actual cost price of produce/service needs to be calculated. This is achieved by totalling all products/requirements purchased and then dividing this into the number of servings/people you will be able to serve. Once this has been established, the table below gives an example of how incorporating other production costs into the price, such as labour and overheads, will affect the selling price.

An example of calculating the cost is as follows.

Selling price for meal for 2	£170.50
Food cost for 2	£80.00
Addition of labour and overheads	£30.50
Linen and crockery	£20.00
Total cost of meal for 2	£130.50
Gross profit	£80.50
Net profit	£40.00

As a percentage therefore, the gross profit is equal to 49 per cent and the net profit is equal to 23 per cent.

A rule that can be used in order to effectively calculate the cost price of a meal is to let the cost of the meal be 45 per cent and fix the selling price at 100 per cent. This enables the selling price of a meal to be calculated as follows;

$$Cost\ of\ meal\ for\ 2 = 900p = 45\%$$
$$Selling\ price = \frac{900 \times 100}{45} = £20.00$$

Selling the meal at £20.00 makes 55 per cent gross profit above the 45 per cent cost price.

Based on a working week, a general example of how this works is as follows:

Food sales for one week	=	£32,000
Food cost for one week	=	£15,000
Labour and overheads for one week	=	£11,500
Total costs for one week	=	£26,500
Gross profit	=	**£17,000**
Net profit	=	**£ 5,500**

This works out as 53 per cent gross profit and 17 per cent net profit for the week.

When controlling and monitoring the food cost of certain items accurately it is much easier to stick to a budget, monitor where any profits and losses are made and control this in turn.

Saving money on costs and staying within a budget is very difficult within the catering industry as most resources are variable in price. Buying items in bulk, taking advantage of special offers/rates and the seasonality of foods can all contribute toward making savings.

As a guideline, the following points should be considered when monitoring cost control.

Quality of produce/resources at a fair price
It is best not to select 'cheaper' alternatives where most items are concerned as generally the quality does not tend to be as good. Rectifying anything, for example having to buy equipment as it has broken or replace poor-quality foods, will cost more in the long term and not just money but labour and other resources.

Portion/serving control
Ensure that all staff are aware of portion/serving sizes per item to be served in order to limit wastage.

Waste control
It is a good idea to check rubbish bins regularly to ensure that it is simply waste that is being disposed of and not quality items or produce that could otherwise be utilised.

Theft
To prevent any items leaving the premises 'through the back door', in addition to completing regular stocktakes it is advisable that any bags, coats

or purses belonging to staff are stored securely out of the working area. Other than main entrances to the premises, doors should be alarmed so that managers will be aware if anyone is entering or leaving the building through these.

Weekly stocktake

Stock should be checked on a weekly basis and it is easier to do this if the job is split into the main departmental categories, i.e. restaurant, bar, kitchen, housekeeping, equipment and other. If costs increase dramatically it will give an insight as to where it has increased.

Ensure prices are correct

When pricing services, at least a 40–50 per cent cost should be incorporated as you will have to cover the cost of the specific product(s) but must not forget other items such as condiments. Inflation needs to be taken into consideration as this will increase yearly and prices will need to cater for this.

INFORMATION SYSTEMS

Various information systems will exist within all areas and all staff should be aware of how these work. 'Information systems' simply is a means of communicating various pieces of information to those working within an establishment.

To gain improved control over the relevant areas computerised systems should be put in place. These allow tracking of produce, resources and financial matters.

Applications are built for your own personal business, providing the tools to potentially increase profitability. Up-to-the-minute information is always available with easily generated reports on labour management, equipment inventory, food/bevarage costs and guest loyalty programmes. It allows you to run detailed financial reporting and analysis and streamlines your ordering and recipe management.

Installing technology in the establishment will remove time management issues and help you to spend time planning for the future.

Ensuring the retention and an increasing customer base is vital for any business but especially so within the hospitality industry. Consumers in this day and age expect to be served with efficiency, professionalism and politeness. Implementing an EPOS system in your area can allow you to reach higher levels of customer service by having all the information you need on a database so that you can maintain real-time information on your stock inventory levels, costs, as well as competitive supplier quotes. You will even have a record of which member of the team communicated with which supplier and even have a record of what was ordered and when.

Electronic or computerised information systems are used by most businesses as they are very flexible to work with, allowing you to email information, securely protect data, and produce spreadsheets and monitoring forms effectively and efficiently. Stock-taking sheets will either be emailed, faxed or posted internally on a daily or weekly basis to the administration department who can update their computer systems accordingly.

By gathering and retaining information about things such as the monitoring of internal and external supplies, staff training, timetables of events and shift patterns, it is much easier to review these procedures and obtain information easily.

For example, by monitoring the external ordering of goods you are able to detail not only what is being purchased but the frequency at which it is purchased and the areas in which there are any discrepancies. In line with this type of procedure, it is advisable to monitor internal ordering effectively so that it can be determined where any left over produce or equipment is being transferred to. This type of information system is known as traceability of goods and is invaluable in the creating and monitoring of budgets and economisation practices.

Assessment of knowledge and understanding

You have now learned about the importance of equipment, colleagues and suppliers as valuable resources within the kitchen. You will have gained an understanding of the importance and need for time management, information systems, cost control, matching resources to work targets and health and safety within this workplace. This will enable you to recognise, assess and implement the skills required to carry these tasks out effectively.

To test your level of knowledge and understanding, answer the following short questions. These will help to prepare you for your summative (final) assessment.

Equipment, colleagues and suppliers as an important resource

1   Name the three main types of equipment found in hospitality-based organisations and give five examples of each.

2   Discuss the benefits of creating a team that work well together and the importance of communication in the workplace.

3   List the five main points that should be taken into consideration when sourcing a new supplier and why these are important.

4   Discuss the benefits of purchasing good-quality products and the importance of regular maintenance.

Time management and cost control

1   Explain the importance of time management.

2   Detail the importance of cost control and how this relates to a budget.

3   Give three examples of the benefits of having a timetable of events.

4   Name the three types of cost that are incurred by a business and what would be classified under these.

Work targets and information systems

1   Note six points that should be taken into consideration when looking to achieve a work target.

2   Discuss the benefits of setting personal targets.

3   Explain why it is important to have information systems in place.

Research task

You now have an understanding of cost control and how to formulate costings.

Complete the table below and cost a meal for two using the information provided and taking the following assumptions into account:

■   The cost of labour and overheads are 55 per cent of the meal cost per portion.

■   The meal cost is 45 per cent and the selling price is fixed at 100 per cent.

	CANAPÉS	DRINK	MAIN MEAL
Selling cost of meal	£	£	£
Produce/service cost	£10.75	£39.75	£86.25
People served	2	2	2
Produce cost per person	£	£	£
Cost of labour and overheads	£	£	£
Total cost	£	£	£
Gross profit	£	£	£
Net profit	£	£	£
Gross profit		%	%	%
Net profit		%	%	%

4

Maintain the health, hygiene, safety and security of the working environment

HS4 Maintain the health, hygiene, safety and security of the working environment

HS4.1 Maintain health, hygiene, safety and security procedures in your area of responsibility

HS4.2 Assess and minimise risks to colleagues and customers

LEARNING OBJECTIVES

This chapter and unit is about maintaining standards of health, safety, hygiene and security to protect staff and customers from harm. This work is essential in preventing accidents, illnesses and thefts which result in difficulties for staff and reduce the efficiency of the business.

After reading this chapter you will be able to:

- Make sure that you have information on health, hygiene, safety and security procedures that apply to your area of responsibility.
- Make sure colleagues have relevant information on health, hygiene, safety and security issues within your area of responsibility.
- Check that colleagues follow the health, hygiene, safety and security procedures that apply to your area of responsibility.
- Monitor your area of responsibility for risks to health, hygiene, safety and security.

■ Deal with risks and accidents promptly, following organisational procedures and legal requirements for safeguarding customers and staff.

■ Record or report risks and any health, hygiene, safety or security action that you have taken according to your organisational procedures.

■ Pass on information relating to how procedures are working and how they can be improved with regards to identified health, hygiene, safety and security risks.

KEY WORDS

Contingency plans
Plans that allow you to identify and plan for things that may go wrong. Back-up plans.

Hazard
This refers to anything that has the potential to cause harm.

Legal requirements
Any law or regulation that governs health, safety and hygiene in the workplace.

Organisation's procedures
The procedures that your organisation has developed to cover health, safety and security in your area of responsibility.

Other members of the public
These may include suppliers who come on to your organisation's premises or business visitors.

Responsible person
The person or persons at work to whom you should report to regarding cash or credit discrepancies or queries; this could be your line manager or employer.

Risk
The likelihood of a hazards potential being realised.

Risk assessment
Deciding how much of a risk a hazard may cause; for this unit, this does not mean carrying out a formal written risk assessment; you should be assessing risks all the time you are working. Take appropriate action to minimise these risks, for example by identifying that there is high risk that a box placed in a doorway could cause an accident and by moving the box to a safer place.

Security procedures

This may include making sure that unauthorised persons do not enter your area of responsibility, making sure that items are protected from theft, following the correct procedures when items go missing.

Statutory authorities

Organisations such as the Health and Safety Executive that have responsibility for ensuring health and safety at work.

Working practices

Any activities, procedures, use of materials or equipment and working techniques that you use when you are doing your job; these might include manual handling, HACCP, use of hazardous substances (COSHH) etc.

Working environment

The working area or areas for which you are responsible.

INTRODUCTION

Health and safety

The Workplace (Health, Safety and Welfare) Regulations 1992 cover a wide range of basic health, safety and welfare issues and apply to most workplaces with the exception of those in or on a ship. They are amended by the Health and Safety (Miscellaneous Amendments) Regulations 2002.

Employers have a general duty under section 2 of the Health and Safety at Work Act 1974 to ensure, so far as is reasonably practicable, the health, safety and welfare of their employees at work. Supervisors of non-domestic premises have a duty towards people who are not their employees but use their organisation's premises. The Regulations expand on these duties and are intended to protect the health and safety of everyone in the workplace, and ensure that adequate welfare facilities are provided for people at work. These Regulations aim to ensure that workplaces meet the health, safety and welfare needs of all members of a workforce, including people with disabilities.

> **! REMEMBER**
>
> Always take time to familiarise yourself with a company's health and safety procedures. This may seem like a time-consuming process but it will not only benefit the employer, but hopefully ensure that you are able to prevent yourself and others from encountering health and safety issues within the workplace.

HEALTH

The measures outlined in this section contribute to the general working environment of people in the workplace.

Ventilation

Workplaces need to be adequately ventilated. Fresh, clean air should be drawn from a source outside the workplace, and be circulated through the workrooms.

Ventilation should also remove and dilute warm, humid air and provide air movement. If the workplace contains process or heating equipment (for example a kitchen) more fresh air will be needed to provide adequate ventilation. Windows or other openings may provide sufficient ventilation but, where necessary, mechanical ventilation systems should be provided and regularly maintained.

© ISTOCKPHOTO.COM/HUCHEN LU

Kitchens should have a good ventilation system

Temperatures in indoor workplaces

Environmental factors (such as humidity and sources of heat in the workplace) combine with personal factors (such as the clothing a worker is wearing and how physically demanding their work is) to influence what is called someone's 'thermal comfort'. For workplaces where the activity is mainly sedentary, for example offices, the temperature should normally be at least 16 °C. If work involves physical effort it should be at least 13 °C (unless other laws require lower temperatures).

Work in hot or cold environments

The risk to the health of workers increases as conditions move further away from those generally accepted as comfortable. Risk of heat stress arises, for example, from working in high air temperatures in a kitchen, exposure to high thermal radiation or high levels of humidity, such as those found in laundries. Cold stress may arise, for example, from working in cold stores, food preparation areas and in the open air during winter.

Assessment of the risk to workers' health from working in either a hot or cold environment needs to consider both personal and environmental factors. Personal factors include body activity, the amount and type of clothing, and duration of exposure. Environmental factors include ambient temperature and radiant heat.

Actions arising from your assessment may include:

1   Introducing engineering measures to control the thermal effects in a
    workplace environment, for example increasing ventilation rates and
    maintaining the appropriate level of humidity. Where workers are
    exposed to cold and it is not reasonably practicable to avoid exposure you
    should consider, for example, reorganising tasks to build in rest periods or
    other breaks from work. This will allow workers to rest in an area where
    the environment is comfortable and, if necessary, to replace bodily fluids
    to combat dehydration or cold.

2   Use of suitable personal protective clothing (which may need to be heat-
    resistant or insulating, depending on whether the risk is from heat or
    cold).

3   Acclimatisation of workers to the environment in which they work,
    particularly for hot environments.

4   Training in the precautions to be taken.

5   Supervision, to ensure that the precautions identified by the assessment
    are taken.

Lighting

Lighting should be sufficient to enable people to work and move about
safely. If necessary, local lighting should be provided at individual
workstations and at places of particular risk. Lighting and light fittings
should not create any hazard.

Automatic emergency lighting, powered by an independent source, should
be provided where sudden loss of light would create a risk.

Cleanliness and waste materials

Every workplace and the equipment, furnishings and fittings should be kept
clean and it should be possible to keep the surfaces of floors, walls and
ceilings clean.

Cleaning and the removal of waste should be carried out as necessary by an
effective system of disposal. Waste should be stored in suitable receptacles.

SAFETY
Maintenance

The workplace, including equipment, resources and systems should be
maintained in efficient working order (efficient for health, safety and
welfare). Such maintenance is required for ventilation systems, equipment
and resources which would cause a risk to health, safety or welfare if a fault
occurred.

Floors and traffic routes

'Traffic route' means a route for pedestrian traffic, vehicles, or both and includes any stairs, fixed ladders, doorways, gateways, loading bays or ramps.

There should be enough traffic routes, of sufficient width and headroom, to allow people and vehicles to circulate safely with ease.

WELFARE

Sanitary conveniences and washing facilities

Suitable and sufficient sanitary conveniences and washing facilities should be provided at readily accessible places. They and the rooms containing them should be kept clean and be adequately ventilated and lit. Washing facilities should have running hot and cold or warm water, soap and clean towels or other means of cleaning or drying. If required by the type of work, showers should also be provided. Men and women should have separate facilities unless each facility is in a separate room with a lockable door and is for use by only one person at a time.

Drinking water

An adequate supply of high-quality drinking water should be provided. Water should only be provided in refillable enclosed containers where it cannot be obtained directly from a mains supply.

Accommodation for clothing and facilities for changing

Adequate, suitable and secure space should be provided to store workers' own clothing and special clothing. As far as is reasonably practicable the facilities should allow for drying clothing. Changing facilities should also be provided for workers who change into special work clothing. The facilities should be readily accessible from workrooms and washing and eating facilities, and should ensure the privacy of the user, be of sufficient capacity, and be provided with seating.

Suitable and accessible rest facilites should be provided in the workplace

Facilities for rest and to eat meals

Suitable and sufficient, readily accessible rest facilities should be provided.

Seats should be provided for workers to use during breaks. These should be in a place where personal protective equipment need not be worn. Rest areas or rooms should be large enough and have sufficient seats with backrests and tables for the number of workers likely to use them at any one time, including suitable access and seating which is adequate for the number of disabled people at work.

From 1 July 2007, it has been illegal to smoke in most indoor places in the UK other than private homes. The law affects workplaces, including lorries and vans, and there are few exemptions.

LEGAL REQUIREMENTS OF HEALTH AND SAFETY AT WORK

Over the years many new health and safety regulations have been implemented and it is ensured that existing laws/Acts are regularly updated to accommodate expanding technology, changing working methods and increased numbers of employees within the workplace.

The main regulations that need to be addressed, implemented and monitored by the supervisor and manager in an establishment are as follows.

The Health and Safety at Work Act (1974)

This Act is in place to cover employees, employers, the self-employed, customers and visitors. It lays down the minimum standards of health, safety and welfare required within each area of the workplace. As with all health and safety provisions, it is an employer's legal responsibility to ensure that the Act is fully implemented and that as far as reasonably practicable the health and safety of all those they are responsible for is correctly managed.

The Health and Safety (Information for Employees) Regulations (1989)

Current regulations require that an employer must provide employees with health and safety information in the form of notices, leaflets and posters, all of which are available through the Health and Safety Executive.

Where an employer has in excess of five employees, a written health and safety policy must be in place for the establishment. This should be issued to every employee, clearly outlining their personal health and safety responsibilities to the employer, other staff and/or customers, visitors, the public.

The Workplace (Health, Safety and Welfare) Regulations (1992)

The key message within this Act is to ensure that those working in the hospitality/catering industries maintain a safe and healthy working environment. It sets out necessary legal requirements for those in a working environment, such as indoor temperature, lighting, ventilation and staff facilities.

The Food Hygiene (England) Regulations (2006)

The Food Hygiene (England) Regulations provide the framework for EU legislation to be enforced in England. There are similar regulations in Wales, Scotland and Northern Ireland. The Food Safety (General Food Hygiene) Regulations 1995 and the Food Safety (Temperature Control) Regulations 1995 do not apply any more. Many of the requirements of these regulations are included in the new EU legislation, so this means that what businesses need to do from day to day has not changed very much. The main new requirement is to have 'food safety management procedures' and keep up-to-date records of these.

The Manual Handling Operations Regulations (1992)

The Manual Handling Operations Regulations Act provides employers and employees with guidelines on how to protect oneself when lifting heavy objects. A risk assessment must be carried out for all activities which involve manual lifting. Employees should be trained how to handle heavy items correctly and if applicable how to use any necessary equipment to do this.

The Control of Substances Hazardous to Health (COSHH) Regulations (1999)

This Act is in place to ensure the correct storage, handling, use and disposal of hazardous substances and is relevant to everyday working practices. Most hazardous substances are identified through the use of specific symbols, which should be clearly shown and recognisable on items.

COSHH regulations were consolidated in 2002 and employers are stated as being held responsible for assessing the risks from hazardous substances and for controlling the exposure to them to prevent ill health. Any hazardous substances identified should be formally recorded in writing and given a risk rating. Safety precaution procedures should then be implemented and training given to employees to ensure that the procedures are understood and will be followed correctly.

The Electricity at Work Regulations (1989)

This Act is of considerable importance as the frequent use of electrical equipment in a kitchen means that electrical goods will be more prone to maintenance issues and therefore need to be checked regularly. It states that all electrical equipment items within the workplace must be tested every twelve months by a fully qualified electrician.

Further, a trained member of staff should regularly check all electrical equipment for safety reasons. It is recommended that this is carried out at least every 3 months but most employers will undertake this annually.

The Fire Precautions Act (1971)

This Act states that all staff must be aware of and trained in fire and emergency evacuation procedures for their workplace.

The emergency exit route must be the easiest route by which all staff, customers and visitors can leave the building safely and fire action plans should be prominently displayed throughout the premises to show the emergency exit route. Where there are more than 20 employees it is a compulsory requirement of the Act that a fire certificate is obtained and this further applies where there are 10 or more employees on different floors at any one time.

The Fire Precautions (Workplace) Regulations (1997)

This requires that every employer must carry out a risk assessment for the premises, under the *Management of Health and Safety Regulations 1999*.

■ Any obstacles that may hinder fire evacuation should be identified as a hazard and be dealt with

■ Suitable fire detection equipment should be in place

■ All escape routes should be clearly marked and free from obstacles

■ Fire alarm systems should be tested on a weekly basis to ensure they are in full operational condition

Reporting of Injuries, Diseases and Dangerous Occurrences Regulations (RIDDOR) (1995)

All injuries must be reported to the member of staff responsible for health and safety. This includes injuries involving guests, visitors and staff. The organisation's accident book must be completed with basic personal details of the person or persons involved, together with a detailed description of the incident. Each accident report book should comply with the recent **Data Protection Act 2003**. There may be legal consequences because of the injury and all witnesses must provide a clear and accurate statement of events.

The Act's key message is that you must report:

■ Any fatal accidents

■ Work-related diseases

■ Major injuries sustained whilst at work

■ Any potentially dangerous event that takes place at work

■ Accidents causing more than three days absence from work

Occupational health nurse at work

The government regularly reviews, updates and implements new health and safety legislation and laws so it is important to ensure that this is closely monitored and any necessary changes made.

Employers should be provided with regular updates as and when necessary, although it is a good idea to monitor these personally to ensure that legislation can be enforced in plenty of time.

HSE (Health and Safety Executive) or local authority environmental health officers can carry out spot checks at premises at any time. Strict penalties are in force for anyone who does not comply with legal requirements and these officials have the power to issue prohibition notices, improvement notices, prosecute, seize, render harmless or destroy anything deemed to be of imminent danger.

In addition to health and safety law and utilising the guidelines of those applicable to a particular workplace, it must not be forgotten that if the working duties of staff or premises – whether this be structurally or business methods – are adapted in any way then additional health and safety procedures may need to be considered and implemented to cater for this.

It is a legal requirement that all health and safety procedures in place must also be clearly set out in report form should it be required by other parties, such as the employer, employee or an enforcement officer.

This report will need to comprise of a risk assessment, procedures in place to minimise, reduce or abolish the risk, procedures taken to make all persons aware of the policy and procedures in place for recording information, such as any accidents that may occur.

YOUR RESPONSIBILITY IN THE WORKPLACE

Although employers have a legal obligation to ensure health, safety and security within the workplace, managers, supervisors and employees have their own responsibility and the responsibility of their colleagues and/or other persons to take these issues in hand.

You should ensure that you are aware of all health, safety, hygiene and security procedures and regulations that are in place and abide by these as far as possible at all times, being clear as to what applies to your area of work. Further, it is helpful to monitor colleagues within your own particular area of work to ensure continuity. It is a good idea to familiarise yourself as to who the person responsible for health and safety within the company is so that you may direct any questions, concerns or report any incidents to them.

If you are aware of any member of staff who is not working in conjunction with relevant procedures, your employer or designated health and safety officer should be notified immediately and the relevant course of action taken.

If your employer is in breach of procedures, you should notify the HSE or environmental health officer as soon as possible so that they can deal with this.

If others are breaking health and safety law, it is not just you that is at risk but also work colleagues and possibly the public/visitors.

Any personal responsibility for health and safety within your area will usually mean that you will also be responsible for the health and safety of others within this area.

As well as monitoring staff to ensure that all procedures are being adhered to, regular checks should be carried out on things such as equipment to hopefully limit the risk of any possible safety hazards.

In the event of any health, safety, hygiene or security issue, such as an accident or a burnt hand or case of food poisoning, this must be reported immediately to the health and safety officer or other designated member of staff and recorded appropriately, stating the following:

■ Date and time of incident

■ Name of person(s) involved

■ What happened

■ Where it happened

■ If anyone else was present

■ Why it is believed to have happened

HAZARD ANALYSIS AND THE RISK ASSESSMENT PROCESS

Regular health and safety checks should be made to ensure that safe practices are being used. The Health and Safety Act covers all full-time and part-time employees and unpaid workers (such as work placements for students). Everyone needs to be aware of their legal duties for health and safety in the workplace as required by the **Health and Safety at Work Act 1974**.

The Health and Safety Executive (HSE) is the body appointed to support and enforce health and safety in the workplace. They have defined the two concepts for hazards and risk;

1 A hazard is something with the potential to cause harm.
2 A risk is the likelihood of the hazard's potential being realised.

A hazard has the potential to cause harm and everyone must identify working practices within the kitchen environment which could harm people. All staff are required to make sure that the kitchen equipment and the workplace in general is well-maintained and safe to use.

Two examples of this are:

1 A light bulb that requires replacing is a hazard. If it is one out of several it presents a very small risk, but if it is the only light within a 'walk-in' refrigerator, it poses a high risk.

2 A pot of boiling hot oil on a trolley top is a potential hazard that might fall off, causing spillage onto clothes, causing burns and creating a slippery floor surface unless cleared away immediately. Therefore it is a high risk.

As soon as any hazard is observed, it must be reported to the designated authority or line manager so that the problem can be rectified. Hazards can include:

- Obstructions to corridors, stairways and fire exits
- Spillages and breakages
- Faulty electrical machinery

Below is a hazard and risk assessment table to give an overview of how to spot and deal with potential risks and hazards.

HAZARD	POTENTIAL RISK	ACTION REQUIRED
Wet floors or walkways	Slips, trips or falls	■ Signage to warn customers and employees ■ Cleaning of area ■ Reporting of risk ■ Reporting of any maintenance that may be needed, i.e. leaking roof or sink
Kitchen machinery	Cuts, burns, scalds, electric shock, alien bodies in food products	■ Maintenance reports ■ Regular servicing ■ Staff training
Lifting of heavy items, i.e. boxes, saucepans, equipment	Strains and sprains, slipped discs, cuts, bruises	■ Staff training on manual handling ■ Rearrangement of area so items do not have to be lifted so high or far ■ Buying of lifting equipment if required
Cleaning chemicals in the kitchen	Chemical burns, contamination to food and food handlers, slips and falls, inhalation of fumes	■ Staff training ■ Information sheets about each chemical readily available ■ Storage away from food in its own lockable cupboard
Cross-contamination	Food poisoning, spoiling of food, illness, sickness	■ Staff training ■ Correct storage containers ■ Colour coding of kitchen utensils and equipment ■ Food labelling ■ Regular kitchen checks ■ Sanitisers available

Signage and information should be readily available to all staff or members within an establishment for use. Within catering establishments there are four main areas that need extra or special attention.

- Safe storage of chemicals
- Safe work and customer areas
- Safe and hygienic food preparation and service areas
- Safe customer and staff equipment areas and storage

HACCP

HACCP stands for 'hazard analysis critical control point'. It is an internationally recognised and recommended system of food safety management. It focuses on identifying the critical points in a process where food safety problems (or 'hazards') could arise and putting steps in place to prevent things going wrong. This is sometimes referred to as 'controlling hazards'. Keeping records is also an important part of HACCP systems.

HACCP involves seven steps:

1 Identify what could go wrong (the hazards).
2 Identify the most important points where things can go wrong (the critical control points – CCPs).
3 Set critical limits at each CCP (e.g. cooking temperature/time).
4 Set up checks at CCPs to prevent problems occurring (monitoring).
5 Decide what to do if something goes wrong (corrective action).
6 Prove that your HACCP Plan is working (verification).
7 Keep records of all of the above (documentation).

Your HACCP plan must be kept up to date. You will need to review it from time to time, especially whenever something in your food operation changes. You may also wish to ask your local environmental health officer for advice.

The reporting of maintenance issues

The preparation of food for cookery must be prepared on surfaces that are hygienic and suitable for use. Work surfaces, walls and floors can become damaged, and they too can be a source of contamination and danger to customers and staff alike. This should be reported to your line manager. A maintenance reporting system can easily be designed to suit each establishment and each section in that kitchen. Good practice is to have a weekly maintenance check and set procedures for repairing or replacing equipment. If this is done it can lead to a more economical maintenance programme as it much cheaper to repair little and often than to wait until equipment in dangerous and perhaps risk injury or litigation. Areas for attention are:

- Cracks in walls
- Damage to tables and workbenches
- Cooking equipment such as pots, pans and utensils
- Windows, sanitary systems and lights
- Flooring and any other structural issues
- Electrical equipment relating to that particular operation

SECURITY IN THE WORKPLACE

This theme can cover a range of different headings, but in every instance a risk assessment will have to be implemented by the supervisor in order to assess any immediate dangers or threats that are apparent within an establishment. The hotel and catering industry can be an area of high risk with regard to the many different areas it encompasses and will not just cover customers but staff and the establishment itself.

The main security issues within the catering industry are:

- *Theft* can cover a range of offences, including such things as the dishonest and unlawful taking of food and drink within an establishment (not just by customers but staff as well), equipment and furniture or furnishings and souvenirs or keepsakes that can be of value. All items that are unknowingly and unlawfully taken from premises will have to be replaced at the expense of the company or at your own cost, which can prove expensive. Customers' employees' and employers' property is also at risk

- *Fraud* is an ever-increasing security issue due to the way that technology and the electronic world has evolved and continues to do so. More and more customers and businesses are using credit cards to pay for goods and items, often via means such as the Internet or card machines and as there are no physical exchanges of money it can be easy for computer-based fraudsters to access credit card and account details. The use of counterfeit credit cards and currency is something that all employees and employers should be extra vigilant about. Due to modern advances in technology, counterfeit is becoming increasingly harder to spot. As well as money and card fraud, another growing area of concern is false claims and expenses which can vary from anything such as dry cleaning bills to damages claims. This is where the documentation of incidents and occurrences can save companies and establishments thousands of pounds a year by invalidating fraudulent claims

■ *Assault* of staff or customers who are attacked are very serious security matters, both within an establishment and outside an establishment. Whether this is physical or verbal it should be dealt with and treated with the utmost importance. There should be strict security codes and procedures in place to protect everyone at the premises, and staff should be trained on how to deal correctly with unexpected situations, hopefully to recognise and defuse any situation before it reaches a critical point – foresight can be a very good deterrent and helpful aid to all

■ *Terrorism* has more recently become a threat that customers and staff are very aware of and should be taken very seriously. All threats of this nature should be dealt with very carefully, such as telephone calls or suspect packages and people. Any incidents should be dealt with in the same way as a fire action plan is followed through. Assess the situation, seek appropriate action or help and then evacuate the area in a calm manner

■ *Vandalism* can cover a range of security risks and can be caused by customers, staff or outside influences. The malicious damage of property can be costly and time-consuming to rectify. All areas of vandalism need to be considered, from direct physical damage to property, graffiti and arson, to the internal or external damage of the premises

These are some of the main areas of security that are of concern and companies, employers and establishments should do all they can to reduce the risks and hazards that these may cause. In a lot of cases simple procedures such as taking all staff and customer contact details and logging them will not only prove helpful in the event of an incident but can help to reduce the temptation of an incident actually taking place.

Having monitoring procedures in place for things such as stock rotation and levels and by keeping up to date records of what has come in and gone out of the premises will help you to recognise easily if any major discrepancies occur. In addition to holding staff and customer records, this should mean that any issue(s) can be thoroughly checked and resolved.

The main areas of premises that will require security within an establishment are the front and back doors. With the front entrance there should be some sort of reception desk or person to meet and greet both customers and staff so that information/details can be thoroughly checked. All visitors should sign in and out and be given some form of identification such as a visitors pass to carry round the premises with them. Staff should be trained fully and if at any time they suspect anyone or anything suspicious or irregular then they should phone or notify the correct person/manager or police immediately. With the back door all deliverymen/women should have identification on them and be from a reputable company that has already been nominated or screened for security. All maintenance personal should be booked in and have appointments or a person or point of contact. Every visitor should have no problem if a phone call has to be made to their employer to verify details. If they are not meant to be there then they need to be cleared first to ascertain why as mistakes can happen.

CCTV can prove to be very useful as a security measure. Unfortunately is not only costly but can be offputting to customers and staff. There are some very discreet camera devices nowadays which can blend in to the surroundings.

Signage stating that the premises has CCTV is also a very good deterrent and if this type of system is to be used, there should be procedures in place to monitor the recording of films to ensure that the time, date and area are noted on each film so these can be easily listed and checked, as well as ensuring films are checked before being recorded over on a rotation basis. Video monitoring systems for CCTV should be kept in a secured area or office, with limited access by a minimal number of employees only, whose names should be noted on record.

The amount of cash and moneys in an establishment can be of major concern as this can encourage both petty theft and organised crime. If money is known to be on the premises then this can be a serious security risk. Staff should be trained and there should be procedures in place so that takings and payments are cashed up at the end of each shift. A safe should be used or moneys taken to the bank when possible to prevent large amounts being available. Businesses can encourage customers to pay by credit or debit cards to help reduce the amounts of available cash. This however can also pose a risk as card fraud is now a common scam that is becoming more common in all industries. Staff should be trained to check for signatures and name details with all card or cheque transfers. They should also be taught how to check for counterfeit notes and coins.

General security measures which are effective are good lighting and clear areas around and close by the premises. This means customers and staff can see clearly anything suspicious or potential danger. Leaving lights on or on timers can help to deter potential problems if people are led to believe someone is present in the building. Lock doors and windows and access gates when leaving a premises after close of business.

Within any establishment all of the systems that are in place have to be maintained and managed, whether it is for food orders to security. Policies or systems have to be introduced to cover the range of potential risk that a hazard analysis would have picked up. Therefore all staff will have to be trained on all these elements from security threats to bomb alerts to customer or employee theft. These policies must be strict and adhered to at all times. Make sure there are ongoing checks and assessment for present and new security risks. Resources should be set aside to cover the cost of security as in the long run this can prove very cost-effective whether this is internally by the company or by an external source. Having an understanding of the laws and legislation means the establishment and its employees will know their rights and the boundaries of what they are legally required to do. Security and safety go hand in hand, however they are two separate issues and need to be managed separately but together as a balance between safety and security needs.

Assessment of knowledge and understanding

You have now learned about the health and safety responsibilities for everyone in the workplace. This will enable you to ensure your own actions reduce risks to health and safety.

To test your level of knowledge and understanding, answer the following short questions. These will help to prepare you for your summative (final) assessment.

Health and safety law

1   Discuss the various reasons as to why health and safety laws exist and the benefits that enforcing these provides.

2   State who the Health and Safety at Work Act (1974) covers and why is it in place.

3   Explain why it is a good idea to keep yourself up to date with current health and safety law and legislation.

Personal responsibility in the workplace

1   Detail the procedure you should adopt and follow if (i) you are aware of a colleague who is not carrying out correct health and safety procedure and (ii) an employer is not implementing and ensuring that staff carry out correct health and safety procedures.

2   List five points that need to be covered when reporting incidents that occur within your area.

3   Give four examples of health and safety that you are personally responsible for in your own area.

Security within the workplace

1   Give three examples of security issues within the workplace and why they are of importance.

2   Discuss the importance of addressing and implementing security measures within the workplace, detailing how this can benefit the employer, employee and customers/the public.

5

Lead a team to improve customer service

LEARNING OBJECTIVES

This unit is about looking at both your organisation and your staffing resources and bringing these together in a constructive way to improve overall customer service. You need to give support and guidance to your team to encourage them to improve their customer service delivery. It is about having a passion for customer service and sharing this enthusiasm with your colleagues and staff team. It is about leading by example.

After reading this chapter you will be able to:

■ Explain the roles and responsibilities of your team members and where they fit in with the overall structure of the organisation.

■ Show how team and individual performance can affect the achievement of organisational objectives.

■ Understand the implications of failure to improve customer service for your team members and your organisation.

■ Plan work activities.

■ Present plans to others to gain understanding and commitment.

■ Facilitate meetings to encourage frank and open discussion.

■ Involve and motivate staff to encourage teamwork.

■ Recognise and deal sensitively with issues of underperformance.

INTRODUCTION

Improving customer service is a team effort – one person cannot do it all on their own. This means that as a supervisor you need to know how to get the most out of your team in terms of performance. Staff members need to feel motivated and encouraged to provide good customer service and this starts with recruiting and selecting the right

- Customers in a restaurant want more than a meal
- Guests in hotels want more than a room
- Clients in a transaction want more than a settlement
- Customers want more that just the product or service that is offrered – they also want to be treated well

© ISTOCKPHOTO.COM/XAVI ARNAU

candidate to deliver good customer service, followed by induction and then monitoring through individual appraisals, regular reviews and discussions with the whole team, as well as through continual in-house training. This chapter will look at each of those areas step-by-step to help you learn how to embrace and improve customer service in your team.

TECH SKILLS ✓ THE FIVE CORE TRAITS OF A GOOD LEADER

1 Intelligence – this includes verbal ability, perceptual ability and reasoning.

2 Self-confidence – the ability to be certain about one's competencies and skills. It includes self-esteem, self-assurance and the belief that you can make a difference.

3 Determination – desire to get the job done. Includes initiative, persistence, dominance, drive, proactivity and capability to persevere in the face of obstacles.

4 Integrity – honesty and trustworthiness. It is widely recognised that leaders with integrity inspire confidence because they can be trusted to do what they say they are going to do.

5 Sociability – this is the leader's inclination to seek out pleasant social relationships, which includes being friendly, outgoing, courteous, tactful and diplomatic. Also sensitive to others needs and showing concern for their well-being.

These traits enable a good leader to get the most out of their team and they will be illustrated in more detail throughout this chapter.

RECRUITMENT AND SELECTION OF THE RIGHT CANDIDATE TO ENSURE GOOD CUSTOMER SERVICE

When recruiting the right candidate you should be looking out for employees who demonstrate or have the potential to be trained to demonstrate:

1 a positive attitude and cheerful outlook.

2 that they enjoy working with and for other people.

3 the ability to make the customer the single most important person in the room at the time.

4 the ability to allow customers to always be right (even when they are wrong).

A customer service person should be able to demonstrate:

1 reliability.

2 empathy.

3 responsiveness.

ACTIVITY

How do people in customer service roles demonstrate these attributes?

How do you assess these qualities throughout the interview and selection process?

© ISTOCKPHOTO.COM/JEFFREY SMITH

ELEMENT OF QUALITY SERVICE	HOW CAN THIS BE CHECKED DURING INTERVIEW AND SELECTION?
Reliability – the ability to provide what was promised, dependably and accurately	Turn up on time/early for interview, meet deadlines in the application process, provide examples from previous jobs or scenarios
Assurance – the knowledge and courtesy of employees and their ability to convey trust and confidence	Politeness during interview, role play during interview
Tangible – the physical elements of customer service, for example, keeping workstations clean and neat, in an orderly fashion, dress professionally, and maintain excellent grooming and hygiene standards	Dress and appearance at interview, references. Has the applicant made the effort to dress and groom themselves appropriately for the interview?
Empathy – ability to put yourself in the place of your customer and respond compassionately by offering service to address their needs and concerns	Provide case studies or examples from previous jobs, also carry out role play during interview
Responsiveness – project a positive, can-do attitude. Take immediate steps to help customers and satisfy their needs	Provide examples and questions to challenge the applicant on how they would deal with certain customers' needs or requirements

INDUCTION

Induction is the best opportunity to get your message across about the company's mission statement and customer care policy. By the end of induction a customer service person should know their organisation, products or services and customers (see diagrams).

This can be done through providing training and information on:

1 company's mission statements.
2 company's customer care policy.
3 company's motivators and rewards.

Know your organisation

Know your organisation
- Organisation mission and vision
- Organisation culture
- Customer interaction policy and procedures
- Company support for product/service

Know your product/service

Know your product/service
- Product/service development and quality improvement process
- Product/service configuration
- Performance data and specification
- Maintenance and care
- Price and delivery

Know your customers

Know your customers
- Customer needs
- Customer concerns
- Customer personality

4 product knowledge.

But also through:

5 working around the different roles in the team.

6 backing up members of the team in a supportive role initially.

7 serving the customer and getting to know them.

ENABLING THE TEAM TO WORK TOGETHER

In order to continue to improve customer service you need to ensure your team works together. This includes several elements that are going to be looked at further.

Treating team members with respect at all times

The easiest way to show your team that you respect them is to show them that they are just as important to you as customers are to them. How do you do this? By carrying out a variety of actions that include:

■ Maintaining the same personality traits at all times – staff don't enjoy working for an erratic or chaotic team leader

■ Politeness – thank your team on a regular basis

■ Show you care – remember their birthdays, Christmas or special occasions

■ Empathy – be empathetic to their needs, desires and motivation

■ Create a vision for your team of what perfect customer service will look like and how it will benefit them

■ Share the company's core values and your own with them, during team meetings, during the shift, through your own example in the workplace

■ Have fun – make a joke or have a laugh with your team

■ Empower them – trust your team to do their jobs well and use their initiative

Agreeing their role in delivering effective customer service

All teams need goals. Without goals, a team has no measure of performance. Set the goals of performance based on the company's objectives, customer service policy and the staff's job descriptions, the department that you work in and the service standards for that department.

This could include:

■ Appropriate dress

■ Maintaining appropriate hygiene

■ Product knowledge

■ Company knowledge

- Positive attitude
- Order of events from the moment the customer arrives in your department to the point when they leave. This could include the greeting, seating at the table, offer of water, menus, taking the order, laying down the bill

Once these standards have been set, ask the team to go through them and:

- Add to them
- Discuss them
- Agree them

Once the standards are agreed, the whole team can work to the same expectations.

Involving the team in planning and organising customer service work and allocate work to suit the different needs of the individuals within the team

Once the different roles and standards for the team have been recognised and agreed it is important for these to be allocated appropriately. Make sure you know your team's talents, strengths and weaknesses. Then:

- Play to your team's strengths
- Develop their weaknesses during quiet periods and through on-the-job training
- Evaluate their performance and provide feedback (more of this later)

Team meetings and pre-shift meetings

These meetings can be used to plan effectively and organise while involving your team in the process of allocating work to suit their different needs.

For example:

1 break the team into smaller groups and ask them to allocate the roles for the shift.

or

2 ask them to choose roles for each other that best suit each other's best attributes.

but remember,

- In carrying out this kind of exercise, if you are not entirely happy with the end result or allocation of roles you can change this

or,

- You can let them work through the shift and get them to evaluate the performance at the end, seeing if they would change anything another time

Motivating team members to work together to raise customer service performance

There are some very simple motivators to enable teams to work together. These include:

■ Having fun at work

■ Socialising after work. For example organising sporting activities

■ Working together and sharing good practice

Likewise, there are also some motivators that include more tangible rewards

Below is a case study to illustrate how one London hotel motivates their staff to excel in customer service

CASE STUDY

VISION

'The best 4-star hotel in London with special people creating special experiences'

VALUES

'We set our sights high and deliver great results'

'We do the right thing for our customers to show them we care'

'We're one team, pulling together'

'We're straight forward and have respect for each other'

'It's not The Cavendish unless. . .'

1 OUR PEOPLE
● *Our people are friendly, knowledgeable, professional and always willing to help*

2 SETTING AND ARRIVAL
● *You will find our contemporary British hotel exceeds your expectations and our flair delivers a pleasant surprise*
● *Your arrival evokes excitement and reassures you that you have made the right choice*
● *Signage effortlessly gets you where you want to be*
● *Check in is accessible and makes you feel welcome, comfortable and at ease*

3 IN ROOM
● *We do everything in our power to ensure you get a good night's sleep*
● *Your bedroom is comfortable, safe and offers additional comforts to those you can enjoy at home*

4 FOOD AND BEVERAGE
- *We provide a choice that makes breakfast an indulgence you won't want to miss*
- *Our room service menu offers an in-room dining experience comparable to our restaurant*
- *Your evening meal is a fantastic dining experience that you will remember and talk about*

5 CONFERENCE PRODUCT
- *Your conference or event is tailor-made to your needs and you feel you are conducting business with knowledgeable and friendly staff*
- *Our pricing is transparent with no nasty surprises*

SHINE TRAINING

Each new employee attends SHINE training, which teaches them The Cavendish's vision and values. A presentation is given that illustrates the scheme as fun and helps staff to understand the business framework (with the focus on the customer) and the expectations for customer service.

SHINE REWARDS

SHINE cards are filled out by any team leader who witnesses a member of staff living the values of the hotel.

The member of staff then gets recognition from senior management and a £10 voucher.

That member of staff is put up for employee of the month, which is decided at the monthly Head of Department meeting, using a vote system.

Employee of the Month receives £150 voucher of their choice and a trophy in the shape of a star. It is also a great addition to anyone's curriculum vitae (CV).

Typically The Cavendish release 40 to 50 SHINE cards per month.

PROVIDING FEEDBACK TO TEAM MEMBERS

The easiest way to provide this feedback is to make time to sit down with the individual and follow some guidelines. There are various theories on providing feedback, so here are just two examples to help you as a supervisor. See which works best for you: it may be a combination of the two. If neither works for you, talk to your manager or human resource/ training department for more advice and training.

Example 1: Pendleton's rules (adapted)

1 Check your team member wants and is ready for feedback.

2 Let your team member give comments/background to the material that is being assessed.

3 Let your team member state what was done well.

4 Now you state what was done well.

5 Let your team member state what could be improved.

6 Now you state **how** it could be improved.

7 Make an action plan for improvements that includes deadlines and opportunity for monitoring.

Compliment

Criticism

Compliment

Example 2: The hamburger theory

When offering a critique:

1 You begin with a constructive compliment on something the person does well (otherwise known as the fluffy bun part)

2 You then get to the meat of the matter, which of course is the constructive criticism part

3 Finally, you end with another constructive compliment (i.e. the other half of the fluffy bun)

ACTIVITY

ACTIVITY

Research two other methods (in addition to those in the text of this chapter) that illustrate how to provide feedback effectively. What are the key points to be learnt from each of those methods?

SUMMARY

Remember – as part of this module you are required to show the following behaviours which underpin effective performance:

1 You show respect for the views and actions of others

2 You set demanding but achievable objectives for yourself and others

3 You empower staff to solve customer problems within clear limits of authority

4 You encourage and support others to make best use of their abilities

5 You constantly seek to improve performance

6 You give feedback to others to help them improve their performance

7 You work to develop an atmosphere of professionalism and mutual support

The exercises on the following pages have been designed to help you display these attributes effectively in order to improve customer service in your team.

Assessment of knowledge and understanding

You have now learnt about looking at both your organisation and your staffing resources and bringing these together in a constructive way to improve overall customer service. You need to give support and guidance to your team to encourage them to improve their customer service delivery. It is about having a passion for customer service and sharing this enthusiasm with your colleagues and staff team. It is about leading by example.

To test your level of knowledge and understanding, answer the following short questions. These will help to prepare you for your summative (final) assessment.

1 List the attributes you should be looking for from a successful job applicant who could join your team and embrace the improvement of customer service.

2 What do you understand by the Maslow's theory – Hierarchy of Needs – and why is it important for you to understand as a team leader? (You may need to do some research here in regard to Maslow's theory.)

3   One of your team is:

(a)   Really struggling to improve their sales of wine and provide customers with a good choice of wine to go with their food. What action plan of recommendations would you provide to help them improve this area of their customer service?

(b)   Failing to get the food to customers while it is still hot. What action plan of recommendations would you provide to help improve this area of their customer service?

(c)   Unable to deal with customer complaints. As soon as they hear a complaint, they run for you or the manager. What action plan of recommendations would you provide to help improve this area of their customer service?

4   Role play, working in threes – one is team leader, one is the member of team and one is observer. Swap the roles around for each of these roles plays and at the end of each role play the observer should share their thoughts on how well the team leader and member of team dealt with the feedback.

(a)   A member of the team came into work in a really bad mood and during the shift provided the bare minimum of customer service. Team leader – how are you going to manage providing feedback to ensure this doesn't happen again?

(b)   The member of team was late for their shift and was dressed scruffily still wearing yesterday's uniform and looking unshaven. Team leader – how are you going to manage providing feedback to ensure this doesn't happen again?

(c)   The member of team came into work – they are on a trial month before being made permanent but are in the fourth week of the trial. They still do not know the food menu well enough, particularly flavours, ingredients, design of the dishes and complementing side orders. Team leader – how are you going to manage providing feedback to ensure they successfully complete the trial month?

●   Also consider, what you going to do if they do not gain all the product knowledge but show a genuine talent for customer service?

6

Supervise food production operations

LEARNING OBJECTIVES

This unit is about supervising food production to ensure that the customer receives their order within reasonable timescales and to quality standards. The unit is about making sure your staff have the necessary skills, knowledge and resources required to carry out their work. It is also about monitoring work, dealing with food production problems and supervising operations to ensure the quality of the product.

After reading this chapter you will be able to:

■ Make sure that the stages of food production follow relevant legislation and organisational policies.

■ Ensure your staff have the relevant skills, knowledge and resources required to carry out their work.

■ Encourage your staff to ask questions about any instructions they do not fully understand.

■ Carry out and record regular checks to make sure that your procedures are being followed as planned.

■ Promptly take action to minimise the effect of problems that could delay food production or affect the standard of food service.

■ Make sure that staff's agreed targets are achieved.

■ Implement procedures to meet control points following relevant legislation and organisational policy.

■ Encourage your staff to report any actual or possible problems with the control points.

■ Collect feedback from your customers that may help to identify any problems with procedures.

■ Record relevant information and deal with it according to your organisation's procedures.

KEY WORDS

Communication
This term refers to the transfer of information, verbally, physically or via another means such as email.

Customer relationship management (CRM)
This is a term applied to processes implemented by an organisation to handle contact with its customers. CRM software is used to support these processes, storing information on current and prospective customers. Details on any customer contacts can also be stored in the system. The rationale behind this approach is to improve services provided directly to customers and to use the information in the system for targeted marketing.

Customer requirements
Understanding and determining what the customer expectations and needs are on an individual basis.

Effectiveness of procedures
This is used in a quantitative way to measure how effective the procedures are in a food service operation.

Food service
Food service includes those places, institutions, and companies responsible for any meal prepared outside the home. This industry includes restaurants, school and hospital cafeterias, catering operations, and many other formats.

Monitor
To check, track or observe processes and procedures.

Organisational procedures
A set of procedures that usually relate to health and safety in the workplace.

Sous vide
French for 'under vacuum'; is a method of cooking that is intended to maintain the integrity of ingredients by heating them for an extended period of time at relatively low temperatures.

INTRODUCTION

The food production system can be summarised into three specific areas; the input, the process and the output. The objectives of a food production system supervisor are to control the quality through the monitoring of standards, skills, procedures and the motivation of the team. Also the control of costs is of the utmost importance to establish an economical method of producing and serving food. This is achieved by implementing systems of measurement in portion control and identifying and implementing processes that cut wastage and excess costs. Effectiveness through efficiency will result in the operation meeting their targets, goals and maintaining standards.

Using this system as a plan of the production structure certain quality control elements need to be deigned to monitor this process and maintain standards. During the **input phase** the control elements are the designing of job specifications and the recruitment of individuals with specific skills sets. Subsequent training and skills development will be required to update the team as often as possible. Based on the technology and equipment available as your resource menus, recipes and ingredient sourcing can now be designed and identified. Stores and inventory management standards need to be set, purchase specifications will also need to be agreed and communicated to suppliers and the team.

Keeping records of products, product testing and dish specification cards that include photographs of the finished product will help the **process phase** run smoothly. The provision of an organised and safe environment is paramount to this phase to ensure that the produce received is efficiently turned into safe, clean and controlled food for the final **output phase** which introduces the finishing of the dishes and the eventual presentation to the customer. It is in this phase the cooking is again monitored and the service is conducted professionally with strong communication strategies.

> **! REMEMBER**
>
> In the late nineteenth century Auguste Escoffier devised the *partie* system, in which different sections of the kitchen were delegated to carry out specific jobs, whether it be preparing or cooking the fish, meat or vegetables. Some kitchens today – particularly in large hotels – still adhere to Escoffier's traditional system, while others have had to adopt their own systems to accommodate smaller brigades of chefs and less elaborate menus.

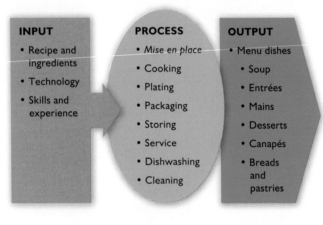

The food production system flow diagram

FOOD PRODUCTION METHODS

The definition of food production is the provision of food flow principally concerned with the processing of fresh, raw, semi-prepared or pre-prepared food stuffs. The consequential product may be in a ready to be served state or it may undergo some sort of preservation process, for example cook-freeze, before eventually being served to a customer.

In the examination of food production methods currently in operation, reference has to be made to the traditions of catering which have had a profound effect on the production methods in operation today. The design of the traditional kitchen was centred on the division of tasks into *parties* or sections. This was the development of the *partie system* and this rigid segregation between these sections meant that the staffing ratio was high in comparison to the amount of meals served.

The traditional methods of food production were maintained and are still used in some hotels and restaurants. However, encouraged by the rising costs of space necessary to house large traditional kitchens, many new operations looked towards different methods of production. By 1966 the first cook-freeze operation had appeared which then gave rise to cook-chill operations later. It is important to note that change has also happened because of the necessary adaptations to food safety law, especially in the form of the Food Safety Control of Temperatures Act 1990.

Conventional food production methods
Traditional partie system
In this method the majority of the food purchased is raw and is then produced on a daily basis for the different service points. The use of labour is alternating, rising to a peak just before the service of each mealtime. The same circumstance is apparent for the use of resources such as cooking equipment, with a good utilisation for short periods of time but generally poor utilisation of resources such as electricity and gas which are often turned on in the morning and left on during the day, although only efficiently used for a few hours. This system is considered an expensive way of running a kitchen in terms of manpower needed to operate it and resource requirements.

The size and complexity of the menu, and the systems used to prepare that menu, will determine the system that is employed to deliver the menu. A kitchen using the traditional partie system with a large brigade of chefs can offer an extensive dinner menu. At service time, a number of skilled chefs will then be able to carry out the final preparation, cooking and presentation quickly and efficiently. A kitchen with a smaller brigade will necessitate an offer of a smaller menu with dishes that can be assembled efficiently.

To ensure this system runs effectively, from the instant fresh supplies are delivered to the kitchen to the position where finished dishes are presented to the customer, distinct areas should be defined. Commodities arriving in the kitchen should be stored quickly into the appropriate storage area (such as the cold store for all perishables), a vegetable store, dry goods store, equipment store or cleaning store for chemicals.

The main food preparation area where meat, poultry, game and fish are prepared should be close to the store area and kept separately from all

Working in a professional partie system

> **! REMEMBER**
>
> A kitchen will only operate efficiently if it has clear leadership from the kitchen supervisor, chef de partie, sous chef or head chef. You must be able to communicate, coordinate, delegate, motivate, organise, inspire and make quick decisions.

vegetable and salad preparation areas. Usually, a separate pastry area should be designated with its own resources for baking, ice cream making and cold storage.

If the kitchen is large enough, all cooking carried out at the point of service will be in a separate area adjacent to the preparation sections, this is where all cooking and the final presentation and service is carried out.

If the preparation and cooking areas occupy the same space, there is a greater necessity for the completion of an efficient *mise en place* system. Dirty tableware should be removed from the restaurant direct to the wash-up area, avoiding the food preparation and cooking areas.

The traditional partie system hierarchy

■ **Executive chef** Highest level possible in the kitchen. Often more time spent undertaking organisational duties than actually cooking. Co-ordinates all kitchen functions and communicates directly with other departments

■ **Chef de cuisine** Manager of the kitchen, resources and kitchen staff

■ **Head chef** The person in authority in the kitchen. Title refers to those who have professional cooks working directly for them

■ **Sous chef** Second in command from the head chef. Responsible for the physical operation of the kitchen, including supervision as well as preparation. If the kitchen is large enough the **head pastry chef** will have the same level of responsibility as the sous chef

■ **Chefs de partie**

- *Saucier:* fish, sautéed dishes, stews, hot hors d'oeuvres, hot entrées and sauces. Commands after the sous chef
- *Rotissieur:* prepares items roasted in the oven and on the spit. Works under the saucier
- *Friturier:* fry cook – responsible for deep-fried foods. Works under the saucier
- *Grillardin:* responsible for grilled foods. Works under the saucier
- *Garde manger:* processes raw meat, cold dishes, forcemeat, pies, galantines and cold hors d'oeuvres
- *Charcutier, and butcher:* work under the garde manger
- *Entremetier:* vegetable cook, responsible for soups (although sometimes saucier does this), vegetables, pasta, and foods made of flour, eggs and cheese
- *Potager:* soup cook, originally was under the supervision of the entremetier
- *Patissier:* pastry chef: all basic desserts, hot desserts, cold desserts, frozen desserts and hot and cold pastries
- *Boulanger and glacier:* work under the patissier

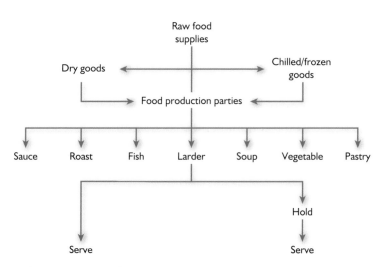

A flow diagram of the main activities in a traditional partie food production system

- Other cooking stations are tournant (relief cook), de garde (duty chef), de nuit (night chef), banquet chef, etc.
- *Commis:* assistants to the chefs de partie
- *Apprentices:* training in each of the parties in turn to learn the entire kitchen

Conventional system for convenience foods

The conventional system has the capacity to facilitate the introduction of convenience foods. This system may range from a partial use to a complete reliance on the wide variety of convenience foods that are now readily available. The best use of such convenience foods is only possible with a specifically planned system however.

In this traditional system if the majority of the food purchased is convenience replacing the previous fresh produce the effects upon labour, equipment, space and the customer should be considered. The reasons that convenience products are used are predominantly cost-based and they will help to ensure that a derived standard and consistency is easier to reach and maintain from the kitchen to the customer. There are minimised set-up costs within the kitchen utilising labour saving equipment and multi-task equipment such as combination ovens, pasta cook units and blast chillers.

Centralised production methods

This system involves the separation of the production and service components of the food flow system. Food that is centrally produced is either then distributed to the point of service in batches or it can be pre-portioned and transported in a ready-to-serve state, either hot or cold dependent on the dish specification, and served with minimal final preparation.

Smaller version centralised production units (CPUs) are gaining popularity in the commercial sector, especially with restaurant chains as a mechanism of

Serving food at a satellite service kitchen in a CPU

providing standardisation of product across outlets. The advantages of the centralised production method are:

1 The separation of the production and service facility allows the unit to work at a consistent level of efficiency as opposed to the traditional partie system.

2 The introduction of a storage phase between the production and service phase allows the production unit to work to maximum efficiency with an economical utilisation of staff and equipment resources.

The disadvantages include:

■ High capital investment of planning and constructing a CPU

■ Unless the system is fully utilised the cost per meal can rise dramatically

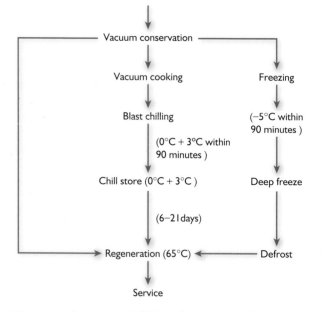

Diagram of the possibilities of the sous vide method

Sous vide

The sous vide food processing technique (meaning under vacuum) was developed in the late 1970s as a way to help reduce shrinkage in foods during cooking whilst maintaining the flavour, moisture and texture values of the food. The method was developed by Georges Pralus for the Restaurant Troisgros (of Pierre and Michel Troigros) in Roanne, France. He discovered that when cooking foie gras in this manner it kept its original appearance, did not lose excess amounts of fat and had a better texture. Another founder in the science of sous vide is Bruno Goussault, who further researched the effects of temperature on various foods and became well known for training top chefs in the method. This system involves the preparation of quality raw foods, pre-cooking such as searing or browning where required, placing the raw food into special plastic pouches, vacuuming and sealing these pouches and either steaming or poaching to complete the cooking process.

The food product can be served directly at this stage or rapidly chilled to 3°C or below and stored for a maximum of 21 days.

The use of sous vide is gaining prominence in many of today's leading kitchens because of the emergence of water-bath machines (thermal immersion circulators) which are used to circulate precisely heated water. Differences of even one degree can affect the finished product. Also the flavour, palatability and nutritional value of the food are all improved and the pouches are also a convenient way of packaging food for safe handling and handy storage.

This system also offers a flexible production method to catering units of all sizes with particular emphasis on à la carte menus and function catering for large numbers.

Sous vide allows kitchens to maximise advance preparation. Provided the food is chilled quickly after the cooking process has finished, it can be safely stored until needed.

It also reduces wastage, making sous vide a highly cost-effective cooking method. This method gives kitchens substantial operational benefits:

■ Minimise wastage by advance preparation of controlled portions

■ Minimum shrinkage of contents during cooking process, typically from 30 per cent to less than 5 per cent in most cases resulting in greater yield

■ Cheaper cuts of meat can be used as the sous vide technique dramatically improves tenderness

■ Extra demand can be drawn from cold store or less used in quieter periods

■ Low energy consumption compared with ovens and gas ranges

■ Non-use of gas reduces ambient temperature in kitchen, and fire risk

■ Several meals from starter to dessert can be regenerated simultaneously in the same bath reducing clean up time

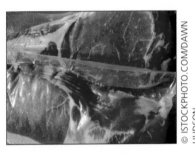

■ With minimal training, unskilled staff can use Clifton Water Baths, this simplifies service and is especially useful for room service during the night

■ Work planning, preparation and cooking outside of service times is improved, e.g. planning ahead for banquet preparation

Vacuum packed meat

When using the sous vide method, it is vital to establish procedures and policies to demonstrate that all efforts have been taken to minimise the risk from anaerobic bacteria e.g. *clostridium botulinum*.

Typical steps to establish a food safety policy

■ Source only the highest quality ingredients from known suppliers and have a system of traceability in place

■ Separate food areas for raw and cooked

■ Establish minimum cooking temperatures for meat and fish

■ Adhere to maximum storage temperatures and times

■ Strict labelling of contents with date (including expiry date) and identification of contents

■ Consider using disposable sterile gloves when filling sous vide bags

■ Use two separate vacuum machines, one for raw and other for cooked foods

HACCP (**h**azards **a**nalysis and **c**ritical **c**ontrol point **p**rogramme) must be implemented as part of the production system. This covers the movement of food from delivery to service. Identify points of risk – some of which may include the following:

- Quality of water in kitchen
- Potential breaks in the 'cold chain'
- Unnecessary 'holding' time
- Potential contamination points with other foods/items in the kitchen environment
- Improper stock identification and rotation
- Time taken to cool cooked food for storage

HYGIENE IN FOOD PRODUCTION: A BASIC GUIDE FOR THE SUPERVISOR

What are the regulations?

The Food Hygiene (England) Regulations 2006 are supported by European Regulation 852/2004.

Who is affected?

Anyone who owns, manages or works in a food business, apart from those working in primary food production such as harvesting, slaughtering or milking, is affected by these Regulations. They apply to anything from a hot dog van to a five-star restaurant, from a village hall where food is prepared to a large supermarket, or to a vending machine. The Regulations do not apply to food cooked at home for private consumption. Every process which deals with preparing or selling food can be classed as a food business activity, including preparation; handling; processing; packaging; manufacturing; storage; transportation; selling; distribution; supplying.

Identifying and controlling food hazards

As the supervisor of a food business, you must:

- Ensure food is supplied or served in a hygienic way
- Identify food safety hazards
- Know which steps in your activities are critical for food safety
- Ensure safety controls are in place, maintained and reviewed

The majority of food businesses will require having a documented food safety management system in place. For catering businesses the 'Safer Food Better Business' pack, published by the Food Standards Agency, may be ideal.

> **! REMEMBER**
>
> The food hygiene regulations apply to all types of food and drink and their associated ingredients.

Basic requirements for food businesses

Food premises should:

- Be clean and maintained in good repair
- Be designed and constructed to permit good hygiene practices
- Have an adequate supply of potable (drinking) water
- Have suitable controls in place to protect against pests
- Have adequate natural and/or artificial lighting
- Have sufficient natural and/or mechanical ventilation
- Provide clean lavatories which do not lead directly into food rooms
- Have adequate hand-washing facilities
- Be provided with adequate drainage

Rooms where food is prepared, treated or processed should generally have surface finishes which are easy to clean, and where necessary, disinfect. This would, for instance, apply to wall, floor and equipment finishes. The rooms should also have:

- Adequate facilities for washing food and equipment
- Adequate facilities for the storage and removal of food waste

Supplies of raw materials

Do not purchase or supply any raw materials if you think that even after sorting or processing they could make food unfit for human consumption. Any material which you suspect or know to be infected or contaminated with parasites or foreign substances to this extent should be rejected.

Monitoring the hygiene of the food production area is essential

Quality of water in food

There must be an adequate supply of drinking water, to be used whenever necessary to ensure food is not contaminated. In the vast majority of cases, this is supplied via the public water supply. If there is any doubt about the quality of a water supply, you should seek advice from your local council environmental health services.

Personal hygiene for food handlers

Anyone who works in a food handling area must maintain a high degree of personal cleanliness, and the way in which they work must also be clean and hygienic. Food handlers must wear clean and, where appropriate, protective over-clothes. Anyone whose work involves handling food should:

- Observe good personal hygiene
- Routinely wash their hands when handling food

■ Never smoke in food handling areas

■ Report any illness (like infected wounds, skin infections, diarrhoea or vomiting) to their manager or supervisor immediately

If any employee reports that they are suffering from any such illness, the business may have to exclude them from food handling areas. Such action should be taken urgently. If you have any doubt about the need to exclude, you should seek urgent medical advice or consult your local council environmental health services.

Preventing food contamination

Food handlers must protect food and ingredients against contamination which is likely to render them unfit for human consumption or a health hazard. For example, uncooked poultry should not contaminate ready-to-eat foods, either through direct contact or through work surfaces or equipment.

Training and supervising food handlers

Food handlers must receive adequate supervision, instruction and/or training in food hygiene. Each food business must decide what training or supervision their food handlers need by identifying the areas of their work most likely to affect food hygiene. Useful guidance may be found in relevant industry guides to good hygiene practice.

A QUALITY MANAGEMENT APPROACH TO FOOD PRODUCTION

To deliver a quality product to your customer the food production operation must adopt some form of systematic approach to quality control. The quality management cycle shown left has been developed from a quality system of

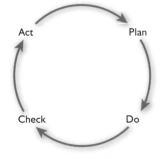

The quality management cycle

> ### ! REMEMBER
>
> Food production operations have many unpredictable elements and added complications to deal with.
>
> 1 Cost structure and high fixed costs in the production and service of food.
>
> 2 Unpredictable demand of sales.
>
> 3 Short production cycle of food preparation. A restaurant may purchase fresh ingredients in the morning to be prepared and offered for lunch service to be consumed. This short cycle allows for little time to correct any mistakes.
>
> 4 The risk of limited shelf life of perishable products and the possibility of bacterial contamination.
>
> 5 Recent and fast-moving developments in food production technology to help increase volume of output, at higher speeds with greater consistency.
>
> 6 The customer expectations that can often be changeable according to external issues such as the time of year, holidays, business or financial climate.

Deming's (1982) Plan-Do-Check-Act cycle. This approach was designed to help identify and correct any errors that occur during production or service in industry and to create a lasting quality improvement plan.

The cycle begins by planning what improvements need to be made based on the illumination of an underlying problem. The 'do' phase implements the move to correct the problem that is then 'checked' through a scheme of measurement. The final phase 'acts' to implement this specific quality improvement to embed it into the working processes of the production team.

Planning

The starting point for any quality strategy should be to establish the specific requirements of customers the food production unit intends to serve. For example: what does a business or local company expect from a lunch during a corporate meeting day and how is that different to normal lunch customers? From this base and many others similar to this question, the operation can derive a detailed operating concept and standardised operating procedure.

Doing

Once the design of the operation has been decided the standards and procedures need to be adopted. Most businesses will create detailed standards of performance which can be built into job roles and standards manuals and that will form the part of an induction process with ongoing training of all employees.

Checking

Checking that the operation performs according to the business plan can be driven at two levels. The first level is creating checks as part of a daily routine. This might include checking the quality of food supplies and deliveries to checking the flavour, consistency and cooking of dishes during the cooking and service stages. Periodic inspection usually identifies whether all procedures are being followed. The method here is some form of operational or internal audit, whereby a detailed checklist is developed to cover aspects of the operation.

Acting

The concluding stage of this cycle is to act on the information collected. Consistency involves acting on any non-compliance to established standards. Quality improvement to move towards zero deficiencies is a continuing process. This cycle focuses on an improving process and to help ensure that the food production concept continues to match the customer's requirements.

Thus at the level of a supervisor or team leader you will typically undertake the following quality control tasks:

1 Plans, organises and supervises the work of dining room and kitchen employees as assigned.

2 Supervises food preparation.

3 Checks and orders supplies.

4 Assists in planning menus.

5 Keeps quality records.

6 Makes quality reports.

7 Performs other related duties as assigned by the operational management.

MEASURING CUSTOMER SERVICE LEVELS

Where possible, systems should be put in place to assess the operation's performance in business areas which significantly affect your customers' satisfaction levels. Identify key performance indicators (KPIs) which reflect how well you are responding to your customers' expectations.

For instance, you might track:

■ The number of queries or complaints about your products or services

■ The number of complaints about your employees

■ The number of dishes returned with complaints

■ The number of contacts with a customer each month

■ Time taken from order to service

Your customers and employees will be useful sources of information about the KPIs which best reflect key customer service areas in your operation or section, making sure that the measures are driven not by how the operation currently runs, but by how your customers would like to see it run.

Customer feedback and contact programmes

Customer feedback and contact programmes are two ways of increasing communication with your customers. They can represent enormous opportunities to pay attention to your customers and to let them know more about what your operation can offer. Customer feedback can provide you with detailed information about how your establishment is perceived. It is also an opportunity for customers to voice doubt, suggest changes or endorse your existing processes, and for you to take note of what they articulate and act upon it. Feedback is most often gathered using questionnaires, administered in the restaurant/service area in person, over the telephone, via email or by post.

The purpose of customer contact programmes is to help you deliver tailored information to your customers. One example is news of a special offer that is relevant to a past purchase – another is a reminder sent at the time of year when a customer traditionally dines at your outlet. Contact programmes are particularly useful for reactivating relationships with lapsed customers. Ensure that your customers sense the added contact is relevant and beneficial to them – inundating customers with unwanted calls or marketing material can be counterproductive. Newsletters and email bulletins allow you to keep in touch with useful information at specifically planned times.

How to deal with customer complaints

Every business has to deal with situations in which things go wrong from a customer's point of view. However you respond if this happens, you should not be dismissive of your customer's problem – even if you are convinced you or your team are not at fault. Although it might seem contradictory, a customer with a complaint represents a genuine opportunity for your business:

■ If you handle the complaint successfully, your customer is likely to prove more loyal than if nothing had gone wrong

■ People willing to complain are rare – your complaining customer may be alerting you to a problem experienced by many others who silently took their custom elsewhere

Complaints should be handled courteously, sympathetically and, above all, swiftly. Make sure that your establishment has a recognised procedure for dealing with customer complaints and that it is known to all your employees. At the very least it should involve:

■ Listening sympathetically to establish the details of the complaint

■ Recording the details together with relevant material, such as a sales receipt

■ Offering rectification – whether by replacement or refund

■ Appropriate follow-up action, such as a letter of apology or a phone call to make sure that the problem has been rectified

TARGET SETTING FOR YOUR TEAM

A new member of your team will be developing their skills over a two- to three-year period and during that time the mentoring and review processes will be helpful in identifying strengths and gaps in the individual's range of skills. The work they are involved in may also be changing over that time. The appropriateness of the targets being set is crucial to the whole process: agreeing targets that are too basic means that the individual will not be working to their full potential, and setting targets that are too ambitious means that undue pressures will be put on the individual.

The least helpful approach to supporting the new member of staff would involve a combination of poorly defined and inappropriate targets that are only discovered to be unhelpful some months into the process, or even worse, during the first annual review discussions.

A simple test of their appropriateness is to review how 'SMART' they are: i.e. to check the agreed target against the following criteria:

Regular meetings with team members help to stimulate positive communication

- Is the target *specific* enough – is everyone involved clear about what exactly needs to be achieved?
- Is the target *measurable* – can you actually demonstrate that a change has taken place?
- Is the target *achievable* – does the target take account of the existing levels of skill, with some sense of progress that is still possible, given the level of skills at present?
- Is the target *relevant* – is it an area the individual can actually have a direct impact on?
- Is the target *time-based* – does everyone involved know when the target has to be achieved by?

If concerns about performance are identified at any time, or if the annual review identifies that the individual has not fully achieved the previous year's targets, the supervisor should consider how to support the individual appropriately and advice should be sought from the HR manager/advisor at an early stage.

Becoming a better communicator

Your responsibility as a supervisor is to communicate clearly and concisely to all employees and create an environment conducive to openness for others. As the staff becomes more diverse, you may have to take extra time and effort to communicate to all staff members. To become a better communicator:

- **Create an open communication environment in your unit**. Encourage employees to talk about work issues; listen carefully and respond to questions or concerns with actions or answers. If an issue is outside your authority, pass it along to the appropriate person; then be sure to follow up

- **Conduct regular staff meetings**. Tell your staff about decisions that may affect them or the work they do and the reasons for those decisions. Use staff meetings to encourage feedback, generate ideas, solve problems and gain support

- **Set up individual meetings**. Set some time aside periodically to meet one-on-one with employees. Group staff meetings are important; however, meeting separately with your employees shows concern about their individual work issues

Further reading and research

Cracknell, H. L. *et al.* (2000) *Practical Professional Catering*. 2nd ed. Macmillan.

Deming, W. E. (1982) *Quality, Productivity and Competitive Position*. Massachusetts Institute of Technology, Centre for Advanced Engineering Study.

Hunter, G. *et al.* (2008) *The Professional Chef Level 3*. Cengage Learning.

Jones, P. and Lockwood, A. (2004) *The Management of Hotel Operations*. Thomson Learning.

Lillicrap, D. and Cousins, J. (2006) *Food and Beverage Service*. 7th ed. Hodder and Stoughton.

Catering, Hospitality & Leisure – Kitchen Management Jobs http://www.jobsite.co.uk/jobs/cateringhospitalityandleisure/kitchenmanagement

The World Association of Chefs http://www.wacs2000.org/

The Craft Guild of Chefs http://www.craftguildofchefs.org/

The British Hospitality Association http://www.bha.org.uk

The National Restaurant Association http://www.restaurant.org

Assessment of knowledge and understanding

You have now learned about supervising the food production system and making sure that the operational area and method of production meets the service requirements. You have seen how it involves planning, supervising cleaning, checking equipment, liaising with other departments and dealing with problems to ensure that service meets the required standard.

To test your level of knowledge and understanding, answer the following short questions. These will help to prepare you for your summative (final) assessment.

1 How can you communicate standard operation procedures to your team?

2 Explain one way you can clearly communicate with customers to measure their meal experience.

3 How would you organise staff training on an individual basis?

4 What would help you observe trends from your customers?

5 What challenges does your operation face in delivering quality to your customers?

6 Describe what is meant by the phrase 'measuring service satisfaction'?

7 State why understanding the needs of the organisation is important.

8 Using Deming's quality management cycle select what you think would be your three most important areas to increase the performance of your food production team. Justify your ideas for this.

9 How would you correct and report failures according to organisational standards and procedures in the kitchen?

Research task

Training the team in their job roles is important when working in a busy food production outlet. Design one dinner menu based on a new team of four chefs with only one of them qualified to a level 3 and the other three at level 1 standard, preparing and presenting food at a high-class gastropub.

Explain where you might employ each chef in the kitchen and with what basic job role.

7

Supervise functions

HS8 Supervise functions

LEARNING OBJECTIVES

This unit is about supervising a functions, for example: a banquet, corporate entertainment event, reception or conference. The unit covers the preparation, running and closing of the event. As such it includes activities such as briefing, monitoring, clearing up and debriefing staff beyond the close of the function.

After reading this chapter you will be able to:

■ Obtain all the necessary information about the function, customer requirements and your responsibilities.

■ Make sure that the equipment and materials needed for the function are on site in good time and are available to the staff that will need to use them.

■ Inspect the function venue to make sure that it has been prepared as agreed.

■ Familiarise yourself with all the necessary health and safety and other legal requirements and communicate these clearly to customers.

■ Brief your staff about their responsibilities at every stage of the function.

■ Liaise with the relevant people throughout the function to make sure that the arrangements meet customer requirements.

■ Monitor the function to make sure that it is running to plan and deal with any problems that threaten to disrupt operations.

- Make sure the function complies with relevant legislation and your organisation's standards.
- Record all relevant information in a suitable format and make this information available to the relevant people.

KEY WORDS

Active documentation
This term is used to describe the paperwork or files being used at the present time in relation to the function, e.g. the booking sheets, menus.

Adjustments
This term refers to any changes to the pricing structure should the organiser require any additional items or services.

Advanced deposit
This term refers to a set amount of money paid to secure the event. This will ensure the room is not double-booked.

Conference groups
This refers to groups of guests who are attending a conference, this can be internal or external.

Credit check
This check is occasionally used to ensure the organiser has sufficient funds to pay for the event.

Daily running sheet
This is a schedule of events that must occur prior to the event, the list will involve the day's work and checks are made to ensure all tasks are carried out efficiently.

Disclaimer
This limits the liability amount which is payable to the guests, including theft, loss or damage whether in the car park, restaurant, suites or function rooms.

Extras
These are services or products which may be added to the organiser's bill with their authorisation.

Function catering
This term is used to describe the service of a particular event, for a set number of guests, with a set menu with predetermined drinks.

Handover
This important function is carried out by two or more staff members who share information regarding the days work, functions etc. to ensure a smooth transition.

Interconnecting rooms
Most commonly found in function rooms, these fold away doors increase or decrease capacity as required.

Meal plans
These are detailed lists showing what meals the guests require, whether breakfast, lunch or dinner, and any special requirements.

Memorandum (memo)
This is an internal document used to communicate between staff or departments.

Minutes
Function minutes are extremely important as they convey the exact requirements of the organiser. They should be typed and sent to the organiser for their approval prior to the function taking place.

Package
A package designed to encourage occupancy, sometimes a package is offered to the organiser when large bookings are made.

Paging
This is a discreet way to contact staff members who are not located in one particular area; banqueting and function staff use these to co-ordinate their work.

Presentation rooms
This refers to the high standards expected when setting up rooms for an event.

USP
The unique selling point.

INTRODUCTION

Functions are defined as the service of food and drink at a designated place and at a specified time for a set number of people and a fixed cost. Functions such as banquets, corporate entertainment, receptions or conferences are an important part of the hospitality industry.

Each is a special project in its own right, and the organisation providing the service is very much in the public eye. The reputation of the business can grow when things go well or be seriously affected if things go badly.

If you are supervising a function you need to be clear about customer requirements. You will need thorough planning, and unflappable organisation, especially when problems occur.

You will also need a sound knowledge of relevant legislation and regulations if the function is to be successful and 'word-of-mouth' publicity is going to be positive.

The types of activities you might carry out for this unit include:

■ Gathering information about the function, customer requirements and your responsibilities

■ Briefing staff about the function and their responsibilities

■ Liaising with colleagues, staff and customers throughout the function

■ Observing arrangements and making sure that these meet legal requirements and your organisation's standards

■ Dealing with problems, such as supply and staffing, that may disrupt the function

■ Clearing up after the function

■ Debriefing staff after the function

■ Getting feedback from others who have been involved

■ Completing all the necessary records

> **! REMEMBER**
>
> There are numerous types of function:
>
> ■ Social – such as weddings, anniversaries and dances
> ■ Business – working lunches and dinners, conferences and meetings
> ■ Combination of social and business – corporate entertainment

© ISTOCKPHOTO.COM/MIKE CLARKE

A typical function room set for a dinner event

FUNCTION TYPES

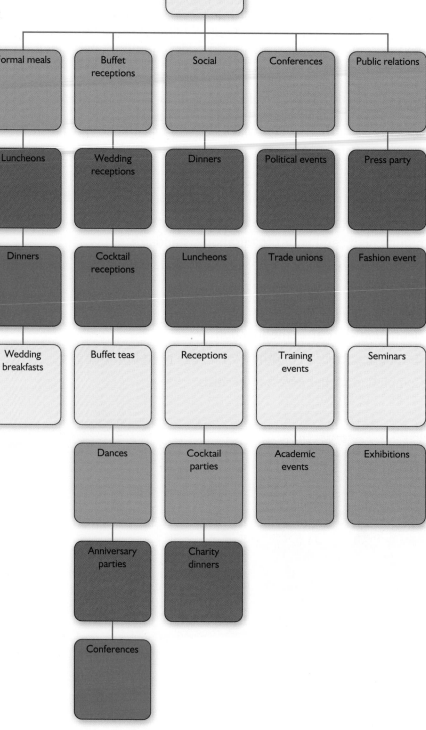

FUNCTION SERVICE STAFF ROLES AND RESPONSIBILITIES

High-end establishments may have a dedicated team whose sole responsibility is the organisation, co-ordination and set up of functions; they will ensure the event is seamless and the guests are happy with the end result.

Smaller establishments will use existing staff to cover the areas and ensure the event is carried out to the best of their ability; this will be undertaken as part of their regular duties.

Sales manager	The promotion of all functions is the responsibility of the sales manager; they will make contact, telephone prospective customers, follow up past organisers and attempt to secure future bookings.
	The sales manager must have a complete understanding of all facilities available and be able to offer the best election to any future customer.
Banqueting/conference manager	These managers are responsible for administration, meeting clients and discussing the finer points of their event. They must ensure that all departments are informed of the events and co-ordinate the process until the event is complete.
Administration office staff	Their responsibility is to work alongside the managers to co-ordinate all correspondence and mail, ensuring it reaches the correct departments prior to the event. These staff members will take provisional bookings and then pass them onto their supervisor.
Banqueting/function head waiter	It is the head waiter who is responsible for the room set-up and organising the front of house team, using experience and leadership qualities to provide a top class service.
Dispense bar	The bar is used to supply all stock for the event. The drinks do not come from the main bar, the control of stock, cash during the service and refilling is the bar manager's area of responsibility.
Banqueting sommelier	This post requires the organisation of staff to deliver the correct wines with each course, they will work with the dispense bar to co-ordinate the event seamlessly.
Permanent staff	Permanent staff are usually experienced in function set-ups and will multi-task, they will ensure the room is set prior to the day.
Casual staff	These staff members are paid hourly and brought into work as required, they will undertake micro training and are usually used as waiting staff.
Porters	The porters will assist in preparing and clearing the room after the function is complete, this is one of the most physical jobs required.

THE ADMINISTRATION

Financial considerations

The designated gross profit margin associated with functions tends to be higher than normal catering in a restaurant or food/drink shop and is usually between 65 and 75 per cent, although this figure can be higher.

The type of function, setting, catering etc. is dependent on the customer's spending power. The average spend of a function usually takes into account the meal and drink during the meal. Pre-dinner drinks, liqueurs and cigars are usually purchased separately.

The semi-fixed and variable costs of the function co-ordination team play a large part; there are prices available for food, drinks, settings, decoration and speakers to name a few.

© ISTOCKPHOTO.COM/
KIRBY HAMILTON

Wine served for a function

Booking and administration

A future function will be clearly documented and key information should be obtained; the questions that need to be asked are:

- The date and time of the function
- The details of the host/organiser
- The type of rooms required and any special requirements such as notification of the need for disabled access
- Food and drink, menus, wine etc.
- What type of service is required: family, buffet, waiter service
- Approximate numbers – which can be finalised closer to the end date
- Size of the tables, seating arrangements
- Price per head or an overall cost
- Cash bar, pre-paid or post event
- Any special requirements
- Equipment hire – speakers, microphone
- Deposit and final payment

Further information that may be sought depends on the type of function required:

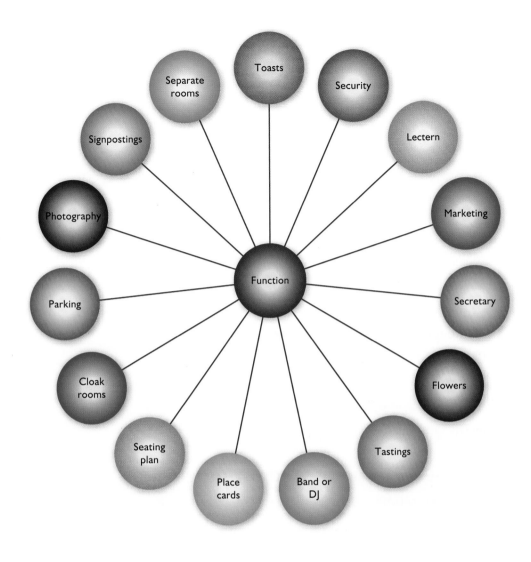

Types of service used

The types of service will vary according to cost, the type of event and the preference of the organiser:

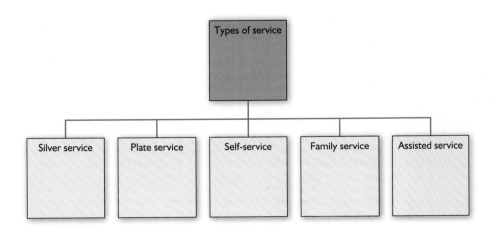

- Silver service is the presentation of food by waiting staff using a spoon and fork, the use of flats and dishes usually made from silver
- Family service – main courses are served plated and the accompaniments and vegetables are served in a dish or bowl and placed onto the table
- Plate service – the meal is plated completely and served to customers
- Self-service – the guests collect their food, usually at a canteen
- Assisted service – this can be a carvery or buffet where guests are offered choices and they move along to complete their meal

The decision is made by the guest with a little help from the establishment; factors which may influence the choice are:

- The guest's wishes
- The type of event
- The food and drink being offered
- The time of the event
- The level of skill the establishment has to offer
- The room set-up
- The equipment available

The seating plans and arrangements

Depending on the type of event it is important to ascertain the following information:

- How many guests on the top table
- Are the ends of the top table being used
- Try to avoid 13 guests (bad luck)
- How many other tables are being used
- What shape of tables – round, oblong, square
  - Numbering the tables, avoiding number 13 if possible; the use of letters will avoid the problem all together
  - The numbers should be set at a height to make it easy for the guests and staff to identify the table location

The seating plans

There are two distinct ways that table plans are produced:

The use of alphabetical lists allows guests to see quickly where their tables are located. Alternatively the tables will be listed with guest's names attached to them; this method is slightly harder for the guest to identify as they must scan all the tables for their name.

A function room set for an event

Recently the use of both allows the organisers, guests and staff to identify seating positions without any problems. Three copies of the lists are produced:

1 To be given to the organiser so they can check they are happy with the arrangements.
2 The guests' copies are left in a key position such as the entrance to the lobby or function rooms.
3 The banqueting team have a copy for reference through the event.

The layout of the tables will be determined by numerous factors including:

■ The type of event
■ The guest's wishes
■ The size of the room and facilities available
■ Number of guests expected

For smaller events and functions the T-shaped table or U set-up may be adopted; as follows:

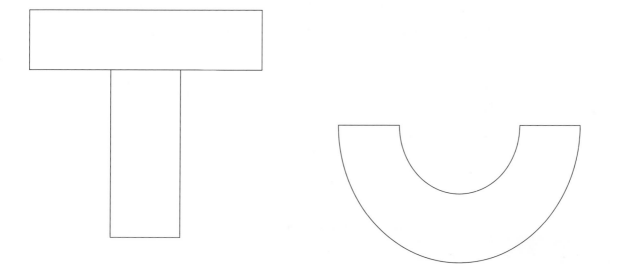

These table plans are ideal for informal events as extra rooms are not required; when the event becomes more formal or the numbers increase then additional break-away tables may be used to facilitate the service.

Large events may use a top table with springs or circular tables:

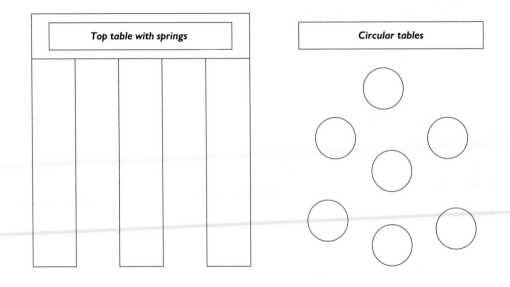

When setting a table the factors which determine spaces are as follows:

■ The minimum space between table springs should be 2 metres (this measurement is made between the backs of the chairs plus the walk way between (1 metre)

■ The average width of tables is between 70cm and 80cm

■ The cover width should be between 50cm and 60cm

■ The distance from any wall to table should be a minimum of 1 metre and 46cm (this is made up of 1 metre walk way and 46cm chair distance from the table)

■ Round tables are:
  ● 1 metre diameter
  ● 1.5 metre diameter
  ● 2 metre diameter

■ When setting up tables for sit-down functions the average area allowed per person is $1m^2$–$1.4m^2$

Clothing the tables (clothing up)

Function cloths for table should be well maintained and laundered; they can set the tone for the event and give the right image the establishment wishes to portray.

The size generally held in stock is 2 metres by 4 metres; longer cloths are available to cover springs, which reduces the need for overlapping or folding.

A clothed table set for a function

The crease should run down the centre of the table with an even over-hang all around the table.

Any patterns should be facing the same way and care must be taken not to mix patterns as this looks unprofessional.

It may take more than one staff member to lay a cloth neatly and to give the desired effect, when clothing a round table a larger size is advisable and two may be used ensure a maximum drop of 70cm is achieved and a 20cm minimum drop.

TABLE DIAMETER	CLOTH SIZE	LONGEST DROP	SHORTEST DROP
1 metre	170cm × 170cm	70cm	35cm
1.5 metre	205cm × 205cm	70cm	27cm
2 metre	240cm × 240cm	70cm	20cm

Clearing and breakdown

The clearing of the tables will occur during the event as plates, crockery and cutlery are removed. This is the normal procedure undertaken in a restaurant environment. Once all guests have left the cloths are removed and sent to be laundered, the tables are dismantled and stored unless the room is being used for another event. The floors should be vacuum cleaned, swept or polished as appropriate and the entire room cleaned to a high standard. These jobs will be shared amongst the waiting staff, porters and housekeepers depending upon the type of establishment.

It is important that a stock take of linen, crockery and cutlery is undertaken to ensure there is sufficient for the next event and to enable any breakages or faults to be repaired or new items purchased.

Marketing

The successful marketing of your function rooms, food, wine, ambience and style will ensure the correct clientele approach the business for their choice of function.

Careful reviews, complimentary descriptions and relevant information help to sell the package.

The function manager/s should create a plan which covers the following points:

- Facilities – these should focus on the good points of the establishment, beautiful settings, disabled access, banqueting halls etc.
- Development – recent improvements such as new rooms, suites, sound systems

■ New product lines – group rates, discounts, clubs etc.

■ Finance – target setting, turnover and gross profit forecasts

■ Productivity – target setting for function utilisation, gross profit and wastage

■ Research – ongoing research of the local area

■ Brochures – colour printed brochures selling your expertise and the 'unique selling point' (USP)

Pricing and costing

The majority of function menus are pre-costed and the gross profit is set: this takes into account staff requirements, equipment and other variables. Additions are occasionally added for little or no additional monies to secure the client's business, this however is a senior management decision. The price for a function should be good value to secure the job; however if the price is too low clients may feel uneasy regarding the quality and decided to go elsewhere.

All functions should be costed to achieve the break-even mark at the very minimum. Gross profit will then start once all costs have been recouped.

There are three factors to consider when pricing a function:

■ Nature of demand – decreasing the price may increase sales whereas an increase in price may affect sales in a negative way

■ Level of demand – flexible pricing is necessary as low demand will result in under-utilisation. Creating deals on functions in low seasons will help utilise the space

■ Competition level – competition is a key factor to pricing and utilisation; monitoring competition will help you stay in touch and establish a larger volume of clients, resulting in higher profits

■ An example of a function cost is:
- 35 per cent food cost
- 25 per cent labour
- 30 per cent additional costs – flowers, linen, cleaning
- 10 per cent gross profit

Flowers supplied for a function

Cost control

Cost control is essential in the running and maintaining of any business. The aim being to obtain and retain as much money as possible, whilst paying out as little as possible in costs.

The cost of employing staff, food produce purchased, equipment repaired, replaced or new items bought in and even the rent on a building must be closely monitored at all times.

First and foremost, any business will need to devise a budget which will allow approximate guidelines of how much money can be allocated (usually on a company financial year basis) to each contributory sector in the running of the business, such as how much money can be spent on staff wages, supplies and equipment.

Based around this budget, a target profit figure will be set which will take costs into consideration and will usually consist of a gross figure (all monies received) and a net figure (minus any expenses paid out).

Knowing the exact cost of each process and every item that is produced, allows you to monitor profits made by each division based on the cost of each meal that is produced. Further, it is possible to see where any necessary changes may need to be made such as over-ordering (wastage of goods), any economising strategies that could be put into place and also allows you to gain an approximate costing knowledge so that you can quote for catering for any special functions such as weddings or corporate events.

Any cost that is paid for will fall under one of three headings.

Food or material costs. The cost of buying these items is variable as several contributory factors will affect this, such as the volume of business, ordering of speciality goods, catering for any functions, any temporary staff that may be required and worst case scenario spoiled goods.

Labour. Labour costs are split into two subelements, the first being *direct labour* cost which will encompass payment of wages for staff directly working in/with the kitchen and includes chefs, housekeepers, waiters, bar staff and any other kitchen workers. *Indirect labour* cost will pay wages to all other staff involved indirectly in the running of the kitchen, such as managers, maintenance persons and general office staff.

© ISTOCKPHOTO.COM

The income within a kitchen will pay all direct labour costs and indirect labour costs will be covered by income from all departments that these employees work for.

Overheads. These costs include expenses such as utility bills, any equipment that may be required and rental of premises.

Further to the above, it must not be forgotten that cleaning materials have to be accounted for and these will be considered an overhead. It is easy to forget that everything within a kitchen will need to be cleaned regularly and there must be sufficient equipment at all times to be able to do this. Therefore a costing will need to ensure enough monies are allocated for cleaning items such as dish cloths, towels, brooms, cleaning fluids etc.

Profit

Gross profit. The monetary difference between the cost of the food used to create a menu and the selling price as a dish purchased by a customer is referred to as gross or 'kitchen' profit.

$$\text{Sales} - \text{food cost} = \text{gross profit (kitchen profit)}$$

Net profit. The monetary difference between the selling price of the food to a customer and the total cost incurred to create the dish including labour, food and overheads is referred to as net profit.

$$\text{Sales} - \text{total cost} = \text{net profit}$$

The costing of each dish is calculated then worked out per day, per week, per month, per year.

Any profit made is always shown or referred to as a percentage of the selling price and this is calculated as follows:

Gross profit

$$\text{Gross profit} \times 100 \div \text{selling price} = \text{sales}$$

Net profit

$$\text{Net profit} \times 100 \div \text{selling price} = \text{sales}$$

When calculating the cost of a dish the actual cost price of ingredients needs to be worked out. This is achieved by totalling all ingredients purchased to create a dish and then dividing this into the number of dishes you will be able to make from all the ingredients. Once this has been established, the table below gives an example of how incorporating other production costs into the price of the dish, such as labour and overheads, will affect the selling price on a menu.

An example of calculating the cost of a dish is as follows.

Selling price for Coq au Vin	£17.50
Food cost for Coq au Vin	£9.00
Addition of labour and overheads	£4.50
Total cost of Coq au Vin	£13.50
Gross profit	£8.50
Net profit	£4.00

As a percentage therefore, the gross profit is equal to 49 per cent and the net profit is equal to 23 per cent.

A rule that can be used in order to effectively calculate the food cost price of a dish is to let the food cost of the dish 45 per cent and fix the selling price at 100 per cent. This enables the selling price of a dish to be calculated as follows;

$$\text{Cost of coq au vin} = 900p = 45\%$$

$$\text{Selling price} = \frac{900 \times 100}{45} = £20.00$$

Selling the coq au vin at £20.00 makes 55 per cent gross profit above the 45 per cent cost price.

Based on a working week, a general example of how this works is as follows:

Food sales for one week	=	£32,000
Food cost for one week	=	£15,000
Labour and overheads for one week	=	£11,500
Total costs for one week	=	£26,500
Gross profit	=	**£17,000**
Net profit	=	**£ 5,500**

This works out as 53 per cent gross profit and 17 per cent net profit for the week.

Accurately controlling and monitoring the food cost of certain items makes it much easier to stick to a budget, monitor where any profits and losses are made and in turn control this.

Saving money on costs and staying within a budget is very difficult within the catering industry as most resources are variable in price. Buying items in bulk, taking advantage of special offers/rates and the seasonality of foods can all contribute toward making savings.

As a guideline, the following points should be considered when monitoring cost control.

■ **Quality of produce at a fair price.** It is best not to select 'cheaper' alternatives where most items are concerned as generally the quality does not tend to be as good. Rectifying anything, such as having to buy equipment as it has broken or replace poor quality foods will cost more in the long term, not just money but labour and other resources

■ **Portion control.** Ensure that all staff are aware of portion sizes per dish to be served in order to limit wastage

■ **Waste control.** It is a good idea to regularly check rubbish bins to ensure that it is simply waste that is being disposed of and not quality items or produce that could otherwise be utilised

■ **Theft.** To prevent any items leaving the premises 'through the back door', in addition to completing regular stocktakes it is advisable that any bags, coats or purses belonging to staff are stored securely out of the kitchen area. Other than main entrances to the premises, other doors should be alarmed so that managers will be aware if anyone is entering or leaving the building through these

■ **Weekly stocktake.** Stock should be checked on a weekly basis and it is easier to do this if split into the main food categories, i.e. fish, meat, vegetables, fruit, dairy, equipment and other. If costs dramatically increase it will give an insight as to where it has increased

■ **Ensure prices are correct.** When pricing dishes, at least a 40–50 per cent dish cost should be incorporated. You will have to cover the cost of the specific food product(s) but you must not forget other items such as condiments. Inflation needs to be taken into consideration as this will increase yearly and prices will need to cater for this

Customer care policy

The most important part of any function is to ensure that the customer is happy from the initial contact, through the event and during the follow up. It is imperative that the customer feels important and that their wishes are achieved to the best of your ability. Your organisation's policy on how customers should be looked after should be adhered to and developed over time.

Legislation

All areas of law and regulations that are relevant to running a function; these include health and safety, hygiene and possibly licensing laws.

The welfare of staff is important ensuring they are all trained in health and safety, hygiene and manual handling. The fire and evacuation procedures must be studied and all staff must be aware of their responsibilities.

It is a company's responsibility to ensure the safety of its clients at all times, and by accepting a function the company enter into a legally binding contract to do everything possible to ensure all customers are safe.

Potent allergens

Ingredients – nuts, shellfish or other ingredients – that can cause potentially dangerous allergic reactions.

Assessment of knowledge and understanding

The following projects, activities and assessments are directly linked to the essential knowledge and understanding for unit HS8.

Make sure that you keep this for easier referencing and along with your work for future inclusion in your portfolio.

To test your level of understanding, answer the following short questions. These will help to prepare you for your summative (final) assessment.

Equipment, colleagues and suppliers as an important resource

1 Name the three main types of equipment found in hospitality-based organisations and list five examples of each.

2 Discuss the benefits of creating a team that work well together and the importance of communication in the workplace.

3 List the five main points that should be taken into consideration when sourcing a new supplier and why these are important.

4 Discuss the benefits of purchasing good quality products and the importance of regular maintenance.

Setting up a function

1 Discuss the different table set-ups available.

2 What factors may determine the type of service available?

3 What function staff are available and what are their roles?

Time management and cost control

1 Explain the importance of time management.

2 Detail the importance of cost control and how this relates to a budget.

3 Give three examples of the benefits of having a timetable of events.

4 Name the three types of cost that are incurred by a business and what would be classified under these.

Health and safety

1 Discuss the importance of a health and safety policy within the workplace.

2 List three health and safety factors each that employers and employees are expected to adopt within the workplace.

3   Give examples of six hazards within the hospitality industry that should be addressed in a health and safety policy.

4   Explain the purpose of the 1974 Health and Safety at Work Act.

Research task

You now have an understanding of hosting an event – put together an event sheet using the following information:

The guest will want the following:

- 200 guests.

- Silver service.

- Top table and springs.

- What size room is required?

- What additions can you offer?

- Five-course menu.

- How many staff are required?

- How many cloths?

- How much will it cost per head total?

- The food cost is £12.50 per person?

- The function date is 21 September – organise a timetable of events that need to take place before, during and after the event.

8

Supervise food services

HS10 Supervise food services

LEARNING OBJECTIVES

This unit is about supervising the food service and making sure that the service area and equipment are suitably clean and ready for use. It involves planning, supervising cleaning, clearing and restocking, checking equipment, liaising with other departments and dealing with problems to ensure that service meets the required standard. A holistic approach to food safety is essential to providing a quality food service.

After you have read this chapter you will be able to:

■ Ensure you have relevant up-to-date information about food safety procedures.

■ Ensure staff have the required skills, knowledge and resources to carry out their work.

■ Check service equipment is ready for use and correctly located and that service areas are stocked in preparation for service.

■ Make sure staff follow the procedures for clearing, cleaning and stocking service areas.

■ Make sure the immediate environment meets customer requirements and any special customer areas are arranged as agreed.

■ Liaise with relevant people and departments to ensure effective delivery of the service.

■ Deal with problems that may affect the standard of food service.

KEY WORDS

Communication
This term refers to the transfer of information, verbally, physically or via another means such as email.

Customer relationship management (CRM)
This is a term applied to processes implemented by an organisation to handle contact with its customers. CRM software is used to support these processes, storing information on current and prospective customers. Details on any customer contacts can also be stored in the system. The rationale behind this approach is to improve services provided directly to customers and to use the information in the system for targeted marketing.

Customer requirements
Understanding and determining what the customer expectations and needs are on an individual basis.

Effectiveness of procedures
This is used in a quantitative way to measure how effective the procedures are in a food service operation.

Food service
Places, institutions, and companies responsible for any meal prepared outside the home.

Monitor
To check, track or observe processes and procedures.

Safety measures and procedures
Safety measures and procedures are activities and precautions taken to improve safety, i.e. reduce risk related to human health.

Service equipment
Specific items required to aid in the service of food to the customer.

INTRODUCTION

The simple definition of food service is the provision of food ready for consumption away from the home. However, this explanation fails to differentiate the diverse types or styles of food service such as the growth of take-away restaurants. Generally a food service outlet is defined as a place selling food that is typically consumed on the premises, where the customer is able to determine the quantity of goods purchased but not usually how it is served. The decision as to which food service system to use in a particular catering operation is taken at the initial planning stage – at this point the market to be catered for and hence the type of catering facility to be offered. This initial planning is critical to the long-term success of the operation. It is important that the food service model chosen is suitable for the type of operation and at the same time meets all the requirements of the food hygiene regulations.

Food safety management systems

The planning of food service operations is complex. This is largely due to some of its distinctive characteristics, such as the high perishable feature of some raw materials and the wide variety of semi-prepared and prepared products available. Some products cannot be stored for any length of time and the served end product is usually consumed on the premises. Another intrinsic problem is the wide variety of customers that can be catered for within the same establishment using a variety of service methods from different service areas, for example a large department store may have many different styles of food outlets. Above all each process has to comply with the HACCP policy. Further information on this is found in Chapter 30.

This is similar to a risk assessment for food production. A risk assessment asks you to think rationally about what might go wrong during the service of food and what you must do to ensure it is safe for your staff and customers. It is based on food safety practices that you will already be familiar with. Risk assessments help to prevent problems rather than reacting to them after they have happened. In order for your food safety management system to work effectively you must have prerequisites in place, otherwise known as good hygiene practice. These would include the maintenance of the premises, structure, equipment, cleanliness, pest control and personal hygiene for your front of house team.

Why have food safety management systems?

■ It is a legal requirement for all food service businesses

■ If your operation is taken to court you should be able to demonstrate that you have exercised all due diligence through arrangements in place to prevent an offence being committed

■ It assists the food service system and helps ensure food is safe for customers to eat

■ It helps you manage a team with specific responsibilities allocated individually

■ It can link to the staff appraisal system and can be monitored effectively

> **! REMEMBER**
>
> When planning the food service operation it is often very helpful to invite the local environmental health officer (EHO) to the premises in advance of installing equipment and setting up systems. At this early stage, forming the basis of a good working relationship for the future will help to minimise any risk of not complying with regulations or best practice.

How do I create a food management system?

■ Identify the process steps involved in your food service operation, from the beginning to the end

■ Identify all the potential food safety hazards in your food service operation for each step, and then decide the points in the operation at which situations could actually go wrong

■ Put in place procedures to stop these situations going wrong (controls), and make sure that you and your staff always carry them out (e.g. serving particular desserts from a dessert trolley for a set time and temperature which is known to reduce bacteria multiplication, or ensuring that food service equipment has been cleaned and sanitised at proper and regular intervals)

■ Establish cleaning schemes and set specific tasks and individual staff names against the particular control wherever possible

■ Decide which of these points are actually critical to making sure the customer is safe, and therefore must be properly controlled (e.g. the hygienic service of raw foods)

■ Establish critical limits for the critical control measures

■ Develop monitoring procedures such as weekly inspections to be undertaken by yourself

■ Establish what corrective action needs to be implemented if the critical limits are not reached

■ Provide some simple documentation to show how you have achieved the above and monitored the controls which are critical to making sure food is safe

■ From time to time you must examine your food service operation to monitor any changes which might need your control measures to alter

HAZARD ANALYSIS SHEET

Step   Date:

| Hazard
What could go wrong? | Control
What are your precautions? | Is it a critical control?
Yes or No | Critical limits
What are the limits?
e.g. temperature and/or time | Monitoring
What do you do to check your controls? | Action on deviation
What to do if something goes wrong. |
|---|---|---|---|---|---|
| | | | | | |
| | | | | | |
| | | | | | |
| | | | | | |

An example of a hazard analysis sheet

(e.g. new menu dishes may have new hazards and need new controls, or new equipment may require different thermostat settings)

THE FUNCTION OF COMMUNICATION FOR FOOD SERVICE SUPERVISORS AND TEAM LEADERS

In an organisation it is often necessary to communicate with people at different levels of the hierarchy, such as a restaurant supervisor needing to communicate with their manager (upward communication) or with one of the service employees (downward communication) or with another supervisor (horizontal communication). The subject matter may be the same, but the actual communication could well be different because of the way a supervisor or manager might use tone of voice and body posture. Generally this is because in a hierarchical structure body language assumes a huge importance all of its own.

For communication to be successful it needs to be received and understood by the listener, but this is fundamentally a two-way process. Listening is a skill that needs to be developed within a supervisory or management role. In communication situations active listeners will each send and receive information with signs of acknowledgement. This acknowledgement can be in the form of confirmation in a verbal sense, or visual signs in the form of positive body language such as eye contact and the nodding of your head to affirm the message is understood. Other communication can be in the form of written messages through emails, letters or memorandums. Using written communication will allow the reader to digest the information over a period of time with clarity and will also act as a reference point for future activities.

The supervision and leadership of others utilises the following processes and skills required to effectively run a food service outlet: planning, organising, coordinating, staffing, directing, controlling and evaluating. The restaurant supervisor's skills need to develop quickly in often busy situations and under these sometimes extreme types of working conditions it is essential that supervisors can at least empathise with their staff in a supportive manner. Supervisors are required to maintain control of their own and their staff's emotions and be receptive to demanding customers alike. Once again body language is an important facet to facilitate calmness of the team during busy periods. Supervision and leadership can be challenging where poor performance of the team or individuals are down to being unprepared, ill informed and having a poor communication system.

Positive body language with eye contact and a smile are important when talking to customers

For the team to fully understand the requirements of the food service operation it is therefore essential that valid and clear methods of transferring information are given. Providing feedback on the effectiveness of set procedures in your area of responsibility to the appropriate person in your organisation is also a supervisor's task. This may be feedback given to your team, or individuals within the team, after having monitored a set procedure such as cleaning and polishing cutlery. You may wish to introduce an alternative method or wish to have an exchange of ideas using your team's experience to develop a new system. There are a number of methods that can be used effectively to communicate standard operating procedures and to enhance both the working environment and customer experience.

Team briefings

The use of briefing is the function of communicating objectives and plans to the team. It usually involves a face-to-face meeting with the team. These briefing sessions must be carried out with clarity and skill. This is generalised as effective speaking and some basic guidelines for a positive briefing experience are:

■ Be prepared by practising the brief. Sometimes the use of visual aids such as a diagram or photograph of how to lay a table is an effective way of communicating the operation's standards

■ Be clear and concise. Double check that what you have said is not vague or ambiguous

■ Keep messages relatively simple without over simplifying the meaning. Avoid the use of too much technical language or management jargon

■ Deliver your message with enthusiasm and confidence to make it potentially stimulating and challenging

Staff training

The basis of good training is the development of a programme with clear objects that can be suited to the needs of individual employees and communicated effectively. There are three elements to a programme:

1 Initial appraisal of an employee to determine and negotiate a training programme.

2 Training the employee to meet the required standard operating procedures.

3 Regular staff performance appraisals and re-training where required.

A good training programme is likely to utilise a variety of methods to achieve its objectives. These may include:

■ Group training sessions on specific tasks

■ On the job training using an external agency such as a college or private training provider

■ Self instruction from the operation's handbook or standard operation procedure manuals

■ Part-time study on a relevant course at a specialised college

■ Interactive learning aids based on the Internet such as the Virtual Kitchen

Further information on the training of staff and setting learning goals is found in Chapter 24.

Setting standards

In most organisations the standards are set by the senior management team and can be embedded in a company policy document. For smaller operations, standards are often implied and fairly informal. However, it is essential for every organisation that there are very clear parameters of standards. These standards will have a direct effect on the experience of the customer.

Standard setting should be clear from the outset of an employee beginning their employment in an organisation. Benchmarks can be set on such areas as personal hygiene, personal appearance and specific standards of preparation before, during and after service. The food service supervisor has three main objectives: to minimise staff turnover, ensure staffing levels are kept as low as possible whilst maintaining the required level of service standard and maintain a friendly, polite and accommodating manner amongst all the team. The first two of these objectives are clearly measurable and the final objective is subjective, although by monitoring the levels of customer complaints, low staff turnover, industrial disputes and appraisal sessions, supervisors may be able to draw conclusions about this last point.

IMPROVING PRODUCTIVITY

There are many motivational theories that explain why people work well. Maslow (1970) introduced the 'hierarchy of needs' and McClelland established a theory of achievement motivation. Such theories emphasise personal rewards and growth where remuneration is also largely ignored. This is contrary to the perspective of employers and organisations that place an emphasis on bonus payments, overtime payments and financial incentives. Process theories are based on how employees are motivated. These models include the role that monetary rewards plays in motivating employees, but the exact relationship between reward, performance, motivation and job satisfaction is not clear. There are some clear guidelines that develop from some of these models for managers, supervisors and team leaders:

1 Employees should be thoroughly trained or developed on a team and individual basis to have the necessary knowledge and skills needed to perform their job roles.

2 Individual employee performance requires monitoring and evaluation.

3 Rewards should relate to individual performance where possible.

4 Organisation policies, systems and technology should be designed to enhance individual and team performance.

5 Barriers to high performance should be minimised, such as stress, co-worker grievance or accidents.

The question of improving productivity is not wholly based on staff motivation and training. There are many alternative options that the manager or supervisor can take to influence productivity within the actual food service operation. When analysing the flow of business in a restaurant for example, it is apparent that there are slow periods sometimes referred to as 'off-peak' where action can be taken to help maximise sales by marketing strategies such as sales promotions.

The review of opening hours of the operation may eliminate unnecessary working hours at the beginning or conclusion of the service period. Supervisors should analyse how reservations are made and at what time so that a decision can be made whether to 'turn over' that table to create two sittings. A simple work study observation can be made to create an understanding of where time is well spent by the food service team and where time can be saved. Standardised lay up plans for sideboards are based on the concept of efficient working procedures and this concept can also be used in the production and service of coffee, tea and tisanes.

! REFLECTION

The preparation for service of a restaurant originally involved all of the service staff beginning their shift at 10.00a.m. The commis waiters were involved in basic activities such as polishing equipment and cleaning sideboards. Station waiters were also present and were laying up tables and their own sideboards. The station waiters were perceived as having a greater job satisfaction because they were responsible for their own section and station.

After reviewing the situation, the supervisor decided to alter the procedure by allocating specific tasks to all the staff. One waiter laid and ironed the table cloths for the entire room and another polished and placed wine glasses. It was deemed a successful change to the *mise en place* of the restaurant because it saved time in setting up.

However, why did this change speed up the *mise en place* session? And how can you use the saved time constructively?

MAINTENANCE AND CARE OF SERVICE EQUIPMENT

A major consideration and responsibility of the supervisor is the maintenance and care of the service equipment. There is a clear impact on quality with poorly cleaned equipment causing contamination of foodstuffs and if observed by customers it may deter them from returning. Cleaning before, during and after service of crockery, cutlery and food service equipment plus the general care is the responsibility of the whole team. Ultimately sound standard operating procedures will reduce potential damage to equipment and maintain the good condition of table settings. The need for effective procedures will help to:

- Meet the requirements of legislation and moral obligations to the customer in ensuring that food items are served in a hygienic manner
- Maintain the appearance of table settings and service items that contribute to the overall positive customer experience
- Reduce capital investment by the organisation

An effective measurement of maintenance and rapid care is the use of maintenance report forms which help to quickly identify which equipment items need repairing or require a service update. Larger organisations now have reporting procedures set up online using an intranet-based procedure. However, smaller restaurant outlets still use reporting forms similar to the example below that is monitored on a daily basis by the supervisor.

> **! REMEMBER**
>
> A recent major road survey investigated why motorists stopped at particular roadside service and restaurant facilities. The principal reason was due to toilet facilities and cleanliness. This resulted in companies spending resources on updating and maintaining the frequency of cleaning these facilities.

RESTAURANT AREA	ITEM	NATURE OF PROBLEM	ACTION TAKEN AND DATE REPORTED	MAINTENANCE COMPLETED AND NOTES	SIGNATURE
Still room	Under cupboard refrigerator	Door seal has perished	Reported to line manager and ordered a new seal from supplier 5 December 2008	Old seal removed and new seal fitted 7 December 2008	
Public toilet area (female)	Second cubicle toilet seat	Toilet seat has become loose and is dangerous to use	Reported to supervisor 6 December 2008	New bolt fitted and tightened to toilet seat 6 December 2008	

Similar types of forms can be designed to describe how certain food service items and equipment need to be cleaned prior to and after the service session. This is good practice to help ensure that a standard operating procedure is maintained and that the organisation's benchmarks are understood by all members of your team. At this stage all restaurant tables, cutlery, crockery and service equipment must always be clean and polished for service and not defective in any way. The diligence of every member of the team is important to ensure that items such as cracked cups or bent cutlery are removed from service immediately.

AREA TO BE CLEANED: RESTAURANT

EQUIPMENT/ SURFACES TO BE CLEANED	FREQUENCY OF CLEANING (DAILY/ WKLY/ MTHLY)	MATERIALS TO BE USED AND DILUTIONS	METHOD OF CLEANING	PRECAUTIONS NEEDED WHEN CLEANING	CLEANING TO BE CARRIED OUT BY	CHECKS ON CLEANING TO BE DONE BY
Restaurant tables	After every service or at least daily	Clean cloth, mild detergent with warm water (1:20)	Clean down any food debris, wash table with a clean cloth, dry table with a different clean drying cloth	Water not too hot. Immediately clear up any spillages	Waitress 1	Supervisor

An example of a cleaning schedule

First impressions always count. Maintaining standards of service is important in maintaining and expanding your customer base. Your area should have relevant methods and documentation to determine standards. In some cases a policy should explain how you intend to do this and should include where appropriate:

■ Cleaning schedule for all public areas including rest rooms, carpets, upholstery, windows, door and external items

■ Cleaning regimes for cutlery, crockery, tables and high chairs

■ Instruction to staff on maintaining displays and keeping aisles/customer areas free from clutter and tripping hazards

■ A dress code for staff (not necessarily a uniform depending on the type of establishment)

■ Instruction to staff on how to address and respond to customers politely and helpfully

■ Instruction to staff on food information, e.g. where a product or ingredient can be sourced, possible allergen content such as nuts, vegetarian, organic and other special dietary options

■ How you will monitor that standards are being maintained

■ Instruction on what to do if there is a threat of violence to themselves or customers

The weekly supervisor checklist shows an average food service operation supervisory checklist that can be adapted to meet the needs and requirements of your own establishment.

WEEKLY SUPERVISOR CHECKLIST

FOOD SERVICE AREA

Date:

CATERING PREMISES	Y/N	ACTION NEEDED/ BY WHOM	CHECKED (signed)
All areas clean and tidy			
Glasses/cutlery/crockery clean			
Staff dress code followed			
Table settings correct			
Toilets clean and stocked			
Maintenance issues			
Customer satisfaction Comments actioned			

SERVICE POINT	Y/N	ACTION NEEDED/ BY WHOM	CHECKED (SIGNED)
All areas clean and tidy			
Displays clean			
Separation of raw and ready to eat foods			
Shelves stocked properly			
Price displays accurate			
Date coding checked			
Aisles clear			
Maintenance issues			
Waste bins clean			
External areas clean			
Customer satisfaction comments actioned			

An example of a checklist for the supervisor

PROVIDING AN EXCELLENT FOOD SERVICE

Interaction between the customer and the food service provider, sometimes referred to as the service encounter, is an important model that tries to identify ways for the service provider to understand very quickly and clearly the needs of the customer. An essential part of this interaction is communication using verbal and body language in a positive manner when taking the food order from a customer. Service is a personal action and employees must get close to customers to take their orders, serve their food and clear their plates. This interaction is task-related and will often set the initial pattern for a good or a bad service experience in the eyes of the customer.

Using scripts to communicate with customers

An area where supervisors and managers have some influence over this interaction is in the provision of scripts. In theory everyone will hold a similar perception to how food service in a restaurant should progress. We all have an understanding, triggered by familiar memories, of how a restaurant visit is structured and customers in particular will have expectations measured against these memories. As long as the interaction between a customer and employee follows in the region of this perception then the food service will be smooth. Any deviations from the accepted customer's perception of normality will result in problems and dissatisfaction.

Being able to script the customer's experience is the key to running a successful food service. These scripts are focused into individual responsibilities where specific employees are tasked to perform certain roles from the initial welcome to the restaurant, through to the actual food service and concluding in the presentation of the bill and farewell to the customer. Fast food operations have very tightly scripted approaches to customer service where the server will say the same to every customer to help efficiently maximise customer choice and speed of service. More formal restaurant establishments may have a looser script but the food server will always understand their responsibility because of their individual script or role within the team.

During training sessions it is imperative that these scripts are visited time and again and also that each employee changes scripts regularly to help with team flexibility during staff sickness or annual holiday leave.

Measuring service satisfaction

To help ensure that strategies implemented by you and your team are having the desired effect on service provision,

TASK

Design and set a script for a member of the food service team to welcome customers to your food service operation. Consider the type of establishment you work in, customer expectations, your service system and the culture of your organisation.

WWW.CANSTOCKPHOTO.COM

Meeting customer needs and exceeding their expectations is what all food service staff should strive for

some monitoring and assessment of satisfaction with service needs to be conducted. Customers tend to measure their experience of a food service outlet against their expectation and their previous knowledge or experiences of restaurants. If the outcome matches their exactly then their confirmation occurs. If their expectations are exceeded, then the meal experience was better than they expected. However, negative confirmation occurs if the outcome is less satisfactory than expected. It is also apparent that the level of expectation will not be the same for every customer.

Differences in the level of satisfaction from one customer to another, or from one meal occasion to another, can result both from changes in a customer's perceptions of the outcome of the experience and from changes in their own expectations. An example of this is that a general decline in customer satisfaction with your restaurant may not mean that you are not performing as well as you used to; it could mean that customer expectations have risen. Therefore restaurant operations may need to raise service standard simply to maintain customer expectations.

Approaches to the measurement of service satisfaction can be divided into three types;

© ISTOCKPHOTO.COM

- ■ Management audit – managers are asked to rate their establishment's performance on a series of factors that relate to customer satisfaction. This audit is completed by managers or supervisors on the basis of their perceptions of how the operations functions

- ■ Customer audit – usually this is in the form of a questionnaire to elicit customer satisfaction with the meal experience. Customers could be asked to score certain items out of ten, or to mark their level of satisfaction by placing a cross against a particular measurement of scale that indicates their level of satisfaction

- ■ External audit – this follows a similar procedure to the customer audit but employs specialists to make an assessment based on their personal experiences in the outlet as a customer. This approach is becoming more widespread

Another potential source of valuable information can be provided by complaints from customers. Many food service supervisors and managers believe that if they are not getting any complaints they must be doing well, however this may not be the case at all. Many customers in the UK are reticent about complaining and many operations make it difficult for their customers to complain at all. The result is that the customer will not return to the food outlet again. At the same time they are likely to tell other people of the bad experience that they had, which will lead to a potential chain reaction of customers looking elsewhere for their next meal experience. Whilst it is clearly important to ensure that customers are satisfied in the first place, it is very poor for an operation not to find out why its customers are dissatisfied.

At all stages in the service, efforts must be made to monitor customer responses and elicit any complaints that they may have. The service employee is the first line of contact but needs support from the supervisor and manager. If a complaint is successfully dealt with at source then the customer will invariably leave the restaurant feeling satisfied. Some companies have now introduced a freephone telephone number for customers to use to discuss their complaints personally by trained staff at customer service centres and other organisations now have an online version of this too.

Developing service excellence for any food service operation is a complex task but one that can bring great advantages and profitability. Developing service excellence will ensure that existing customers are retained and encouraged to use the organisation time and again.

Further reading and research

Adjey, Z. and Hunter, G. (2009) *Food and Beverage Service Level 2.* Cengage Learning.

Cracknell, H. L. *et al. (2000) Practical Professional Catering.* 2nd ed. Macmillan.

Dale, B. (1999) *Managing Quality*. 3rd ed. Blackwell.

Lillicrap, D. and Cousins, J. (2006) *Food and Beverage Service.* 7th ed. Hodder and Stoughton.

Maslow, A. (1970) *Motivation and Personality.* 2nd ed. Harper.

Maslow on Management http://www.maslow.com

The Meat Hygiene Service http://www.food.gov.uk/foodindustry/meat/mhservice

Coeliac Organisation http://www.coeliac.org.uk

British Hospitality Association http://www.bha.org.uk

National Restaurant Association http://www.restaurant.org

McLelland's theory of achievement http://www.netmba.com/mgmt/ob/motivation/mclelland

Assessment of knowledge and understanding

You have now learned about supervising the food service and making sure that the service area and equipment are suitably clean and ready for use. You have seen how it involves planning, supervising cleaning, clearing and restocking, checking equipment, liaising with other departments and dealing with problems to ensure that service meets the required standard.

To test your level of knowledge and understanding, answer the following short questions. These will help to prepare you for your summative (final) assessment.

1 How can you communicate standard operation procedures to your team?

2 Explain clearly how should staff communicate with customers to measure their meal experience.

3 How would you organise a staff rota based on service requirements?

4 What would help you observe trends in levels of demand for a restaurant?

5 What measures can you introduce to maintain the cleanliness and maintenance of restaurant service equipment?

6 Describe what is meant by the phrase 'measuring service satisfaction'?

7 State why understanding the needs of the organisation is important.

8 Using Maslow's hierarchy of needs model select what you think would be your three most important areas to help motivate your food service team. Justify your ideas for this.

9 How would you correct and report failures according to organisational standards and procedures?

10 How would you identify, deal with and report breaches of legislation, regulations and codes of practice?

Research task

Training the team in their job roles and scripts are important when working in a busy food service outlet.

Design three scripts based on serving a main course with silver served vegetables and a matched wine for a dinner at a high class restaurant.

9

Supervise drink services

HS11 Supervise drink services

LEARNING OBJECTIVES

This unit is about supervising the preparation and delivery of the drink service. It is about enabling a friendly efficient service in relaxed safe surroundings, ensuring that the law is fully complied with and that customer behaviour problems are dealt with quickly and correctly.

After reading this chapter you will be able to:

■ Make sure staff follow procedures for preparing and restocking the drink service area.

■ Make sure that the attractiveness and comfort of the drinking areas meet customer needs and expectations.

■ Carry out your preparations in good time to allow the scheduled drink service to be provided.

■ Liaise with other relevant people and departments to ensure the delivery of an effective drinks service.

■ Make sure specified standards and procedures for the service of products is maintained and that the drink service complies with relevant legislation.

■ Make sure that communication with customers takes place in a manner that is appropriate to them and the situation.

■ Carry out all activities with consideration for the comfort and well-being of other customers and local residents.

■ Monitor drink service areas and take prompt and effective action to deal with any problems that may disrupt the drink service to the customer.

KEY WORDS

Ambience

The mix of background noise and other reflected sounds that make up a room's acoustic character. It also refers to the acoustical qualities of a listening space, such as reverberation, echoes and background noise.

EPOS

Electronic point of sale, could be a shop, checkout counter or location where a transaction takes place. It is also data recorded at a checkout and used for forecasting and stock control.

Legislation

Term may refer to a single law, or the collective body of enacted law. Before an item of legislation becomes law it may be known as a bill, which is typically also known as 'legislation' while it remains under active consideration. Legislation can have many purposes: to regulate, to authorise, to grant, to declare or to restrict. In some jurisdictions legislation must not be confirmed by the executive branch of government before it enters into force as law. Under the Westminster system, an item of legislation is known as an Act of Parliament after enactment.

Inputs

The resources needed to carry out a process or provide a service.

Operation

Business operations are the repeated activities involved in the running of a business for the purpose of producing value for its owners. These core activities should take into consideration:

1 Generating recurring income.

2 Increasing the value of the business.

Outputs

Products, services or information supplied to meet customer's needs.

Purchasing

A function concerned with the search, selection, purchase, receipt, storage and final use of a commodity in accordance with the catering policy of the establishment.

INTRODUCTION

Drink service can incorporate a range of activities in a range of hospitality outlets including hotels, bars, restaurants, pubs and nightclubs and be provided through departments like cocktail bars, room service, self-service counters and mini bars. It can involve anything from zero service on a staff's part, through to quite intensive service. The important thing to remember throughout this chapter is what outlet might you be working in during your career, who will the customer be and what are your resources. As a supervisor it is your role to consider the quality of the service, the profitability of the outlet and the control aspects involved in running a bar.

This chapter will consider the human resources involved in drinks service, as well as legislation, profitability, stock control, cleanliness and hygiene. It will ask you to consider a range of different outlets, not just the one you might be working in now, and to consider scenarios and solutions to the outcomes that may arise from being a supervisor in a drinks service area.

TYPES OF DRINKS SERVICE: A REMINDER

First, consider what type of outlet you might work in. It could be a:

- Bar in a hotel
- Room service in a hotel
- Cocktail bar
- Public house
- Wine bar
- Self-service restaurant in a store or food court
- Café
- Morning coffee or afternoon tea in a hotel, restaurant or individual outlet

Second, consider the types of service that may be provided:

- Table service
- Counter service
- Self-service
- Room service

ROLES AND RESPONSIBILITIES OF PEOPLE IN THE DRINK SERVICE AREAS

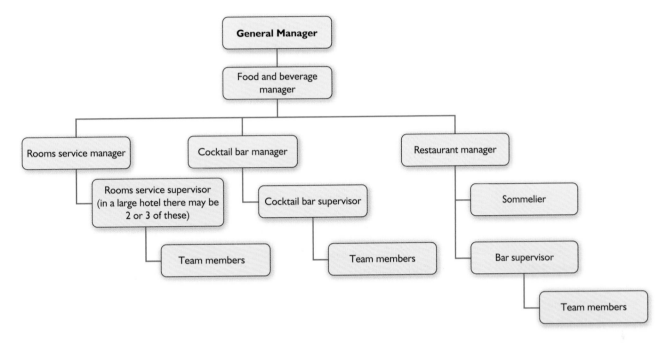

A section of an organizational chart of a hotel to illustrate the beverages operations and roles within each of those outlets

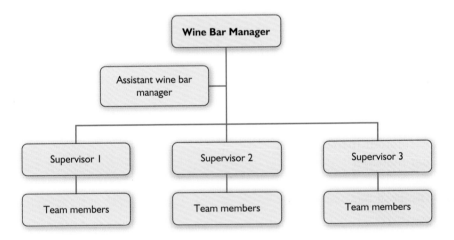

An organizational chart to illustrate the lines of management in a large city-based wine bar

While considering the organisation of any department staffing levels also need to be set. To set staffing levels you need to consider:

■ Opening hours and the number of shifts there will be in a week

■ Number of bars/outlets

TASK

Part 1

1 Do you recognise any of the beverage service roles in the previous chart on page 125?

2 How many have you completed in your career?

3 Are there any roles missing?

4 What are the daily tasks for each of these roles?

Part 2

5 What type of outlet do you work in?

6 What are the beverage service-related roles?

7 What is your role?

8 What are your daily tasks?

■ Number of managers and supervisors needed to cover the shift

■ The forecast sales for each shift

■ Number of staff needed to cover each shift

■ Level of service required – table service, bar service

■ Skills required from staff in light of the type of service

■ Staffing levels at peak times in the business, e.g. Christmas

Examples of staffing requirements for different types of beverage service operations:

1 Medium class hotel.

 (a) Supervisors
 (b) Assistant supervisors
 (c) Wine waiter
 (d) Dispense bar supervisor
 (e) Dispense bar assistants
 (f) Sommeliers

2 Cafeteria.

 (a) Supervisors
 (b) Counter service hands

3 Department store.

 (a) Supervisors
 (b) Dispense bar staff
 (c) Wine waiting staff

4 Industrial beverage service.

 (a) Supervisors
 (b) Steward
 (c) Butler
 (d) Counter service staff

5 Popular mid-range priced restaurant.

 (a) Restaurant manager
 (b) Bar manager
 (c) Supervisor
 (d) Dispense bar assistant

Attributes required by staff who are involved in drinks service include:

■ A professional and hygienic appearance

■ Punctuality

■ Local knowledge

■ Personality

■ Customer focused

- Memory
- Honesty
- Loyalty
- Willingness to help
- Sales ability
- Senses of urgency
- Customer satisfaction
- Ability to handle complaints
- Contribution to the team

DID YOU KNOW?

A professional and hygienic appearance should include:

- Cleanliness
- Aftershave/perfumes shouldn't be too strong
- Sufficient sleep
- Healthy intake of food
- Regular exercise
- Hands should be clean, free of nicotine stains, with clean and well-trimmed nails
- Men should be clean shaven
- Women should only wear light make-up
- Earring should only be studs/sleepers
- Uniform should be clean
- Hair should be clean, well groomed and where appropriate, tied back
- Shoes should be comfortable, clean, polished and plain/neat
- Teeth should be brushed immediately before coming on duty
- Cuts and burns should be dressed appropriately
- Colds/infections should be reported
- Hands should be washed immediately after using the toilet, smoking or dealing with refuse
- Staff should avoid mannerisms, like chewing gum, running hands through hair, etc
- Excessive jewellery should not be worn

Bearing in mind these details, choose one of the other attributes in the bullet list and detail the requirements you would have as a supervisor.

LEGISLATION AFFECTING DRINKS SERVICE AREAS

The biggest overhaul in licensing law legislation of recent times happened in 2003 and came into force on the 24 November 2005. It included:

- 24-hour licensing
- Dual licences – one for the person and one for the premises
- Regulatory crime
- Health and safety
- Food safety
- Underage sales
- Permitting drunkenness in licensed premises
- Disability discrimination
- Door security
- Licensing qualifications

Four underlining objectives to the new Licensing Act were:

1 Prevention of crime and disorder.

2 Public safety.

3 Prevention of public nuisance.

4 Protection of children from harm.

Useful websites

Government website:

Government Licensing Act 2003 http://www.opsi.gov.uk/acts/acts2003/pdf/ukpga_20030017_en.pdf

Other useful websites include:

How the Licensing Act 2003 affects the hospitality industry http://www.licensingact2003.co.uk/home.htm

Evaluation of the impact of the Licensing Act 2003 http://www.culture.gov.uk/reference_library/publications/3574.aspx

Your local council

Other legislation includes:

- Smoking ban legislation: http://www.smokefreeengland.co.uk/
- Sale and Supply of Goods Act 1994. A customer can refuse to pay if:
  - The goods supplied do not correspond with the description
  - A displayed item is not what it seems
  - The goods are inedible

- The Trade Descriptions Act 1968/1972 makes it a criminal offence to mis-describe goods or services. Care should be taken with:
  - Wording wine lists
  - Describing menu items
  - Describing conditions
  - Describing the service provision

- Weights and measures

  http://www.businesslink.gov.uk/bdotg/action/layer?topicId=1074003284

  - Sale and Supply of Goods Act 1994. According to the Act the customer can refuse to pay or can demand replacement if:
    - The goods supplied do not correspond with the description, e.g. a fried egg which has in fact been scrambled
    - A displayed item is not what it seems
    - The goods are inedible

- The Trade Descriptions Act 1968/1972 makes it a criminal offence to mis-describe goods or services. Care must therefore be taken when:
  - Describing rooms in promotional materials
  - Wording menus and wine lists
  - Describing menu and drinks items ot customers
  - Describing conditions, such as cover and service charge or extras
  - Describing the service provision

- Price lists. Price Marking (Food and Drink Services) Order 2003: the price of food and drink must be clearly illustrated and displayed

- Customer Property and Customer Debt. Hotel Proprietors Act 1956:
  - Establishments have liability for guest's property for those who have booked overnight accommodation
  - If customers are unable to pay, no right of lien exists except in an inn, i.e. the right to hold property against non-payment of an account

- Health, safety and security
  - Occupiers Liability Act 1957
  - Health and Safety at Work Act 1974
  - Fire Precaution Act 1971
  - Food Safety Act 1990

EQUIPMENT NEEDED IN THE DRINKS SERVICE AREA

Significant equipment is required in setting up a drinks area. The following lists give just some of the equipment required to get started.

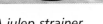

A julep strainer

Cocktail stirrers

Glassware

- Water glass
- Mixed drink glass
- Champagne glass
- Red wine glass
- Soft drink glass
- After-dinner drinks glass
- White wine glass
- Fortified wine glass
- Cocktail glasses
- Beer glasses
- Riesling glass
- Liqueur glass

Linen

- Napkins
- Tablecloths

Ice bucket

Crockery and cutlery

- Cups
- Teaspoons
- Forks
- Saucers
- Knives
- Spoons

Disposables

- Napkins
- Wipes
- Cleaning cloths
- Tablecloths
- Aprons

Other specialist equipment

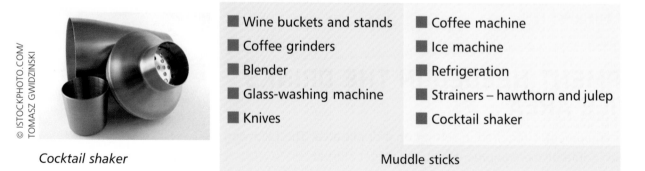

Cocktail shaker

- Wine buckets and stands
- Coffee grinders
- Blender
- Glass-washing machine
- Knives
- Coffee machine
- Ice machine
- Refrigeration
- Strainers – hawthorn and julep
- Cocktail shaker

Muddle sticks

Procedures for preparing and restocking the drink service area, prior to service

1   Requisition beverage stock.

2   Requisition consumables – fruit, milk, sugar, cream etc.

3   Restock service points.

4   Rotate stock as appropriate using first in first out (FIFO).

5   Polish glasses and crockery.

6   Clean, tidy, wipe down and mop still room and bar areas.

7   Clean, wipe out and replenish fridges and display cabinets.

8   Switch on coffee machine, dishwasher, glass-washer, etc.

9   Switch on post mix.

10   Change gas cylinders, kegs.

11   Check, clean and replenish shelves.

12   Replenish linen.

13   Set up tables and arrange chairs.

14   Dust, wipe or polish all hard, glass and mirrored surfaces.

15   Vacuum carpeted areas.

16   Sweep and mop all tiled areas.

17   Collect and check floats for tills.

18   Check menu availability.

19   Write specials boards.

20   Wipe menu covers.

21   Set up bar work station and counters.

22   Attend pre-opening briefing.

23   Switch on lights and music.

24   Make final check of bar, still room, toilets and other areas.

25   Open doors at appropriate time.

TASK

The role of the supervisor

As the supervisor, how are you going to ensure that all the jobs listed are completed prior to the doors opening?

Cleaning the drink service area after service

1   Clean, wipe and polish all bar tables, counter, work stations and work surfaces.

2   Pack, wrap and store all garnishes, fruit, milk, cream, etc. in the appropriate fridge or other location.

3   Disconnect key beers, rinse beer lines, turn off gases etc.

4   Write a requisition order for the next shift to replenish stock and garnish items.

5   Switches off, empty, rinse and clean glass washer.

6 Reconcile till, float and takings.

7 Switch off till, lights and other items of equipment.

DRINKS SERVICE: PROFITABILITY

The purchasing function

The internal control objectives which have to be addressed by the system are to make sure that the company only pays for goods and services which have been authorised and received:

■ Goods and services can not be received without an expense to the business being recorded

■ Only authorised purchases of goods and services are made

■ Only authorised goods are accepted on delivery

■ Only authorised purchase invoices are processed

Methods of purchasing

■ Wine shippers

■ Wholesalers

■ Cash and carry

■ Auctions

BEVERAGE CONTROL PROCEDURES

BOOK	USED TO RECORD
Order book	Orders made to suppliers
Goods inwards/goods received book	Goods received from suppliers
Goods returned book	Goods that are sent back to suppliers
Returnable containers book	Returnable containers sent back to suppliers
Cellar stock ledger	Stock movement in and out of the cellar
Bin cards	Stock of individual lines in the cellar
Requisition book	Re-stocking orders for individual service areas
Daily consumption sheets	Usage of stock in individual service areas
Ullage book	Breakage, spillage, wastage
Off-sales book	Items sold off at the off-sale price
Transfers book	Movement of stock between different service areas

Use of computers

Electronic point of sales (EPOS) can control and record all of the above through the use of the front of house (sales) and back of house (stock) systems. It will then give you a total of the stock that should be on your shelves and in your fridges over the time frame you want – i.e. daily, weekly, monthly, etc.

DRINKS SERVICE: CUSTOMER SATISFACTION

Attention to detail

Environment	Consistency of products and service
Staffing levels	User-friendly products and services
Staff skills	Value for money
Staff knowledge	Welcome and recognition
Social skills	Customer reward programmes
Hygiene standards and cleanliness	Safety and security
Speed of service	Staff morale: happy staff = happy customers

Ambience

The mix of background noise and other reflected sounds that make up a room's acoustic character. It also refers to the acoustical qualities of a listening space, such as reverberation, echoes, background noise.

COMMUNICATION

Did you know that 70 per cent of all communication is non-verbal and uses gestures, including

■ Shrugs
■ Tears
■ Laughter
■ Raised arms
■ Eyebrows
■ Arms folded?

To understand this language is important and it takes a special kind of supervisor to be intuitive.

TIP

If you don't have an EPOS, this can still all be tracked using a spreadsheet package.

TASK

Remember an experience where there was a poor ambience.

Remember an experience where there was a great ambience.

In each case describe the:

■ People – how many, who were they, etc.

■ Music

■ Style of service

■ Establishment

■ Occasion

Staff – mood, look, energy

As a supervisor, how can you:

■ Control the ambience?

■ Improve the ambience?

■ Change the ambience?

■ What other things might be missing that could impact on the ambience?

TECH SKILLS

Shrug

Frown

Did you know that 20 per cent of communication is done by language (the second most common form of communication)? This includes:

■ Pitch and level of voice

- Monotone to highly excited
- Screaming and shouting to a raised voice
- Whispers

The last 10 per cent of communication is based on the words we actually use.

Barriers to communication

It takes a lot of hard work to communicate with people. More effort needs to be put into hearing the information you are receiving, as opposed to the information you are giving. To be effective in communicating with your customers and team you must work hard on developing a speaking style that effectively communicates. This includes:

■ The tone of your voice

■ The speed at which you speak

■ The style of your body language

COMMUNICATION	SKILLS REQUIRED
Speaking (vocal)	Volume, pitch, tone, pace
Non-verbal	Facial, eyes, posture, gestures, body movement
Writing	Active short sentences
Listening	Focus, eyes, posture, gesture, body, movement

ROLE PLAY

Work in groups of three.

This role play is designed to help a supervisor learn the skills to discipline/reprimand a member of the team while also ensuring that member of staff's commitment to the remainder of the shift and to the workplace.

■ One person is the supervisor

■ One person is the member of staff

■ One person is the observer

The supervisor needs to tell off the member of staff for being late for shift for the second time that week.

The supervisor is looking for a change in the person's behaviour as opposed to dismissing them or upsetting them.

The staff member feels the need to defend themselves.

Before starting the role play the observer should write down what they expect each person – supervisor and staff member – should be getting from the meeting.

At the end of the role play, review together whether that was achieved and how. If it wasn't achieved, why not?

Also consider, were the observer's expectations realistic or should they have expected more from the situation, or less.

ROLE PLAY

Work in groups of four.

■ One person is the supervisor

■ One person is the member of staff

■ One person is the customer

■ One person is the observer

The customer is complaining about the poor quality of their cocktails and the fact that they don't believe they are being made to the traditional recipe.

The member of staff is trying to deal with the complaint, but the customer isn't content with the response.

The member of staff has gone to get their supervisor and this is where the role play is picked up. The customer is reiterating their complaint to the supervisor. Supervisor – handle the complaint, and then follow it up with the team member.

Observer – you should look out for the following:

1 How is the supervisor dealing with the complaint?

2 What is the member of staff doing while this is going on?

3 How does the supervisor react towards the member of staff once the complaint has been dealt with?

Before starting the role play the observer should write down what they expect each person – supervisor and staff member – should be getting by the end of the role play (situation).

At the end of the role play, review together whether that was achieved and how. If it wasn't achieved, discuss why not? Also discuss, were the observer's expectations realistic or should they have expected more from the situation, or less.

Having now carried out these role plays, consider the following:

1 What effective skills/attributes do you have in relation to communication?

2 What skills/attributes do you need to develop to improve your communication?

In preparing your responses to these questions, you may also include feedback from your tutors, from the people you work with, your family, friends and perhaps other members of the class.

Further role plays to consider in relation to developing communication skills:

1 Dealing with customer behaviour in relation to alcohol consumption and responsible drinking.

   (a) You are training your team to handle customers who have consumed enough alcohol and you are not willing to serve them any more alcohol. You want your team to suggest that they either go home or have a soft drink.

   (b) The second stage of this role play would be to train your team to remove a customer from the premises who has consumed too much alcohol but won't have a soft drink or leave the premises voluntarily.

2 Restriction on information given to customers.

(a) How would you and your team handle a situation where there is a VIP (pop star) in the function room right next to the cocktail bar? Customers keep coming up to say they have heard rumours of who is in there – how do you convincingly dispel those rumours?

(b) Can you think of any other situations where you might have to restrict the information you give to customers? How would you handle it? Design a role play around the situation.

3 Selling techniques

(a) You are running a train session again and as the supervisor you are going to be the observer. Your team needs to work in pairs – one is the customer, one is the team member.

(b) The team member needs to convincingly sell using two methods: the first is suggestive selling, the second is upselling. For example, for suggestive selling they could suggest an appropriate aperitif or pre-dinner drink. For upselling, they could attempt to persuade the customer to upgrade their bottle of cava to a bottle of house champagne.

(c) As the supervisor, you need to consider the effective skills displayed in each of these methods of sales. Second, you need to consider the skills that weren't displayed that perhaps made it an unsuccessful attempt at selling.

(d) Then you need to inform the member of staff about each of these strengths and weaknesses in their sales techniques and make suggestions for how it could be improved.

(e) When you have completed this role play, discuss with the team member and customer how effectively they thought you handled giving the feedback and how you could improve your communication for future use also.

Assessment of knowledge and understanding

You have now learnt about some key elements involved in drinks service – including the setting up of the drinks area, the cleaning of it, some aspects in relation to the control of stock in the bar service areas, legislation and how to communicate effectively with both your team and customers in relation to some of these aspects.

As you have gone through the chapter you have already tried out some role plays and discussed some elements of supervising the drinks service, but now to test your level of knowledge and understanding further, answer the following short questions. These will help to prepare you for your summative (final) assessment.

1 Legislation.

(a) What are the consequences if you should choose to deviate from any of the aspects of legislation laid out earlier in the chapter?

(b) What policies and procedures does your organisation have in relation to legislation?

(c) List a series of references – websites, books and journals – where you could find more information in relation to legislation relevant to the hospitality industry and useful to you as a supervisor.

2   Purchasing.

(a) What are the main requirements of the purchasing function in the service of drinks?

(b) What are the main objectives in relation to the purchasing of drinks?

(c) How can stock control improve profitability?

(d) What systems and procedures does your organisation have in relation to control and profitability? Can you see how these fit in to the purchasing cycle?

(e) Recognise and list the areas where there is less control or procedures and policies are not followed correctly.

(f) Discuss how these policies and procedures (or their execution) could be adapted to improve the overall profitability of the drinks service areas.

3   Clearing and cleaning the drink service area.

(a) List the equipment in your drinks service area. Now consider, is there anything missing? How would you go about requesting the missing equipment? What policies and procedures do you need to follow?

(b) What policies and procedures are in place or could be in place to monitor the effective preparation of the drinks service area in a timely fashion, ready for opening time?

(c) How can these roles be allocated effectively to the team to ensure standards are met?

(d) How would you handle a situation where not all these roles and activities had been carried out to the appropriate standards?

(e) Are there any contingency plans in place for when the drinks service area hasn't been effectively prepared? If yes, what are they? Are there any missing? If no, what contingency plans would you consider putting in place?

Research task

Consider the purchasing cycle of the whole outlet in which you work. It would be worth job shadowing a purchasing manager for a day if that is possible.

Now consider, how do the day-to-day tasks and paperwork that are carried out in your drinks service area contribute towards the profitability of that outlet? This can include deliveries, transfers in and out of the department, recording of wastage, complimentary drinks, effective use of EPOS by all staff, stock-taking, etc.

Are there any aspects of the day-to-day tasks that are not carried out effectively and could put the profitability of the outlet at risk? If so, what are they?

Finally, how would you deal with ensuring those tasks are carried out effectively in future and improve the profitability of your outlet, as well as the service standards and communication within your team?

10

Supervise housekeeping services

LEARNING OBJECTIVES

This unit is about the maintenance of the housekeeping service. This unit deals with the preparation, supervision and review of the service, involving the planning of equipment and supplies, preparing staff rotas, briefing staff and collecting customer feedback.

After reading this chapter you will be able to:

■ Allocate staff and brief them on duties, relevant procedures and any variations relating to their work routines.

■ Make sure staff have the necessary skills, knowledge and resources when they are needed to carry out their duties.

■ Ensure staff are aware of the standard of behaviour acceptable to the organisation.

■ Ensure staff are aware of how they should communicate with customers and other staff members whilst at work.

■ Schedule housekeeping procedures to take place at intervals which are suitable for maintaining the standards of the housekeeping service.

■ Monitor and review the service to ensure that staff follow the correct housekeeping procedures and that the housekeeping service meets the needs of customers.

■ Inform your staff and customers about any changes to the service that may affect them.

■ Take effective action to manage problems that may disrupt the housekeeping service when they occur.

■ Collect feedback on the service from staff and customers.

■ Pass on feedback and recommend improvements to the relevant people according to your organisation's requirements.

■ Make sure the required records are completed and processed.

KEY WORDS

Cleaning frequencies
The amount of time an area or item needs cleaning and how often.

Deep cleaning
A thorough clean, that would normally create disruption to an area, requiring the removal of furniture. Cleaning areas that are not cleaned thoroughly on a daily basis, due to accessibility.

Induction
A formal introduction to the company you are working with, which includes instruction, training and orientation. An induction can be for a period of time.

Periodic cleaning
Cleaning that is carried out on a cycle or regular basis. Normally this cleaning is not required on a daily or weekly basis, and requires some pre-planning.

Preventative maintenance
Precautionary maintenance carried out to prevent a breakdown, or the piece of equipment failing.

Schedule
A programme or plan listing all of the actions to be completed.

Supplies
The materials, goods, food or provisions required to perform the task, job or role.

INTRODUCTION

Good housekeeping within an organisation is key to a successful business. The first impression upon entering a building that is clean and tidy is a positive one giving customers confidence in how well the organisation is run.

Housekeeping generally covers all areas of the building, from reception to the dining room, lounges, corridors and of course the bedrooms. Attention

© ISTOCKPHOTO.COM/YONG HIAN LIM

Good standards of cleanliness

to detail is paramount to ensure the best surroundings for guests at all times. A deficiency in this area, however small, can make the difference as to whether the guests enjoy their visit or not, and whether they return.

From most customer surveys, guests indicate that room cleanliness ranks very high in determining their level of satisfaction. Reception staff will tell you the comments they receive from guests at checkout, which can be important feedback to monitor standards. Other comments reception staff feedback on are the complaints from guests if their rooms are not ready when they arrive to check in.

The success of an organisation is to achieve high room occupancy levels. Housekeeping can have a measurable effect on the success of these efforts.

CREATING THE SERVICE

It is important to understand the areas to be cleaned by your team. Areas of responsibility are different in each organisation. In some organisations the housekeeping team are not responsible for the cleaning of the kitchen or restaurant, this falls within the relevant departments.

Once the areas have been identified the frequency of cleaning needs to be agreed. This is basically how often the task will be carried out in each area.

AREA: STANDARD BEDROOM

DUTY	FREQUENCY	COMMENTS
Checkout	D as occurs	Must complete by 4p.m.
Change bed linen	D as occurs	
Clean bathroom	D	
Make beds	D	
Re-stock guest supplies	D	
Clean all glass/mirrors	D	
Hoover	D	
Damp dust	D	
High-level dust	W	
Change curtains	Q	
Remove radiator covers to clean	A	
Hoover furniture upholstery	W	Move furniture to hoover under
Clean and defrost fridge	W or at departure	Move fridge out to clean behind

Some organisations display the cleaning frequencies so that guests are clear about what to expect from the housekeeping service. In public areas, such as corridors, lifts and public toilets consideration is required for the best cleaning time, with minimal traffic.

AREA: PUBLIC AREAS

DUTY	FREQUENCY	COMMENTS
Main lobby	D	By 8a.m.
Empty bins	3 D	
Clean toilet areas	4 D	By 8a.m., 11a.m., 1p.m., 4p.m.
Spot check for litter	3 D	
Door glass	3 D	

> **CONSIDER**
>
> ■ How often should public areas be policed or spot cleaned, and when?
>
> ■ How often will the carpets need cleaning?
>
> ■ What specific duties need to completed daily?

Understanding the frequencies for each area enables the work schedules for the housekeeping staff to be devised.

Work schedules

Different organisations arrange these in different ways, but the information required within the schedule includes:

■ Task

■ Frequency

■ Method

■ Equipment

■ Health and safety

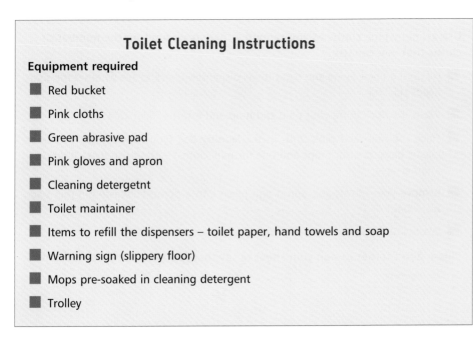

Toilet Cleaning Instructions

Equipment required

■ Red bucket

■ Pink cloths

■ Green abrasive pad

■ Pink gloves and apron

■ Cleaning detergetnt

■ Toilet maintainer

■ Items to refill the dispensers – toilet paper, hand towels and soap

■ Warning sign (slippery floor)

■ Mops pre-soaked in cleaning detergent

■ Trolley

Health and safety

■ Never mix any of the cleaning chemicals that you use

■ Take care when cleaning behind the toilet and underneath pipes, beware of foreign objects

■ Report any faults to equipment or the area that you are working in to your supervisor

■ Ensure that you display warning signs when you are cleaning floors

■ Leave all equipment clean, dry and tidy after use

Procedure to follow to clean a toilet area

■ Wash your hands with hot water and soap

■ Open the door and window, and leave open while you are cleaning

■ Squirt the toilet maintainer around the inside of the toilet bowl and under the rim Allow to soak and leave the toilet brush in the bowl

■ Fill the red bucket with hot water and detergent

■ Soak the pink cloths in the bucket

■ Use your pole and pad to damp dust and clean walls, ledges etc.

■ The areas within a toilet should be cleaned in this order. Using a pink cloth, clean

- Mirror
- Toilet tissue, soap and hand towel dispensers
- Handrails and fittings

■ Using a new pink cloth

- Sink
- Back of the door and door frame

■ Using a toilet brush clean around the inside of the toilet bowl

■ Clean the toilet brush and holder

■ Using a new pink cloth clean the chair, door plate and handle, toilet cistern and seat, and finally outside the toilet pan

Use as many pink cloths as you require – there is no limit on the number of cloths that you can use

■ Fill up the toilet tissue and hand towel dispenser. Check to see whether the soap needs refilling

■ Wash the floor using your pole and mop and exit the toilet area

■ Place the mop and pink cloth in the laundry bag (you should have two clear plastic bags, one for mops and one for pink cloths) – never use these items in another area

■ Remove your gloves and apron and place into a domestic waste bin (bin with black bag)

■ Wash your hands in hot water with soap

Please don't forget to sign your sheet to say that you have completed all duties

Staff need to be clear about how to carry out each task and this can be achieved by issuing job cards to new staff. Laminate the cards so that they can be used by the staff for as long as they need, and can be wiped over when necessary.

Other methods of detailing the tasks of each member of staff is to create a document which lists:

- The time that each task should be completed
- Duties to be performed
- A signature from the member of staff
- A signature from the supervisor once the room has been checked

This documentation gives accountability to each member of staff, and provides a good tool to performance-manage staff.

HEAD HOUSEKEEPER/SUPERVISORY ROLE

How does the housekeeping department know which rooms to clean?

The reception team will provide a daily report of rooms occupied, which guests are leaving or staying, and the expected arrivals. Additional information received would include special requirements i.e. additional pillows, blankets, well-ventilated room etc.

!	REMEMBER
Acknowledging regular guests makes them feel comfortable and a valued customer.	

How does the above information get to the team cleaning the rooms?

Many organisations still use paper reports for housekeeping staff to follow, so they know what type of service is required in each room, whether the guest is staying, leaving or a new arrival.

The head housekeeper/supervisor duties include allocating the team of staff to areas of the organisation. Some staff may have the same areas every day, but they need to be covered on their days off or holiday period. Once the staff are allocated to their areas they can receive the reports that detail the room status.

!	REMEMBER
It is important to have all staff working to the same standard to ensure the service does not deteriorate when the regular member of staff is off, and their duties are covered by someone else.	

Preparing staff rotas

Once the work schedules are confirmed for your team, rotas can be created to staff the areas to achieve the standards that you have set. Housekeeping staff generally work between the hours of 7.00a.m.–5.00p.m. over a seven-day period.

Establishing the amount of time to complete each task can be carried out either by observing someone carrying out the duties and timing them, or working by the type of area and the area it occupies. Adopting a scientific approach to the amount of time to be allocated to an area ensures consistency across the site.

This scientific approach requires the following information:

Type of area

List all the types of areas that need cleaning, in order of complexity. For example, you will observe that toilets take longer to clean than a corridor, due to complexity of the clean and the amount of fixtures and fittings in the toilet area.

The size of area

Knowing the room floor size (m^2), enables the correct allocation of time to be allocated. However, the type of area depicts the amount of time to be allocated. For example a toilet and a cupboard both measuring the same floor area would have a different time allocated to each area. The toilet would have more time allocated due to the complexity of the clean required and the number of fittings to be cleaned.

Not all organisations use an exact approach and for example would cover the cleaning of a standard double room from anything from 20–40 minutes depending on the size of the room and the standards of cleanliness set to achieve. As a supervisor you will need to ensure that you have allocated sufficient time for your staff to complete their duties to the standard you require. You also need to make sure that you have consistent time allocation across your team to prevent staff being treated unfairly.

Once you are clear about the amount of time needed to complete the cleaning, you can allocate staff to areas by the use of a rota. The rota normally consists of:

- All staff listed
- The hours that they are planned to work (start and finish time)
- The area they are allocated to
- Cover required for holidays and sickness

Rotas are normally 'live' documents that change daily in order to cover the service requirements. Changes can be as a result of more rooms sold than expected, staff illness, training and holidays. There should be flexibility in your staff establishment to have a pool of staff that can be called upon for holiday and sickness cover.

Allocation to areas can be managed in two ways:

1 **Staff allocated to their own areas and are rarely moved.** This is a popular method that allows staff to have ownership of an area, or a certain number of rooms. It enables staff to take pride in 'their' rooms and they are competent in the daily routine they are required to complete. Regular guests can enjoy having the same housekeeping member of staff servicing their room. Difficulties occur if staff become unfamiliar with other areas, and so less flexible when trying to cover the service required.

2 **Staff are regularly moved to different areas.** This is normally less popular with staff as they are never sure which area they are going to work in. Sometimes standards of work can be reduced as staff are less sure of what to do in each area. This option does give staff more familiarity of the site, and the different areas to be cleaned.

> **! REMEMBER**
>
> Monthly team meetings need to be fun as well as informative. Listen to your team and help with any difficulties they have with their duties. Feedback any compliments or complaints received. Reflect on anything that went well and how it can be achieved again, and what went wrong, and how it can be prevented from happening again.

MANAGING THE HOUSEKEEPING STAFF

Depending on the size of the organisation, housekeeping teams tend to be large, with a number of part-time staff.

Supervisory skills required to manage a diverse mix of people should include training around equality and diversity, and training techniques for staff with English as a second language. The organisation should have policies in place to cover training, equality and diversity and skills for life training.

Communication to your team of staff is vital. Keeping them informed of new practices and procedures as well as news about the organisation, improves team work and raises standards. Most teams find monthly meetings beneficial, enabling staff to raise issues with you and discuss any concerns that they have. The supervisor can use the time to gauge morale, check on knowledge, inform on new practices and update on feedback received about the housekeeping service.

> **! REMEMBER**
>
> Even though you communicate new procedures to staff, ensure that you have checking mechanisms in place to establish whether they have understood the information that you have given them.

Recruiting staff

It is vital to have thorough cleaning staff that take pride in their work. Encourage staff to aim for their rooms to be the best standard, a room that they would pay to stay in.

> **! REMEMBER**
>
> Keeping staff motivated reduces staff turnover, which in turn saves time and money.

Keeping the housekeeping team motivated

In order to keep the housekeeping team motivated the establishment should:

■ Train them well and ensure that they understand what is expected of them

■ Pay them correctly and on time

Housekeeping staff

- Give them sufficient uniforms
- Remember their names and acknowledge them when passing in the corridor
- Keep them informed of changes within the organisation, cleaning practices and anything that affects them. Meet with them regularly as a whole team and allow them to raise any issues
- Value them. Thank you costs nothing but goes a long way
- Ensure the housekeeping team understand the importance of their role and how it fits into the organisation
- Performance-manage poor performers or staff that do not attend on a regular basis. Teams become less effective if they have to carry the work of poor performers

STAFF TRAINING

Large organisations will hold corporate inductions for all new staff as they join the company. Smaller organisations tend to have a less formal approach, carrying out departmental inductions on a one-to-one basis.

All induction training should include:

- Welcome
- Information about the company
- Who's who in the organisation
- Fire training specific to the organisation and area of work
- Health and safety at work
- Use of chemicals
- Uniform policy and issuing of uniform
- Pay and pension details
- Training required

A supervisor will be responsible for the training of new staff and their performance.

Keep training records of the tasks staff will be trained in, the date that they demonstrate that they are competent and the signatures from the staff member and supervisor. This record is useful to revisit for any future training or performance issues.

On the first day of employment a new member of the housekeeping staff must know how to work safely. On the job training can be achieved by the new employee working alongside a competent member of the team.

ACTIVITY

Create a departmental induction booklet which covers all of the above induction training. To interest all staff make sure that it is easy to read, and includes colour and pictures.

! REMEMBER

Different training skills may be required to be effective with some staff.

! REMEMBER

Working safely:

Display slippery floor warning signs

Following the correct lifting techniques

Do not mix chemicals

Know the location of the fire assembly point

All duties to be covered should be listed on the training schedule. Remember to refer to the frequency schedules to ensure the training schedule covers all duties. We have shown an example of a training schedule here.

A TRAINING SCHEDULE FOR NEW HOUSEKEEPING STAFF

PROCESS	TICK	DATE	TRAINEE SIGNATURE	SUPERVISOR SIGNATURE
Paperwork/administration				
Time sheets				
Signing in and out				
Security (ID badge, etc.)				
Payment of wages				
Car parking				
Reporting of illness				
Booking annual leave				
Reporting accidents				
Fire drill/reporting procedure				
Department induction				
Appraisal – 14 days				
Safety				
Manual handling				
Use of warning signs, cones				
Use of protective clothing				
Usage of chemicals (COSHH)				
Storage of chemicals (COSHH)				
Basic cleaning				
Gloves and the importance of them				
Infection control cleaning procedures				
Kitchen cleaning and maintenance				
Removal of rubbish sacks				
Use of colour coded sacks				
Domestic cupboard and equipment				
Disposal of soiled mops				

PROCESS	TICK	DATE	TRAINEE SIGNATURE	SUPERVISOR SIGNATURE
Customer care				
Miscellaneous				
Security call				
Basic cleaning				
High dusting				
Damp dusting				
Cleaning of beds				
Skirting boards				
Static mopping				
Internal glass				
Kitchen cleaning and maintenance				
Cleaning of still				
Cleaning and use of dishwasher				
Cleaning fridge				
Setting up tea service				
Cleaning of tea pots, etc.				
Bottle sack				

© ISTOCKPHOTO.COM/ IMAGEDEPOTPRO

CAUTION WET FLOOR!

© WWW.CANSTOCKPHOTO.COM/

Mandatory training

Fire

Fire kills. All staff should know what to do when the fire alarms sound and how to evacuate the building.

Health and safety

All staff should know how to work safely and how to report faulty equipment to the supervisor. Training must be given in moving and handling, how to move furniture to clean and how to lift items correctly. The correct uniform must be worn along with the protective clothing required.

Cleanliness

Staff should understand how to clean areas using a colour-coded system for cloths, buckets and mops, to avoid cross-contamination from one area to another. The colours should be predetermined by the organisation. See the table for an example.

AN EXAMPLE OF COLOUR CODING

Red

All toilets and bathroom areas

Red cloths

Red buckets

Microfibre mop

Blue

Blue cloths

Blue bucket

Microfibre mop

All bedroom areas and other areas
(does not include toilets/bathrooms /
kitchens or bedrooms)

Green

Green cloths

Microfibre mop

Kitchens

> **! REMEMBER**
>
> Make sure staff are aware of the notices that can appear on door handle to the guest's room, i.e. do not disturb.

Customer care training

Ensure staff understand the importance of customers, and the fact that without them they wouldn't have a job.

SUPPLIES AND EQUIPMENT

It is important to have the right equipment and cleaning product for the job. A regular review of all products is important to keep up to date with the latest technology.

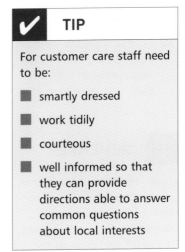

© WWW.CANSTOCKPHOTO.COM/

As a guide you will need a few products to maintain the areas you clean:

1 Polish.
2 Glass cleaner.
3 Toilet cleaner.
4 Toilet descaler.
5 General detergent.

Most companies provide products already packaged or as a concentrate to decant into spray bottles. Suppliers often offer greater discounts if all products are purchased from one supplier, but the important consideration is that all products meet your needs.

> **✔ TIP**
>
> For customer care staff need to be:
>
> ■ smartly dressed
> ■ work tidily
> ■ courteous
> ■ well informed so that they can provide directions able to answer common questions about local interests

Typical types of equipment used by housekeeping services include:

■ Vacuum cleaners

■ Floor-buffing machines

■ High-level dusters

■ Steam cleaning machines

■ Mops systems for wet and dry use

■ Colour-coded cloths and buckets

The amount of the above equipment required depends on the size of the organisation and the number of staff that you have. You need also to take into account how the rooms are located, ensuring sufficient equipment on each floor. It is time-consuming for staff to be searching for equipment or waiting to share.

Larger pieces of equipment such as floor-buffing machines or mechanical floor cleaners can be purchased or leased. Details should be obtained from the supplier and the offer for purchase or lease evaluated. Leasing arrangements normally cover the maintenance costs, a consideration if you do not have a maintenance team on site.

The safety of your staff is paramount and it is the responsibility of the employer to ensure that all staff are trained to recognise, understand and deal with these risks. Your staff have an equal responsibility to ensure that they take note of this training and carry out their work as they have been shown, with due regard to health and safety legislation.

As a supervisor you are required to build in daily checks to ensure that your staff are working safely.

To ensure that your staff work in a safe way and comply with legislation you must make sure that they:

■ Maintain a high level of personal hygiene and appearance

■ Report any hazards that they notice in the workplace

■ Follow the health and safety procedures of your organisation

Bed linen

Normally provided by linen services, an adequate supply of bed linen and towels is required to provide an efficient housekeeping service. Items should be checked as beds are made and towels replaced for stains and damage.

Complimentary products

Most organisations provide soap, bath and shower gel and shower caps free of charge. Housekeeping staff should be trained to know which products go in which standard of room, and the frequency with which they are changed.

Trialling products

Identify staff that are able to give an opinion regarding the suitability of new products. Once they are committed to a product it is easier to implement new products with the rest of the team.

When trialling equipment consider the following:

- Will the item live up to the daily demands?
- Is the item constructed to last?
- Are electrical leads long enough to be able to carry out the task in most areas?
- Ease of cleaning the actual equipment
- Practicalities of using the product by the housekeeping team
- Service available for repairs and maintenance
- Cost versus performance

CONTROLLING SUPPLIES AND EQUIPMENT

Have one person responsible for the dilution of products if concentrates are used. They should also be responsible for the filling of the bottles. This is best done on the evening shift so that all products are ready to use when the team arrives in the morning.

Employees should be taught how to use products and equipment during their induction, and at further training sessions, using them safely and according to manufacturer's instructions.

For strict control, staff can be instructed to sign their cleaning trolleys in and out of an area. Ensure staff are instructed to return all items, even empty bottles. Their equipment should be clean and cloths returned to be laundered.

Supplies and equipment play an important role in staff satisfaction and their ability to perform properly. Supplies and equipment are the 'tools of the trade' for the housekeeping staff. If staff have to hunt for supplies, fill up their own bottles, and have difficulty finding a vacuum that works, their attitude will be 'they expect me to do all this work, but I never have the tools'.

Fault reporting of equipment

Your team should be trained to know what to do in the event of their equipment failing or if it is unsafe to use. As a supervisor you should carry out regular checks on equipment to ensure it is safe for

! REMEMBER

Monthly briefing sessions are useful to check the knowledge of your staff and reinforce the health and safety rules. Use each session to cover a different topic, trying to keep the session fun and informative.

Complementary products

✔ TIP

Resist changing products too frequently as this can cause confusion within the team, who will become unsure of what product to use where.

! REMEMBER

Remind staff at regular training sessions about the use of chemicals.

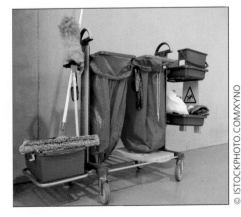

Housekeeper's trolley

ACTIVITY

Consider how you would trial new products and the way you would collect feedback from your staff.

REMEMBER

If equipment is waiting to be repaired, ensure that it is labelled with the fault to prevent anyone using the item.

REMEMBER

Regularly check at your staff meetings that staff are aware of the reporting procedure for faulty equipment. They may need to know how to contact you to inform you of the problem.

REMEMBER

Each piece of electrical equipment should be PAT- (portable appliance test) tested. This is for portable items of equipment that are electrically tested for safety. A sticker should be applied to the piece of equipment once that it has been PAT tested, detailing the date of the test and the due date of the next test. These tests must be carried out by a qualified electrician. Your staff should be checking that the piece of equipment is within the next PAT test date, before using it.

use, but train your staff to follow a fault reporting procedure. This should be managed through the supervisor, by asking the staff to notify you immediately of any faults or unsafe equipment. A procedure should be in place for you to then notify the maintenance team or maintenance contractor.

ACTIVITY

Produce a form to record faulty equipment to allow for the following information:

- Date
- Reported by
- Type and number of equipment
- Fault reported
- Action taken
- Date sent for repair
- Date returned

Maintaining equipment

Some establishments have their own maintenance teams to repair equipment, others have contracted maintenance companies to carry out repairs.

Each piece of equipment should be labelled with a unique number so that records can be maintained. Information kept should include:

- Date of purchase
- Supplier
- Maintenance record
- Expected life of the equipment

From your records, you are able to identify pieces of equipment that are regularly breaking down, allowing decisions to be made about repairing versus replacing.

PERIODIC CLEANING AND PREVENTATIVE MAINTENANCE

All organisations require deep cleaning at an agreed interval.

This cleaning will require housekeeping and maintenance teams working closely together to achieve this without disturbing guests or having the room out of order for a long period.

ACTIVITY

Design a schedule for all the items that require periodic cleaning and maintenance within a bedroom. Consider the frequency they are to be cleaned and a schedule of completion dates.

Carpet cleaning

Carpets require cleaning on a daily basis, but deep cleaning should be built into the housekeeping schedules. Working closely with the maintenance team to achieve this cleaning is important, especially if rooms are being redecorated, and the carpets can be shampooed prior to being re-let.

Good customer care

© ISTOCKPHOTO.COM/DAVID GILDER

CUSTOMER CARE

It is important that guests receive a quality service, enjoy their stay and feel that they have received value for money. All of this will encourage them to return for a further visit. There are a number of factors under the customer care heading that contribute to guests and visitors feeling satisfied with their stay and the way that they are looked after. The following information details the areas that contribute to providing a good experience of your establishment. As a supervisor you should visit these on a regular basis to ensure that the service is at the required level for the standards you have set.

Communication

What behaviours should the housekeeping staff adopt?

■ Acknowledge guests wherever they see them around the building

■ Be helpful and informative with questions from guests

■ Understand the contribution made by other departments

■ Be considerate and friendly to everyone

■ Communicate in a way that is easy to understand

■ Be approachable and positive

■ Share ideas for improving their work environment

	ACTIVITY
	Think of an occasion when you have been disappointed by the standards in a hotel bedroom that you have stayed in – how did it make you feel? Think of an occasion when you have seen good standards – what was the difference good standards made to you?

REMEMBER

!

Give your staff the opportunity to come up with better ways to improve services for guests. This may be by informal meetings or by just chatting to them whilst they work.

Lost property

Systems should be in place to record any items left by guests. Lost property should be kept in a safe place, tagged with details of who found it and where. Attempts should be made to contact the guest the item belongs to. Policies should be in place for the period that the establishment keeps the lost property. Included in the policy should be the procedure to follow once the period of time has lapsed for keeping the items, and the process of disposing of items. Some establishments offer the item to the person who found it, ask for a donation for the item or donate to charity.

Do not disturb signs

These are a common feature in many hotels. Staff need training on the reason for these signs, establishing at what point of the day they enter to clean the room, as some guests forget these signs have been left out on display. Train staff to contact their supervisor if they are unsure whether they should enter the room or not.

Other signs used include 'Available for Cleaning'.

© ISTOCKPHOTO.COM/JON SCHULTE

Do not disturb sign

TECH SKILLS ✓

QUALITY ASSURANCE

Quality assurance is what you do to ensure that your guests receive the service they expect, with no errors. For the housekeeping service it means a clean environment/room, completed on time.

How can you measure quality?

- Comments/complaints received at the reception desk
- Direct complaints to the housekeeping department
- Internal/external cleanliness audits carried out by independent assessors
- Repeat business – high level of customers returning on a regular basis
- Supervisory audits of areas, checking on staff performance
- Guest questionnaires

REMEMBER

An inspection should include:
- all standards of cleanliness
- any maintenance issues
- check on TV, telephone, electrical items, lights
- complimentary products are in place

The key element of quality control is that the work of the housekeeping staff should be inspected by someone, every day for every area. However, a programme should be in place so that all rooms are checked over a period. Most organisations check all departure rooms daily to ensure acceptable standards for new arrivals.

Staff or supervisors that carry out the inspections are key personnel performing a valuable role. They are the last people to be on duty usually, before a guest arrives. An excellent inspector, who flags up issues, can raise the housekeeping performance to the utmost in quality.

There are a number of computerised quality systems to carry out inspections, against the criteria that you set, via a handheld device. All of these systems require the programme to include the standards set by the housekeeping department.

Whether the organisation uses a paper audit system or a computerised system the criteria will be the same and will follow the lines as the example of the criteria required for a bathroom area in the table.

ACTIVITY

1 Devise a checklist that can be used when carrying out a cleanliness audit

2 Convert the checklist into a form that can be used to record the cleanliness audit

CRITERIA FOR A BATHROOM AREA

ELEMENT	REQUIREMENT
Showers	The shower, chair, wall-attached shower, walls, tiles and grout should be visibly clean with no scum, dust, limescale, stains, deposit or smears.
Toilets and bidets	The toilet and bidet should be visibly clean with no scum, dust, limescale, stains, deposit or smears.
Replenishment	There should be plenty of all consumables and soap.
Sinks	The sink and wall-attached dispensers should be visibly clean with no dust, dirt, debris, limescale, stains or spillages. Plugholes and overflow should be free from build-up.
Baths	The bath should be visibly clean with no dust, dirt, debris, limescale, stains or spillages. Plugholes and overflow should be free from build-up.

Collecting customer feedback

It is important to receive feedback about your service, both positive and negative. Feedback can be obtained from:

- Comments received by the reception team at checkout
- Letters or emails received from guests
- Questionnaires, comment cards made available in the bedrooms
- Telephone surveys to guests
- Direct to the housekeeping team by the guest

If you have questionnaires or comment cards in the rooms you will need to consider how these will be collected.

ACTIVITY

Design a questionnaire/comment card for guests to complete. Consider how you want guests to return them, and how you are going to communicate the information back to your team.

REMEMBER

Always share complaints received about your service with your manager, so that they can offer support and advice to rectify issues.

REMEMBER

Complaints can be used to raise standards, by sharing the complaint with staff and putting in procedures to ensure that the complaint does not happen again.

For complimentary letters received about your service or the service offered by the establishment, it is good practice to acknowledge the letter by writing back to the guest and thanking them for taking the time to write. For letters concerning housekeeping standards, it would be appropriate for a response to come from the supervisor or manager of the area.

For all formal complaints, the complaint must be acknowledged with the customer. The customer should be satisfied that an investigation will take place to establish the facts, the issue dealt with and an offer of recompense if appropriate. Complaints should be shared with the affected person or team and if appropriate used as a training aid to raise standards. Complaints can be as a result of poor performance by an individual. Procedures should be in place to provide support and additional training to staff in this position. For staff that do not continually perform to the required standards, procedures should be in place to performance-manage them.

Further reading and research

Robert J. Martin (1998) *Professional Management of Housekeeping Operations*, 3rd edn. John Wiley.

O. G. Goring and David Gee (eds) (1970) *Hotel and Institutional Housekeeping*, 2nd revised edn. Barie and Jenkins.

BICS The British Institute of Cleaning Science: http://www.bics.org.uk

ISSA The International Sanitary Suppliers Association: http://www.issa.com

UKHA UK Housekeepers Association: http://www.ukha.co.uk

CHSA The Cleaning and Hygiene Suppliers Association: http://www.chsa.co.uk

Assessment of knowledge and understanding

You have now learnt about the responsibilities involved in supervising the housekeeping services, ensuring standards are maintained to provide the customer with a clean environment and a comfortable stay.

To test your level of knowledge and understanding, answer the following short questions. These will help to prepare you for your summative (final) assessment.

1 List the importance of creating a clean environment.

2 What customer care skills would you expect of the housekeeping staff?

3 How would you monitor good standards of cleaning?

4 What methods can be used to monitor standards of cleanliness and customer satisfaction?

5 How would you address customer complaints and poor performance?

6 How would you inform staff of customer feedback?

7 How would you deal with a member of staff that was not achieving the standards that you expect?

8 What departments are directly connected to housekeeping, requiring good working relationships?

9 Why is pre-planned maintenance important to the guest and housekeeping staff?

10 What benefits are there in using a colour-coded cleaning system?

11 List four considerations you would make before changing the cleaning products.

Research task

Consider the design requirements for a new hotel, from a housekeeping prospective. Consider what you would have to do to enable the housekeeping service to provide an efficient, quality service.

11

Supervise portering and concierge services

HS20 Supervise portering and concierge services

LEARNING OBJECTIVES

This unit is about supervising the portering and concierge service. It includes preparation, supervision and review and therefore covers making sure that the portering and concierge service has all the necessary staff, equipment and supplies, that procedures are in place for running the service and ensuring that staff are properly briefed, trained, overseen and supported.

After reading this chapter you will be able to:

■ Allocate staff and brief them on duties, relevant procedures and any variations relating to their work routines.

■ Encourage staff to ask questions if there is information that they do not understand.

■ Ensure staff conduct and presentation promotes goodwill and understanding with customers and complies with organisational policy.

■ Make sure staff have the skills, knowledge and resources when they are needed to carry out their duties.

■ Monitor and review procedures to ensure the service meets the needs of customers and complies with relevant legislation and organisational policy.

■ Inform your staff and customers about any changes to the service that may affect them.

■ Collect feedback on the service from staff and customers.

- Take effective action to manage problems that may disrupt the portering and concierge service when they occur.
- Pass on feedback and recommend improvements to the relevant people according to your organisation's requirements.
- Complete records to support the service according to your organisation's procedures.

KEY WORDS

Accommodation services
This term can also be referred to as 'room division'. This refers to individual departments who are responsible for the upkeep and selling of rooms within the establishment.

Actual arrivals
This term is used to describe guests that arrive at the establishment and who have already checked in.

Actual departures
This term refers to guests who have already checked out of their rooms.

Blacklisted
This term refers to guests who have been systematically barred from the establishment for non-payment of the bill or unacceptable behaviour.

Bulk checkout
This refers to groups of guests whose accommodation and any other authorised services are charged back to the tour operator.

Communication barrier
This refers to poor communication skills such as poor language, listening, noise, prejudice or verbal skills.

Concierge
This name refers to the person or persons who are in charge of the portering team; the service includes numerous responsibilities regarding the guest's satisfaction.

Correspondence
This refers to the written communication between the establishment and its guests.

Demographics
Refers to selected population characteristics including race, age, income, disabilities, educational attainment, home ownership, employment status and even location.

Extras and Extras account

This refers to additional services offered which are purchased on top of the base products. These are then invoiced to the extras account – this is sometimes referred to as cross-selling.

Loyalty cards

This is a programme that rewards guests who use the establishment's facilities frequently, offering free items, discounts and additional services.

Occupancy level

This refers to the number of rooms occupied within the establishment; the figures are usually represented as a percentage.

Porterage

This refers to the charged service or storing and delivering luggage to and from the guest's room as required.

Porters

Staff members who form part of the concierge team responsible for luggage delivery.

Rack rate

This refers to the standard rate assigned to rooms; they are usually the top end rate which is then negotiable at the supervisor's discretion.

Target market

The market segment to which a particular good or service is marketed.

> **! REMEMBER**
>
> Always ensure the customer's expectations are exceeded as a guest will feed back on average four times with a good experience and up to 20 times if they are not satisfied.

The concierge desk

INTRODUCTION

The role of a concierge is to provide face-to-face contact with the guests, ensuring their expectations are not only met but exceeded.

The concierge will have different roles and responsibilities in each establishment; a small hotel may rely on its reception team to deliver the role where as a large international hotel will have a dedicated team available.

THE PORTERING TEAM

The portering team fall under the responsibility of the concierge; they may operate within this team or in a smaller establishment will report directly to the front of house manager. The role of a porter requires their presence 24 hours a day, 7 days a week, and 365 days a year.

Smaller establishments may use the night reception team to manage this role as the majority of guests will be asleep and the requirements for luggage transportation or valet parking are reduced.

The porter will use his/her knowledge to recommend services offered by the establishment which will earn the business added revenue, they will also use their contacts to arrange tickets, restaurants, cars and other services required by the guests.

The term concierge may simply mean 'door keeper', but it is a skilled job that requires years of research and dedication to achieve. The simple tasks of parking cars, fetching luggage and providing general information can be achieved within a short period of time; the broader job requires good contacts that are able to provide services at sometimes very short notice.

In large international establishments the concierge will hold the position of head of department and will be ultimately responsible for interviewing, hiring and firing staff; they will be responsible for rotas, overtime and training. The concierge will deputise a head porter or captain who will continue to maintain the highest possible standards of customer service.

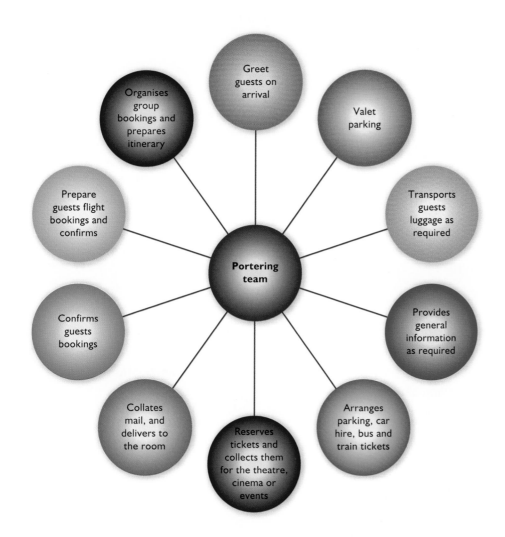

The portering team's responsibilities

A guest will have more contact with the portering team than any other department. It is not unusual for guests to be on first-name basis with the porters and as such the guests will see the porters as a major part of the hotel or establishment.

A guest may choose to return based on the porters performance so it is essential they perform to the best of their abilities.

A porter must be extremely proactive and ensure they have the answers ready before the questions are asked.

Porter meeting a client

© ISTOCKPHOTO.COM/TOM HAHN

To become a successful porter the following attributes are recommended:

- Organisation skills
- Well-groomed and excellent personal hygiene
- Very discreet, sympathetic and tactful
- Good product knowledge and resourcefulness
- Excellent selling skills
- Good understanding of the market and the establishment's requirements
- Courteous and attentive
- Excellent communication skills

THE CONCIERGE

Becoming a concierge is an extremely difficult task, one that requires patience, attention to detail, sound knowledge and usually a minimum of 5 years' portering experience with 2 years in charge of the team.

Becoming a concierge is an honour and as such comes with a membership to the 'Les Clefs D'Or', which translates as the golden keys.

Les Clefs D'Or

The membership founded in France in the 1950s and was set up by a small community of porters whose aim was to create an association based on quality and service.

Once you are a member you can wear the famous cross golden keys on your lapel indicating you have achieved membership of this renowned organisation.

The association's website is: http://www.goldenkeysconcierge.co.uk

To become a member requires a dedication to the industry and continual striving for excellence.

Below is a list of the organisation's aims:

THE CONCIERGE AND PORTERS' RESPONSIBILITIES TO THE GUESTS ARRIVING AND DEPARTING

Generally the concierge desk is situated next to the main reception; the location, usually near the door, is important as this is the first contact a guest will have with the establishment.

The fact that the concierge is situated near the front door does not mean the porters are constantly based there; due to their ever-changing tasks the porters are always moving so a degree of physical fitness is required.

The arrival of the guests

The concierge and the team are instrumental during the cycle of service, as the diagram to the right demonstrates.

The porter will check the booking sheets for the day, porter's diary and front office diary. The porter's diary is an essential tool which allows detailed communication within the team; it highlights guest requirements, preferences and any other piece of valuable information which the team can use to excel in their role.

Planning and checking are key words which a good concierge team will never take for granted; they are aware of the establishment's daily activities and movements of the guests.

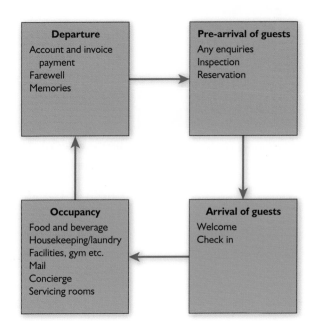

The team plan the following carefully:

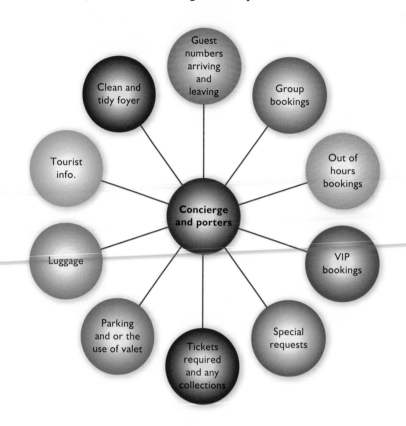

Chauffeur service

During this time the guests may arrive; prompt and professional greetings are essential as the first impression always counts.

If the guests arrive by car, ensuring the door is opened and their luggage collected will set the tone for the guest. The guest is escorted to the reception and the luggage is taken to their room, if the room is not ready then the luggage will be tagged and stored for the guest's convenience.

If a guest arrives in their own car then the porter will open the door, remove the luggage as above then arrange for the car to be taken and parked, the keys kept securely in the concierge area and the parking fee charged to the guest's invoice.

Taxi arrivals can be dealt with in two ways: the guest will pay and the procedure for greeting guests will commence, alternatively the porter will pay the fare and charge this to the guest's invoice.

Coach or bus arrivals require supervision and careful planning. The coach may be guided to a safe disembarking area, the luggage ported in a logical controlled fashion and the guests taken to check in. The establishment must not become congested and blocked so a professional organised manner is required.

Sufficient staff levels are required to ensure the smooth transition of welcoming, checking in and arrival in the room with luggage.

Escorting guests to their rooms

This part of the porter's job is extremely important; once the guest has checked in the process may commence. This is an interactive time with the guest and care must be taken to ensure the correct image is portrayed:

■ Answer the guest's questions as accurately as possible; if unsure of the answer inform the guest you will return with the answer

■ Build a professional relationship with the guest

■ Highlight key services and facilities available to the guest

■ Comment on the room's facilities

■ Instruct the guest on the emergency evacuation policy

The cycle of service – occupancy

During this part of the cycle the porter has the opportunity to highlight their abilities as a professional.

The level of information offered will depend on the establishment's standing within the industry; a high-end establishment may comment on the following points:

■ Facilities and services offered by the establishment

■ Housekeeping and laundry

■ Messaging service

■ Transportation

■ Tickets and events

■ Restaurants and bars

■ Emergency evacuation procedures

■ Local history and information

■ Baby sitting and crèche

■ Business centre hours of operation

■ Shopping and local attractions

■ Gym, swimming pool and sauna

■ Toiletries

Being proactive with guests

A porter is on call 24 hours a day and as such is required to respond instantly to guest's requests; it may not be the porter's direct responsibility but they must ensure the request is followed up and completed as soon as possible. The porter is the guest's first and last port of call and is the link to the establishment.

The concierge assisting a guest

The guest may choose to contact the porters directly face to face, telephonically or through other departments such as the main reception desk.

An experienced porter/concierge will build a portfolio of past issues or requests that required action; these can be use in future to ensure the smooth running of the department.

Guests departing

The job of the porter is almost complete; the guest however may still make numerous requests such as:

- Collecting the luggage
- Organising transport
- Collating and forwarding any mail for a set period of time
- Working out travel and future directions

If there are groups involved then the porter needs to organise the coach parking area, luggage transfer, group checkouts and any other queries; ensuring that all guests receive a first class service, lose no luggage and feel at ease will help to create a positive impression of the establishment.

LUGGAGE – HANDLING, TAGGING, COLLECTING AND STORAGE

As previously discussed the requirement for porters to have a good level of physical fitness is important. The day-to-day carrying and distribution of guest's luggage can be very tiresome. The correct posture and training is essential.

Manual handling

The majority of days lost to illness and injury are caused by poor manual handling as a porter. Ensuring the team have undertaken effective manual handling courses and continue to update their skills is an important part of their job. The main areas affected during manual handling are back strains due to incorrect lifting, pushing and pulling.

If the following points are observed then the number of incidents of injury should be reduced:

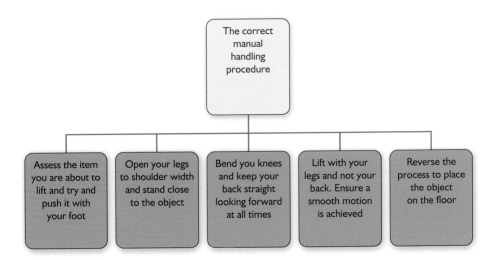

| Assess the item you are about to lift and try and push it with your foot | Open your legs to shoulder width and stand close to the object | Bend you knees and keep your back straight looking forward at all times | Lift with your legs and not your back. Ensure a smooth motion is achieved | Reverse the process to place the object on the floor |

The correct manual handling procedure

Trolleys

It is commonplace for establishments to use trolleys to transport luggage; there is still a degree of lifting on and off of the trolley involved. Modern trolleys have a selection of hooks along the centre to carry suit holders and other items on hangers.

These trolleys come in a wide selection of shapes, colours and sizes. They must remain in good order and be spotless in appearance like the staff operating them; this will help achieve the correct image which the establishment wishes to portray.

Tagging luggage for guests

Tagging is the procedure used by the porters when the guest's room is not quite ready for occupancy. Tagging is essential when dealing with group bookings and coach parties. The luggage may be delivered prior to the guests arriving in their rooms; the tag is attached to the piece of luggage and the rip of tag given to the guest so they can track their luggage.

The tags will vary in size, shape and information attached. As a rule the following should be used as best practice:

- The tag number on both sides
- Room number
- Guest name
- Date
- Time
- Items – how many bags the guests has

An example of a porter's trolley

© ISTOCKPHOTO.COM/ROBERT SIMON

Tag Number:

023788

Concierge luggage tag: 023788
Room No…
Guest name……
Date…… Items…..
Time……

When filling out the tags it is important to complete all the details thoroughly and accurately; it is also important that the names are filled in fully as there may be more than one person staying with the same surname. In an ideal situation all luggage should be delivered within 10–15 minutes; guests then feel they are being looked after and are not just another number staying in the establishment.

When a guest leaves they may also want their luggage collected and sent to the lobby or placed into a waiting car. Large high-end establishments will do this as part of the service. The task of transferring luggage, opening doors and other tasks will occasionally end in the porter receiving remuneration 'tips' for their work; this may vary due to the guest, staff work or type of establishment worked in.

Keys and assisting security

Keys and security are essential parts of a porter's day-to-day responsibility; a porter may take the room keys from a guest but must then pass them to reception. They must not issue keys to guests as mistakes can be made; the fewer the people who deal with keys the less chance there is of loss or theft.

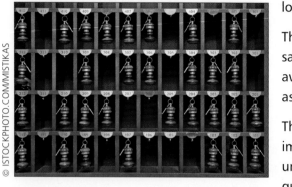

© ISTOCKPHOTO.COM/MISTIKAS

Hotel keys

The concierge and porters do not keep spare keys for the same reason; they do however keep car keys securely locked away; the keys are tagged in a similar fashion to the luggage as the car may be requested at any time by the guest.

The security of an establishment has never been more important than in today's climate; suspicious behaviour is an underlying aspect of this. It may come in the form of staff, guests, suppliers or any other random persons entering the area. Key points to notice are:

- Avoiding eye contact
- Nervous
- Fidgeting
- Excess checking of surrounding area

It is important that the appropriate security team are notified immediately, that the supervisor is informed and they are never left alone. This is a great responsibility, however care must be taken not to confuse a lost person requiring assistance from a potential threat.

Assessment of knowledge and understanding

You have now learned about supervising the portering and concierge service.

To test your level of knowledge and understanding, answer the following short questions. These will help to prepare you for your summative (final) assessment.

Responsibilities of the porter

1   There are numerous responsibilities of a porter when dealing with guests; list five of them.

2   Explain the porter's area of responsibility when in the cycle of service.

3   Explain what the porter must do when a coach or group booking arrives.

4   If as guest makes a request for a particular service, what should the porter do and explain his/her role in this task.

The concierge

1   Detail the requirements of becoming a concierge and name the correct French title given to them.

2   Describe the aims of the concierge association.

3   Explain the roles of a concierge in a large high-end establishment.

Handling luggage

1   Describe the correct way of manual handling.

2   Describe the process of tagging luggage and its importance.

3   Explain why luggage may not be taken to a room immediately.

Research task

The concierge has asked the head porter to train a new recruit in the day to day responsibilities within the establishment.

Produce a detailed list of:

■   The responsibilities.

■   Who is overall in charge of each task.

■   The guests' expectations.

■   Resources that may be required.

■   Establishment security.

12

Supervise reception services

HS21 Supervise reception services

LEARNING OBJECTIVES

This unit is about supervising the reception service to ensure that it has all the necessary staff, equipment and supplies. It involves ensuring that procedures are in place for running the service and that staff conduct themselves appropriately and are properly briefed. The unit also covers the monitoring and improvement of the service.

After reading this chapter you will be able to:

■ Allocate staff and brief them on duties, relevant procedures and any variations relating to their work routines.

■ Make sure staff have the skills, knowledge and resources they need when they need them.

■ Encourage staff to ask questions if there is information that they do not understand.

■ Ensure staff are aware of how to present themselves and of the standard of behaviour acceptable to the organisation.

■ Make sure that your staff follow the reception procedures and maintain the appearance of the reception area according to organisational requirements.

■ Make sure your staff communicate with customers in a manner that promotes goodwill and understanding.

■ Make sure the reception service complies with relevant legislation and organisational policy.

■ Inform your staff and customers about any changes to the service that may affect them.

■ Take effective action to manage problems that may disrupt the reception service when they occur.

■ Collect feedback on the service from staff and customers and monitor and review procedures to ensure the service meets the needs of customers.

■ Pass on feedback and recommend improvements to the relevant people according to your organisation's requirements.

■ Complete the required records and report on performance and procedures as required.

KEY WORDS

Audit
A review, check or inspection of something, such as a process or goods.

Complex
Something that could be difficult, with other factors attached to it.

Establishment
Another word for a business, organisation or group.

First impressions
The first thing someone experiences which makes up their mind or influences them and can produce a positive or negative opinion.

Organisation
A business or group.

Receipt
A copy of a transaction of goods or services.

Reservation
Booking of a room or service within an organisation.

Transaction
An operation that takes place, sometimes classed a business deal.

INTRODUCTION

Reception staff are likely to be the first employees that guests come across, therefore providing guests with their first impressions. As the supervisor/manager of reception it is important to ensure reception staff give a professional and efficient impression.

Reception is not only the place that guests check in or out, but a busy area providing information to guests and visitors about

Reception staff

local attractions, directions, theatre and taxi bookings and of course details about the hotel's facilities.

A good reception team consists of staff that can work under pressure, remain calm and polite at all times and look smartly dressed at what ever time of the day. Reception is normally the hub of the organisation, a contact point for information and an area that responds to emergency situations i.e. calling of the fire brigade, police or ambulance services.

RECEIVING AND ASSISTING VISITORS

Receiving visitors is one of the most important duties your reception team will perform for the organisation. However the visitors are dealt with, whether they are internal or external, expected or unexpected, it is essential that the team maintain a degree of professionalism to maintain standards and security.

The visitors' impression of the organisation is created by your team as much as the environment. Creating a good first impression is vital, especially on reception. Many companies have recognised the importance of creating a good impression and have developed detailed procedures for dealing with visitors.

PROMOTING BUSINESS

It is important that you train your staff to know about the products that your organisation offers. An example of this would be to ensure that staff offer to book a wake-up call, breakfast, papers and a meal in the restaurant. Information about the restaurant's menu, specialities and opening times should be to hand. When a guest arrives at the reception desk staff may need to tell the guest about all of the organisation's facilities.

The benefits for the team

- It makes them feel part of the organisation that they work in
- It allows them to act professionally and confidently
- It creates good team spirit

The benefits for the organisation

- It creates a good impression for customers
- It maintains security
- It is cost-effective
- It promotes sales

! REMEMBER

Promote customer care training: 'Guests are the reason for our work, not an interruption'.

! REMEMBER

Ensure your team treat visitors well by:

- Greeting promptly
- Understanding the nature of their business
- Directing them to the appropriate people, products or services within the organisation
- Acknowledging any difficulties and seeking assistance from the most appropriate person

ACTIVITY

Devise an induction schedule, listing all the services a new receptionist needs to know. Include internal facilities as well as external attractions, interests and services.

The benefits for the customer

◼ It creates a good first impression

◼ The external customer is likely to return, the internal customer is likely to be more helpful towards the team

◼ They are likely to return or contact the team again

COMMUNICATION

The reception team needs to choose the most appropriate method of communication when dealing with any person that they come in to contact with. They need to take into account:

◼ Who they are

◼ What they want

◼ If they have any special needs i.e. if they are foreign speaking, hearing impaired

Routine enquiries

Most of the time enquiries dealt with by the reception team will be routine. One example of this would be directing people to another area of the building. For this the team must be trained in the layout of the building.

Complex enquiries

Reception staff are likely to have to deal with people in complex situations. These may include angry, upset, aggressive, drunk or distressed visitors.

You will be required to give your staff the skills to deal with these situations by working with the organisation's policies, ensuring that they are practical for staff to follow and implement. Professional advice can be sought to demonstrate the skills required to deal with aggressive and abusive behaviour.

TASK

Prepare laminated cards of the building for your staff, for easy reference.

! REMEMBER

Train your staff to understand the establishment's policies. For example, the need for confidentiality around who is staying.

! REMEMBER

Basic guidelines for staff:

◼ Always try to stay calm

◼ Try to move an angry customer to a quiet area

◼ If they are very angry, let them have their say – this will give you or your staff time to think about a reply

◼ Try to identify what the customer's needs are

◼ Don't argue – try to speak softly, but be firm. This is likely to calm them down and it is more difficult to argue with someone when they are speaking softly

◼ Encourage staff to contact their supervisor or manager as quickly as possible if the customer continues to be upset

ACTIVITY

List some 'what if' scenarios and have a group discussion with staff on how to handle the scenarios.

1 What if a drunk person comes into reception and uses unacceptable behaviour?

2 What happens if someone will not pay their bill?

3 What if a guest collapses in reception?

4 What is my role if the fire alarms sound?

> **! REMEMBER**
>
> Build up a good relationship with the local police. Encourage them to walk through the building regularly and provide them with refreshments.

> **! REMEMBER**
>
> Train your staff to identify a sign from you if the police are to be called discreetly.

> **! REMEMBER**
>
> Train the reception team to project professional messages across the audible system. Create standardised messages for them to use.

CCTV

> **! REMEMBER**
>
> Keep a log of security incidents reported by the reception team. Detail what happened and how the incident was dealt with.

Supervisor/managers response to dealing with complex enquiries

It is likely that by the time the supervisor or manager arrives to deal with a situation, the customer has run out of steam. The same rules apply about keeping the customer calm and talking softly to them. Once the customer has got their problems off their chest they can be reasoned with and a solution agreed. For quality issues, this would normally be in a reduction to their bill.

Dealing with customers who continue to be aggressive or are drunk, the police may need to be called.

Following a complex situation, always debrief the staff, talk through what happened, how it was handled and what could be learnt from the situation. Staff should expect support when dealing with difficult situations.

Paging systems

Paging systems, bleeps or mobile phones are used in many large organisations, where people have to be contacted but there is no telephone extension near to where they are working. There are two common types of paging systems:

1 An electronic bleep that identifies that the person is required and should report back to a central point, often reception.

2 An audible message transmitted using strategically placed speakers. This type is usually used in reception and public areas.

MAINTAIN A SECURE ENVIRONMENT FOR CUSTOMERS, STAFF AND VISITORS

Maintaining effective security should be the concern of everyone. There may be security staff or porters with a responsibility for security, but as a supervisor/manager you must ensure your staff are trained to deal with security issues.

Profitability can be affected both by direct loss of property or damage to the building, which can damage the business through loss of custom. Most hotels have many entrances into the building, providing difficulties in maintaining a secure environment. A number of organisations install CCTV systems to record key areas, often linking back to an area near to reception, for cameras to be viewed.

Reception staff should be trained to follow basic security practices:

■ Handle all cash transactions away from the customer and other unauthorised persons, preferably out of sight

■ Follow the company's policy for cash handling, ensure two personnel always verify the amount of cash counted

■ Keep security issues and procedures confidential

- Never accept or return guests' property unless it has been properly recorded
- Keep their own belongings, such as handbags or wallets, secure and out of sight in a locker
- Keep alert to anything or anyone looking suspicious, i.e. fire exits left open, a car parked in the car park for a period of time
- Keep keys under close supervision. It is normal to have a log book for keys
- When visitors arrive for staff or guests, check that they are expected before giving them directions

Cash handling

Cash handling is an important part of a receptionist's role. It is also a very vulnerable area in that it is temptation to theft, fraud and violent behaviour. For these reasons it is important that the supervisor/manager has procedures in place for security for handling cash. Cash handling procedures must be designed to reduce the risk of fraud and theft, and the team's vulnerability.

TASK

Put regular audits in place to check that the cash handling procedures are being adhered to.

Shift handover

Most reception teams work a shift pattern to cover the opening hours of the organisation, often over a 24-hour period.

Each shift will take responsibility for cash for that shift. At the start of the shift staff will receive and count the float. The amount received should be counted and countersigned by the person handing it over to the shift.

All transactions from the previous shift should have been closed down before the new shift starts.

DEALING WITH CUSTOMER BILLS AND AN AUDIT TRAIL

Whenever anyone handles cash or any other payment methods, there should be an audit trail to back up the action. It enables any future query to be traced back to the source and understood.

There are three ways to complete this information:

1 Manual system.
2 Computerised system.
3 Combination of manual and computerised.

REMEMBER

Devise incident cards as a quick reference for staff, with details of how to contact key staff, managers.

Cash handling

© ISTOCKPHOTO.COM/© OLEKSANDR GUMEROV

REMEMBER

Put training in place for new staff in cash handling procedures.

REMEMBER

Shift patterns may resemble:

Early	7.00a.m. – 3.00p.m.
Late	3.00p.m. – 11.00p.m.
	9.00a.m. – 5.00p.m.
Night	11.00p.m. – 7.00a.m.

Traditional till

© ISTOCKPHOTO.COM/ GUILLERMO LOBO

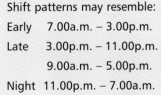

DEALING WITH CUSTOMER BILLS AND AN AUDIT TRAIL

> **! REMEMBER**
>
> Ensure you have a full understanding of how your systems work and how to access the audit trail.

> **TASK**
>
> Review the audit rolls, receipts and customer bills used in different organisations.
>
> ■ Decide which ones represent what you would use
>
> ■ Make a list of the personnel who would have access to audit rolls or programs. Decide how you would monitor this

On a traditional electronic till there will be two rolls of paper. One will be the till roll and one is an audit roll. When payments are made details are collated on both rolls. The receipt roll can provide a receipt for the customer and the audit roll is kept as a permanent record of transactions.

If a computerised system is used, a program records the audit trail.

> **! REMEMBER**
>
> ■ Whenever a transaction takes place there should be an audit trail
> ■ It is a legal requirement that whenever a good or service is purchased a receipt must be given
> ■ Procedures should be in place to restrict staff access to audit trails and paperwork

Preparing a customer's bill

In many retail establishments customers' bills are created with the use of barcodes, scanning items over a computer reader which automatically produces a bill. In hotels and restaurants, rooms and meals/drinks cannot easily have barcodes attached to them. This means that receptionist staff need to be accurate when compiling a bill and know exactly what price to charge for each good or service.

The basic components of a bill in an establishment that provides accommodation are:

■ Accommodation

■ Food

■ Drink

■ Telephone

Further items may be:

■ Video or television channels

■ Laundry

■ Newspapers

■ Mini bar

Every day the reception team will keep the customers' bills up to date by posting charges to the bill as the services are used.

> **TASK**
>
> Compile a checklist for the reception team to ensure daily charges are made. This will be required for manual systems and a reference for computerised systems.

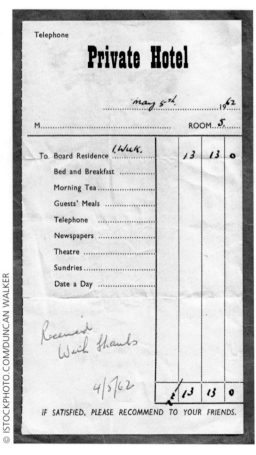

Example bill

In most organisations charges for drinks and food are automatically made at the bar/restaurant to the customer's bill by a computer link to the main reception system. Ideally the bar and restaurant areas should collect signatures from guests as items are added to their bills.

CHECKLIST

Bill checklist

■ It is illegal to charge a price other than the one advertised for any good or services

■ Before a customer pays a bill they have the right to check its accuracy

■ Once a bill has been checked and agreed, the customer and the establishment have made a legal contract about the amount which is to be paid

■ Once a transaction has been made, a printed receipt must be provided as proof of that transaction

Presenting a customer's bill

Most customers ask for their bill. When a customer asks for their bill it should be presented to them in a written or printed format. This gives the customer a clear indication as how the total was calculated. The customer should be allowed time to study the bill, if they choose to do so, before payment is collected.

When creating or totalling a bill it is essential that the correct price or codes are used, otherwise the bill will not be correct. The correct price must be entered so that:

■ The correct change can be given, if applicable

■ The reading on the reception roll and audit roll matches the amount of payment received

■ The customer is charged the correct amount of money

The correct code or ledger information (if a bill is not being paid immediately and is sent, for example to a company for payment, it is called a ledger payment) must be entered when receiving payment so that the accounts department will know how much money to expect in cash and how much in other forms of payment.

Once payment has been made, even if it is a non-cash payment, the customer must receive a machine-printed receipt showing the amount that they have paid. For ledger accounts it is usual practice that the guest checks and signs the bill, to agree the amount to be paid.

! REMEMBER

If once the customer has checked the bill, and the receptionist then identifies a mistake in calculating the bill it cannot be added at a later date. The money is lost.

! REMEMBER

Train your staff to present the bill discreetly. The customer may be with guests that they do not want to disclose the contents or amount of the bill to.

A customer's bill

! REMEMBER

Train your staff to be familiar with ledger codes used for payments.

Build in your own checklist to ensure compliance with the codes.

© ISTOCKPHOTO.COM/PAUL GARDNER

Types of payment

Taking payment

Once a customer is satisfied that the bill is accurate, they will pay. Ensure the reception team are aware of the law that requires a receipt to be issued for the services that the customer has received.

Different types of payment:

- Cash
- Ledger
- Token or voucher (used for promotions or cashless systems)
- Cheque
- Credit/debit card

TASK

Ensure staff are aware of the vouchers/tokens accepted by your organisation, and the procedure to handle and store them.

Receipts

Normally the customer's bill is also their receipt, produced in a triplicate format. The copies of the bill are divided as:

- Top copy – customer copy
- Bottom two copies – kept by the establishment and used by the accounts department

! REMEMBER

- Train reception staff to keep cash draws tidy
- Notes should be stored in the correct denomination, facing the same way to aid counting

Cheques

! REMEMBER

- A bank card issued by a bank or building society contains information for the receptionist to verify the ownership of a cheque
- Bank, building society and euro cheques should be supported by the relevant bank card
- The bank card will contain an issuing amount or value to support the cheque
- The bank card signature should match the customer's signature on the cheque

© ISTOCKPHOTO.COM/PALI RAO

Payment by cheque

TASK

Produce a checklist of cheques that your staff may be presented with, and a policy on how to process them.

CHECKLIST

Points to consider when receiving cheques:

- Date is correct
- Amount is in writing and figures, and is correct
- Signature is the same as the bank card
- Bank card is valid
- Total does not exceed guarantee figure on card
- Bank card and sort code are the same as the cheque

Traveller's cheques should be supported by the owner's passport. The receptionist should look at the passport photograph and signature to identify the customer.

Credit cards

CHECKLIST

Have in place procedures to accept traveller's cheques, to include

■ Cheques dated and signed in front of reception staff

■ Customer ID

■ Storage of traveller's cheques

Credit cards

Not all establishments accept all credit cards. This is because they have to pay commission to the issuing company, and these rates vary. A credit card payment is guaranteed by the card's printed limit, by the floor limit of the establishment and by the authorisation code.

Authorisation or payment is needed whenever the bill total is for more than the card's stated limit, the establishment's floor limit, or both. Most establishments use 'chip & PIN' machines to process credit/debit cards.

Dealing with customers requiring refunds

Most organisations have a limited number of personnel that have the authority to refund. All refunds should have an audit trail.

Reasons for refund:

■ Something has gone wrong – the customer is dissatisfied

■ Error in charging

■ Customer may be 'trying it on'

On all occasions an investigation should be undertaken by the supervisor/manager authorised to give refunds, to establish the facts.

! REMEMBER

Floor limit is the establishment's credit limit without authorisation.

■ If the total of a bill exceeds the floor limit, an authorisation or payment must be sought from the issuing company

■ Be aware of the length of stay of guests and ensure procedures are in place to guarantee payment as the bill exceeds the floor limit

---

CHECKLIST

Have in place procedures for staff to follow if the card is declined for payment.

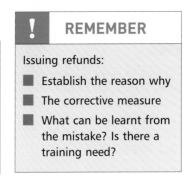

Chip & PIN machine

! REMEMBER

Issuing refunds:

■ Establish the reason why

■ The corrective measure

■ What can be learnt from the mistake? Is there a training need?

ACTIVITY

Test your staff on how to handle guests who are complaining. Include questions around:

1 Customer care and the initial response by your team.

2 Who to contact.

MAINTAIN CUSTOMER RECORDS

Customer records play an important part in any organisation. The most successful establishments maintain detailed records, training staff to recall their customers' likes and dislikes.

Enquiry information records

Information from an initial telephone call can be retrieved again if a reservation is made. These details can be stored on a computerised database.

! REMEMBER

Customer records should be:
- ■ Accurate
- ■ Regularly updated

CHECKLIST

Have procedures in place for the service to continue should computerised systems fail

TASK

Design an enquiry form for your staff to use to gain all of the information required for your database. Remember data bases are only as good as the information fed in.

ENQUIRY FORM

Top of Form

Your Details:

Title   **Surname**   **First Name**

Address

Town   **Country**

Post Code

Email

Phone Number

Nature of Enquiry, include date and no. in party.

Send

Clear

Bottom of Form

© ISTOCKPHOTO.COM/CRISTIAN LUPU

Reservation records

When a booking is taken, either by using a paper form or a computerised system, a booking number is created for the reservation. It is at this point that all of the information required about the guest can be recorded.

Billing and guest information records

Dockets used to prepare accounts, summary sheets and invoices, paying-in books, cash and trading accounts have to be readily available for customers and management of the establishment.

Guest history information normally includes:

- Name and address of guest
- Dates and length of stay
- Room they occupied
- Price charged
- Special requests
- How they paid
- Comments/complaints
- Preferences, e.g. type of room/extra pillows etc.

! REMEMBER

All accounts, invoices and dockets have to be kept for six years for the Inland Revenue and VAT inspector.

TASK

Ensure your establishment has a systems back-up procedure in place to maintain computerised records.

DEALING WITH RESERVATIONS

Some organisations have a separate team taking reservations, either on-site or based centrally. Smaller organisations include reservations within the reception duties.

Reservation enquiries

Bookings are made:
- By telephone
- Face-to-face
- Repeat bookings
- By email, letter or fax

TASK

Ensure your staff know your organisation's procedures for bookings, whether deposits are required and how bookings are guaranteed.

TASK

Are all of your staff aware of the sales targets and how to achieve them?

Taking reservations by phone

! REMEMBER

Some organisations offer incentives to staff with excellent customer care and sales targets.

TASK

A supervisor/manager demonstrates good practice by identifying previous customers prior to arrival and greeting them on arrival.

TASK

Produce a pie chart for your organisation, detailing the mix of business your establishment has.

! REMEMBER

Ensure that your staff are aware of the facilities available for disabled guests. Take the staff to see the bedrooms and toilets with disabled access.

! REMEMBER

Consider the needs of guests from the different types of bookings that you have. What facilities and service would a coach party require? What is being offered as part of their package?

! REMEMBER

Ensure procedures are in place to:
- Check bookings are legitimate
- Take deposits

Most organisations use computerised systems to take bookings. At a touch of a button you can see whether there is the required type of room available for a particular date.

The system will also provide the registration card for the guest's arrival.

Sources of reservations

- Booking agencies
- Repeat bookings
- Customers using your establishment's facilities i.e. conference, function
- Internet
- Tourists
- Business people
- Guide books
- Families

All of the above are important customers to maximise room occupancy.

Customer group bookings

A group of people reserving accommodation will normally expect a discounted rate in return for their business. This could also attract free accommodation for the organiser and coach driver.

When deciding whether to accept a group booking the following should be considered:

- Size of party
- Type of accommodation required
- Time of year
- Length of stay
- Days of the week
- Bed and breakfast or dinner, bed and breakfast
- Price you can offer
- The type of party

Over-booking

In some organisations a high proportion of people who book rooms do not arrive. It is important to maintain a high occupancy, and many organisations over-book to achieve it. The supervisor/manager leads at what point this happens, and decides upon which guests are to be booked elsewhere.

TASK

Over-booking can potentially lead to dissatisfied guests, so have procedures in place for staff to follow, to be prepared for guests arriving without a room available. Work closely with other hotels to book guests into and arrange travel arrangements.

Tight procedures

Care should be taken when accepting bookings from customers who have sent confirmation by fax or email, and whose bills are to be settled by account at a later date. This booking could be in the name of a company which does not exist and the address could be false.

Confirmation by email or fax a deposit is encouraged in some establishments so that customers are more likely to honour their bookings.

Booking details

Details are taken using a computerised system. This will retrieve information about previous bookings or information about the customer.

The system should contain the following details:

■ Customer's name, title and initials

■ Address including postcode

■ Telephone number

■ Type of room required

■ Duration of stay

■ Number of rooms required

■ Terms required

■ Price

■ Booking status

■ Special requests

Guaranteed reservations

If the period of time between the booking being made to the arrival time is short, i.e. the same day, many establishments request the customer guarantees the reservation with a credit card. This means that charges can be made even if the customer does not arrive.

> **! REMEMBER**
>
> Train staff to know what to do when they receive a cancellation.

Booking cancellations

Cancellations can be difficult to overcome, especially at short notice. This is the reason deposits are taken for large parties and functions. Some

TASK

Have in place procedures to check unconfirmed bookings. Decide how much in advance you will do this to maximise occupancy.

organisations take credit details for all bookings and make charges for short notice cancellations.

Working closely with other organisations or agencies can help to re-book rooms, following cancellations, maximising the occupancy levels.

DEALING WITH THE ARRIVAL OF CUSTOMERS

Customers who arrive without making a booking in advance are known as 'chance bookings' or 'walk ins'. Clearly no advance preparations can be made for them so the procedures for the reception team to follow are slightly different and have to be done with speed.

Reception

Reception environment

This area gives the first impression of the organisation. If it looks untidy and chaotic, a bad impression is immediately formed with the customer. This could lead to doubt in the efficiency of the rest of the establishment.

Registration (without a booking)

If a customer arrives without a booking the following should be carried out:

- Check availability for the request made
- Give the customer details of the accommodation available, charges etc.
- Take customer details and enter onto the system
- Check customer in
- Inform housekeeping and other departments that an additional room is occupied
- Take payment for accommodation

! REMEMBER

Excellent customer care skills are required by the reception team. Ensure all guests are greeted in a way that makes them feel welcome and special.

! REMEMBER

Train staff to be alert to customer's needs and identify whether the room allocated is suitable, before the customer knows.

! REMEMBER

A registration card must be completed on arrival for several reasons:

- By the Immigration (Hotel Records) Order 1972 it is a legal requirement that everyone over the age of 16 who books sleeping accommodation in return for payment, completes a registration form giving full name and nationality
- Customers who are not British have to give additional information such as passport number, place of issue, next destination and full address
- Customer accounts can be accurately made up
- Helps internal audit processes
- Information can be gained for the sales department
- In an emergency, an exact record of customers is required

Registration (with a booking)

Documentation can be prepared prior to arrival for customers with bookings. Before arrival, the arrivals for the day can be checked for accuracy and special requests to ensure details are correct. Key cards and registration cards can be printed to speed up the check-in procedure and once completed the customer has only to check the details and sign the registration form.

On arrival

- Give the registration form to the customer
- Some organisations alert customers to the fire/emergency procedures at this point
- Issue the key and key card. Give directions to the room

6p.m. release

One way of re-letting short notice bookings is to hold them until 6p.m. on the day of arrival. This gives the opportunity for the rooms to be reallocated after this time.

PREPARE CUSTOMER ACCOUNTS AND DEAL WITH DEPARTURES

As soon as a customer arrives it is usual to open an account or bill in their name or company. Charging items to a customer's bill is known as 'posting'. Charges may include:

- Food and drink
- Leisure facilities
- Theatre tickets
- Telephone calls
- Newspapers

Customer accounts

The reception team receive notification of any charges incurred by the guest around the establishment, either manually or electronically.

When a customer checks into an establishment a credit limit is usually set up for regular or known customers. For 'chance' bookings, a pre-payment is normally asked for.

Long-term customers will be asked to pay their account at regular intervals, to make sure they are able to pay and provide the organisation with a constant flow of money.

TASK

Work with the reception team to handle 'unexpected situations' i.e. a guest believes that they have made a booking, but the team is not expecting them.

How would the team deal with a drunk guest arriving for accommodation?

! REMEMBER

If a customer does not arrive, the law states that an establishment may charge two-thirds of the total cost if the accommodation remains unlet.

Key card

© ISTOCKPHOTO.COM/EVA SERRABASSA

! REMEMBER

The key card plays an important part with the accounting process. It confirms the rate being charged to the customer, and allows them to charge items to their room account wherever they produce it within the organisation.

! REMEMBER

As supervisor, build in daily checks on customer accounts and identify those required to make payments.

Deal with the departures of customers

How guests are handled when departing after settling their accounts is just as important as how you handle them on arrival, as a bad experience at this time could completely spoil their stay.

Sometimes a customer is unable to pay their account, because they may have lost their wallet or they may have no intention of paying. To obtain food, accommodation and services without the means to pay is against the law and the police should be called. You are within your rights to confiscate any luggage they have, but not their vehicle. This is called the 'Right of Lien' and if the account is not settled within six weeks you have the right to sell their possessions.

> **TASK**
>
> Consider how feedback can be collated by your team to improve the reception team's performance and feedback to other departments about their performance.

> **! REMEMBER**
>
> Customers checking out do not expect to be kept waiting for their bill to be made up.
> - Present the bill to the customer so that they can agree the total
> - Take payment from the customer
> - Once the customer has vacated the room, ensure that the room key is returned

A 'walk out' poses similar problems and you will be required to give a full description of the customer to the police.

Customer comments

> **! REMEMBER**
>
> The supervisor/manager should be available to assist at busy checkout times, to talk to customers and receive feedback about the services.

When presenting the bill, it is good practice to ask the customer if they have enjoyed their stay. This gives customers the opportunity to give feedback on their stay and enables the organisation to improve their services, if required.

Bidding customers farewell

This is as important as greeting customers as they arrive. It is a further opportunity to encourage customers to return.

Further reading and research

> **TASK**
>
> Decide how you want your team to greet and bid farewell to your customers. Train them and regularly review how successful the team is at this.

Colin Dix and Chris Baird (1998) *Front Office Operations*. Longman.

Jeremy Huyton and Sue Baker (2001) *Principles of Front Office Operations*, 2nd revised edn. Thomson Learning.

Denney G. Rutherford and Michael J. O'Fallon (2006) *Hotel Management and Operations*, 4th edn. Wiley.

Peter Jones and Andrew Lockwood (2002) *Management of Hotel Operations*, revised 3rd edn. Thomson Learning.

Assessment of knowledge and understanding

You have now learnt about supervising the reception service to ensure that it has all the necessary staff, equipment and supplies. You know how to ensure that procedures are in place for the running of the service and that staff conduct themselves appropriately.

To test your level of knowledge and understanding, answer the following short questions. These will help to prepare you for your summative (final) assessment.

1 Why is it important as a supervisor to ensure that your team has a professional image?

2 If you sell additional rooms that have not been pre-booked, why is it important to tell other departments?

3 Describe how you would monitor the sales achieved by each member of staff.

4 How would you train your team to identify a problem before it happens?

5 List the legal requirements for registration.

6 List the payment methods that organisations accept.

7 How would you handle a customer that could not pay their bill? What factors would you consider?

8 Why is it important to maintain customer satisfaction?

9 Describe the procedure you would have in place to deal with being over-booked.

10 What skills would you look for when recruiting a new receptionist?

Research task

Establish the business mix for your organisation and the revenue achieved for the mix.

Compare this information with three other organisations and decided which is the best mix to have to optimise revenue.

13

Supervise reservations and booking services

LEARNING OBJECTIVES

This unit is about organising the reservation and booking service to ensure the development and maintenance of the necessary resources and procedures essential for operation. It also involves monitoring the service and suggesting improvements.

After reading this chapter you will be able to:

■ Brief staff on duties, relevant procedures and any variations relating to their work routines.

■ Encourage staff to ask questions if there is information that they do not understand.

■ Ensure staff are aware of how to present themselves and of the standard of behaviour acceptable to the organisation.

■ Make sure that your staff follow the reservation and booking procedures.

■ Make sure your staff communicate with customers in a manner that promotes goodwill and understanding.

■ Make sure staff have the resources they need when they need them.

■ Make sure the reservation and booking service complies with relevant legislation and organisational policy.

- Inform your staff and customers about any changes to the service that may affect them.
- Take effective action to manage problems that may disrupt the linen service when they occur.
- Collect feedback on the service from staff and customers and monitor and review procedures to ensure the service meets the needs of customers.
- Pass on feedback and recommend improvements to the relevant people according to your organisation's requirements.
- Complete the required records and report on performance and procedures as required.

KEY WORDS

Bona fide
In good faith; without dishonesty, fraud or deceit.

Computer
An electronic device for the storage and processing of information.

Database
A collection of data which has been organised so that a computer program can quickly select desired items. This could be something as straightforward as a list of names in alphabetical order or an ascending list of numeric stock codes. The secret to the successful use of database technology is the way in which data or information is structured to enable efficient processing.

Ergonomics
An applied science concerned with the human characteristics that need to be considered when designing things that people use. This is to ensure that the interactions between people and the things they use are effective and safe.

Over-booking
This is when there are too many reservations for the number of rooms available for any one night.

Reservation
Booking of a room or service within an organisation.

INTRODUCTION

The reservation and booking service offered by a hospitality outlet is often the first experience the customer will have of a company. Therefore, if you work on the 'first impressions last' concept you can be assured that it is also the most important service offered. If it all goes wrong the customer won't make a booking at all, or start off their visit to your outlet with niggling complaints, and it will go downhill after that.

This chapter aims to address the policies and procedures, legislation and staffing resources required to run an effective reservation and booking service in any one of many different types of hospitality outlet.

ROLES AND RESPONSIBILITIES OF THOSE INVOLVED IN THE RESERVATION AND BOOKING SERVICE

In a hotel environment there may well be a rooms division manager. The organisational chart could look something like this:

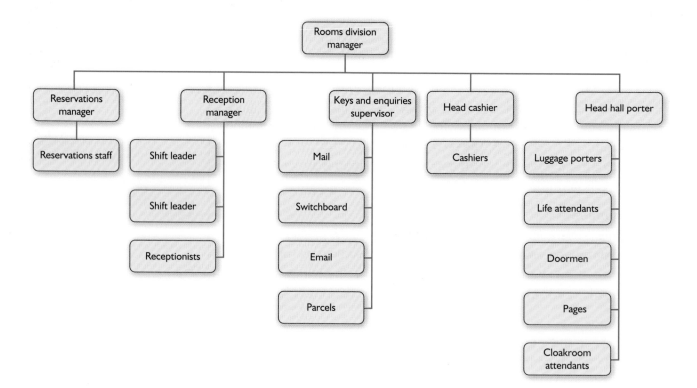

You are more likely to find this type of structure in a five-star hotel as it is quite comprehensive and includes a wide range of job roles and teams. As you can see, all of them have a front-facing role where they have communication with the customers and need to make an impression.

In a restaurant, your reservations and bookings team may look more like this:

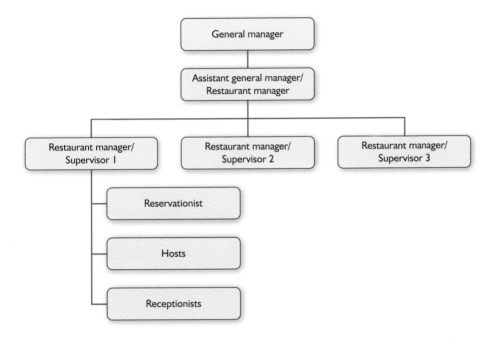

Here you can see it is a more simplified structure and includes a front of house team that includes responsibilities for **reservations** (often out of normal opening hours via a **telephonist**), **hosts** who will meet and greet the guests and a **receptionist** who will take reservations and answer queries while the restaurant is open.

In a bar, it is often the *doormen* who have that first contact with your customer. A typical impression can be of someone who is surly, unfriendly and at times threatening, because they also have a security role.

In a self-service environment it may be that the cashier is the first point of contact for the customer, or the person serving the food, or the chef cooking the food.

So, before continuing, it is worth pausing to think about the following. In your place of work:

■ Which members of staff are having the first contact with the customer?

■ What impression are they giving to that customer?

■ Is that impression good or not?

■ How could it be improved/adapted or changed?

As a supervisor, what do you think you should be doing to identify these roles and ensure that the guest is getting the best *first impression* possible from your outlet?

ACTIVITY

Try drawing an organisational chart to highlight the front of house roles in your organisation and how they fit in with the rest of the outlet. Then highlight which of them meets the customer first.

POLICIES AND PROCEDURES INVOLVED IN THE RESERVATION AND BOOKING SERVICE

Policies and procedures in place

Some of the policies and procedures you might find as part of the reservations and booking service include:

■ Reservation policy – this could include:

- Information that should be taken when receiving a booking (name, address, contact details, special requirements, etc.)
- What information should be given the customer when they make their booking
- Deposits taken or credit card details taken at time of booking
- Forms that need to be completed by the member of staff taking the booking: this might also include how the reservation is tracked. For example in a diary, or on the computer

An example of Best Western's booking policy is as follows:

Booking policy

To make a booking, you may telephone our Reservations Centre on **08457 74 74 74** or telephone the hotel concerned direct on the number given within the hotel description.

The person making the booking ('the party leader') **must be at least 18** and must be authorised to make the booking on the basis of these Booking Conditions by all persons named on the booking. By making a booking, the party leader confirms that he/she is so authorised and that all party members agree to be bound by these Booking Conditions.

The party leader is responsible for making all payments due to us. Subject to availability, we will confirm your break by issuing a confirmation invoice. This invoice will be sent to the party leader or your travel agent.

Please check this invoice carefully as soon as you receive it. Contact us immediately if any information which appears on the confirmation or any other document appears to be incorrect or incomplete as it may not be possible to make changes later.

We regret we cannot accept any liability if we are not notified of any inaccuracies in any document within ten days of our sending it out. Booking confirmations will either be sent by Royal Mail or, if your email details are taken on making the booking, will be sent by email.

It is **your** responsibility to ensure that you regularly check your email account and check any confirmation documents sent to you.

■ Deposits – as mentioned above

- Do you take a deposit when the booking is made?
- Do you take credit card details? What do you do with those? Do you store them safely? Or do you reserve a credit amount on their card?

■ Cancellation policy

- How much notice does the customer have to give in cancelling their reservation?
- What happens if they don't give enough notice? How much do you charge them?

This is Best Western's cancellation policy:

Should you or any member of your party need to cancel your chosen break once it has been confirmed, the party leader must immediately advise our Reservations Centre. Your notice of cancellation will only be effective when it is received by our Reservations Centre, at which time you will be given a cancellation number relating to the date and time of your call. This must be kept by you for reference. Where we incur costs from the time we confirm your booking, we will charge you a sum to cover the costs, expenses, charges and losses that we incur as a result of your cancellation. In the case of breaks that include a health and beauty treatment, this will be the full cost of the health and beauty treatment in question. In the case of breaks which include an activity, the following charges will be payable:

Period before departure within which written notification of cancellation is received	Cancellation charge
29 days or more	Activity deposit
15–28 days	50 per cent of the cost of the activity
0–14 days	100 per cent of the cost of the activity

Breaks including an activity

In addition, with all breaks, you may be charged an amount to cover the cancelled accommodation element of your break. If our reservations department receive notice of your cancellation more than 48 hours prior to the date that your chosen break is due to commence, there will be no cancellation charge.

If they receive notice 48 hours or less before the date your break is due to commence, then you will be required to pay 100 per cent of the cost of the accommodation element of the break. In all cases, any amendment charges which have already been incurred are not refundable in the event of the person(s) to whom they apply cancelling.

Depending on the reason for cancellation, it is sometimes possible to reclaim these cancellation charges (less any applicable excess) under the terms of certain insurance policies. If you have purchased such an insurance policy and this applies to you, claims must be made directly to the insurance company concerned. Please ensure that you return to us any vouchers or tickets in your possession that relate to the cancelled break.

If any member(s) of your party is/are prevented from travelling, the person(s) concerned will be able to transfer their place to someone else (introduced by you). An amendment fee may be charged. Should you wish to make any changes to your confirmed break, you must notify us in writing as soon as possible. Whilst we will endeavour to assist, we cannot guarantee we will be able to meet any such requests.

■ Storage and security of data – please see the legislation on pages 197–198

You may use a whole host of forms to help store this information. For example:

■ Reservation forms

■ The bookings diary

■ The blacklist/unwanted persons list

■ Room availability records

■ Arrivals list

■ Rooms status records

■ Guest indexes

Or, you might use a computer.

© ISTOCKPHOTO.COM/COSTINT

Manual vs computerised – advantages and disadvantages

ADVANTAGES	DISADVANTAGES
■ **Speed** – computers work at electronic speeds and can process thousands of transactions per second	■ **Breakdowns** – systems aren't always 100 per cent reliable and can 'crash' at awkward moments
■ **Accuracy** – computers always do exactly what they are told to do	■ **Audit trail requirement** – written audit trails are often still required in case anything goes wrong or for the purposes of financial audits. This means that 'paperless' work environments are further off from happening that we would like
■ **Discipline** – computers can perform the same tasks over and over again and never get tired, bored or distracted	
■ **Capacity** – computers can process large amounts of data easily, meaning they can perform more in-depth analysis and consider more variables	■ **Memory restrictions** – a computer's memory is finite
■ **Reduction in the amount of clerical work** that is carried out	■ **Training time** – it can take a lot of time to train individuals to use computer systems
■ Boring repetitive tasks can be **automate**d, making employees' jobs more varied and fulfilling, increasing job satisfaction	■ **Speed restrictions** – data entry by the operator of the computer can be slow
■ **Increase productivity** – same amount of work completed with less effort	■ **Compatibility and expandability** – not all computers talk to one another and it can be frustrating when they don't link up
■ **Cost savings** in reducing staff numbers or, more importantly	
■ Staff can concentrate less on routine work and have more time for **personal interacting with the guest**	
■ **Networking** – can cope with a number of transactions or inputs going on all at the same time	

A computer is only as good as the investment made in it.

An old computer can be slow, short of memory and not have the most up-to-date software to speed up a transaction. It may 'crash', thereby interfere with your work. **A new computer** won't 'crash': it is fast, dependable, has up-to-date software and can integrate various elements of software to provide more useful information.

The diagram below illustrates how the right computer with its hardware, software and communication can improve the work environment.

TIP

If you have a night auditor or night manager in your place of work, then ask them what their job entails. You may find that a lot of their work is making sure that various computer systems link up. You may not!

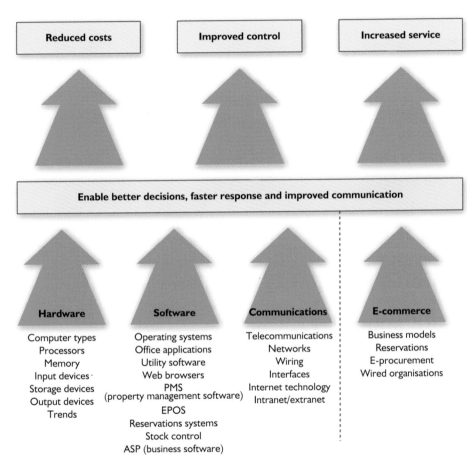

Examples of the forms often found in relation to bookings

A Hotel Arrivals List

A Booking Form

Feedback from staff and customers

How do you receive feedback from guests?

■ Verbally

■ Questionnaires

- Lack of service charge
- Body language

In a hotel, who do guests go to first when they have a problem or complaint?

- Reservations/concierge

In a restaurant, who do guests go to first when they have a problem or complaint?

- Waiter
- Then, supervisor
- Or on their way out they will comment to the host, doorman, manager?

What are you doing with that feedback?

- Recording it? If so where?
- *At this stage it may be worth referring to Chapter 22, Monitor and Solve Customer Problems*

LEGISLATION

There is a variety of legislation that has a significant impact on the reservation and booking service. It may include some of the following:

Health and safety

The regulations have been designed to ensure that reservations and bookings can be a safe and stress-free operation. It covers aspects including seating, positioning of equipment, absence of noise, glare and dangerous radiation.

At Wembley Stadium during a concert the bar staff on the pitch are required to wear ear plugs to protect their hearing.

Have you ever considered the ergonomics of sitting at your computer? It is important that you sit properly with your feet and the keyboard in the right position and that you rest your eyes from time to time. Your teachers will explain this to you in more detail.

Have you ever considered the impact of standing on your feet for an 8-hour shift?

Contracts for accommodation

When a hotel accepts a booking from a guest, it enters into a binding contract. The guest is expected to turn up and the hotel must provide the agreed accommodation. If either

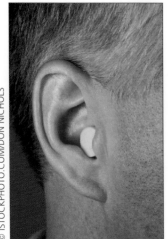

party fails to honour their side of the bargain, it must compensate the other for any loss suffered.

The Hotel Proprietors Act 1956

A hotel is defined as an 'inn' and therefore has an obligation to accept a bona fide traveller who 'appears able and willing to pay a reasonable sum for the services and facilities provided, and who are in a fit state to be received'. A guest may be put on a blacklist if the hotel has had an unfavourable experience with them in the past.

Sex Discrimination Act 1975

Prohibits any outlet discriminating against any person on the grounds of sex, race, colour, nationality, race or ethnic origin.

Right of lien

Part of the Innkeepers Act 1878 allows a hospitality outlet to seize a guest's belongings and sell them to defray costs if their bill is not paid. It does have a number of restrictions though, and a guest who was thinking of leaving without paying probably wouldn't bring anything with them that was worth seizing.

Price display orders (food, accommodation and bar tariff)

If you have serviced accommodation premises and supply food or food and drink to non-residents, you need to comply with the Price Marking (Food and Drink Services) Order 2003. Amongst a number of responsibilities, this states you must display the prices charged, including VAT.

Data Protection Act

The Data Protection Act gives individuals the right to know what information is held about them. It provides a framework to ensure that personal information is handled properly.

The Act works in two ways. First, it states that anyone who processes personal information must comply with eight principles, which make sure that personal information is:

1 Fairly and lawfully processed.
2 Processed for limited purposes.

3 Adequate, relevant and not excessive.

4 Accurate and up to date.

5 Not kept for longer than is necessary.

6 Processed in line with your rights.

7 Secure.

8 Not transferred to other countries without adequate protection.

The second area covered by the Act provides individuals with important rights, including the right to find out what personal information of theirs is held on computer and most paper records.

IDENTIFYING THE ORGANISATION'S PRODUCTS, FACILITIES AND SERVICES

In being able to provide the right service for bookings and reservations you need to be very clear about what you are providing and who the first point of contact is for any customer.

Are you:

■ A busy wine bar with doormen monitoring customer flow?

■ A busy Michelin star restaurant who takes bookings only up to 2 months before and the phones will be busy every day and you may have to turn away 70 per cent of those who call, without a reservation?

■ A self-service canteen for workers who come in every lunchtime and will probably see the chef or the cashier first?

■ A local pub and the bar person is the first point of contact?

■ A hotel with a big reservations team where first point of contact will be via the phone or even the Internet?

In addition to who the first point of contact is, you also need to consider what else do you provide that requires reservations and bookings? Are you a:

■ Pub that also has a restaurant?

■ Hotel with a leisure club or spa?

■ Hotel with a thriving restaurant?

■ Work canteen that also does special functions for the workers?

© ISTOCKPHOTO.COM

TASK

List all the services you provide as a hospitality outlet and highlight each of the areas that require reservations and bookings services.

TAKING A RESERVATION
Communication
Monitoring staff performance in relation to communication – e.g. mystery diners, etc.

We have already recognised that communication to all customers at the reservations and bookings stage is vital. But first a task:

Did you recognise the following areas?

Polite	Smartly dressed and well-groomed
Friendly	Clarity of voice
Smiling	Understands their duties
Courteous	Professional

It is important to realise that you need to be very clear about the standards of service you and your company expect from people working in your team in a reservations and bookings role. Only then can you monitor their skills and expertise in relation to those qualities.

It is important that you can monitor them and use a variety of methods to do that:

1 Self-observation when you are around.

2 Observations from other members of the team or supervisors and managers from other teams.

3 Mystery diners/guests – have you ever looked at the job role of a mystery diner? Try this out:

The Mystery Dining Company

We want to attract great diners. That means people who enjoy dining out and who can provide accurate, insightful and reliable feedback on every aspect of what they find. You'll need an eye for detail and be able to work to deadlines too.

https://www.mysterydining.co.uk/Pages/diners-about-you.aspx

4 Questionnaires may highlight both good and bad performance and name particular staff who were very friendly and helpful, or who perhaps weren't.

ACTIVITY

Write down the top 10 most important aspects/qualities needed when taking a reservation/ booking.

1

2

3

4

5

6

7

8

9

10

Here is a sample questionnaire that can be found online:

Dear Guest,

Your opinion on our services is of utmost importance to us, therefore we kindly ask you to take a few moments and fill in our questionnaire. Your feedback will help us improve our services and adapt them according to your suggestions and wishes. Thank you very much for your help.

Information about your stay

Hotel *

Your Name

Check In

Length of stay [   ] night(s)

Room number

Questions

How did you get to know about our hotel?

- ◯ from an acquaintance
- ◯ from advertising
- ◯ from a travel agency or catalogue
- ◯ from the Internet
- ◯ other

Any remarks

Purpose of your visit

- ◯ business
- ◯ conference
- ◯ sightseeing
- ◯ relaxation/wellness
- ◯ health
- ◯ other

Any remarks

☹ ☹ 😐 ☺ 😊

Arrival & welcome at the hotel   ◯ ◯ ◯ ◯ ◯

Any remarks

Check-in procedure ○ ○ ○ ○ ○

Any remarks

Friendliness of reception/concierge staff ○ ○ ○ ○ ○

Any remarks

Atmosphere and peace and quiet of your room ○ ○ ○ ○ ○

Any remarks

Cleanliness of the room and bathroom ○ ○ ○ ○ ○

Any remarks

Technical conditions/thermostat control of the room ○ ○ ○ ○ ○

Any remarks

Room service and minibar content ○ ○ ○ ○ ○

Any remarks

Atmosphere/cleanliness of public areas ○ ○ ○ ○ ○

Any remarks

Standard of restaurant services   O   O   O   O   O

Any remarks

Quality of food & beverages served   O   O   O   O   O

Any remarks

Choice and quality of breakfast   O   O   O   O   O

Any remarks

Services of the coffee shop and the bar   O   O   O   O   O

Any remarks

Banqueting services and function rooms   O   O   O   O   O

Any remarks

Service, quality and cleanliness of the Spa, Fitness and Wellness centre   O   O   O   O   O

Any remarks

Check out procedure   O   O   O   O   O

Any remarks

Would you recommend our hotel to friends/family?

○ Yes

○ No

Any remarks

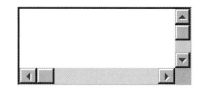

Do you have any other comments, which may help us improve our service, the product we offer or our marketing efforts?

Security Code *

Please enter the text You can see in the picture.

5   Monitoring sales levels can often indicate good and bad performance too. A good reservationist or host will generate more sales generally than someone who is not so good.

Taking corrective action – solutions, training

There are several methods of corrective action that can be taken. It is worth considering the following:

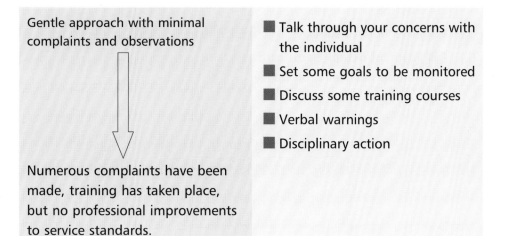

Gentle approach with minimal complaints and observations

↓

Numerous complaints have been made, training has taken place, but no professional improvements to service standards.

■ Talk through your concerns with the individual

■ Set some goals to be monitored

■ Discuss some training courses

■ Verbal warnings

■ Disciplinary action

TASK

What training events could you put on to help increase staff awareness to their impact on sales and performance within a reservations and bookings role?

Further training

Limits in relation to your authority

Are there limitations in your role or job in terms of how far you can take training or disciplinary action? If there are, then discuss these with your manager and communicate together to work out how far you can manage a situation and at what point you should take it to them to be dealt with. Also discuss how you will continue to communicate difficult situations like this. For example, through:

■ Shift handovers

■ Weekly meetings

■ Email

■ Log book

Equally, recognise your own training needs.

Information required in taking a reservation

So what information is required in taking a reservation? Well, this can be different depending on the environment that you are working in.

HOTEL	RESTAURANT	BAR
■ Date of arrival	■ Date required	■ Date
■ Number of nights	■ Number of guests dining	■ Number of guests
■ Time of arrival	■ Time of table	■ Area of the bar/private room
■ Number of people	■ Special menu/table d'hôte/À la carte	■ Free bar/cash bar
■ Number of rooms	■ Name	■ Special requirements
■ Type of room	■ Contact details – phone number/email address/address	■ Contact details
■ Room rate	■ Reservation taken by	■ Booking made by (staff)
■ Name	■ Payment details/credit card number (cancellation policy)	■ Payment details
■ Phone number	■ Special requirements	
■ Address		
■ Email address		
■ Who reservation taken by		
■ Guaranteed/confirmed		
■ Special requirements		
■ Date the reservation was taken		
■ Payment details		

Monitoring and utilising the information recorded (databases) to maintain and improve the service offered

The success of a business in modern times is frequently dependent on the accurate gathering, processing and use of information relating to the operations. Even something as simple as a customer mailing list needs to be managed appropriately if it is to be kept up to date and accurate. Therefore, any tools or applications that can make the tasks involved easier and more efficient need to be given serious consideration.

Most businesses recognise that the more you know about your customers, suppliers and competitors, the better, but many businesses do not have the time or resources available to gather and process large quantities of information. Therefore they may lack information about how their business is performing, how profitable their product lines are, whether customers are making repeat purchases, etc.

Note that your gathering, storage and processing of customers' personal data must comply with data protection legislation. Please see the legislation section above.

TIP

Training can be very draining for the trainer/supervisor, so make sure that as well as feeding others, you are being fed yourself.

The alternative? You will become drained and unable to be clear and fair in how you manage others.

Take time out for yourself and your own professional development.

Assessing customer needs

Assessing your customer's needs involves gathering and recording all relevant factual information together with their aims, social demographics and expectations from you as a service provider. That is easier said than done. So how do you assess a customer's needs?

1   Use your database. Have they been before, what were their patterns of business and reservations?

2   Use your brain...

   (a)   What do you supply?

   (b)   What is your policy on service?

   (c)   If it fitted in with a classification how would you grade the style and service of your hospitality environment?

   (d)   Now, *exceed* those expectations that the guest has when they come in

COMMISSION

In this instance there are two types of commission:

1   An agent's compensation for performance of the duties of his agency; in real estate practice, a percentage of the selling price of the property, or percentage of rentals, etc.

Or

2 A fee for services rendered based on a percentage of an amount received or collected or agreed to be paid (as distinguished from a salary); 'he works on commission'.

An agent's compensation

For example, if you are a hotel and have a marketing strategy that includes using third parties to help sell your rooms you would pay them a form of commission. This could include:

■ A flat rate per room sold, or

■ A percentage of the revenue from the sale of the room

Such third parties could include Internet-based companies such as lastminute.com, hotels.com or expedia.

Alternatively it could include marketing companies such as:

■ Leading Hotels of the World

■ Hip Hotels

Some companies act as a third party to mediate between a venue and the guest using it, for example wedding planners, events' organisers.

OVER-BOOKING

The concept of over-booking is to book for more than you have available. The reason for doing this is to compensate for no shows and cancellations, thereby maximising occupancy and revenue.

© ISTOCKPHOTO.COM

Policy

There is no official policy in regard to over-booking. Many companies do have a policy however and this is set usually by the revenue manager of a hotel or by the general manager in a smaller outlet or restaurant.

It is worth considering the legislation in relation to this – refer to contracts in the **legislation** section of this chapter.

Procedures

There are few procedures for over-booking, but they are as follows:

1 Decide by how much you are prepared to over-book for each separate date/shift.

2 Take all the contact details for each booking.

3 Decide how you are going to prioritise the bookings if they all turn up.

4 What are you going to do with the reservations that you really cannot facilitate, i.e. not provide a room or table. Where are you going to send them? How are you going to compensate them?

Prioritising

TASK

Class discussion

1 What do you think needs to be taken into consideration in allocating rooms or tables when you are over-booked and it is looking very likely that they will all turn up?

2 What are you going to do with the ones that have been turned away?

Assessment of knowledge and understanding

You have now learnt about some of the supervisory aspects of the reservation and booking service, including the roles and responsibilities, legislation, how to supervise the reservations and bookings service and managing over-bookings.

To test your level of knowledge and understanding, answer the following short questions. These will help to prepare you for your summative (final) assessment.

Roles and responsibilities

1 Consider your front of house team and produce an organisational chart to illustrate their roles.

2 Make a note of the various customer service tasks involved in their daily duties.

3 Finally, evaluate how effective they are at meeting the needs of the customers making the reservations. Can you spot any gaps in the service?

Policies and procedures

1 Does your company have any procedures and policy in relation to reservations and bookings?

   (a) If so, note down the key points of this paying particular attention to the tasks involved for the front of house teams

   (b) If not, research a company that does have procedures and policies and then go back to (a)

2 How do you manage the legislative aspects within these policies and procedures?

3 Research a company that has an overbooking policy, then consider:

   (a) How does it work, explain the details of it to the rest of your class or, if appropriate, to your team

   (b) Is it clear?

(c) Can it be easily disseminated into practice?

(d) What is the company's contingency plan?

Technology

1   What technology do you use in the reservations and bookings service environment?

2   How do you ensure that your staff know how to use it and the importance in terms of the accuracy of the information they need to input?

3   How could the use of technology be improved in your hospitality outlet?

Customer service

1   How long do you think it takes on average to take a booking? With this in mind, list the tasks involved in taking a booking or reservation in your work environment.

2   How well do your team look after the customer? How can you ensure they all go the extra mile?

3   How could you use performance statistics from third parties such as mystery diners or guest questionnaires?

4   What does that information say about you?

5   Unfortunately, where customer service is concerned, 100 per cent of guests are rarely 100 per cent satisfied. What do you think you need to do with your team to improve performance in relation to customer service when taking reservations and bookings?

Research task

Taking reservations

1   Consider this...

You are an events organiser and a couple have to see you about arranging their engagement party.

Now decide:

■   What information do you need to get from the couple in relation to the booking?

■   Once you have all the information you feel necessary, what are you going to next? How do you communicate this important information to third parties so ensure that the party goes off without any hitches?

14

Contribute to promoting hospitality services and products

HS6 **Contribute to promoting hospitality services and products**

LEARNING OBJECTIVES

This unit is about the promotion of services and products. It is geared towards those in a supervisory role who are well placed to offer new ideas for promotional activities. Promotion may be through regular activities such as posters, leaflets and discounts as well as more irregular innovations such as special timely events.

After reading this chapter you will be able to:

■ Identify possible activities to promote the services and products in your area of responsibility.

■ Identify promotional activities and the likely sales improvements activities could generate.

■ Consult with relevant colleagues about your ideas for promotional activities.

■ Make sure these activities are consistent with your targets, your organisation's objectives and values and legal requirements.

■ Collect and organise relevant information to support your ideas for promotional activities, taking account of the resources that will be available.

■ Help to develop and implement plans effectively.

■ Monitor activities to make sure that targeted customers are being reached and promotional activities are run according to agreed plans and standards.

■ Collect information about the promotional activities and evaluate their effectiveness.

KEY WORDS

Competition
Competition is the rivalry of two or more parties over something. Competition occurs naturally, and gives incentives for self improvement. Rivals will often refer to their competitors as 'the competition'.

Market segmentation
A market segment is a subgroup of people or organisations sharing one or more characteristics that cause them to have similar product needs.

Mnemonic
A mnemonic device is a memory aid. Commonly met mnemonics are often verbal, something such as a very short poem or a special word used to help a person remember something. Mnemonics rely on associations between easy-to-remember constructs which can be related back to the data that is to be remembered, e.g. PEST (see below).

PEST analysis
PEST stands for 'political, economic, social, and technological analysis' and describes a framework of factors used in environmental scanning. It is a part of the external analysis when doing market research and gives a certain overview of the different factors that the company has to take into consideration. It is a useful strategic tool for understanding market growth or decline, business position, potential and direction.

Promotional activities
The types of activity that take place to increase sales and profit for a business. Examples may include fliers, emails, Internet sites, loyalty cards, advertisements, etc.

Resources
The machines, workers, money, land, raw materials and other things that a business uses to produce goods and services and to make its economy grow.

Sales mix
A sales mix is the proportions of sales coming from different products or services. Changes in sales mix often affect profits because different products often have different profit margins, therefore a change in the sales mix can have an impact on profits even if total revenues are unchanged.

SWOT analysis
SWOT analysis is a strategic planning method used to evaluate the strengths, weaknesses, opportunities and threats involved in a project or in a business venture. It involves specifying the objective of the business venture or project and identifying the internal and external factors that are favourable and unfavourable to achieving that objective.

Target market

Market specialisation is a business term meaning the market segment to which a particular good or service is marketed. It is mainly defined by age, gender, geography, socio-economic grouping, or any other combination of demographics. It is generally studied and mapped by an organisation through lists and reports containing demographic information that may have an effect on the marketing of key products or services.

INTRODUCTION

The sales and promotional activities of any business, including hospitality, can make or break them financially. Alongside managing the finances of the business, marketing and promotions is probably the next most important aspect for a manager and their team if they are going to achieve their budget and profit margins.

The activities to promote sales in a business can vary hugely and only a decade ago were restricted to advertising in newspapers and magazines, radio and television. The Internet has now taken over and become the most important advertising medium.

This chapter will continue to cover these areas, including target market and sales mix. It will give you tools to understand your business and provide recommendations and appropriate activities to enable you to increase your sales and profitability.

> **! REMEMBER**
>
> Most sales and promotional activities are carried out to:
> - Increase profitability
> - Increase average spend
> - Increase number of guests coming into your business
> - All three

RESOURCES

There are some important factors to consider in relation to resources and their use in sales and promotional activities, including:

- Financial targets
- Human resources – the staff and their expertise

Financial resources

When considering financial resources and their impact on marketing and promotional activities you must take the following factors into account:

1 How much money do you have available to spend on sales and promotions?
2 How much profit are you trying to make or increase through your sales and promotional activities?

© ISTOCKPHOTO.COM/VICKI REID

3 Are you trying to increase guest flow into your outlet, increase the average spend, increase profitability, or all three?

4 Are you trying to bring in new clientele or encourage people to return?

Each of these will impact on the best possible way to promote your business.

Human resources

When considering human resources and their impact on marketing and promotional activities you must take the following factors into account:

1 Is your team skilled enough yet to promote your business internally?

2 Is your team skilled enough yet to promote your business externally?

These two resource areas will be returned to later in this chapter when you begin to strategise the best forms of marketing for your business. In the meantime, it is important to begin to understand your guest.

TARGET MARKET

It could be said that the guest (or customer) is your third resource. Without them you cannot make any sales or profit. In order to have a successful promotional campaign for your business, you need to understand who they are.

Each customer/guest that comes into your business has a different set of expectations. These expectations are based on a whole host of things and can include:

- The occasion – is it a special occasion or celebration, or not?
- Their budget – how much do they want to spend?
- Their tastes – is this a treat or do they go out regularly? Do they like your style of product or are they experimenting from their norm?
- Their mood – are they in a good or bad mood? Have they had a good or bad day? Are they tired or stressed? Or are they on holiday?
- Their culture – their background, ethnicity, upbringing, etc.
- Their experiences – do they go out a lot and know what they like? Or are they less experienced and more easily pleased?

When reviewing the customers that come into your business you can break them down in a variety of ways. These include:

- Socio-economic groups – There are two methods to highlight socio economic groups illustrated on the next page

SOCIAL CLASS	
I	Professional, etc. occupations
II	Managerial and technical occupations
III N	Skilled occupations – non-manual
III M	Skilled occupations – manual
IV	Partly skilled occupations
V	Unskilled occupations

A	Upper/middle class
B	Middle class
C1	Lower middle class
C2	Skilled working class
D	Other working class
E	Lowest level of subsistence
F1	Large farmers (50+ acres)
F2	Small farmers (50– acres)

■ Average spend – revenue per guest or customer, calculated as follows:

Restaurant/Bar

$$\frac{\text{Revenue or sales}}{\text{No. of guests}}$$

Hotel/Accommodation

$$\frac{\text{Total revenue for room sales}}{\text{No. of rooms sold during same period}}$$

■ Time of day – at what time of day do they come into your establishment?

■ Duration of stay – how long do they stay in your establishment?

■ Type of customer – business, tourist, local, etc.

■ Age, sex and/or ethnicity

SALES MIX

Once you have defined the types of customers that come into your business you can then determine what they consume using 'sales mix'. Sales mix determines the consumer-purchasing decisions that result in total revenue. This can also be important in determining aspects like cost of sales and gross profit. In this instance though, sales mix helps you to determine what your customers are consuming.

The breakdown can include:

■ How much drinks revenue is from beer, how much from wine, how much from soft drinks and how much from spirits?

■ How much food revenue is coming from starters, main courses and desserts?

■ How much starters revenue is coming from starter 1, from starter 2, from starter 3? Equally this could be used for main course and dessert choices on the menu

■ How much revenue is coming from food? How much revenue is coming from beverages?

✔ TIP

Selling less of a more profitable product but making up the sales with a less profitable product stills leaves you with lower profits!

■ How much revenue is coming from sales of double rooms? How much revenue is coming from sales of standard double rooms, how much is coming from suites?

■ How much revenue is coming from rooms, versus food, drink, banqueting, leisure club?

Below are some examples of how this would be illustrated. Note that each example adds up to 100 per cent.

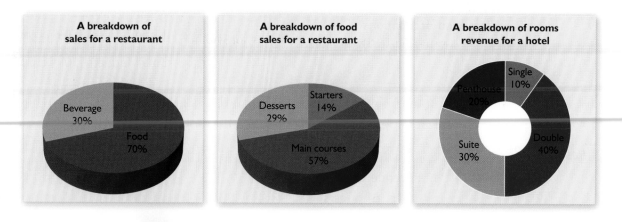

A breakdown of sales for a restaurant — Beverage 30%, Food 70%

A breakdown of food sales for a restaurant — Starters 14%, Desserts 29%, Main courses 57%

A breakdown of rooms revenue for a hotel — Single 10%, Penthouse 20%, Double 40%, Suite 30%

TASK

■ Can you think of any other types of breakdown of sales mix that are relevant to your business? (For example, revenue generated per week per each individual member of staff – this breakdown would help you to work out who is better at sales)

■ Calculate how your total sales are made up in relation to the various elements of sales in your outlet?

■ Now break one of those revenue areas down further, e.g. food, and calculate your breakdown again?

DID YOU KNOW

An Excel spreadsheet could do a lot of these calculations for you.

⊿	A	B	C	D
1	TOTAL ROOMS REVENUE	£100,000		
2	Single	£10,000	10%	
3	Double	£40,000	40%	
4	Suite	£30,000	30%	
5	Penthouse	£20,000	20%	
6				

PROMOTIONAL ACTIVITIES

Sales promotion is a series of activities and materials used to create sales of goods and services. These activities could include any of the following:

■ Developing customer loyalty schemes

■ Offering meal deals or packages

- Children's menus
- Drinks promotions possible in association with your suppliers
- Links with other special occasions – local, regional or global. For example, linked with the Olympics, football competitions, country festivals, music festivals, pre-theatre
- Products to complement seasons and/or specific calendar dates

Sales promotion can be carried out in three ways:

1 Through advertising – this is based on contacting and engaging with existing or potential target markets for your business, providing information and encouraging buying.

2 Through merchandising – this is largely based on increasing the average spend of existing customers by promoting particular services and goods.

3 Through personal selling – this is largely based on increasing the average spend of existing customers through upselling and suggestive selling, These terms will be defined later in the chapter.

© ISTOCKPHOTO.COM/DNY59

Advertising

The various mediums for advertising include:

- Broadcast – radio and television
- Print – newspapers, magazines
- Postal advertising – direct mail, hand drops
- Consumer publications – directories, guides, business publications, professional journals
- Other – transport, stations, airports, cinema, billboards

© ISTOCKPHOTO.COM/ SONYAE

Merchandising

VARIOUS MEDIUMS FOR MERCHANDISING

■ Menus	■ Blackboards
■ Posters in the windows and around the walls of the business	■ Tent cards on the tables
	■ Fascia boards
■ Trolleys	■ Brochures
■ Buffets	■ Drink coasters and placemats
■ Window displays	■ Directional signs
■ Aromas	■ Floor stands

© ISTOCKPHOTO.COM/TRAVELIF

Personal selling (also called face-to-face selling)

Did you know that if you follow the right sequence you could be a lot more successful at face-to-face selling?

Try DIPADA – it is a mnemonic for define, identify, prove, acceptance, desire, ask.

1 *Define* – who is your customer and how much are they looking to spend?

2 *Identify* – what are they looking for? A children's menu, a party menu, à la carte, a suite, penthouse, etc.

3 *Prove* – prove to your customer why you are the best and why they have to buy from you.

4 *Acceptance* – is the customer ready to move on or do they still have questions about what you have been telling them? You could ask 'are you happy with that?' or 'would that solve your problem?' or 'would you like anything else?'

5 *Desire* – make your customer want what you are selling. Tell them what makes what you're selling the best.

6 *Ask* – if you have done all this right they should have enough information and be ready to make the order or booking.

You also need the right techniques. In order to sell effectively you have to know everything there is to know about your product. For example:

■ Description of the dish

■ Explanation of how it is served

■ Where the produce has come from – source, organic, local (ethics and environment)

■ What are the specialities of the region and the establishment

■ What makes that dish or drink special? Is there a good story behind it?

To encourage your team to improve this knowledge you could consider:

■ Regular tastings of the menu and new specials

■ Training and briefing sessions (particularly during pre-shift meetings)

■ Trips out to the suppliers

■ Trips to the competition in the surrounding area

■ Visits to other competitors and similar businesses away from your region – *sampling alternative experiences can bring back new ideas*

In order to sell effectively your team need to be able to:

■ Sell in an appealing way (this goes back to *desire*) – make the customers want what you are describing – use the right adjectives for the right product (see the table)

■ Promote the right product to the right person (*define*)

■ Seek information from the customer in order to define them and sell them the right product

■ Use opportunities to sell additional items – for example: use of the gym or spa, a table in the restaurant, a cocktail in the bar, garnishes, side orders, share a dessert, coffee and petit fours, etc.

■ Provide the right service for the right customer and seek your customer's view on the acceptability of the food, drinks and service

	BEDROOMS	FOOD	DRINK
Some examples of adjectives that could be used to enhance what you are selling	Luxurious Branded cosmetics Soft Warm Scenic views Design – contemporary, luxury, traditional	Mouthwatering Delicious Tasty Meaty	Lively Sparkly Fruity Punchy Sophisticated

Upselling is a technique whereby you try to encourage your customer to upgrade their choice.

■ You are exposing the customer to other options they may otherwise not have considered

■ In the process, you must identify why they would want to upgrade and this is the key to successful upselling

■ For example:
  ● 'A double deluxe has the bigger bathroom with bath and separate shower as well as fantastic views of the coastline'
  ● 'The fillet steak is more succulent and tender with a melt in the mouth feeling as compared with the rump steak'

Suggestive selling is when the salesperson suggests additional items that are related to the original item being purchased.

■ For example – would you like a side order of green beans or salad? Would like to book a massage in our spa? Would you like to reserve a table for dinner tonight? Would you like a glass of champagne while you look at the menu?

■ Once again you are opening the customer up to choices they may otherwise not have considered

---

TASK

Add more adjectives to this table that could be used to sell each type of hospitality product identified above.

 TIP

Did you know that some of us are extrovert and some of us are introvert – this can impact on the way we sell.

Extrovert	Introvert
Sociable	Less sociable
Active	Less active
Impulsive	Cautious

We can use our characteristics to help us to sell effectively – by identifying similar or different traits in our customers we can adapt to their needs and personality

Look, listen and try to understand which your client is and then you can be empathetic to their needs.

■ The outcome is to enhance their experience in your restaurant, bar or hotel and hopefully increase your profits

■ By expanding their experience beyond what they came in for it is also likely that they will enjoy it more, thereby improving the 'wow' factor, and they will be more likely to talk about it and tell all their friends

Identifying training needs in relation to effective personal selling

The following programmes are examples of training sessions that could be run to help all your team in effective personal selling:

■ Identifying standards of performance required

■ Product knowledge

■ Wine tasting

■ Cocktail tasting

■ Job swaps – working in a different department for the day, e.g. reception working in housekeeping

To make these sessions effective, you must identify:

1   The gap between the knowledge, skills and attitudes displayed by people in their jobs and the knowledge, skills and attitudes needed for them to achieve the results the job required.

2   Are the staff aware of the results and standards expected of them?

3   Identify your staff and recognise:

  (a)   Where do they fit in?
  (b)   How long do they stay and why?
  (c)   Where do they come from?
  (d)   How are they chosen?

Other factors to consider in promotional and marketing

Legislation

There are several areas of legislation to be aware of to ensure effective promotional and marketing in your business. These are:

Licensing laws

(a)   Permitting drunkenness in licensed premises – it is an offence to serve people who are drunk or to permit people who are drunk to remain on licensed premises

(b)   Disability discrimination – it is now a requirement to make 'reasonable adjustments' to premises to afford access to disabled persons

(c)   Door security – all door staff must be trained and registered

(d) Weights and measures – Sale and Supply of Goods Act 1994 – according to the Act the customer can refuse to pay or can demand replacement if:

  i The goods supplied do not correspond with the description
  ii A displayed item is not what it seems
  iii The goods are inedible

(e) The Trade Descriptions Act 1968 /1972 makes it a criminal offence to mis-describe goods or services. Care must therefore be taken when:

  i Describing rooms in promotional materials
  ii Wording menus and wine lists
  iii Describing menu and drinks items ot customers
  iv Describing conditions, such as cover and service charge or extras
  v Describing the service provision

(f) Price Marking (Food & Drink Services) Order 2003 – prices of food and drink must be displayed in a clear and legible way by persons selling be retail for consumption on the premises

(g) The Consumer Protection Act 1987 deals with misleading prices including service, cover and minimum charges

PEST analysis

PEST analysis is a simple, useful and widely used tool that helps you understand the 'big picture' of your Political, Economic, Sociocultural and Technological environment. It helps to provide a vision for the future of your business and when used alongside SWOT (strengths, weaknesses, opportunities and threats) can help you to identify how to improve the profitability of your business.

To use this tool, follow this three-stage process:

1 Brainstorm the relevant factors that apply to you.
2 Identify the information that applies to these factors.
3 Draw conclusions from this information.

An example matrix that could be used to document your findings.

STRENGTHS	WEAKNESSES
• P	• P
• E	• E
• S	• S
• T	• T
OPPORTUNITIES	**THREATS**
• P	• P
• E	• E
• S	• S
• T	• T

Financial resources

In considering your sales and promotional activities you must examine the financial resources available to you. You cannot afford to use all your spare resources to set up an expensive advertising campaign that is then not very successful.

You must consider the following:

■ How much money is in the budget for sales and promotional activities?

■ How much of the expected increase in forecasted profits should be spent on sales and promotional activities?

■ How much extra sales will each type of activity generate? And therefore which is the most effective?

Types of sales and promotional activities can be categorised by cost, as shown in the table.

CHEAP	MEDIUM	EXPENSIVE
Staff training to improve product knowledge and encourage effective use of selling techniques	Flyers handed out in local residential areas	Television and radio
Emails to client database	Direct mail and newsletters	Press – local, national, specialist
Telephone	Internet site	Brochures
Networking	Third-party websites	
Tent cards and drinks mats		
Loyalty cards		

© ISTOCKPHOTO.COM/ALEKSANDR LOBANOV

Other resources to consider in promoting hospitality and related activities

Time

■ How much does your company have available to invest in the promotion of hospitality services? This could include:

- Time needed to organise promotional activities
- Time needed to distribute information on promotional activities
- Time needed for training

Staff skills

■ What skills do you have in your team that will help with the promotion of hospitality services?

Facilities and materials

This could include the resources you have available to:

■ Offer new products onto the market

■ Financial budget to introduce promotional activity

■ Printing facilities

■ Internet access and website

■ Competitors and clients to promote your activities

Competitors

It is a good idea to network with your competitors in order to look at their areas of strength, weaknesses, opportunities and threats – both to themselves and your business. By identifying their strengths and weaknesses you can assess your own and be more strategic about how you want to improve your business and build your strengths based on their weaknesses.

PLANNING PROMOTIONAL ACTIVITY

To promote your business effectively you must plan how you are going to do this:

1 List the groups of customers who currently use your business and identify who you would like to use your business, in other words who you need to promote your business to.

2 Try to find out why certain groups of people are not using your business. Then decide what type of promotional activity would be best for each group (see below), and what promotional materials you will need to support this activity.

3 Draw up a budget and detailed plan, including a plan of how you will evaluate the promotional activity.

4 Produce any materials to support the promotional activity, such as leaflets, posters or signs.

5 Organise the activity.

- Set a priority list – who are you going to target first and for how long?
- Who will you target as your second priority and at what point after the first group have been targeted?
- How will you target them and what type of material will you use for each target?

Costing a promotional activity

There are several factors to consider when costing a promotional activity:

■ Graphics and design – printed materials and website

■ Printing

■ Distribution – labour, post, Internet, email

■ Advertising costs

■ Set-up costs i.e. decoration and design required for promotion

TASK

1 Find out how much it would cost to:

(a) run an advert in your local newspaper

(b) run an advert in a monthly magazine

(c) get an external company to design a simple website

(d) do a print run of coloured flyers to distribute

2 Now set a budget for carrying out a promotional activity. Take into consideration the cost of preparing the promotion as well as its distribution and spreading the message to your 'target customer'. Also consider where you might be able to save costs but keep the quality and integrity of the promotional activity.

3 Now consider how much revenue you need to make in order to cover the cost of your promotional activity as well as the other day-to-day costs incurred in running your business.

EVALUATE AND MEASURE EFFECTIVENESS OF PROMOTIONAL ACTIVITIES

How can you evaluate the effectiveness of your promotion?

1 Look for an increase in sales following the promotional activities.

2 Ask customers if they have seen your advertising – fliers, posters, adverts.

3 Have customers fed back to you on the quality of your advertising and promotion?

4 Is the increase in sales a prolonged activity or short lived for just a week or so?

5 What increase is there in profit? Ultimately this is more important than any increase in sales.

Having completed this type of evaluation it is worth putting it into a SWOT matrix.

Strengths	Weaknesses
■ Increased brand awareness ■ Good uptake on special offer	■ People only came back the once to use the special offer and haven't returned
Opportunities	Threats
■ Database of contact details to use for future targeting of activities	■ Competitors have started to use similar methods to promote their businesses

These are just examples of SWOT: they can be developed or moved into different sections.

Assessment of knowledge and understanding

You have now learnt about some of the types of sales and promotional activities that take place in hospitality-based businesses to help effectively increase sales and profit as well as the business's reputation. This should give you some thoughts and ideas on how you could promote your business and reflect on its promotional activities.

To test your level of knowledge and understanding, answer the following short questions. These will help to prepare you for your summative (final) assessment.

1 What is the difference between upselling and suggestive selling?

2 Who is your existing market in terms of customers and how would you like to change this and identify new markets appropriate to your business?

3 How would you use sales mix to identify gaps in your sales activities and potential profitability?

4 Identify five possible and appropriate activities that your team could undertake to promote the services and products in your area of responsibility and identify your responsibilities in implementing and supporting these activities and their successful execution.

5 Identify appropriate promotional activities and the likely sales improvements activities could generate taking into consideration the resources available to you.

6 How would you consult with relevant colleagues about your ideas for promotional activities and seek their support, taking into consideration the consistency with your targets, your organisation's objectives and values and legal requirements, as well as how to implement the plans effectively? You may wish to consider the use of SWOT and PEST in the planning, monitoring and executing of the effective promotional activity.

7 Identify how you would monitor activities to make sure that targeted customers are being reached and promotional activities are run according to agreed plans and standards.

8 Lay out a plan of how would you embark on a review of your sales and promotional activity, from the beginning where you would review the existing activities, through to a strategic plan of embedding new activities into the business and reviewing their effectiveness.

9 Name five implications that the identified legislation have on your business in relation to the sales and promotional activities.

10 Your restaurant wants to introduce a 'theme night' once a week to increase sales on what is traditionally otherwise a quiet night. Decide on your theme and then consider the budget costs that would be incurred in promoting this. Also consider how much sales revenue you would require in return to pay back these initial promotional costs.

Research task

Training is imperative to the successful embedding of sales and promotional activities.

Prepare a training plan that you would use to improve the sales and promotional activities that occur within your business.

15

Contribute to the development of menus and recipes

HS9 Contribute to the development of menus and recipes

LEARNING OBJECTIVES

This unit is about developing or introducing new menu items. It involves research, implementation and review.

After reading this chapter you will be able to:

■ Take account of food combinations, flavours and dietary requirements when introducing new recipe and menu suggestions.

■ Identify ingredient ratios, cooking times and temperatures for producing the recipe in varying quantities.

■ Identify methods of presenting, holding and distributing the product.

■ Register and pass on relevant information about the suitability of the new menu item according to organisational systems in your place of work.

■ Introduce recipe suggestions in accordance with the style and policy of your organisation, available resources and the expectations and standards of your customers.

■ Make sure staff have the information, skills and resources required to support the introduction of the new menu item, according to the individual jobs that they do.

■ Collect and take account of feedback from staff and customers.

KEY WORDS

Allergy
An acquired, abnormal immune response to a substance that can cause a broad range of inflammatory reactions.

Bill of fare
Menu: a list of dishes available at a restaurant.

Diet
A regulated daily food allowance.

EPOS
Electronic point of sale, could be a shop, checkout counter or location where a transaction takes place. It is also data recorded at a checkout and used for forecasting and stock control.

Food intolerance
A condition whereby a person is unable to tolerate certain parts of foods. This is different from a food allergy because the immune system is not involved.

Gross profit
The profits before overhead (fixed operating expenses) have been deducted.

Gueridon
A style of service which food items are prepared in the dining environment.

Net profit
The profits remaining in a business after all expenses have been taken out, but before tax.

Nutrition
A source of materials to nourish the body.

Seasonality
Products that are available for a limited or seasonal period.

Silver service
The method used to deliver food to the table on a platter held by the waiter and served to the customer's plate using a fork and spoon.

! REMEMBER

The development of recipes and menus should be based around numerous factors:

- Staff ability
- Cost
- Seasonality
- Feedback
- Resources
- Dietary requirements
- Time of day

INTRODUCTION

Menus were originally simple lists of food available and were put together in an unstructured order.

The use of an organised menu began in the nineteenth century and this saw the introduction of separate courses such as soup, starters, fish courses, main courses and the like.

The twentieth century has seen many new cultures influencing the UK and this has resulted in a wide variety of restaurants and a plethora of available food items.

Working in hospitality can be a rewarding experience; skills, experience and confidence play a part in a person's development.

A key area for development is assisting the kitchen staff when new menus are required. As a chef becomes secure with the pace and structure of an existing menu, it is natural to want to improve or change the content, structure or design. To be able to do this, a thorough understanding of menu planning and implementation is imperative.

A chef's strength can lie in understanding what the customer really wants; by working with and using the experience and knowledge of the front of house team (bar, restaurant and reception) a detailed and well-rounded menu can be developed.

There will be very few menus created in a chef's life which are labelled 'perfect'.

© ISTOCKPHOTO.COM/SEAN LOCKE

Input from third parties allows the menu to develop to suit the needs of the business and customers similarly. When developing new ideas for a menu certain considerations should be taken into account.

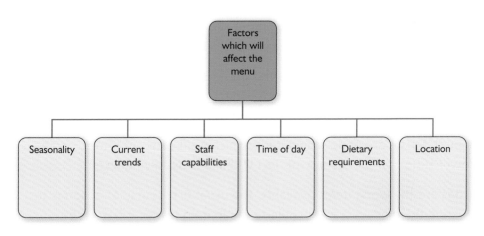

Factors which will affect the design of the menu

MENU ENGINEERING

Managers, waiters, chefs, porters and all other staff working in hospitality require knowledge of menu engineering. There are two factors which affect this:

■ The popularity of the items
■ The gross profit

There are four matrixes:

- Plough horses
- Stars
- Dogs
- Puzzles

and are laid out in the following manner:

Plough horse	Stars
Dogs	Puzzles

- Stars are defined as high popularity with a high cash gross profit
- Plough horses are defined as high popularity but with a low cash gross profit
- Puzzles are defined as low popularity with a high cash gross profit
- Dogs are defined as low popularity with a low cash gross profit

This simple strategy offers you the chance to identify which items are selling and which need rethinking in relation to menu and dish development.

Category interpretation

Puzzles are named simply because that is exactly what they are; low-cost, high-profit items which sell occasionally, such as gueridon work.

Stars are the highest yielding items both in sales and profit; these items cost little to produce in relation to the selling cost. They are made features of to ensure a good high turn over.

Plough horses are good selling items which yield a decent return, and have a lower status on the menu with less visibility is usually adopted.

Dogs are the worst items available; the usual first course of action is to change them as soon as possible to minimise a loss of gross profit. Combining these items with others to create a set menu will allow a sales increase and potential profit increase.

This tried an tested way of assessing the best dishes to serve on a menu still has its place in the workplace, however, the up to date EPOS system gives a faster more accurate report on all dishes and menus.

The system processes data on dish costs, selling prices and gross profit, highlighting poor selling dishes and ones that are losing the business money.

DISH SPECIFICATION

Producing a detailed dish specification sheets will ensure that all dishes on the menu are costed correctly and can therefore be checked to ensure they reach the targets set.

The table gives an example of a dish specification for a beef stir fry.

BEEF STIR FRY: INGREDIENTS FOR 16 PORTIONS

MEAT AND FISH - MEAT LARDER						
PRODUCT NAME	PRODUCT SPECIFICATION	QTY	UOM	COST	DISP	RET
Beef skirt	Cut into 4cm strips	3000	g	12.00		
Order instruction For stir fry			Total:	12.00		

FRUIT AND VEGETABLES - FRUIT/VEG						
PRODUCT NAME	PRODUCT SPECIFICATION	QTY	UOM	COST	DISP	RET
Herbs Chervil	-	100	g	1.32		
Herbs Parsley curly	Split	100	g	0.20		
Lemons	-	9	ea	2.25		
Onion spring	Bunch	8	ea	4.00		
Pak Choi - ea	-	8	ea	12.80		
Order instruction None			Total:	20.57		

DRY AND FROZEN - DRY						
PRODUCT NAME	PRODUCT SPECIFICATION	QTY	UOM	COST	DISP	RET
Bicarbonate of soda	-	200	g	4.25		
Cornflour 3663	-	400	g	0.42		
Oyster sauce	-	510	ml	1.68		
Rice basmati Tilda easy cook	-	3000	g	5.83		
Soy sauce	Kikkoman	1000	ml	2.85		
Order instruction None			Total:	15.03		

Grand Total: £47.60

Food costs for 16 portions = £47.60

Gross profit example = 50% (£47.60 ÷ 100 × 50) = £23.80

Selling price = food cost + gross profit = selling price (16 portions)

Selling price = £47.60 + £23.80 = £71.40

Per portion (selling price ÷ 16 =) £71.40 ÷ 16 = £4.47

This standard formula works for all food cost, gross profit and selling prices. The only variables are the percentages set by each establishment.

SEASONALITY

Certain foods are seasonal, such as fruits, vegetables, game, fish and certain meats. Fruit and vegetables can be purchased throughout the year because if they are not in season in this country they can be in season somewhere else in the world and will be delivered quickly via airlines. However, locally sourced foods are generally cheaper, more environmentally friendly and flavoursome than commodities that are sourced from overseas.

© ISTOCKPHOTO.COM/ SANDRA CALDWELL

Fish that are about to breed and are full of eggs (roe) will have less flavour and flesh yield than fish that is in season. This will obviously affect portion control and costs for the overall dish.

© ISTOCKPHOTO.COM/ ARNE THAYSEN

Game can only be killed when not breeding or raising young. Each type has an allocated season. It should be noted that at the very start of game season the flavour of the flesh can be a little characterless.

Seasonality of **meat** is usually restricted to lamb. With spring lamb being very tender and also quite expensive to purchase, the development of the menu should take this into consideration.

© ISTOCKPHOTO.COM/SERGE VILLA

We are able to find a full range of food produce sourced from all over the world and readily available all year round. This has offered a choice and convenience for the chef to produce an eclectic menu, but there are many benefits to returning to the seasonal cycles of nature and buying fresh, seasonal produce from local suppliers.

The increasing awareness of health-related issues, and concern about the quality, source and type of food which we consume is increasingly influencing consumer opinion. Concerns over the environmental impacts of transporting food produce long distances, through excessive 'food miles' which can also have a detrimental effect on the food we consume along with its 'traceability', are also key factors in influencing our buying behaviour. The implication of 'food miles' indicates how far ingredients travel from the farmer who produces it to the consumer who eats it. This concept is sometimes known as 'farm to fork'. That includes the journey from farm to processor, then from processor to retailer and finally from retailer to consumer. It includes travel within the UK as well as between countries. The further food has to travel, the longer it spends in shipment. That means vital vitamin content can be lost and nutritional values of fresh foods inevitably decline. Transporting food large distances will consume a

© ISTOCKPHOTO.COM/ERIC ISSELÉE

lot of fuel, whether it travels by lorry or plane. This inevitably increases carbon dioxide emissions and contributes to global warming.

CURRENT TRENDS

Not everybody can be a trendsetter or molecular gastronomist, but current trends and fashions in food should be monitored. Hospitality staff should always be aware of what other competitors, restaurants and trends are doing. Studying the restaurant reviews and reading media comments about the attitudes of the customers to the new trends is an important education in writing your new menu. Speak to your own customers, suppliers and team to consider creating new dishes for your menu to meet the needs of the customer and to attract new clients.

There are many other aspects to consider, and some of them are shown in the menu consideration cycle below.

Understanding the cycle will help to ensure profit margins are achieved. Using the cycle as a checklist will aid any establishment; there is no definitive start point to the cycle as all the points should be considered prior to the menu being implemented.

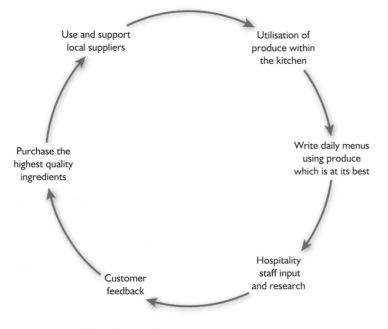

Menu consideration cycle

THE CAPABILITIES OF THE KITCHEN AND FRONT OF HOUSE TEAM

When planning a new menu the capabilities of the kitchen and front of house team should be carefully considered. A menu should stimulate the chefs and the service team but should not stretch them beyond capability to render the

new menu ineffectual. It is important that training is given to the team so that they understand the menu complexity and how to produce and serve each dish. A menu that is too simple can become boring to produce, but a menu that is too complicated can lead to the team becoming confused.

Type of menu

- **À la carte** items on the menu are individually priced and are cooked or finished to order; this allows the guest to construct their own menu. This sort of menu can sometimes require upselling from the waiting staff due to the increased price

- **Table d'hôte** a set menu, with a set price. Table d'hôte menus have limited choices, such as a meat fish or vegetarian option, but usually they have little choice except for an option for people who have special dietary needs. The menu can range from a single course to a nine- or ten-course 'grazing menu'. The portion sizes should reflect the size of the menu. With a single course the portion size should satisfy the appetite, and with a multi-course menu the entire menu should also satisfy the appetite without the guests feeling too full or being unable to finish their meal. Banquets and function menus are usually table d'hôte menus and should be carefully designed with the needs of the customer in mind. Care should be taken not to include dishes that take to long to assemble or contain food that will not hold for service without deteriorating quickly

- **Cyclical menus** are designed to be repeated at given intervals, usually on a weekly, monthly or seasonal basis. They are usually used in canteens and educational institutions, within facilities that have groups of people for set periods of time e.g. training facilities. In canteens and staff restaurants where the customers eat every day the cycle should be longer and start on different days of the week so that the customers will not feel bored by the repetition of the food on offer

  Stock control can be more efficient because the level of stock will be lower as the cycle predicts purchases. In large operations long-term agreements or forward purchasing can lead to further discounts with suppliers.

- **Breakfast menus** can be an extremely important part of a hotel's repertoire of food service. Generally, the last impression a guest gets of the food of a hotel establishment is the breakfast service. The menu can be à la carte, buffet style or continental. The offer can include a selection of the following:

  - Cereals/porridge and yoghurts
  - Fruit juices, fresh and preserved fruit
  - Egg dishes
  - Smoked fish
  - Fried meats such as sausage, bacon, black pudding, kidney dishes

- Cold meats
- Sauté potatoes
- Selection of breads and morning goods such as croissants and Danish pastries
- Preserves
- Tea, coffee or chocolate

Dietary requirements

Understanding the various requirements for people who have special dietary needs is a requirement of all hospitality staff from a commis waiter up to the manager.

Coeliac

No gluten is allowed in the diet (e.g. breads, biscuits and foods that contain wheat flour). Soya flour, which does not contain gluten, can be used as a substitute for wheat flour in most cases.

Diabetic

Avoid foods that contain sugar or glucose, inform the people of the sugar content of dishes, or provide alternative courses that allow the guest to choose dishes that are high or low on the glycaemic index. Most diabetics can moderate their medication to suit menus as long as they know the menu in advance.

Nut allergy

Some people have an extreme intolerance to nuts; they can go into anaphylactic shock with even the slightest trace of nuts consumed and will require immediate medical help to overcome this state. Menus should indicate clearly where nut products have been used.

Shellfish allergy

Similar to nut allergy in reaction, the guest may have slight symptoms such as a rash to a more problematic anaphylactic shock.

Dairy intolerance

The use of soya-based products can replace dairy products for cooking.

Vegan

These are individuals who will eat no animal products at all as part of their daily diet.

Vegetarian

These are guests who will eat no animal products but will consume egg products and dairy products such as butter and cream.

Ovo-lactarians

Similar to vegans but will eat eggs and milk.

Oysters should be avoided by those with a shellfish allergy

Lactarians

Vegans who will eat dairy products.

Hospital patients

Any menu in a hospital should be written by both the chef and a dietician. The dietary requirements of the patient are of paramount importance in this case.

Schoolchildren

There is a renaissance in the need to correctly supply schoolchildren with a healthy diet that is free from excess fatty and processed foods. The budgetary restrictions placed upon school caterers can be very restrictive in the production of these menus.

College/university students

Similar to schools, the menus on offer should be healthy but substantial to allow for the higher metabolic rates. Menus should reflect a diversity of styles and ethnic cuisine.

People at work

Consideration should be taken about the occupation of the recipients of the food, e.g. are they soldiers in training, manual workers from a building site, or the office worker that can use less calories and require a more healthy diet. For chefs that work in the financial and corporate business sector; you should consider the fact that a 'lunch requirement to help secure a big deal' within the professional banking or the legal sector may indicate a substantial contract so the menu should be discussed with the client or principal butler to ascertain the requirements of the clients.

WRITING AN INFORMATIVE AND BALANCED MENU

When writing a menu consider the following points:

■ *Avoid jargon* Do not use unnecessary jargon that might intimidate the guest and do not over-embellish the description of each dish

■ *Use local and understandable language* Certain words will not translate into English from a menu planning point of view such as *mayonnaise* or *sauerkraut*. These are words that have become part of the English language over time. If foreign language is used, sometimes it is best to state a simple explanation in English underneath or ensure the food service team can translate the menu perfectly for the customer

■ *Keep it simple* Use menu descriptions that are simple to understand. Avoid using too many dishes as the customer will have difficulty in choosing

Development of the menu

As discussed earlier, menus must evolve with the needs of the customer and the business. These changes should be structured to allow for smooth transitions and the following points should be considered. For most establishments, change is important. It keeps interest and ambition alive. Make a critical evaluation of the menu. Check the sales mix of each dish and write recipes that fit in with the structure of the existing menu and compliment dishes that you intend to keep. The recipes should be costed to fit into the business plan and achieve the required profit margin.

Marketing the menu

The menu changes can work in the favour of the business if it is marketed correctly:

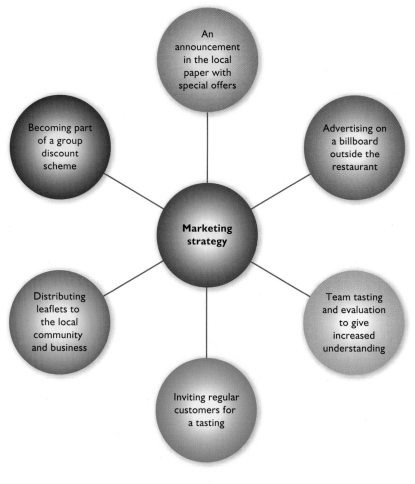

An announcement in the local paper with special offers

Advertising on a billboard outside the restaurant

Becoming part of a group discount scheme

Marketing strategy

Distributing leaflets to the local community and business

Team tasting and evaluation to give increased understanding

Inviting regular customers for a tasting

Marketing strategy

Implementing the menu changes

1 Design the recipes taking into account all previously mentioned factors and correct food costing.

2 Produce an accurate specification sheet for each dish.

3 Test cook the dishes.

4 Taste test the dish.

5 Discuss the merits of the dish and make any changes that are deemed necessary.

6 If the dish is approved, present the dish to the service team to sample and describe the dish exactly. It is important that the service staff have an understanding of new dishes as their recommendations can lead to the dish being a success.

7 Meet with some of the customers who have tried the new menu for feedback. This has the advantage of making them feel included and building a rapport with your clientele.

KEY TYPES OF MENU

À la carte menus

Table d'hôte menus

Cyclical menus

Breakfast menus

! REMEMBER

The development of recipes and menus needs to backed up with a suitable marketing campaign.

Feedback, loyalty bonuses, offers, newspapers, television and radio will all help to secure the revenue required to maintain a financially viable business.

CHECKLIST

✔ Staff ability

✔ Feedback from customers

✔ Seasonality

✔ Current trends

✔ Cost

✔ Resources

Assessment of knowledge and understanding

You have now learnt about some of the things to consider when planning a menu, and the importance of costing and marketing your menu.

To test your level of knowledge and understanding, answer the following short questions. These will help to prepare you for your summative (final) assessment.

Make sure that you keep this for easier referencing and along with your work for future inclusion in your portfolio.

Developing new recipe ideas

1 State **three** stages in the development of new recipes.

2 Identify **two methods** of receiving customer feed back from a new menu item.

3 Explain **why** it is important to give an in-depth briefing to service staff when introducing new menu items.

4 Give **two** reasons why a menu might be changed.

5 Explain **why** is it important to consider the customer's needs when developing new recipes.

6 Explain what a **table d'hôte menu** is.

Costing recipes

1 When costing menus **why** should seasonality of ingredients be considered?

2 What are the financial advantages of a **cyclical menu?**

3 Explain the term **gross profit.**

Recognising dietary requirements

1 Describe the term **vegetarian.**

2 List two different types of **vegetarian.**

3 Name **two** allergies the can bring on anaphylactic shock.

4 **Who** should compile menus for hospitals?

5 Explain **why** it is important to consider the job roll and lifestyle of customers when developing menus.

6 Explain **two** factors to consider when planning dishes for school children.

Writing an informative and balanced menu and marketing the menu

1 Explain **why** you should avoid the use of foreign languages when writing a menu.

2 Explain **why** it is important not to have too many dishes on the menu.

3 List **two** methods of marketing a menu.

Support the implementation of the menu

1 **List** the stages that should be followed when testing a recipe.

2 Explain **why** a new recipe should be discussed after a test cook.

Research task

Using your knowledge of a professional kitchen devise four simple menus which could be used in each of the following places:

■ School.

■ College.

■ Restaurant.

■ Hotel.

16

Supervise off-site food delivery services

HS12 Supervise off-site food delivery services

LEARNING OBJECTIVES

This unit is about delivering food for consumption off-site, monitoring and maintain the quality of food items before despatch and supervising the delivery of food. 'Off-site food delivery' is any food, hot or cold, which on being delivered is deemed ready to eat.

After reading this chapter you will be able to:

■ Establish and maintain the correct procedures when taking and recording food orders.

■ Implementing and monitoring the correct food hygiene, health and safety and industry codes of practice procedures.

■ The roles and responsibilities of yourself and your colleagues in delivering food to the customer and how you should work together.

■ Implement contingency plans when foods fail to reach required standards.

■ Know what packaging and containers are available and how they maintain the quality of the food items you are responsible for.

■ Advise customers promptly of any difficulties or where it will be impossible to fulfil agreements.

■ Identify and sort out conflicts of interest and disagreements with deliveries that minimise damage to the work being carried out.

■ Ascertain what information needs to be collected and how to present it in an accepted format.

KEY WORDS

Contingency plans
Plans that allow you to identify, and plan for things that may go wrong. Back-up plans.

Monitor
To check, track or observe processes and procedures.

Processing food orders
Taking and recording the food order and passing it on to those responsible for food production.

Relevant information
The records regarding food orders and delivery that you need to keep up to date.

Relevant legislation
All areas of law and regulations that are relevant to food delivery.

Team communication
Giving and receiving information within the team (this applies to you as the supervisor) and making sure that members communicate effectively with each other.

Team leadership
Giving the team clear and effective instructions and being a positive role model to other team members.

INTRODUCTION

Delivering food for consumption off-site is a complex operation that requires careful planning, preparation and co-ordination. It is important that your food arrives as ordered, on time and in the best possible condition. All staff must follow the correct procedures for taking and recording orders, observing all the necessary requirements for hygiene and the condition of food, and for meeting customers' delivery requirements.

> **! REMEMBER**
>
> The reputation of the establishment rests on the performance of the off-site food delivery service.

Off-site food delivery services are one of the most competitive markets in the hospitality sector, catering to a very fickle market of consumers who have a wide choice of establishments. The assortment of eateries ranges from the welfare sector 'meals on wheels' for the elderly or infirm who are unable to cook for themselves, to the commercial sector of pizzerias, burger and ribs eateries to Chinese and Indian restaurants.

WWW.SXC.HU

Any caterer who is able to produce food is able to offer an off-site food delivery services, expanding their customer market, catering in marquees at weddings, to church halls, maximising the use of their production kitchens.

Issues that can damage your organisation's ability to perform include poor record keeping of food orders. Food hygiene is a major factor in any food delivery service due to food leaving the premises and passing out of the control of trained catering personnel.

To work in an off-site food delivery business, you have to be able of keeping up to date and accurate records of food orders, supervise the food safety practices of the catering team, ensure compliance with food hygiene and health and safety procedures and industry codes of practice. You must have knowledge of and be able to take control of the entire delivery system from the preparing of the food to the customer's door, having the relevant contingency plans in place for when problems may occur.

OFF-SITE FOOD DELIVERY SYSTEMS

A system can be largely defined as an integrated set of tasks that accomplish a defined objective. In any off-site food delivery business it is important to have a system in place that all the staff are familiar with. Familiarity can be achieved through staff training using a variety of methods: on-the-job, computer-based training (CBT), or through organised staff training days.

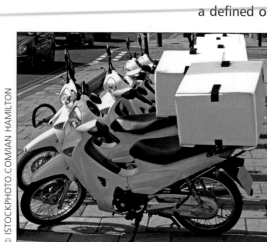

© ISTOCKPHOTO.COM/IAN HAMILTON

What equipment should I use?

There are three generally recognised types of food deliveries: hot, cold and room temprature or ambient. Various methods of transportation are used on aeroplanes, trucks, vans, cars or indeed mopeds. To decide on the most appropriate method certain questions need to be answered:

■ What volume of provisions needs to be transported?

■ Quality and robustness of the transporting food?

■ At what temperature does the food need to be maintained while being transported?

■ What temperature dose the food need to be when arrives at its destination at?

When transporting foods that are kept at ambient or room temperature you must ensure that the transport is clean, hygine and fit for purpose.

Cold food needs to be transported with temperature controls in place, such as chiller or freezer conditions. Thermal insulated containers for short distances may suffice, but temperature checks would need to be made upon delivery.

It is a requirement by law that all food be served safe and fit for purpose, therefore all food must be produced and served in line with current food hygiene legislation. There are a number of systems that will allow you to

---

! REMEMBER

It is a requirement by law that all food be served safe and fit for purpose.

achieve this due to advances in technology in recent years. The two main methods used are insulation and self-heating, which are now explained.

Insulated thermal boxes are designed to keep food that is already hot at a suficiently high enough temperature to serve. One of the more modern self-heating methods is the use of induction technology using preheated thermal bags for keeping food hot while being delivered.

WHAT RECORDS SHOULD I KEEP?

Food order records

The majority of food orders in most establishments will come over the telephone, it is therefore important that a record be taken immediately of the necessary details. These details could include the following:

- What time was the order taken
- Time of delivery
- Delivery address
- Order requirements
- Cost

This information is recorded either electronically or on a paper pad.

There is a growing trend is for off-site food orders to be taken online through a verity of Internet sites. There are many such sites and this has the added benefit of keeping a record off all your orders taken online.

A food order taken over the phone

All orders and information such as special offers must then be communicated to the following personnel:

- Food production staff
- Delivery drivers

> **! REMEMBER**
>
> A record of all your orders must be kept by law.

Financial records

The law says that everyone who pays tax must keep the records they need to fill in a tax return. If you don't keep records, how can you show what you've earned and what you've spent? Tax-registered businesses are legally required to keep certain types of business records.

HM Revenue & Customs (HMRC) might decide to look into your tax returns or claims. If they do, they may want to look at your records. It will save you time if you can show that the records you have kept are full and accurate. It can also save you money – you can be issued fines if records are not kept properly.

Page 1

Company Tax Return form

HM Revenue & Customs

CT600 (2006) Version 2

for accounting periods ending on or after 1 July 1999

Your company tax return

If we send the company a Notice to deliver a company tax return (form *CT603*) it has to comply by the filing date or we charge a penalty, even if there is no tax to pay. A return includes a company tax return form, any Supplementary Pages, accounts, computation and any relevant information.

Is this the right form for the company? Read the advice on pages 3 to 6 of the Company tax return guide (the *Guide*) before you start. The forms in the CT600 series set out the information we need and provide a standard format for calculations. Use the *Guide* which contains general information you may need and box by box advice to help you complete the return form.

Please note that some boxes on form *CT600* are not in order, reflecting changes made since the form was first published in 2004.

Company Information

Company name

Company registration number

Tax Reference as shown on the CT603

Type of Company

Registered office address

Postcode

Keep any information and documents that you may need to help you fill in your tax return or to make a claim.

Most of the time, you'll be looking at records for the current or previous year, but sometimes you'll need to go back a bit further. For example, you may need to work out your profit or loss on the sale of something you've owned for a long time (such as a delivery vehicle, or special equipment). At the very least you may need a record of the amount you originally paid for that asset. There are other times, too, when you will need to refer to old records.

Food hygiene systems and records

All food hygiene laws apply to off-site food delivery, as the service falls into the category of a food premises, with the delivery system seen as just an extension of this. To this end food labelling regulations do not apply for products such as pizza delivery, but if it was sold to other premises to be cooked and served they would have to be labelled.

A full hazard analysis critical control point (HACCP) system must be in place and the relevant control in place with records kept, such as delivery monitoring house rules, temperature control house rules, off-site temperature record, cleaning schedules, stock control rules forms and temperature controls.

The HACCP flow chart in the table would be needed for an off-site food delivery service. This would run in conjunction with the HACCP system that would be in place for feeding on the premises.

> **! REMEMBER**
>
> A HACCP system must be in place, and the appropriate records kept.

SERVICE – HOT-OFF SITE SERVICE TO CUSTOMERS (FOOD SERVED IN OTHER LOCATIONS SUCH AS HOME DELIVERY AND OUTSIDE CATERING)

HAZARDS(S) AT CCP(S)	CONTROL MEASURES AND CRITICAL LIMITS	MONITORING AND RECORDING	CORRECTIVE ACTION
What can go wrong?	What action has to be taken to effectively reduce or get red of the hazard? What are the critical limits?	How are the control measures checked and recorded?	What should be done if the control measure fails and/or critical limits are not met?
Growth of harmful bacteria Cooked/ready-to-eat foods/home delivery/buffet	■ Make sure that food is dispatched at a suitable temperature AND/OR ■ Make sure that food arrives on site at a suitable temperature OR ■ Transport food and reheat to a suitably high temperature OR ■ Transport food and hot hold at a suitable temperature until service The above temperatures need to be sufficient to discourage the growth of harmful bacteria	■ Check temperature of food prior to despatch OR ■ Check temperature of food on arrival OR ■ Check that your specified reheating temperature is reached AND/OR ■ Check that your specified hot holding temperature is maintained	■ If the food is below your specified temperature on despatch reheat to a suitable high temperature ■ If the food is below your specified temperature on arrival, consider if the food is safe to use ■ If the food is below your specified temperature reheat to a suitable temperature ■ Consider if food is safe to use
	What you need to do: Keep to your **temperature control house rules**	**What you need to do:** Complete **off-site temperature record**	**What you need to do:** Refer to your **temperature control house rules**
Other contamination e.g. from vehicle, equipment, customers	Use good personal hygiene practices Keeping delivery vehicle and contact equipment clean Make sure that food is protected and/or covered	Observe and supervise personal hygiene practices Observe and supervise the cleanliness of the vehicle and delivery containers Observe and supervise protection of food	■ Dispose of food which may be contaminated ■ Review staff training

HAZARDS(S) AT CCP(S)	CONTROL MEASURES AND CRITICAL LIMITS	MONITORING AND RECORDING	CORRECTIVE ACTION
	What you need to do: Keep to your **personal hygiene house rules** Keep to your **cleaning house rules** Keep to your **stock control house rules**	**What you need to do:** Complete **weekly record** Complete **cleaning schedule**	**What you need to do:** Refer to your **training, personal hygiene, cleaning and stock control rules**

The food standards agency provides many HACCP templates for small business.

WHAT ARE CONTINGENCY PLANS?

REFLECTION

Can you think of a situation that relied on the use of a contingency plan. Would you make any changes?

A contingency plan is a plan that is devised for a specific situation for when things go wrong. They are required for businesses or individuals to recover from incidents in the minimum time with minimum cost and disruption.

Due to the nature of off-site food delivery service it is important that there are a number of contingency plans in place should anything go wrong, such as:

- Traffic congestion
- Vehicle breakdown
- Non-availability of resources
- Staffing problems

REMEMBER

A contingency plan is a plan that is devised for a specific situation for when things go wrong.

Once contingency plans have been formulated, it is important to then communicate them to staff so that all personnel know the route to take should problems occur.

In the event of a problem needing the implementation of a contingency plan it is important to notify the establishment manager, food production staff, delivery drivers and most importantly your customers immediately.

Identifying and addressing a conflict of interest

A conflict of interest could be such as:

- The order is not correct, for what the customer has implied he has requested
- The customer's expectation of waiting time has been exceeded
- The delivery has failed to arrive

What must be made clear to the delivery drivers is that the situation must be resolved with the minimum damage to the reputation of the delivering establishment. Contingency plans must be in place to resolve these situations that may arise. This would help to reduce the risk of a conflict of interest and a disagreement with the delivery.

How to deal with problems

A problem is the name given to the process of getting from one situation to another preferred one, which contains uncertainties or difficulties.

There are two types of problems: maintenance problems that exist where the current situation is not as it should be. The second group is achievement problems, where the current situation could be better, but there are reasons why it is not. These can be divided into the following three categories:

1 Where the current objective has not been achieved.

2 Where the current objective has been exceeded.

3 Where an opportunity exists.

To help solve problems we need to understand the problem-solving process and systematically apply the appropriate skills and techniques. The problem-solving process is broken down into five main subprocesses:

AN EXMPE OF A ROBEM-SOLVING ROCESS

STAGE OF PROBLEM SOLVING	EXAMPLE
1 Recognising the problem	Food has failed to be delivered.
2 Defining the problem: • Current situation • Desired situation • Objective	Delivery vehicle has broken down.
3 Analysing the problem	The vehicle is 20 minutes away and has been broken down for 15 minutes.
4 Possible solutions	Send a replacement vehicle to collect food and take to destination. Replace food straight away and send direct to destination. Phone customer to inform of the inability to deliver food.
5 Implementing the solution	Replace food straight away and send direct to destination. Also phone the customer to inform them of the situation.

Recognising and defining a problem

Problems often go unnoticed due to us not having the techniques or systems in place to detect them. To help focus our search for further information we need to label and define it.

> **! REMEMBER**
>
> In order to analyse a problem you need to have all the relevant information.

Analysing the problem

In order to analyse a problem you need to have all the relevant information, representing it in a meaningful way so that relationships between information can be seen. This analysis helps you decide what the ideal solution will be.

Developing possible solutions

You need to fully understand a problem before you can develop a solution and devise a course of action to deal with any obstacles to achieving the objective. You need to combine and modify ideas to develop a workable solution.

Evaluating solutions

If there is a range of solutions each one will need to be evaluated, to decide which will be the most effective. For this you will need to identify the features of the desired outcome, eliminating solutions which do not meet constraints. Then decide which solution is best to implement. A problem is only solved when a solution has been implemented.

Implementing the chosen solution

Implement requires the use of a plan, describing the actions required. The most common method is through the use of an 'action plan' detailing objectives, timescales, resources required, remedial actions and further actions should the objective not be achieved.

Action plans can be created in many forms, a simple method is shown here:

	ACTION	ACTION BY	REVIEW BY	RESOURCES NEEDED	DIVERGENCE FROM THE EXPECTED COURSE
(a)	(b)	(c)		(d)	(e)
1.					
2.					
3.					
4.					
5.					
6.					
7.					
8.					

	ACTION	ACTION BY	REVIEW BY	RESOURCES NEEDED	DIVERGENCE FROM THE EXPECTED COURSE
9.					
10.					
11.					
12.					
13.					

Problem-solving requires manipulating information using analytical and creative thinking skills, analytical being processes such as ordering, comparing, contrasting and evaluating. Creative thinking uses the imagination to create ideas; it involves looking beyond the obvious. Solving problems is a complex process with each individual better at solving some problems than others. Some of the reasons people fail include:

REMEMBER

Solving a problem sometimes involves looking beyond the obvious.

- Not being methodical
- Lack of commitment
- Misinterpreting the problem
- Lack of knowledge

Further reading and research

Stevens, M. (1997) *How to be a Better Problem Solver*. The Industrial Society.
Advice on workplace conduct http://www.worketiquette.co.uk/
Food legislation http://www.food.gov.uk

Assessment of knowledge and understanding

You have now learned about the responsibilities you have to work effectively in an off-site food delivery service and the importance of record keeping and contingency plans.

To test your level of knowledge and understanding, answer the following short questions. These will help to prepare you for your summative (final) assessment.

1   State the responsibilities you have in delivering food to the consumer.

2   Explain clearly what you understand by the meaning of organisational procedures.

3   Describe how you lead your team by example.

4   List five records that need to be kept and how to present them in an accepted format.

5   State how to monitor that the quality of food is maintained before and during delivery.

6   Describe briefly how to review and evaluate your operations and make recommendations to management.

7   State when you implement contingency plans and who to notify.

8   Using the principles of HACCP, describe how to implement the requirements of food hygiene.

9   Explain the packaging and transportation methods used to transport hot food in your establishment.

Research task

Food hygiene is important when working in an off-site food delivery business.

State five considerations you would make as a supervisor to ensure that you comply with current regulations.

17

Supervise cellar and drink storage operations

HS13 Supervise cellar and drink storage operations

LEARNING OBJECTIVES

This unit is about supervising cellar and drink stores to ensure that drinks are available for use in the best possible condition. It involves monitoring procedures, operations and equipment and dealing with any problems that might occur.

After reading this chapter you will be able to:

- Make sure your staff follow agreed cellar and drink storage procedures to maintain the quality of drink products.
- Suggest ways of improving the efficiency of procedures to the relevant person in your organisation.
- Make sure all activities in the cellar area comply with relevant legislation and organisational policy.
- Encourage your staff to look for and report problems when they occur.
- Take effective action to address problems relating to cellar and drink storage.
- Implement contingency plans to minimise any risks resulting from problems.
- Record details of problems and corrective action taken in a suitable format and make them available to the relevant people according to organisational systems and procedures.

KEY WORDS

Cask-conditioned beer
The cask is a barrel made of aluminium, stainless steel or oak, used to store beer.

Cellar
A room used to store beer and drinks, sometimes found in the basement, underground.

Environment
The surroundings that you are working in, which includes the atmosphere and location.

Keg
This can be the word used for a barrel, cask or drum to store beer or lager.

Quality
Character with respect to fineness, or grade of excellence. Offering a product or service at their best.

Rotation of stock
Ensuring that old stock be used before new.

Ventilation
Ventilation can be simply described as air circulation. This is the extraction of stale, overheated and contaminated air, and the supply and distribution of fresh air in amounts necessary to provide healthy and comfortable conditions for the occupants of the space being ventilated.

INTRODUCTION

Drink stocks and bar equipment are high value items and an efficient system for storing and issuing of drinks is a priority for bar managers. An efficient system provides the customer with the drink that they have ordered, delivered in the condition that they expect.

The cellar is usually in the basement of an older establishment. The precise layout will vary, but the ideal cellar or store room provides separate storage areas to suit each type of drink. There should be a main area for cask-conditioned and keg beers, a dark draught-free area for wines, or separate wine store, and a store room for bottled drinks i.e. beer, spirits and minerals.

The cellar will contain the dispense equipment (including cylinders of carbon dioxide or mixed gas) which propels the beer and cider from the cask, keg or tank to the service point in the bar. Some soft drinks are also dispensed from the cellar, from concentrated mixes.

Newer establishments tend to be built with temperature controlled cold rooms in which to keep lagers and other drinks that need chilling.

CELLAR ENVIRONMENT

The cellar must be adequately lit and ventilated, and maintained at the right temperature and humidity for the drinks kept there. If you discover the cooling system is not working or has been turned off without explanation you must act upon this immediately. As a supervisor/manager you will be required to deal with this following the organisation's procedures, contacting the nominated engineer to deal with faults or breakdowns.

© ISTOCKPHOTO.COM/RAMSEY BLACKLOCK

MAINTAINING A HYGIENIC ENVIRONMENT

Dust, mould, rodents and insects are all common factors within a cellar, if the environment is not maintained. They can all lead to an effect on the quality of the drinks stored and ultimately cause a health hazard.

Pest control must be implemented to ensure a safe environment, either by your organisation setting independent pest devices or by employing an external company with expertise in this area.

High standards of hygiene are essential to protect the quality of the drinks. The Food Safety Regulations 1995 class cellars as food rooms and therefore they must meet the standards. Nothing should be stored in the cellars which might taint the drinks, give off strong smells, introduce dirt or bacteria, encourage dust to collect, or bacteria and mould to grow.

What are good cleaning practices?

Good cleaning practices ensure a safe environment for the storage of drinks.

1 All beer and drink spillages must be wiped up and the area cleaned immediately.

2 Follow safety instructions and the warning labels given on cleaning agents and wear the personal protective equipment required.

3 Clean in a logical order, so that you do not make areas you have cleaned dirty.

> **! REMEMBER**
>
> Maintaining good practices within a cellar affects the quality and availability of products for your customers.

> **! REMEMBER**
>
> Know your organisation's procedures to deal with faulty equipment and the contingency plans to implement when equipment fails.

> **! REMEMBER**
>
> Under the Food Safety Act 1990, proprietors of food businesses (which include pubs and bars) commit an offence if they serve a food (which includes drink) that is harmful to health.

> **! REMEMBER**
>
> In older buildings walls and floors should not be left wet; this would encourage the growth of mould.

4 Daily floor cleaning using an appropriate detergent. The detergent must not be strongly fragranced as this could taint the beer.

5 On a weekly basis floors, walls, drains and gullies should be washed down. Drains and gullies collect and carry away waste water. Sumps are found in cellars that are below level of the main drainage system. They collect waste water, which is then pumped up into the drains. Weekly cleaning will prevent dirt from accumulating, and the water in sumps from giving off unpleasant smells (which harm the drinks).

6 The grilles of the cellar cooling equipment need regular cleaning with a soft brush, to remove dust, dirt and fluff which has gathered there. If the fluff is not removed, the hot air generated by the equipment would not be able to escape freely.

7 Racks, shelves and the platforms that the gas cylinders stand should be cleaned frequently and kept dry.

8 Clean the equipment after you have finished each task, and put it away in the correct place.

9 Mops must be washed and dried after use.

Cleaning the equipment

The layout of the establishment and the position of the cellar will affect the length of the beverage pipe work used to transport the beer from the cellar to the bar. Whatever the length, the system of pipes, traps and pumps which brings the beer from the cellar to the bar must be cleaned regularly. If the pipes are not cleaned this will affect the quality and taste of the beer that you serve. A collection of yeast and other contaminants in the equipment will make the beer cloudy, sour or over-frothy.

Once the beer pipes are cleaned with the recommended pipe cleaner, the pipes should then be cleaned through with fresh water, to avoid any contamination between the beer and cleaning fluid.

Once the cleaning is complete the beer should be checked for appearance, smell and taste.

Coolers and pumps within the cellar should be cleaned and maintained regularly.

! REMEMBER

Safety with cleaning products:

1 Never mix cleaning agents with other cleaning agents.

2 Never put cleaning agents into containers designed for other products.

3 Never use a drinking glass for measuring cleaning agents.

4 Always wear gloves and follow instructions on use of further personal protective equipment.

5 Beer line cleaner is corrosive and reacts in contact with acids, aluminium and your skin or eyes. If breathed or swallowed it will cause great harm.

ACTIVITY

1 Produce job task cards as a reference for new staff, covering the cleaning requirements of your cellar. Detail daily, weekly and ad hoc cleaning activities and the health and safety issues attached to the duties.

2 Devise cleaning schedules for your staff to record the cleaning that they have carried out, requiring a date and signature from staff when the cleaning was carried out. You can use this record to monitor standards and staff performance.

RECEIVING DRINK DELIVERIES

Drink stocks and bar equipment are high-value items. If mistakes go unnoticed at the time of delivery, and your supplier is paid for items that were not received, the profits are affected. There can also be a risk that poor checking systems encourage dishonesty, creating suspicion and harming working relationships.

Delivery preparation

The driver of the vehicle delivering your products will want to deliver quickly and move on to the next delivery. Receiving of the delivery and the return of unwanted stock needs to be done safely and items should be checked.

During delivery

Staff should be trained in safe methods of handling (refer to chapter 4 on health and safety).

■ Keep the area safe to move around in, both for your staff and the delivery staff

■ Cellar flaps and hatches must be properly secured when open, with a safety barrier in place

■ Leave the specialist tasks to the trained delivery crew

■ Use lifting equipment

Checking and signing for deliveries

It is important that this procedure is followed correctly. Even if you have the same supplier and delivery staff regularly, it is a necessity to check and verify the delivery. Most suppliers refuse to consider claims for missing or faulty items, unless it is identified at the point of delivery.

1 Collect the delivery note from the driver, sometimes the supplier may issue an invoice with delivery.

2 Check that the items on the delivery note correspond with what was ordered.

3 Staff should be aware that they must inform the supervisor/manager if the supplier has not delivered the quantity, brand or size requested. The supervisor will decide what items to accept. Alternative arrangements may have to be made to source some stock from an alternative supplier.

4 Check as each item is unloaded that the quality is acceptable. Examine the date mark, packaging and appearance of each item, that crated and boxes contain the amount stated, bottles are full and seals intact.

5 Put to one side any items which cannot be accepted.

! REMEMBER

Have in place checking mechanisms to ensure that stock invoiced for has been delivered.

! REMEMBER

Before the delivery arrives:

■ The delivery area should be clear

■ Empties and returns are counted and set aside for collection

■ Trolleys and lifting devices are available

■ Safety is risk assessed e.g. tripping or slipping hazards, weights to be lifted

■ The record of what was ordered is available to check against

! REMEMBER

■ Check the products as they are delivered

■ Record any discrepancies

■ Take action if stock is not delivered and is required

■ Keep walkways unobstructed

■ Clear up breakages or spillages immediately

■ Stack cases and boxes to no more than shoulder height

■ Ensure all the paperwork is sent immediately to the office/person dealing with accounts and that there are no discrepancies

6 Count the number of each item and tick off against the delivery note.

7 Record on the delivery note any discrepancies or shortfalls.

8 Sign the delivery note. In most cases the delivery note is a carbon and the supplier and customer each retain a copy.

9 The customer copy should be sent immediately to the office/person that deals with the accounts.

Dealing with delivery problems

When items are not what were ordered – wrong size, brand or quality or quantity problem – the delivery note has to be altered so that the supplier and the customer paying the invoice know what has happened. Usually the delivery person will write changes on the delivery note, which is signed by them and the customer.

© ISTOCKPHOTO.COM/DEMONOID

Delivery note

Some suppliers have returns notes for items not accepted at the point of delivery. The delivery person will complete this with the quantity and description or code number of each item, the reason for the return, and the customer details.

If a returns note is given it should be attached to the delivery note and sent to the person/office dealing with accounts.

Any disagreements with the delivery driver over quality or quantity or any other issue of the delivery should be resolved by the supervisor or manager.

Storing and issuing drinks

Why is an efficient system for storing and issuing drinks a priority for bar managers?

■ If stored too long the quality of most drinks deteriorates

■ Drink stock is valuable, tight control reduces the risks of items being stolen

■ Most drinks are preferred cool and chilled, less energy is required to get them to the correct service temperature if the cellar is cool

■ All drinks fall into the same category as food under food safety law, so the cellar and drinks storage areas have to meet the requirements for food premises. They must be kept clean and hygienic

CONTROLLING STOCK LEVELS

In order that stock does not run out and to avoid over-stocking it is usual to have a system in place of a minimum and maximum stock levels. An order is placed when the minimum level has been reached.

Some companies/suppliers offer discounts for bulk buying or a discount if the order achieves a certain value. Consideration should be made as to whether a sufficient saving is made to achieve a benefit against higher stock levels and stock rotation.

Computer-based stock control systems are used in most organisations, to highlight what needs ordering. This is an efficient and quick way of ordering what is required. Some systems work on a re-order by barcode, or by the physical inputting of stock levels into a handheld device. Older establishments may use a cellar book to record in coming and outgoing stock for each item, and the balance. From this the order is placed.

Monthly stock checks

This is a physical check of all stocks within the cellar and drink storage areas, normally carried out at the end of a 4-week period or the end of a calendar month. Figures are received from the bar tills for the number of each product sold and compared with the stock in the storage areas and the amount of stock ordered within the month. This is a tight control to ensure that all security measures are in place and any discrepancies between what has been ordered and consumed are investigated. This is a further deterrent to prevent theft.

The documentation used for recording physical stock checks can normally be generated by a computerised stock management system, which records the opening and closing stock, item by item. Manual systems can be used by simply recording all items to be stock-checked with the amount recorded by each item. An Excel spreadsheet can be developed to cover the necessary items, enabling the closing stock to be carried over to the next recording period.

PREPARING GAS CYLINDERS AND KEGS FOR USE

Kegs are stored in the cellar, upright, with the keg closure valve at the top (as illustrated in the photograph to the right).

The coupling head fits into the well, making the connection to the beer line (which transports the beer or cider to the bar) and to the carbon dioxide or mixed gas supply. As the contents of the keg are drawn off, the gas:

- Fills the air space left above the beer or cider, otherwise there would be a vacuum
- Helps the beer or cider maintain its condition, if the air was let into the keg this would harm it
- Prevents the carbon dioxide which is in the beer or cider from escaping. It is the gas which gives the drink its sparkle

Beer barrels

Kegs come in various sizes, the commonly used are 50 and 100 litres, which serve 88 and 176 pints respectively, if there is no wastage.

At the end of service

The gas supply to the kegs should be turned off overnight each time the bar closes. This is a safety measure.

Changing a keg

Some establishments have only one keg connected at a time. Larger, busy establishments have a system that allows several kegs of the same beer to be connected. When one keg is empty the system automatically diverts to the next full keg.

Kegs must be connected to the dispense system in date order, the oldest first. Each keg will have the date it was brewed on displayed, or the best before date.

1 Choose the keg to be connected. Ensure the oldest stock is used first.

2 Turn off the gas supply to the empty keg.

3 Pull the lever on the coupling head out and upwards until it clicks. Turn the coupling head anti-clockwise to unlock it from the keg.

4 Remove the protective seal which covers the closure valve of the new keg. Check that the fitting is clean and undamaged.

5 Check the coupling head is clean and insert into the spear head and turn clockwise. It is important not to over-tighten.

6 Pull the level on the coupling head out and push downwards until it clicks. This allows the beer to flow.

7 Check the connection to the gas and turn on.

8 Check that there are no leaks at the coupling head. You should not see any leakage of beer or hear the hissing of gas.

Changing a gas cylinder

Between the gas cylinders and the keg is a pressure release valve. This will be set up by the brewery. Each type of beer has its own pressure requirement to keep it at its best condition.

1 Close the main valve of the empty cylinder. Have a look at the gauge to ensure that the cylinder is empty.

2 Using a spanner undo the nut on the reducing valve of the empty cylinder, and pull it free.

3 Place the empty cylinder to one side.

4 Place the new cylinder in position.

! REMEMBER

Have in place checks on the following:

1 Staff are connecting the kegs correctly.

2 Stock is being rotated, the latest date first.

! REMEMBER

The company supplying the beer should provide training in maintaining the quality and the use of their products. Keep records of staff that have received this training.

5 Remove the protective cover or tape from the outlet valve.

6 To clear any dust or moisture in the valve, open and immediately close the outlet valve. The jet will clear any dust.

7 Connect the reducing valve to the new cylinder by hand, ensuring the washer is in place and in good condition. The nut should go on easily, if not remove it and start again (this will avoid damaging the thread). Tighten the nut with a spanner, but do not over-tighten.

8 Fully open the main valve of the new cylinder.

9 Check for minor leaks. The gas is invisible and has no smell, but will make a hissing sound if it is escaping.

Gas cylinder pressure gauge

! REMEMBER

The company supplying the gas should provide training in the use of their cylinders.

! REMEMBER

Safety when changing gas cylinders

1 Never leave full or empty cylinders unattended in the cellar unless they are clamped to the wall in an upright position.

2 Do not adjust the setting of the pressure releasing valve yourself.

3 Never connect cylinders that have been damaged or exposed to high temperatures.

4 If your staff suspect there is a leak but cannot hear the gas hissing ask them to squeeze some washing up liquid over the joint – if the liquid bubbles it means there is a leak.

5 If your staff find a minor leak, turn the gas off at the main valve and investigate the cause.

6 Do allow anyone to touch a gas cylinder which is leaking from its main valve. The casing becomes very cold and will burn skin. Ensure your staff induction training covers what to do if they find a leaking cylinder, instruct them to leave the cellar immediately and request urgent help.

Dealing with empty kegs and gas cylinders

Both of these should be stored in a different place to the full containers. This is best practice to avoid confusion and stock being mixed.

Empty kegs and cylinders should be stored in a secure place and away from moisture or exposed to extremes of hot or cold.

CHECKLIST

Create a system so that you are sure that staff are segregating old and new casks i.e. use a colour-coded system.

 **ACTIVITY**

Test your staff on how to move a keg

Include questions around:

1 The protective equipment they require in relation to footwear and gloves.

2 The posture they should have before moving the keg.

3 Describe the movement needed to move the keg, rather than lifting it.

STORING AND PREPARING CASK-CONDITIONED BEER

Cask-conditioned beer is not ready to drink when it first arrives. It requires a few days in the cellar for fermentation to be complete and the sediment to settle at the bottom of the cask.

Barrels

Conditioning equipment

The cask can be made of aluminium, stainless steel or oak. The delivery staff usually put each cask into position so it can lie with little disruption. The casts sits on a raised platform called a stillage. The cask lies on its side, held in position by a wooden wedge on either side.

When the cask is first put in place, a block has to be put on the front bearer, so that the cask is level. Later, the cask can be tilted by removing the block.

At one end, and this should be the end facing into the cellar, is the fitting which will take the cask tap. The cask tap will dispense the beer to the bar. When the cask is delivered, this fitting is closed by a wooden or plastic plug. Later the tap will be hammered into this plug with a mallet so that the connection can be made to the beer line. The cask should be positioned with the plug at the bottom.

On one side of the cask, at the top when the cask is resting horizontally, is the bung hole. This is closed with a wooden plug or bung. The bung has a small hole in the centre to take a spile or vent peg.

The spile is used to open or shut the hole in a wooden plug or bung. There are two types of spile. The soft spile, usually made of cane, is porous, so it does not make an air-proof seal. It is used until the beer stops fermenting, and replaced as necessary, so that carbon dioxide can escape. Once this stage is complete, the soft spile is replaced by a hard spile, usually made of hardwood or plastic. This is either pushed firmly, to make an air-proof seal, or pulled loose to allow some air into the cask.

> **! REMEMBER**
>
> Wooden spiles should only be used once and then thrown away. Other types can be re-used as long as they are thoroughly cleaned between use (use beer line cleaner to soak them).

Conditioning the beer ready to use

The process takes between a few days, depending on the type of beer. During this time the beer is vented, so that carbon dioxide created by the fermentation can escape. The beer also needs time for the sediment to settle.

The cask should be placed onto its stand as soon as it is delivered, and it will remain there until the beer has been sold. The only time the cask should be moved is to slightly raise the end furthest from the tap after about a third of the beer has been sold. This process should be treated with care to ensure that the sediment is not disturbed.

> **! REMEMBER**
>
> Venting beer, ensuring your staff are competent in the following:
>
> 1 Scrub and rinse the wooden plug or bung with clean water.
> 2 With a mallet, tap a soft spile into the hole in the wooden plug.
> 3 Leave the beer to complete its fermentation (usually a few days). Froth will form around the spile.
> 4 Twice a day wipe away the froth and replace the spile with a new one.
> 5 After wiping away the froth, if no more bubbles appear the beer has stopped fermenting. Remove the soft pile with pliers.
> 6 Tap a hard spile into the wooden plug. This allows the carbon dioxide to build up inside the cask, until the beer has cleared and is ready to drink. To prevent too much gas building up the hard spile should be tapped gently.

Changing a cask

1 Turn the tap off at the empty cask, and disconnect the beer line.

2 Allow any beer in the line to run into a bucket.

3 Test that the beer in the new cask is ready to use.

4 Connect the beer line to the tap on the new cask, tightening the nut loosely.

5 Half open the tap to allow any air in the line to escape through the loose connection.

6 Hand-tighten the connection.

7 Open the tap fully.

8 Loosen the spile.

Maintaining cask-conditioned beer

Looking after the beer during use helps keep it in better condition for a longer period. It is important to slow down the escape of carbon dioxide from the beer, otherwise the beer become flat, and to avoid disturbing the sediment as this will make the beer cloudy.

The level of beer is checked using a dipstick, similar to checking the oil in a car. It is important that the dip stick is clean prior to being inserted into the beer, to avoid contamination.

Remove the spile, carefully push the dipstick through the wooden plug until it touches the bottom of the cask, withdraw the dipstick and note the mark left by the beer.

At the end of each bar service, push the hard spile firmly into the bung hole. This protects the beer from any contamination, as the air in the cellar may contain bacteria. It also slows the release of carbon dioxide from the beer.

> **! REMEMBER**
>
> You need to make sure your staff check the amount of beer left in the cask regularly to:
>
> 1 Avoid pulling sediment from the bottom of the cask to the bar, which cause the pipes to block.
> 2 Judge when the cask can be tilted. This gets as much beer as possible from the cask without disturbing the sediment.

> **! REMEMBER**
>
> Before every session insist that your staff loosen the hard spile, so that air can be drawn into the cask as the beer is drawn off. If this isn't done the sediment can be disturbed.

© ISTOCKPHOTO.COM/
DIETER SPEARS

Test of beer quality

Preparing and storing empty casks

As soon as possible after a cask is empty, make sure it is made airtight:

■ Apply a hard spile into the bung hole

■ Remove the tap, gently tap it to loosen it

■ Block the keystone with a cork

TASK

Set up six glasses of beer all with quality issues, and encourage your staff to identify the problem with each. Include a dirty glass as an unacceptable standard.

BEER QUALITY CONCERNS

A customer demands the perfect pint every time, and the quality of the beer is achieved from the way the beer has been stored, prepared for service and the condition of the pipes it has travelled in. The following tips may help to identify any problems that are identified with the condition of a pint of beer

Cloudy beer – the beer lines have not been cleaned adequately or often enough. The cellar temperature control system may not be working properly or there is a problem with the gas supply.

Poor head retention – the beer lines are not clean. The cellar may be too warm, affecting the temperature of the beer as it is poured into the glass. The beer may have been on tap for too long, or the cask-conditioned beer has been used before it was ready.

Fobbing – this is when the beer is too frothy. It may occur in hot weather if the cellar cannot be maintained at the correct temperature. If the temperature is ok then the cleanliness of the pipes is most likely to be the problem. Check the gas supply is working correctly.

Further reading and research

John Cousins and Dennis R. Lillicrap (2006) *Food and Beverage Service*, 7th edn. Arnold.

John Cousins, David Foskett and Cailein Gillespie (2002) *Food and Beverage Management*, 2nd edn. Longman.

Bernard Davis, Andrew Lockwood and Sally Stone (1998) *Food and Beverage Management*, 3rd edn. Butterworth-Heinemann.

Food Hygiene Regulations http://www.opsi.gov.uk/si/si2005/20052059.htm

Manual Handling Regulations http://www.hse.gov.uk/pubns/indg143.pdf

Research the country's leading breweries for their training guidance

Assessment of knowledge and understanding

You have now learnt about the responsibilities to maintain the drink and cellar storage operation, ensuring standards are maintained to provide the customer with the drink that they ordered, in the condition that they expect.

To test your level of knowledge and understanding, answer the following short questions. These will help to prepare you for your summative (final) assessment.

1 State three reasons why the cellar should be hygienically clean.

2 How would you build into your daily routine to monitor cleanliness in the cellar?

3 Why is good security important? Describe how you would monitor security.

4 Describe how you would monitor your staff's performance to ensure standards are maintained.

5 What systems would you have in place to ensure any beer quality issues are rectified before a customer has cause to complain?

6 List the checks needed to be in place to ensure stock that has been invoiced for has been received.

7 List five health and safety facts to consider when managing a cellar/drink store.

8 Consider the relationship required between the drink supplier and organisation, ensuring that you hear of the latest offers and receive the best value for money.

9 Detail the outline of a contingency plan should a supplier fail to deliver.

10 Consider the role a supervisor would play to ensure a smooth service for the customer in the event of the cellar being flooded.

Research task

Visit three different organisations and view their drink and cellar arrangements. Consider all the designs and then design a layout that you would consider was best practice.

18

Manage the receipt, storage and dispatch of goods

HS14 Manage the receipt, storage and dispatch of goods

LEARNING OBJECTIVES

This unit covers the competence that hospitality supervisors require to manage the receipt, storage and dispatch of goods.

After reading this chapter you will be able to:

- Confirm the quantity and types of goods being managed.
- Determine the storage conditions and equipment required to manage the goods.
- Assess the capacity of the storage facility, and identify appropriate areas for receiving, storing, or dispatching goods.
- Organise the movement or rotation of goods to assist receiving, storing, or dispatching goods.
- Ensure any monitoring activities, tests, and other storage arrangements required for the goods are carried out in accordance with organisational procedures.
- Identify and confirm requirements for facilities and equipment to be used with the goods.
- Utilise and maintain the organisation's logistics resources effectively to manage the receipt, storage, and dispatch of goods.
- Provide information on the goods and their requirements to all relevant people.
- Identify any relevant health, safety and security issues relating to the management of the goods.

■ Identify any problems with managing the goods.

■ Take the appropriate action to deal with any problems with managing the goods.

■ Report and record work activities in the appropriate information systems according to organisational procedures.

■ Comply with all relevant work and safety legislation, regulations, standards and organisational procedures.

KEY WORDS

Purchase order

A commercial document issued by a buyer to a seller, indicating the type, quantities and agreed prices for products or services the seller will provide to the buyer. Sending a PO to a supplier constitutes a legal offer to buy products or services. Acceptance of a PO by a seller usually forms a once-off contract between the buyer and seller so no contract exists until the PO is accepted.

Purchase requisition

An authorisation for a purchasing department to procure goods or services. It is originated and approved by the department requiring the goods or services. Typically, it contains a description and quantity of the goods or services to be purchased, a required delivery date, account number and the amount of money that the purchasing department is authorised to spend for the goods or services. Often, the names of suggested supply sources are also included.

Purchase specification

Detailed description of the measurable characteristics desired in an item to be purchased, such as quality, size, weight, performance parameters, safety requirements, etc.

Stock rotation

The practice of moving products with an earlier sell-by date to the front of a shelf (or in the cooler if the item is on repack so they get worked out before the new product), so they get picked up and sold first, and of moving products with a later sell-by date to the back.

INTRODUCTION

To manage the receipt, storage and dispatch of goods covers a wealth of products in the hospitality environment. It can include food and beverages, but also linen, laundry, cleaning chemicals and any other type of goods that come into the workplace. The control of each of these three areas is

ACTIVITY

Write a list of as many goods as you can think of that a hospitality environment may receive into their workplace over the course of the year.

important as in turn they can affect the profitability of the company. This chapter will consider some of the types of goods that a hospitality workplace uses, as well as give consideration to the receiving of those goods, the storage of them and the dispatch to the various departments in the workplace. It will also take into consideration the security of storage of those goods, some of the legislative aspects of storage of those goods and the procedures needed to maintain control.

TYPES OF GOODS PURCHASED

Perishable and non-perishable

Perishable

© ISTOCKPHOTO.COM/
REBECCA ELLIS

These are mainly foodstuffs but some beverages have a short lifespan. They need to have a fast turnover in order to maintain their quality. Low levels of stock are possible with daily deliveries, which is usual in large cities but may be less common in rural areas. Minimum stocks need to be maintained so that freshness is ensured, but without compromising on customer service. Some sectors have converted to longer-life products (packaged or frozen) to reduce loss and help with portion control.

Non-perishable

© ISTOCKPHOTO.COM/CARLOS ALVAREZ

These tend to have larger holdings as deliveries are generally less frequent.

- Liquor may have a large number of stock items, depending on the type of operation and the length of the wine list
- Supplies include a range of departmental and administrative expenses – guest supplies, paper goods, cleaning material, printed items
- Plant includes china, glass and cutlery and sometimes repairs and maintenance items

TECH SKILLS ✓

HOW IS PROFITABILITY AFFECTED BY THE RECEIPT, STORAGE AND DISPATCH OF GOODS?

There are several factors that can affect profitability while taking into consideration the receipt, storage and dispatch of goods. These include:

- The correct receiving of goods:
  - (a) Ensuring the correct delivery details are provided
  - (b) Ensuring the correct quantities are delivered
  - (c) Checking the quality of the goods delivered
  - (d) Ensuring the goods delivered are not damaged in any way

■ The correct storage of goods, this includes:

(a) Ensuring the goods are stored correctly according to legislation

(b) Ensure goods are securely stored to avoid loss or theft

(c) Ensure the correct volumes of goods are stored so that the outlet does not run out of key items needed to run the day-to-day operation

(d) Ensure that stock is accounted for and recorded appropriately

■ The correct dispatch of goods, this includes:

(a) Ensure that the right goods are delivered to the right department at the right time

(b) Ensure the right quantity of goods are delivered

(c) Ensure that delivery to a department is safe and secure

(d) Ensure that the correct paperwork has been completed

WHOSE RESPONSIBILITY IS IT TO MANAGE ALL OF THIS?

If you work in a large hotel you may well have a purchasing team who manage and look after each of these areas, supplying you (the department) with your every requirement. Equally if you are a large bar or restaurant you may also have a slightly smaller purchasing team.

What if you are a small hospitality outlet? Who looks after it then?

■ You, or

■ Maybe the general manager or the head chef, or the head housekeeper, or

■ A combination of the above

The role of the purchasing manager

■ In some establishments you will find a purchasing manager – they will be in charge of all the purchasing cycle and oversee its application and execution to all the departments in an establishment

■ As a supervisor you may find yourself involved in any number of the following aspects:

● Responsible for the management of purchasing, procurement and keeping purchasing records, recording the receiving and correct storage of goods

● The purchasing of all commodities within their responsibility

● Ensuring continuity of supply of those items to use or departments

● Finding cheaper and more efficient sources of supply

● Keeping up to date with all the markets being dealt with and evaluating new products

● Research into products, markets, price trends

- Co-ordinating with production departments to standardise commodities and reduce stock levels
- Liaising with production, control, accounts and marketing departments
- Reporting to senior management through established communication channels

Policies set by management	Determine market segment aimed at, target price to be paid, the quality required and the price to be charged to customers. Set standard operating procedures (SOPs) to regulate purchasing function
Menu	Determines the choice of items available to customers
Volume forecasting (see also purchasing and storing)	Determines the quantity to be purchased
Requisition (paper or electronic)	Indicates the particular requirements of each sales outlet
Purchasing	Selects suppliers, contracts, minimum and maximum quantities and quantity discounts available. Ensures adequate temperature controlled storage is available. Specifications for individual items and to ensure continuity of supply
Receiving	Inspects for quantity and quality reports to control any discrepancies, checks conformity with required temperature statutes and maintains records for HACCP. Checks delivery vehicle temperatures as laid down in SOPs
Storing	Correct storage for each item, ensures that all temperature sensitive items are stored quickly and correctly and ensures freezers and refrigeration are not overloaded
Production	Preparation of items purchased
Selling	Provision of satisfactory products at the correct selling price/cost and quality
Control	The measurement of performance of all outlets involved, adherence to company policy and SOPs and provide feedback to management

The purchasing function

The purchasing cycle

Purchasing cycle

The purchasing procedure

1   Each section of the organisation will have established stock levels and a procedure for stock replacement. This may include requisition forms, but with modern computers and EPOS, the system may alert you to low stocks and be raised orders automatically.

2   The selection of the source of supply is agreed in advance by the department manager and contracts made, which include:

(a)   Price to be paid

(b)   Delivery performance, particularly including time, date and place of delivery

Cycle for purchasing goods

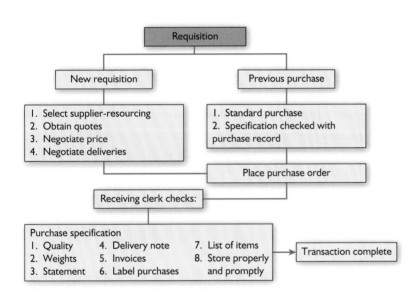

This cycle considers how the goods are purchased in the first place, starting with a requisition from a department or outlet within the workplace. The stages that follow include:

■   The requisition is checked to see if all the goods are in stock. If they are then the next control point is the dispatch of goods which will be considered later in the chapter

●   As part of an organisation's internal financial controls, the accounting department requires a purchase requisition process to help manage requests for purchases. Requests for the creation of purchase of goods and services are documented and routed for approval within the organisation and then delivered to the accounting group

ABC COMPANY
123 Main Street, Anytown, Country 00000   TEL 000-000-0000   FAX 000-000-0000
SUPPLY REQUISITION
(Please fill in blanks)

Requested by: _____

Authorized by:

Department: | **Bar** | |

Date:

Division and no.:

Requisition #:

Div.	I
Div.	2
Div.	3
Div.	4
Div.	

Page #:

Quantity	Item (please be specific)	Vendor* & catalogue number	Price each

*Submit separate requisition for each vendor.

ACTIVITY

What core pieces of information are required in the completion of the purchase order on the right?

■ A purchase order – this is used to raise an order with the supplier. If it is a new supplier required for the goods then see box labelled 'new requisition' in the flowchart on page 267. If it is an existing supplier then the box labelled 'previous purchase' in the flowchart

● A purchase order allows buyers to clearly and explicitly communicate their intentions to sellers, and to protect the seller in the event of a buyer's refusal to pay for goods or services

An Example Purchase Order

<table>
<tr><td>Your logo here</td></tr>
</table>

[Your company name]
[Your company slogan here]

Date: ###############
P.O. #: [100]
Customer ID: [ABC12345]

Vendor [Name]
[Company name]
[Street address]
[City, Post code]
[Phone]

Ship to [Name]
[Company name]
[Street address]
[City, Post code]
[Phone]

Shipping method	Shipping terms	Delivery date

Qty	Item #	Description	Job	Unit price	Line total

	Subtotal	
	Sales tax	
	Total	

1. Please send two copies of your invoice.
2. Enter this order in accordance with the prices, terms, delivery method, and specifications listed above.
3. Please notify us immediately if you are unable to ship as specified.
4. Send all correspondence to:
[Name]
[Street Address]
[City, Post code]
[Phone]
[Fax]

_____ _____
Authorized by   Date

[Street Address], [City, Post code] [Phone] [Fax] [E-mail]

■ If it is a new supplier and/or new goods, it will also require a purchase specification which details the quality required for the goods This includes details about the quality of the goods, the size of the goods, the amount required, frequency and delivery details. See example below for oven-fried chicken legs

OVEN-FRIED CHICKEN LEG

Breaded, fried UK Grade A. The batter/breading shall consist of a flour-type base with other ingredients as needed to produce desirable texture, flavour, and colour. The pick-up of batter and breading prior to frying shall be approximately 14–16 per cent of the weight of the chicken. Chicken should be processed in vegetable oil for at least two minutes at 325°F. The finished fried chicken should have an internal temperature of 185°F – dark meat. After frying, the chicken should be immediately chilled and quick-frozen. The finished product should be uniformly covered with batter and breading and have a uniform brown colour. The product should be free from burnt areas. The edible portion of the chicken exclusive of breading, skin, and bone must be two ounces cooked weight.

Manual vs. computerised ordering of goods

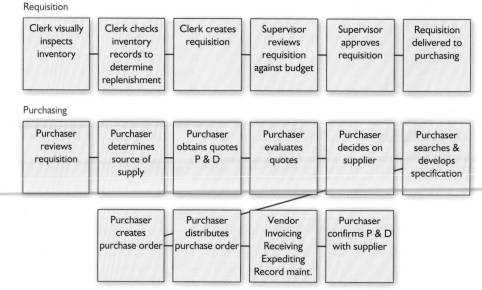

Manual process – duration five working days

Requisition

| Clerk visually inspects inventory | Clerk checks inventory records to determine replenishment | Clerk creates requisition | Supervisor reviews requisition against budget | Supervisor approves requisition | Requisition delivered to purchasing |

Purchasing

| Purchaser reviews requisition | Purchaser determines source of supply | Purchaser obtains quotes P & D | Purchaser evaluates quotes | Purchaser decides on supplier | Purchaser searches & develops specification |

| Purchaser creates purchase order | Purchaser distributes purchase order | Vendor Invoicing Receiving Expediting Record maint. | Purchaser confirms P & D with supplier |

P & D = Price & delivery

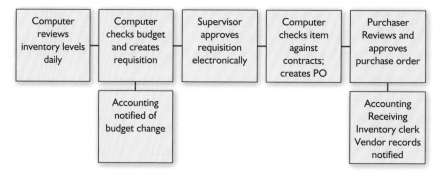

Computerised process – duration 1 to 2 hours

| Computer reviews inventory levels daily | Computer checks budget and creates requisition | Supervisor approves requisition electronically | Computer checks item against contracts; creates PO | Purchaser Reviews and approves purchase order |

| | Accounting notified of budget change | | | Accounting Receiving Inventory clerk Vendor records notified |

TECHNOLOGIES USED BY BUYERS INCLUDE:

1 Fax machines.

2 Personal computers.

3 POS – point of sale.

4 Barcode reader.

5 Product ordering.

6 Inventory tracking and storage management.

7 Internet.

8 Email.

9 News group and mailing list.

10 World Wide Web.

11 Instant and text messages.

TECHNOLOGIES USED BY SUPPLIERS INCLUDE:

1 Customer database (CRM).

2 Ordering system (Web ordering).

3 GPS (routing).

4 RFID (radio frequency identification).

RECEIVING OF GOODS

Once goods have been ordered, they will then be delivered to the workplace. There are three key aspects that have to be checked at this stage, before receiving of goods is finalised:

1 The acceptance of goods ordered and the adjustments of any discrepancies in quality or quantity of goods ordered.

2 Checking the condition of packaging or containers and rejecting those not in good condition.

3 Transfer of commodities to the ordering departments or to stores or cellar.

When receiving a delivery, it is important that you check the following:

■ The quantity on the delivery note is the quantity that you receive

■ Write down any anomalies between the delivery note and the actual delivery

■ Ensure the delivery person and the person receiving the order both sign the delivery note to confirm what was actually delivered

ACTIVITY

■ Why do you think it is important that the three aspects on the left are checked?

■ What might happen if the three aspects above were not checked?

■ How would this affect the outlet and the organisation as a whole?

STORAGE OF GOODS

FIFO and stock rotation

FIFO stands for first in – first out, which basically means that the stock delivered first should be used first (before more recent deliveries). This is to avoid wastage in the form of stock that has deteriorated or gone beyond its sell-by date.

In relation to perishability of goods then food is the most obvious example, but after that comes any form of drink stock.

In addition, linen and laundry can also deteriorate:

■ If they get stuck at the back of a shelf they can get creased beyond use, or

■ Dusty from being left on the shelf too long, or

■ Damp

Likewise, stationery, chemicals and furniture all need to be carefully considered in relation to storage.

TIP

Receiving a delivery

1 Check crates randomly to ensure that the delivery people have filled the whole crate and not left gaps in the middle of the crate.

2 Make sure you get a signature for what was delivered and any missing items.

3 Chase up the credit note from the company.

ACTIVITY

■ Can you think of any other forms of deterioration to stock and what happens to that deterioration?

■ How can deterioration of stock be avoided?

Example of food storage in a fridge

Recommended layout for
your refrigerator if it has to
be multi-purpose.

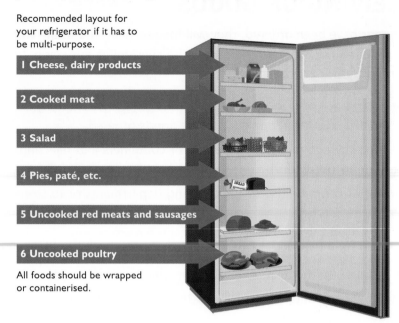

1 **Cheese, dairy products**

2 **Cooked meat**

3 **Salad**

4 **Pies, paté, etc.**

5 **Uncooked red meats and sausages**

6 **Uncooked poultry**

All foods should be wrapped
or containerised.

Example of temperature storage and cellar layout for wines

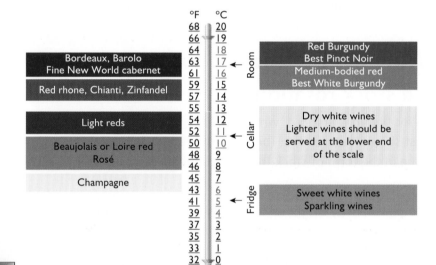

	°F	°C	
	68	20	
	66	19	
	64	18	Room
Bordeaux, Barolo Fine New World cabernet	63	17	
	61	16	
Red rhone, Chianti, Zinfandel	59	15	
	57	14	
	55	13	
Light reds	54	12	
	52	11	Cellar
Beaujolais or Loire red Rosé	50	10	
	48	9	
	46	8	
Champagne	45	7	
	43	6	Fridge
	41	5	
	39	4	
	37	3	
	35	2	
	33	1	
	32	0	

Red Burgundy
Best Pinot Noir

Medium-bodied red
Best White Burgundy

Dry white wines
Lighter wines should be
served at the lower end
of the scale

Sweet white wines
Sparkling wines

Example of cellar storage

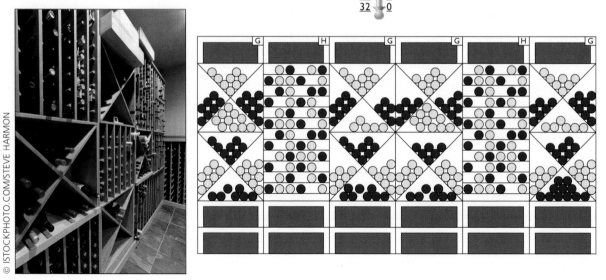

Aspects to consider in the storage of any goods

- ■ HUMIDITY
- ■ DARKNESS
- ■ CALM
- ■ CLEANLINESS and VENTILATION
- ■ ANGLE OF STORAGE
- ■ SPACE UTILISED FOR STORAGE OF GOODS
- ■ FREQUENCY OF DELIVERY
- ■ SAFETY

ACTIVITY

What other considerations need to be given to aspects of storage of goods?

Stock control

There are a variety of methods used to help control stock, particularly in relation to its storage, these include:

- ■ Stock-taking – this is the counting of stock on a regular basis. Once stock has been counted it is reconciled with what should actually be there
- ■ Allocation of space for stock (e.g. bin numbers for wine, shelves for dry foods, etc.) – this helps to avoid stock hiding or going missing
- ■ Paperwork – including requisitions, delivery notes, credit notes and purchase orders. By completing paperwork appropriately you are making personnel in the workplace accountable for stock movement in the building

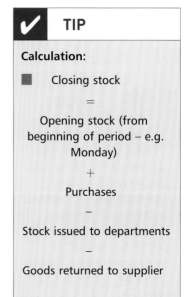

TIP

Calculation:

- ■ Closing stock

=

Opening stock (from beginning of period – e.g. Monday)

+

Purchases

–

Stock issued to departments

–

Goods returned to supplier

Par levels

1 Par levels – you must ensure that every product has a minimum and maximum par level. This is the correct levels of stock required to ensure that you don't over-stock during quiet periods of business or understock during busy periods.

2 Once par levels are set, these need to be maintained. Within the cellar, when orders are made the following must be taken into consideration:

(a) Level of business – busy or quiet
(b) Par levels
(c) Orders from the individual outlets your cellar may supply (i.e. in a hotel)

Security is vital in the safe storage of any goods. Goods have a resale value to anyone who can obtain them and sell them on for their own personal gain. So to be sure to avoid temptation, security and the vigilance of security is imperative. Here are a few methods to consider in assuring the security of your stock:

1 Locks – cellars must be kept locked at all times when the cellar/store person is not in the nearby vicinity.

2 Paperwork – logs must be kept to track goods in and out of the cellar.

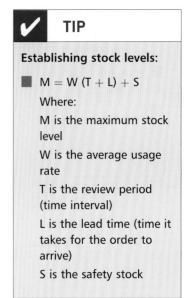

TIP

Establishing stock levels:

- ■ $M = W (T + L) + S$
  Where:
  M is the maximum stock level
  W is the average usage rate
  T is the review period (time interval)
  L is the lead time (time it takes for the order to arrive)
  S is the safety stock

© ISTOCKPHOTO.COM/
ISAKOVICH ALINA

✔ TIP

You will need these websites ready later for the Research task.

🥄 ACTIVITY

The duty manager of a big hotel is given responsibility for the keys to the storage areas outside of the purchasing team's normal working day. The duty manager is very busy and someone needs more stock for their bar. The DM gives the member of staff the keys.

■ What could go wrong in relation to the security of the storage of areas, requirements for paperwork, etc.?

■ What other things might go wrong?

■ How would you find a solution to this?

3 Par levels – maximum and minimum levels of stock should be logged and maintained at all.

4 Authorised personnel – only allocated and authorised personnel should be allowed into the cellar at any time.

5 CCTV to monitor the comings and goings from the cellar.

Legislation

There is various legislation in regard to the storage of stock and these include:

COSHH Care of Substances Hazardous to Health http://www.hse.gov.uk/coshh/

Health and Safety at Work Act http://www.hse.gov.uk/pubns/law.pdf

Food safety and hygiene http://www.food.gov.uk/safereating/

DISPATCH OF GOODS

This area literally takes into consideration the safe delivery of goods from the storage area to the appropriate departments.

This may include:

1 Delivering food to the kitchens:
  ● Ensure the paperwork is signed correctly by the chef receiving the goods
  ● Ensure that goods are not kept out of refrigeration unduly causing foods to enter into the danger zone of temperatures
  ● Ensure that goods don't leak, burst or get damaged enroute to their destination
  ● Check par levels of stock after delivery to ensure there are enough goods for the next time a requisition is likely to be made (e.g. daily, weekly, next month, etc.)

2 Delivering drinks to the bar:
  ● Carry out same procedure as 'delivering food to the kitchens'

3 Delivering laundry to housekeeping:
  ● Carry out same procedure as 'delivering food to the kitchens'

4 Delivering linen to the restaurant:
  ● Carry out same procedure as 'delivering food to the kitchens'

5 Delivering stationery to one of the administration offices
  ● Carry out same procedure as 'delivering food to the kitchens'

6 Delivering hired furniture to conference and banqueting:
  ● Carry out same procedure as 'delivering food to the kitchens'

COMPUTERISED SUPPORT APPLICATIONS

HOSPITALITY-SPECIFIC APPLICATIONS

PMS – property management system	Stores data about guest activities, their portfolios and compose several reports essential for all departments in hospitality unit. Mostly is used in hotel industry or larger restaurant chains where many departments are involved in operation.
Reservation system	Manoeuvre with reservation enquiries, tracks availability and rates and provides management and supervisors with essential reports.
Stock-control system	Controls and manage level of stock and use of stock, provide supervisors and management with report such as using rates, sale, stock ratios.
Recipe costing system	In relation with stock control system or independently provide management with accurate costing for individual dishes.
Conferences and banqueting system	It is similar to reservation system although is specialised on booking of conferences facilities. It provides management with several essential reports.

Assessment of knowledge and understanding

You have now learnt about how to manage the receipt, storage and dispatch of goods from storage points in an outlet.

To test your level of knowledge and understanding, answer the following short questions. These will help prepare you for your summative (final) assessment.

Receipt of goods

1 What key pieces of information should be checked when receiving a delivery of goods and why?

2 How can a computerised system of ordering assist the purchasing team?

3 What problems do you think could be incurred during the receipt of goods and how would you overcome these difficulties?

Storage of goods

1 Earlier in the chapter you were given examples of how to correctly store food in a refrigerator, wine in a cellar and a beer cellar. Now consider how the following types of goods should be stored correctly and under what conditions (e.g. humidity, etc.).

(a) Dry foods

(b) Linen and laundry

(c) Stationery

(d) Furniture

(e) Chemicals

2 Bearing in mind your answers to question 3 above and the examples given earlier in the chapter, make a list of all the equipment needed to assist in the correct storage of goods for a pub or bar.

3 Identify how a stocktake should be carried out appropriately and effectively to ensure that *all* goods are counted correctly and accurately.

4 Having identified how a stocktake should be carried out, ask at your workplace to actually carry out a stocktake with one of the supervisors. Ask them to check you to ensure you are correctly carrying out the task.

Dispatch of goods

1 How can information be shared amongst the whole organisation in relation to goods, including information about the goods themselves, as well as the stock levels available and any special requirements of the goods or ordering details?

Research task

Taking into consideration the aspects of receipt, storage and dispatch of goods, you are required to research more information on the legislative implications of storage of goods and write a list of 10 legislative tips that an employer could use to ensure the appropriate storage of goods and be legal.

Don't forget to use Government-based websites for factual information, guidelines and factsheets. You may want to keep those factsheets in your study file to show your assessor at the next assessment point.

19

Supervise the wine store/cellar and dispense counter

LEARNING OBJECTIVES

This unit is about supervising staff to maintain wine in the best possible condition. It also deals with the maintenance of stock at the dispense counter.

After reading this chapter you will be able to:

- Carry out regular inspections to make sure your staff are following established cellar and dispense counter procedures.
- Store wine and dispense counter stock under the correct environmental conditions.
- Make sure you and your staff handle wine and dispense counter stock in a way that minimises damage to bottles, containers, packaging or their content.
- Deal with damage, deterioration and loss of wine and dispense counter stock correctly.
- Make sure service equipment is clean, free from damage and stored in the correct place.
- Deal with unforeseen situations and problems.
- Make sure that your staff follow relevant legal requirements.
- Record information and make it available to the appropriate people as required.

KEY WORDS

Deterioration
When wine is no longer in a condition to be served to the customer.

Dispense counter
The bar area where staff will order and prepare drinks to serve to customers.

Environment
The surroundings that you are working in, which includes the atmosphere and location.

Environmental conditions
The temperature, lighting and humidity under which wines should be stored.

Industry codes of practice
Guidelines drawn up by the drinks industry which show how businesses should follow the law and deliver high standards to the customer.

Legal requirements
All aspects of law and regulations that affect the storage of wine; these would include laws and regulations covering hygiene and health and safety.

Quality
Character with respect to fineness, or grade of excellence. Offering a product or service at their best.

Rotation of stock
Ensuring that old stock be used before new.

Stock rotation
A system that ensures that wine is withdrawn from storage when it is in peak condition.

Unforeseen situations and problems
Availability and quality of ingredients, equipment or power failure, staff problems, customer problems.

Ventilation
Ventilation can be simply described as air circulation. This is the extraction of stale, overheated and contaminated air, and the supply and distribution of fresh air in amounts necessary to provide healthy and comfortable conditions for the occupants of the space being ventilated.

Wine cellar
A room used to store wines, spirits and drinks, sometimes found in the basement, underground whilst technically a wine cellar situated above the ground is often called a *wine room*, while a small wine cellar (less than 500 bottles) is sometimes termed a *wine closet*.

INTRODUCTION

Wine stocks and bar equipment are high-value items. An efficient system for storing and issuing of wines is a priority for supervisors and managers and provides the customer with the drink that they have ordered, delivered in the condition that they expect.

Wine cellars protect alcoholic beverages from potentially harmful external influences, providing darkness and a constant temperature. Wine is a natural, perishable food product. Left exposed to heat, light, vibration or fluctuations in temperature and humidity, all types of wine can spoil. When properly stored, wines not only maintain their quality but many actually improve in aroma, flavour and complexity as they mature.

The cellar is usually in the basement of an older establishment. The precise layout will vary, but the ideal wine cellar provides separate storage areas to suit each type of wine such as separating white from red wines and champagnes. There should be a dark draught-free area exclusively for wines.

The wine cellar will contain the dispense equipment (including cylinders of carbon dioxide or mixed gas) which propels the beer and cider from the cask, keg or tank to service point in the bar. Some soft drinks are also dispensed from the cellar, from concentrated mixes.

Newer establishments tend to be built with temperature-controlled cold rooms which keep lagers and other drinks which need chilling.

© ISTOCKPHOTO.COM/FILONMAR

> **! REMEMBER**
>
> Maintaining good practices within a cellar affects the quality and availability of wine for your customers.

THE WINE CELLAR ENVIRONMENT

Wine can be stored satisfactorily between 7 and 18°C (45 and 65°F) as long as any variations in temperature are gradual. A temperature of 13°C (55°F), much like what is found in the caves used to store wine in France, is ideal for both short-term storage and long-term ageing of wine. Note that wine generally matures differently and more slowly at a lower temperature than it does at a higher temperature. Between 10 and 14°C (50 and 57°F), wines will age normally. Wine cellars can be either active or passively cooled. Active wine cellars are highly insulated and need to be properly constructed. They require specialised wine cellar conditioning and cooling systems to maintain the desired temperature and humidity. In a very dry climate, it may be necessary to actively humidify the air, but in most areas this is not necessary. Passive wine cellars must be located in naturally cool and damp areas with minor seasonal and temperature variations, for example, a basement in a temperate climate. Passive cellars may be less predictable, but cost nothing to operate and are not affected by power surges or loss.

Some wine experts debate the importance of humidity for proper wine storage. A French study has claimed that the relative humidity within a bottle

> **! REMEMBER**
>
> Know your organisational procedures to deal with faulty equipment and the contingency plans to implement when equipment fails due to a power supply loss.

© BRANNON THERMOMETERS

A wine cellar thermometer

> **! REMEMBER**
>
> Under the Food Safety Act 1990, proprietors of food businesses (which include pubs and bars) commit an offence if they serve a food (which includes drink) that is harmful to health.

© ISTOCKPHOTO.COM/INA PETERS

of wine is maintained at 100 per cent regardless of the cork or screw cap used or the orientation of the bottle. However, other informed arguments specify that low humidity can be a problem because it may cause organic corks to dry prematurely. An inch of gravel covering the floor periodically sprinkled with a little water was recommended to retain the desired humidity.

If you discover the cooling system not working or turned off without explanation you must act upon this immediately. As a supervisor/manager you will be required to deal with this following the organisation's procedures, contacting the nominated engineer to deal with faults or breakdowns.

MAINTAINING A HYGIENIC ENVIRONMENT

Dust, mould, rodents and insects are all common factors within a cellar, if the environment is not maintained. They can all lead to an effect on the quality of the wine and dispense equipment stored and ultimately cause a health hazard.

Pest control must be implemented to ensure a safe environment, either by your organisation setting independent pest devices or by employing an external company with expertise in this area.

High standards of hygiene are essential to protect the quality of the drinks. The Food Safety Regulations 1995 class cellars as food rooms and therefore they must meet the standards. Nothing should be stored in the cellars which might taint the wine, give off strong smells, introduce dirt or bacteria, encourage dust to collect, or bacteria and mould to grow.

What are good cleaning practices?

Good cleaning practices ensure a safe environment for the storage of drinks.

1 All wine and drink spillages must be wiped up and the area cleaned immediately.

2 Follow safety instructions and the warning labels given on cleaning agents and wear the personal protective equipment required.

3 Clean in a logical order, so that you do not make areas you have cleaned dirty.

4 Daily floor cleaning using an appropriate light detergent. The detergent must not be strongly fragranced as this could taint the wine or dispense equipment.

5 On a weekly basis floors, walls, drains and gullies should be washed down. Drains and gullies collect and carry away waste water.

6 The grilles of the cellar cooling equipment need regular cleaning with a soft brush, to remove dust, dirt and fluff which has gathered there. If the

fluff is not removed, the hot air generated by the equipment would not be able to escape freely.

7 Racks, shelves and the platforms that the wine bottles are laid in should be cleaned frequently and kept dry.

8 Clean the equipment after you have finished each task, and put it away in the correct place.

9 Mops must be washed and dried after use.

A supervisor's checklist for cleaning the wine cellar

This should be carried out periodically and particularly when new equipment is introduced, or new work methods changed. Once you have decided on how often you are going to clean, where you are going to clean, how often and with what, your next decision is how to set out the schedule.

One example is to have a grid, although this is only an example and there are many other ways of achieving a well-designed schedule. Many of the cleaning chemical manufacturers produce schedules which you can adapt to your own needs.

GENERAL RISK ASSESSMENT OF THE WINE CELLAR

- ■ Warning signage to alert staff of risks is clear to everyone who enters the wine cellar
- ■ Good and clear access to the wine cellar is always maintained
- ■ Ventilation in the wine cellar is clear
- ■ Full wine bottles are stacked or stored in racks and handled safely
- ■ Empty wine bottles are stored appropriately
- ■ Eye protection and gloves are available and used for cleaning the wine cellar
- ■ Wine cellar door is securely fixed when open
- ■ Appropriate and effective lighting is in good working order
- ■ Evacuation procedure is situated on a wall that is easy to identify and to follow

CLEANING CHECKLIST

- ■ All flooring and surfaces are clean of wine and drink spillages
- ■ Personal protective equipment required for cleaning is correctly stored in a cabinet away from the wine storage area
- ■ All floor areas are clean and dry
- ■ All walls are clean and dry
- ■ All drains and gullies have been washed and no residual water or chemicals are left
- ■ The grilles of the cellar cooling grilles and external areas are clean and free of dust
- ■ Racks, shelves and the platforms that the wines bottles are laid in are clean and dry

ACTIVITY

1 Produce job task cards as a reference for new staff, covering the cleaning requirements of your wine cellar. Detail daily, weekly and specific cleaning activities and the health and safety issues attached to the duties.

2 Devise cleaning schedules for your staff to record the cleaning that they have carried out, requiring a date and signature from staff when the cleaning was carried out. You can use this record to monitor standards and staff performance.

3 Include the monitoring of the condition of the bottles and boxes of wine so that the staff will check for cracks and breakages in glass and inspection of exposed corks.

! REMEMBER

Have in place checking mechanisms to ensure that stock invoiced for has been delivered.

! REMEMBER

Before the delivery arrives:

- The delivery area should be clear
- Empties and returns are counted and set aside for collection
- Trolleys and lifting devices are available
- Safety is risk assessed e.g. tripping or slipping hazards, weights to be lifted
- The record of what was ordered is available to check against

RECEIVING WINE DELIVERIES

Wine stocks and counter dispense equipment are high-value items. If mistakes go unnoticed at the time of delivery, and your supplier is paid for the items that were not received, the profits are affected. There can also be a risk that poor checking systems encourage dishonesty, creating suspicion and harming working relationships.

Delivery preparation

The driver of the vehicle delivering your products will want to deliver quickly and move on to the next delivery. Receiving of the delivery and the return of unwanted stock needs to be done safely. Items should be checked upon delivery whilst the driver is still on site.

During delivery

Staff should be trained in safe methods of handling.

- Keep the area safe to move around in, both for your staff and the delivery staff
- Cellar flaps and hatches must be properly secured when open, with a safety barrier in place
- Leave the specialist tasks to the trained delivery crew
- Use lifting equipment if necessary

Checking and signing for deliveries

It is important that this procedure is followed correctly. Even if you have the same supplier and delivery staff regularly, it is a necessity to check and verify the delivery. Most suppliers refuse to consider claims for missing or faulty items unless it is identified at the point of delivery.

1 Collect the delivery note from the driver, sometimes the supplier may issue an invoice with delivery.

2 Check that the items on the delivery note correspond with what was ordered.

3 Staff should be aware that they must inform the supervisor/manager if the supplier has not delivered the quantity, brand or size requested. The supervisor will decide what items to accept. Alternative arrangements may have to be made to source some stock from an alternative supplier.

4 Check as each item is unloaded that the quality is acceptable. Examine the date mark, packaging and appearance of each item, that crates and boxes contain the amount stated, bottles are full and seals intact.

5 Put to one side any items which cannot be accepted.

6 Count the number of each item and tick off against the delivery note.

7 Record on the delivery note any discrepancies or shortfalls.

8 Sign the delivery note. In most cases the delivery note is a carbon and the supplier and customer retain a copy.

9 The customer copy should be sent immediately to the office/person that deals with the accounts.

Dealing with delivery problems

When items are not what were ordered – wrong size, brand or quality or quantity problem – the delivery note has to be altered so that the supplier and the customer paying the invoice know what has happened. Usually the delivery person will write changes on the delivery note, which is signed by them and the customer.

Some suppliers have returns notes for items not accepted at the point of delivery. The delivery person will complete this with the quantity and description or code number of each item, the reason for the return, and the customer details. If a returns note is given it should be attached to the delivery note and sent to the person/office dealing with accounts. Any disagreements with the delivery driver over quality or quantity or any other issue of the delivery should be resolved by the supervisor or manager.

STORING AND ISSUING THE WINE

Why is an efficient system for storing and issuing wine a priority for bar managers?

- If stored too long the quality of some wine might deteriorate

- Drink stock is valuable, tight control reduces the risks of items being stolen

- White wine and champagnes are preferred cool and chilled, less energy is required to get them to the correct service temperature if the cellar is cool

■ All drinks fall into the same category as food under food safety law, so the cellar and drinks storage areas have to meet the requirements for food premises. They must be kept clean and hygienic

■ Wine becomes 'light struck' when exposed to bright natural or fluorescent light. This is the primary reason to use darker glass for bottling, and if wine is bottled in clear glass you should exercise particular caution to keep it out of bright light

■ Store the wine either on its side or upside down if you want to keep it for any period of time. This will keep the cork wet and protect against oxygen. Keep it out of the light, as bright light will damage the wine

Controlling stock levels

In order that stock does not run out, and to avoid over-stocking it is usual to have a system in place of a minimum and maximum stock levels. An order is placed when the minimum level has been reached. This is managed normally by the supervisor, and is worked out so that there is time for new stock to come in before the product runs out.

Computer-based stock control systems are used in most organisations, to highlight what requires ordering. This is an efficient and quick way of ordering what is required. Some systems work on a re-order by barcode, or by the physical inputting of stock levels into a handheld device.

Older establishments may use a cellar book to record in coming and outgoing stock for each item, and the balance. From this the order is placed. The person responsible for the ordering will back up the information from any system with a physical check to see what is running low. There is also a double-check at monthly stock checks. Most computerised systems incorporate all stock movements, order requirements, delivery and invoice systems, all linked to the accounts person/office.

Monthly stock checks

This is a physical check of all stocks within the wine cellar and drink storage areas, normally carried out at the end of a 4-week period or the end of a calendar month. Figures are received from the dispense counter tills for the number of each product sold and compared with the stock in the storage areas and the amount of stock ordered within the month. This is a tight control to ensure that all security measures are in place and any discrepancies between what has been ordered and consumed are investigated. This is a further deterrent to prevent theft.

Issuing stock to the dispense counter

The issuing of beverages such as wine generally takes place at set times during the day and may require a requisition note signed by an authorised person. When stock is transferred from storage to sales point it may be entered onto the sales database depending on the system in use. The importance of recording the transfer of wine to the dispense counter only becomes necessary when either the person responsible for the stock changes or additional people has access to stock (i.e. bar staff). In these cases a duplicate copy of the transfer may be used, one for each party concerned.

MAINTAINING THE DISPENSE COUNTER

There is a variety of equipment found at the dispense counter for the making, selling and dispensing of cold beverages both alcoholic and non-alcoholic.

Bar coolers

While serving beer, lager or ale, draught or pilsner, take care of the temperature consideration for the customer. Different kinds of liqueur are enjoyed at different temperatures. While cooler temperatures are the norm, the customers are more often than not fastidious when it comes to the temperature range of their drinks.

Having a display that catches your customer's eye can translate into instant sales. So be particular with your display arrangement and ensure the right kind of bar equipment is used to give you a suitable mix of style and utility.

Beverage dispensing

This is a useful service aid for the quick and measurable service of beverages. Cold beverages that create cocktails can easily be stored in these dispensers that come with two to three dispenser options. Once stocked, these dispensing units can work through a large number of orders in a short span of time.

There is another set of cocktails and frozen drinks that require slush and frozen beverages for preparation. Adding a frozen beverage dispenser according to your sales mix can reduce cocktail preparation time significantly.

Bottle coolers

If there is a small space set aside for the dispense counter, an innovative piece of bar equipment that facilitates bottle storage and acts as a cooling device for accompaniments to drinks can also be placed underneath the counter. This system is stackable for bottled beer and wines that require a certain cold service temperature.

© ISTOCKPHOTO.COM/DAN IONUT POPESCU

Glass-washers

Managing the flow of glassware in any one service point can be a problematic affair. So how does one manage the numbers? Using disposable options is not usually a luxury one can afford in a small restaurant or bar business. The use of a glass-washer situated in the dispense bar or counter will maintain the effective flow of glassware for use during the service time.

Ice bins or ice-makers

In the business of serving cold drinks, there is an absolute requirement for the use of clean ice. However, a continual supply can be difficult with the refrigerator being opened frequently. The use of an ice bin or bucket is essential, but better still is the machine that produces ice and fits under the counter. These are ideal for parties where you cannot afford the time to keep running back into the kitchen for more ice cubes.

Dispense counter preparation checklist

This is an example of a checklist that the supervisor could use when preparing the dispense counter for each service session.

THE DISPENSE COUNTER	PREPARATION
Counter tops	Clean and remove all residues
Beer taps	Clean and remove all residues
Display shelves	Clean and remove all residues
Garnishes and accompaniments, hygienically presented	Prepare garnishes and store
Dispense counter stock	Check all stock and requisition stock
Storage shelves	Clean and remove all residues
Refrigerators	Clean and remove all residues from shelves, rotate stock and check use-by dates
Glasses	Wash and polish, where appropriate
Small equipment	Disassemble, clean, remove all residues, and reassemble
Bottle skips	Empty and wipe out
Point of sale	Obtain float
Staff	Check personal appearance, health and hygiene
Menus	If available, clean
Promotional displays	Clean and remove all residues and set up, where appropriate

Restocking the dispense counter

Before each main service period the stock in the dispense counter must be replenished.

Each of the dispense counter outlets has to stock a particular amount of each product: this is called *par stock*. At all times the stock must be kept at these levels. Par stock levels will have been decided by the management in order to have enough stock for the running of the dispense counter.

There are many systems that can be used when restocking the bar. Listed below are some of the steps involved.

- Check the stock that is already in the dispense counter
- Compare the amount of each stock item that is already in the dispense counter to the par stock figures
- If the stock on hand is less than the par stock, then that item must be ordered from the stores department
- Write the items needed into a requisition book and submit to the stores department

Rotating stock

When restocking the dispense counter it is necessary to make sure that any new stock is rotated with the old stock.

As discussed previously, the new stock should always be put to the back and the old stock put to the front. This is a system used in all bars and restaurants

The system is referred to as **FIFO – first in first out.** If the FIFO system is followed in conjunction with monitoring your sales, the products that you sell will always be of the freshest and highest quality. Always check for use-by dates as you are restocking to ensure that this quality level is always maintained.

Stocktake

A stocktake is a method used by the supervisor to monitor stock and the amount of money that should be returned for the stock and can be performed on a weekly, fortnightly or monthly basis, depending on the management system in place.

All stock must be counted. It is important to have an organised storage system to enable you to do this accurately. Two people should participate in stock-taking. One person will count out the number of items and the other person completes the records.

Stock should be called in shelf order and should also be recorded in that way. By doing this you ensure that all stock is recorded and none is missed.

Here is an example of a stocktake record sheet.

DATE		BAR OR DISPENSE COUNTER		STAFF MEMBER	
Beverage stocks					
Description of goods	Size	Brand name	Quantity	Cost price	Stock value

Opened bottles of beverages are recorded in tenths of a bottle. The way to achieve this is to lay the bottle on its side: it can then be divided into tenths.

Record the amount in the bottle. For example:

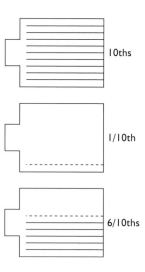

10ths

1/10th

6/10ths

Preparing garnishes for service

A garnish is a decoration. In any bar or dispense counter, many of the drinks served to customers are garnished. The best type of garnish is often a simple one; garnishes should not be overpowering to look at. If they are large and cumbersome they look unattractive and detract from the presentation of the drink rather than enhancing the presentation.

The garnish used on a drink will depend on the drink being served. Some drinks do not have garnishes. Scotch, Bourbon, Coke and wine are examples of drinks that are never garnished, unless they are used in a cocktail.

Your dispense counter should have a list of standard garnishes that are used for each particular beverage. Cocktails are usually served with more elaborate garnishes than other simple beverages. If a cocktail is not on your menu then you may have an optional garnish.

Some of the garnishes that can be used in a dispense counter are:

- Fresh fruits
- Powders and condiments, e.g. cinnamon, chocolate powder, Tabasco sauce
- Colourings mixed with sugars for the rims of glasses
- Non-edible items, e.g. plastic animals, umbrellas, straws

When choosing an optional garnish you should take into consideration:

- The flavour of the drink to be garnished
- The colour of the drink
- The concept of the drink

Handling garnishes

- Always use clean utensils when preparing garnishes
- Always check fruit to ensure that it is of good quality. Poor-quality fruit will only detract from the presentation of the drink
- Dispose of fruit that has spoiled or dried through exposure to air
- In powdered condiments such as coconut, salt, sugar, powdered chocolate, always look for foreign particles
- Never re-use swizzle sticks, umbrellas or fruit
- Always keep the garnish preparation areas clean and tidy
- If a garnish stains the cutting board make sure it is cleaned thoroughly
- Do not forget: bacteria lurk wherever food is prepared. Clean as you go and use hot soapy water

Check environmental control systems

- Environmental control systems include: heating, ventilation or air conditioning, lighting and music
- This equipment is all electrical therefore the plugs should be checked for any damage
- Heating, ventilation and air conditioning temperatures should be set to the required level should these be used
- Check all lighting switches for any malfunction

© ISTOCKPHOTO.COM

MAINTAINING THE DISPENSE COUNTER

> **! REMEMBER**
>
> The reason for using a garnish is to enhance the overall presentation of the drink to be served. This should ultimately increase sales through 'visual selling'.

> **! REMEMBER**
>
> When preparing garnishes it is important to remember that they should always be fresh and prepared hygienically. After preparation the garnishes should be covered, sealed and refrigerated if they are edible.

■ Music equipment should be checked prior to use

■ Adjust the volume after switching it on according to the required level

■ Make sure that after service all equipment and lights are switched off and secured from unauthorised access

■ Should any extension leads or cords be in areas where customers are, these must be secured in such a way not to cause any danger

ACTIVITY

Make a list of the environmental controls in your organisation, and what their optimum settings are.

TYPE	SETTING

Further reading and research

Lillicrap, D and Cousins, J. (2006) *Food and Beverage Service*, 7th ed. Hodder & Stoughton.

Davis, B. *et al.* (2008) *Food and Beverage Management*, 4th ed. Butterworth Heinemann.

Lichine, A. (1967) *Alexis Lichine's Encyclopedia of Wines and Spirits.* Cassell & Company Ltd. Chapter 6, pages 22–24.

Kramer, M. (2007) Seeking Closure. *The Wine Spectator* October, 36.

Food Hygiene Regulations http://www.opsi.gov.uk/si/si2005/20052059.htm

Manual Handling Regulations http://www.hse.gov.uk/pubns/indg143.pdf

Assessment of knowledge and understanding

You have now learnt about the responsibilities involved in maintaining the wine cellar and dispense counter operation, ensuring standards are maintained to provide the customer with the drink that they ordered, in the condition that they expect.

To test your level of knowledge and understanding, answer the following short questions. These will help to prepare you for your summative (final) assessment.

1 State three reasons why the wine cellar should be hygienically clean.

2 Describe three examples of good cleaning practices.

3 Why is regular stock-taking important? Describe how you would undertake a stocktake.

4 Describe how you would monitor your staffs' performance to ensure standards are maintained.

5 What systems would you have in place to ensure any wine quality issues are rectified before a customer has cause to complain?

6 List the checks needed to be in place to ensure stock that has been invoiced for has been received.

7 List five health and safety facts to consider when managing a cellar/drink store.

8 Consider the relationship required between the wine cellar staff and the dispense counter team.

9 Detail the outline of a contingency plan should a supplier fail to deliver.

10 Consider the role, as supervisor, that would play to ensure a smooth service for the customer in the event of the wine cellar losing power (electricity).

Research task

The new supervisor hired to look after the wine cellar and restaurant bar area soon realised that the stock control of the premises she was hired to manage was so disorganised that it was one of the reasons that custom was falling.

During the first audit it became clear that her team would order wine on an ad hoc basis without keeping any clear stock records. When deliveries arrived at the premises the staff appeared too busy to count the items or even check for quality and would simply sign the delivery note without checking the delivered products.

There were no monthly stocktakes and the wine stored in the cellars would reach 20°C. A recently installed EPOS system was not linked to any stock-taking system so that no stock reports seemed to exist.

Consider the implications of the situation described above in terms of:

1 Health and safety.

2 Sales control.

3 Quality of product.

What steps would you undertake to ensure that the quality of the service and product is not jeopardised?

20

Supervise vending services

HS16 Supervise vending services

LEARNING OBJECTIVES

This unit is about the maintenance of the vending service. It deals with the monitoring and supervision of the service and involves briefing staff on procedures and work schedules, reviewing sales, inspecting vending machines and dealing with problems. The unit covers work to ensure food is maintained and dispensed in the best possible condition, meets the necessary requirements for food standards and hygiene and is adjusted to cater for requirements.

After reading this chapter you will be able to:

■ Ensure staff follows procedures and work schedules to ensure the vending service complies with legislation and your organisation's policies.

■ Help to develop procedures and work schedules and ensure staff are updated on any new requirements.

■ Make sure the resources you need to maintain the vending service are available to your staff.

■ Carry out inspections to make sure procedures are being followed.

■ Monitor and review the service to identify how the service could be improved.

■ Take effective action to manage problems that may disrupt the vending service.

- Inform your staff and customers about any changes to the service that may affect them.
- Collect feedback on the service from staff and customers.
- Record information as required and make it available to the relevant people.

KEY WORDS

24-hour service
Round the clock continual service for consumers.

Food hazards
A hazard is anything that could cause harm to the consumer. There are three main hazards that may arise with food or drink from vending machines. These are contamination by:

- Bacteria or other micro-organisms that cause food poisoning
- Chemicals, for example, cleaning materials or pest baits
- Foreign materials such as glass, metal or plastic

Maintenance
Regular servicing and upkeep of the vending machine.

Merchandising
This refers to the methods, practices and operations carried out to promote and sell certain products.

Vending
A vending machine is a machine that provides various snacks, beverages and other products to consumers. The idea is to vend products without the use of a cashier. Items sold via vending machines vary by country and region.

INTRODUCTION

The style of organisation and type of service expected from your customers will determine to a large extent the delivery and service system requirements. Those where large numbers of people must be served quickly such as educational establishments, industrial plants and hospitals will usually provide a cafeteria-style service. However, automatic vending will be used as a supplement service for irregular hours catering such as a 24-hour service.

This chapter will consider the human resources involved in the vending service, as well as legislation, profitability, stock control, cleanliness and hygiene. It will ask you to consider a range of different outlets, not just the one you might be working in now, and to consider scenarios and solutions to the outcomes that may arise from being a supervisor in a vending service area.

Types of vending machine

There are basically four types of vending machine.

1. Beverage vending – can either mix ingredients to produce a specific beverage or will already have a pre-mixed beverage inside each cup to be selected.

2. Chilled food vending – can be for the selling of sandwiches and snack foods that require refrigeration.

3. Merchandise vending – these are usually glass-fronted vending machines so that the customer can view the products for sale. An example of this type is a vending machine selling confectionery.

4. Micro-vending system – this system provides a range of hot or cold foods from which the customer can make a selection and then heat in an accompanying microwave oven.

The role of a vending services supervisor

1. Monitors the daily activities of a vending operation.

2. Maintains records to ensure proper service of equipment and stocking procedures.

3. Supervises personnel in maintenance, repair and sanitation of equipment and in stocking and rotating products.

4. Supervises cash collections.

5. Trains and evaluates staff.

6. Assists in the development of proposals for new equipment.

7. Conducts test panels to obtain customer suggestions or reactions on products.

TYPES OF VENDING SERVICE TO CONSIDER

Knowing the right questions to ask, and choosing the right functions, is easy for those whose 'day job' is purchasing vending machines. Some of the following criteria may not apply to your operation, but the information below gives various guidelines that need to be considered when determining the right vending solution for your operation.

Small company: 30–50 personnel

Companies are typically looking to vending as an answer to ease of service and to health and safety concerns. Many have analysed the full savings vending offered over the 'kettle and cup' system and discovered that they can actually save money via the use of vending. Almost all companies want to manage drinks for staff and customers themselves – avoiding the need to schedule and pay for outside caterers – and are driven by relieving the burden and distraction for their staff.

Medium company: 50–250 personnel

Mid-sized companies are generally driven by two factors. Either they face the same issues identified by their smaller counterparts or their existing vending machine is unsatisfactory in terms of drinks and food quality or reliability. In the latter case the solution is all about discovering the optimum balance of quality drinks and food with reliable, low-maintenance machines.

Enterprise: 250+ personnel

The larger site typically employs a range of drinks and food solutions, combining cafeteria-based operations with 'local' vending machines throughout the site. The driver here is to achieve a quality level that is acceptable to a discerning employee base but that still offers the most efficient, low-maintenance operation.

> **TASK**
>
> Review the vending operation in your own place of work. Consider the types of service that may be provided from the information box above that could potentially stimulate a better service for your customers and help to stimulate higher sales.

THE CLEANING OF VENDING MACHINES

Good hygiene practice is required to be followed by all food handlers and servers. Regular cleaning and supply of stock is always required through demand and this might necessitate numerous daily visits to the vending machine to clean and restock the items that have been used. Staff should be trained in the techniques of cleaning and restocking of all types of vending machines. However, the following list of key features needs to be considered when undertaking this task.

1   Always try to clean and restock the vending machine when demand is at its lowest which will help to minimise potential loss of sales.

2   Always wear the correct protective clothing to minimise potential accidents or help to safeguard against spillages.

3   Where possible before cleaning the vending machine should be isolated from the mains supply to avoid any electrical accidents.

The vending service in a factory

VENDING MACHINE BUYERS' GUIDE

What are your criteria?

Work environment benefits

- Eliminate mess
- Reduce complaints
- Health and safety

Financial benefits

- Saves time
- Improves efficiency of the workforce
- Can replace water coolers

Staff benefits

- Quality branding of products
- Wide choice available
- Affordable drinks
- Reliability and consistency

Operational efficiency

- Quick to clean
- Quick to restock
- Rapid response service
- Reliable

4 The vending machine's supplier will always have a set of written recommendations and instructions for use, cleaning and maintenance. These should always be followed especially with reference to nominated cleaning agents.

5 Select the nominated cleaning agents and prepare them for use. Always ensure that the sanitisers and sterilisers are used correctly.

6 Temperatures must be monitored during this process to ensure that the limit has not been exceeded with reference to refrigeration temperatures and the temperatures for hot beverages and foods. The monitoring of temperatures should always be undertaken to assure the temperature limit is not surpassed. Food that has been exposed to unsafe temperatures should be discarded immediately.

7 Clean the vending machine according to the manufacturer's recommendations.

8 Dismantle any internal working parts for cleaning according to the health and hygiene standards.

9 Always wipe down the internal and external surfaces of the vending machine to maintain the clean outlook of the service. Ensure that the external surfaces are clean, dry and smear free.

10 Test the vending machine to ensure that it works correctly.

11 Complete any records especially those that the environmental health officer may want to inspect.

12 Always leave the area around the vending machine clear of any rubbish and in a clean condition.

> **! REMEMBER**
>
> It is important that the food safety management system is reviewed when new types of products are introduced to a vending system, different vending machines are used, or new types of clients acquired.

SUPERVISING THE VENDING OPERATION

There are a variety of duties that a vending supervisor must undertake in line with standard operating procedures.

Servicing issues

Servicing your vending machines will be a continuous problem. To maintain sales volume, you must keep the machines clean and supplied at all times. The frequency of refilling will depend on the number of machines you have and the amount of customer you have on a daily basis. In addition to keeping the machines supplied, you must ensure that certain cleanliness standards are maintained. For example, if you happen to have a cup-type vending machine as part of your operation, you should advise your member of staff to be careful when the machine is being filled. Any syrup that is spilled in the process will soon attract insects. Daily cleaning of the cup-drop will keep insects away and will help you to maintain an attractive and sanitary appearance for your customers.

Machine management and administration

■ Nominate and train key personnel to take responsibility for duties specifically related to vending machines

■ Encourage catering staff to see vending as a part of their overall service and recognise that there are substantial benefits to be gained from healthy vending

■ Check that the electrical supply is safe and secure

■ Establish a comprehensive maintenance and repair contract for the machine(s)

■ Ensure that common or recurring problems are understood and addressed to prevent a lack of confidence in the machine by users

■ Active and efficient management of the machine is needed to keep waste figures low

■ Provide large, secure, attractive litter bins for each vending machine

Marketing and promotion

■ Discuss and agree a marketing and promotion strategy to popularise the vending service and ensure that customers are involved in this process

■ Market through posters and newsletters where possible

Monitoring, evaluation and review

■ Regular and reliable data collection is essential to manage both choice and profitability of machines

■ Nominate and train specific personnel to collect and collate data in order to monitor the use and commercial success of the machine

FILLING A VENDING MACHINE

It is important to always supply enough stock to meet the demand of your customers. You should always carefully check the condition of all stock in the vending machine to ensure it is in the optimum condition. Key features of monitoring the stocking vending machines are:

1 Isolate the electricity supply for safety.

2 Remove and dispose of any stock that is in the vending machine that has passed its expiry date or is not in optimum condition.

3 Check the dates on all the stock and always place the older items at the front of the vending machine so that these are used first – following the principle of stock rotation.

4 Always supply enough stock to meet the demand and ensure that all labelling and packaging is correct.

5 Check the slow-selling items very carefully for the correct expiry dates on the packaging and for signs of deterioration in the commodity.

6 Refill all appropriate containers with the relevant powders and products and ensure that all correct cups, plates and napkins are available in or near the vending machines.

7 Check that the vending machine is in full working order.

8 Complete any records especially those that the environmental health officer may want to inspect.

With a service system that fulfils the cleaning and restocking, the following areas must also be covered by the supervisor to help ensure a smooth and responsive service to the clientele.

■ Provide a total beverage or snack vending service

■ Fill and maintain level of ingredients and vending cups and utensils

■ Clean and sanitise the whole machine to a very high standard on a regular basis

■ Attend to minor adjustments and maintain the vending quality for drinks and food

© ISTOCKPHOTO.COM/ANDREAS STEINHART

Coffee machine

! REMEMBER

The up-to-date results of the procedure must be available for inspection by an environmental health officer as required.

Charts which detail times and regularity of checks and cleaning will suffice when accompanied by supporting documents such as details of HACCP.

TASK

Design an organisational chart for your workplace taking into consideration the levels of management and supervisory support as well as the number of staff required to maintain the vending service.

■ Collect any cash and credit if applicable to the vending solution

■ Send monthly accounts showing machine sales and usage

THE PURCHASING ROLE OF THE SUPERVISOR

■ In some establishments you will have a purchasing manager – they will be in charge of the purchasing cycle and oversee its application and execution to all the departments in an establishment

■ However, where an establishment is not large enough to justify the role of the purchasing manager, you may find the roles subsumed into other job roles

■ For example:

● The senior chef will place orders with suppliers
● The restaurant manager or food and beverage manager will place orders too

■ As a supervisor you may find yourself involved in any number of the following aspects:

● Responsible for the management of purchasing, procurement and keeping purchasing records, recording the receiving and correct storage of goods
● The purchasing of all commodities for the vending service
● Ensuring continuity of supply of those items for the vending service
● Finding cheaper and more efficient sources of supply from time to time
● Keeping up to date with all the markets being dealt with and evaluating new products to maximise potential sales
● Research into products, markets, price trends and new technology
● Liaising with production, control, accounts and marketing departments
● Reporting to your line management through established communication channels

The procedure for purchasing stock

1 You will have established stock levels and a procedure for stock replacement. This may include requisition forms, but with modern computers and EPOS, the system may alert you to low stocks and orders will be raised automatically.

2 The selection of the source of supply is agreed in advance by the department manager and contracts made, which include:

(a) Price to be paid
(b) Delivery performance, particularly including time, date and place of delivery

3 The ordering process is electronic, by telephone or via written order.

4 The acceptance of goods ordered and the adjustments of any discrepancies in quality or quantity of goods ordered.

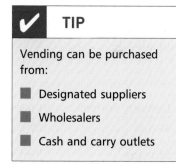

TIP

Vending can be purchased from:

■ Designated suppliers

■ Wholesalers

■ Cash and carry outlets

TIP

Establishing stock levels

- $M = W(T + L) + S$

  Where:

  M is the maximum stock level

  W is the average usage rate

  T is the review period (time interval)

  L is the lead time (time it takes for the order to arrive)

  S is the safety stock

ACTIVITY

Using the control chart try and create your own version for foods that must be kept chilled or frozen.

5 Checking the condition of packaging or containers and rejecting those not in good condition.

6 Transfer of commodities to the ordering departments or to stores.

Procedures for restocking the vending service

1 Requisition of drinks and food stock.

2 Requisition of associate consumables – milk, sugar, UHT cream, cups, cutlery, etc.

3 Rotate stock appropriate using first in first out (FIFO).

4 Reconcile float and takings if applicable.

5 Clean, tidy, wipe down and secure the vending machine.

6 Clean, wipe out and replenish stocks and display windows of the vending machine.

7 Switch on the vending machine and test for correct working.

Hazard analysis chart

A hazard analysis chart should be used to help with the maintenance, cleaning and supply of vending machines. The table is an example of the type of documentation to use for ambient temperature ingredients in vending machines.

PROCESS STEP	HAZARDS	CONTROLS	MONITORING	CORRECTIVE ACTION
Purchase of products	Presence of micro-organisms, toxins or foreign matter	Buy from a reputable supplier	Check supplier has accreditation from reputable audit organisation	Warn or change supplier
Delivery to the stores	Presence of foreign materials	Visual check of delivery vehicle	Delivery record check	Reject delivery
Storage	Pest infestation	Pest control in place FIFO in the warehouse	Pest control contract Warehouse check	Reject product Review with clerk
Transport to a vending machine	Presence of foreign materials	Vans cleaned to schedule	Cleaning record	Reject product Review with driver
Filling and cleaning vending machine	Microbiological growth in machine	Operator trained to clean properly and with sufficient frequency	Operators audited	Retrain operator Clean machine
Storage and dispensing	Microbiological contamination of water	Connect to a source of drinking water	Site survey form ensures water source is drinking water	Disconnect machine

THE DISPLAY OF VENDING GOODS

During the restocking of the vending machine it is important that you consider how the vending goods should be displayed. With a vibrant display of the goods contained in the machine it is probable that this form of marketing will help to increase sales.

© ISTOCKPHOTO.COM/SHAWN GEARHART

If certain products have sold out and suitable replacement products are used it is important to provide correct information on the vending machine to inform the customer of the change of product. The label must be visible at all times so an informed selection can be made.

The use of menus can be employed to help give information to customers, and these have become a successful way of selling products in sophisticated vending machines which sell hot and cold meals.

Some vending machines have computerised displays which will give price information. The operator should always check that these prices are correct alongside any pricing information that may also be displayed.

TASK

Remember an experience where there was a poor vending service.

Remember an experience where there was a good vending service.

Describe the:

- Quality – brands used, flavour, etc.
- Speed of service
- Ease of control of the machine
- Cleanliness of the machine and service area
- Occasion – why did you use the service?

As a supervisor:

1 How can you:

   (a) Control the quality of the product available?

   (b) Improve the speed of service?

   (c) Increase the cleanliness?

2 What other things might be missing that could impact on the ease of controlling the vending operation?

Assessment of knowledge and understanding

You have now learnt about some key elements involved in the vending service – including the setting up of the area, the cleaning of it, some aspects in relation to the control of stock and hazard analysis. As we have worked through the chapter we have also discussed some elements of supervising the vending service. To test your level of knowledge and understanding further, answer the following short questions. These will help to prepare you for your summative (final) assessment.

Legislation

1   What are the consequences if should choose to deviate from any of the aspects of legislation laid out earlier in the chapter?

2   What policies and procedures does your organisation have in relation to legislation?

Purchasing

1   What are the main requirements of the purchasing function in the vending service?

2   What are the main objectives in relation to the purchasing of ingredients for a vending machine?

3   How can stock control improve profitability?

Clearing and cleaning the drink service area

1   List the resources required to service your vending service area. Now consider, is there anything missing? How would you go about requesting the missing equipment? What policies and procedures do you need to follow?

2   How can the roles of your team be allocated effectively to individuals to ensure service standards are met?

3   Are there any contingency plans in place for when the vending service has broken down? If yes, what are they? Are there any missing? If no, what contingency plans would you consider putting in place?

Research task

Your organisation has used the services of a small counter system to serve tea, coffee and home-made sandwiches. This is an accepted system and the person who runs and delivers the service is also popular and has been employed in this role for many years.

However, this person is about to retire and your managers are considering replacing this service with a vending operation.

Write a brief plan which considers both the process that you would use to implement the new vending system and the potential issues you might face when undertaking this task.

21

Supervise linen services

HS18 Supervise linen services

LEARNING OBJECTIVES

This unit is about the maintenance of the linen service. Guests expect clean, fresh linen during their stay. The linen service has the responsibility for making sure that this happens, and that guests expectations are met, or exceeded. This unit deals with the preparation, supervision and review of the service, involving the planning of equipment and supplies, preparing staff rotas and briefing staff and collecting customer feedback.

After reading this chapter you will be able to:

■ Allocate staff and brief them on duties, relevant procedures and any variations relating to their work routines.

■ Make sure staff have the skills, knowledge and resources when they are needed to carry out their duties.

■ Encourage staff to ask questions if there is information that they do not understand.

■ Ensure staff conduct and presentation promotes goodwill and understanding with customers and complies with organisational policy and legal requirements.

■ Monitor and review procedures to ensure the linen service meets the needs of customers and complies with relevant legislation and organisational policy.

■ Inform your staff and customers about any changes to the service that may affect them.

■ Collect feedback on the service from staff and customers.

■ Take effective action to manage problems that may disrupt the linen service when they occur.

■ Pass on feedback and recommend improvements to the relevant people according to your organisation's requirements.

■ Complete records to support the service according to your organisation's procedures.

KEY WORDS

Contingency
The possibility of an eventuality. Back-up plans.

Durable
Tough, hard-wearing and long-lasting.

Hired
On loan, not belonging to the organisation.

Inanimate load
A lifeless load, often heavy.

Inventory
A record, list or account.

Logo
Badge or symbol of the organisation.

Synthetic
Man-made fibre.

INTRODUCTION

The management of linen services can cover bed linen, towels, shower curtains, restaurant table linen, uniform and guest laundry. In all establishments the service is to provide clean, well-laundered linen to the bedroom and restaurant staff.

As with all services, the impression it leaves with guests is vital. Beds should be made with clean, crisp linen and towels arranged in bathrooms inviting use.

BED LINEN

The fabric for bed sheets and pillowcases is usually a blend of cotton and polyester. Items made solely of cotton are not recommended for commercial use because they are not as durable as those with blended synthetic fibres. Usually sheets with a blend of cotton and polyester withstand over 500 washes.

The way fabrics are woven is an indicator of quality. Before linens are sold to commercial buyers, the fabric is normally washed.

Sheets and pillowcases must fit the mattresses and pillows they are to cover. It is beneficial to standardise mattresses and pillows to limit the number of sizes, to minimise the cost of sorting, counting and storing them.

Bed linen

Common bed linen sizes

SHEETS	SIZE (INCHES)
Twin	66 × 104
Double	81 × 104
Queen	90 × 108
King	108 × 110

PILLOWCASES	SIZE (INCHES)
Standard	20 × 30
Large	20 × 40

CONSIDER

Consideration is required when choosing the colour of linen. White bed linen gives a clean, crisp appearance and is durable to washing processes.

ACTIVITY

Devise a checklist to form part of the induction for new staff, detailing the different sizes and types of linen your establishment uses.

BATH LINEN

Towels and bath mats are made of a pile fabric with loops on both sides, called towelling. The quality of the towel is determined by the weight of the item. The heavier the item, the thicker it will be.

Common bath linen sizes

TOWELS	SIZE (INCHES)
Bath towel	20 × 40
Bath sheet	24 × 50
Hand towel	16 × 26
Bath mat	18 × 24

! REMEMBER

Thick, fluffy towels in a bathroom give the feeling of luxury. Consideration should be given to the colour, to maintain the look of luxury. Dark-coloured towels fade quickly through washing processes.

Bath towels

! REMEMBER

Have good housekeeping standards, check the condition of the shower curtains after each departure.

! REMEMBER

Ensure your staff are trained to handle linen. Linen can be extremely heavy and staff should be trained in moving and handling of inanimate loads.

 **ACTIVITY**

Within your organisation, find out who is responsible for linen services, and plot on your organisation's structure chart.

Shower curtains

Most shower curtains are made of synthetic fibres, such as vinyl or nylon. Nylon curtains are resistant to mildew and are less likely to become brittle after washing.

LINEN SERVICES RESPONSIBILITIES

In most establishments linen services is the responsibility of the head housekeeper/manager. The distribution of linen services is normally covered by linen porters or housekeeping staff.

In hotels that use a laundry company for the supply of their linen, the linen/housekeeping staff will be responsible for:

■ Receiving linen and housekeeping deliveries
■ Counting and checking linen
■ Keeping linen records in good order
■ Storing linen and keeping the linen storage area in good condition

Depending on the size of the establishment, the usage of linen can be of considerable amounts. In establishments with restaurants, coffee shops, room service and banquet services, the amount of napkins and tablecloths used can be substantial.

Tablecloths

TABLE LINEN

Like bed linens, blended fabrics last longer than just cotton materials. The size of a tablecloth should be level with the chair's seat or fall to at least 12 inches below the table's edge.

 **ACTIVITY**

Devise a system so that staff can easily identify which cloth to use on which table. Colour-coding the labels can ease identification.

COMMON TABLECLOTH SIZES

TABLE CLOTHS	SIZE (INCHES)
Table for 2	54 × 54
Table for 4	64 × 64
Table for 6	72 × 72
Table for 8	90 × 90

PURCHASING VS HIRING OF LINEN ITEMS

The following options are available to establishments regarding the linen stocks:

1 Purchase of own linen and washing facilities on site.
2 Purchase of own linen and a contractor collects soiled linen for laundering off-site.
3 Linen is hired and washed by the contractor.

Purchase of own linen and washing facilities on site

Smaller establishments prefer this option. The main factors to consider when purchasing linen are the durability of the linen, laundering costs and the cost per item price. Although the life expectancy of an item can be pre-established by the manufacturer, the final results are generally determined by the chemicals used to launder the item and the number of times it is washed.

> **! REMEMBER**
>
> Hotel-owned linen with a logo is often attractive to guests as a souvenir.

Purchase of own linen and a contractor collects soiled linen for laundering off-site

This option reduces the cost of a laundry/washing facility on-site, and through the service specification the establishment can determine stock levels, delivery and collection times. The finish of the linen can also be determined.

If the contractor provides a wash service to similar establishments, with the same type of linen, losses of stock may occur with your linen being sent to other establishments. This would create additional costs by having to replace stock on a regular basis.

>  **ACTIVITY**
>
> Write a service specification for a laundry company detailing the requirements of your service.

> **! REMEMBER**
>
> To aid the laundry contractor, ensure that your linen is labelled with your establishment's name or logo.

> **TASK**
>
> Have a system in place to record the number of items sent to the contractor's laundry and the number of clean items returned.
>
> Keep to one side any linen items returned that do not belong to your establishment. Discuss with the contractor how this has happened and the likelihood that your stock is being sent to other establishments.

Linen is hired and washed by a contractor

This option can be the most efficient service, but comes with a premium cost. Stock items, levels, finish and delivery/collection times can be agreed with the contractor. The contractor is responsible for maintaining stock levels in the event of losses or damage.

> **TASK**
>
> Have in place a contingency plan to cope with the supplier failing to deliver. Ensure your staff know what to do.

STOCK LEVELS

All establishments must hold sufficient linen inventory to ensure that sheets, pillowcases, towels, bath mats, napkins and tablecloths are available when needed.

Linen

© ISTOCKPHOTO.COM/KAY RANSOM

When setting stock levels the following factors should be considered:

- The size of the establishment
- Occupancy rates
- Restaurant usage
- The number of times the sheets are changed in guest rooms

In normal circumstances the following stock level would be in place:

- A supply of linen in all bedrooms available for occupancy
- A supply of linen on the restaurant tables
- A supply of linen in the store cupboards, at floor level if applicable
- One supply being washed
- One supply in reserve (contingency)

REMEMBER

Insufficient stock creates complaints and additional work for staff.

Most organisations use two sheets per bed and provide two bath towels, two hand towels and one bath mat.

ENVIRONMENTAL FACTORS

Bed linen and towels are changed frequently in guest rooms. This is expensive and not very environmentally friendly.

Many hotels have introduced a towel exchange system, where guests are asked to leave their towels hanging on the towel rail if they wish to use them again or leave them in the bath or on the floor if they would like them replaced.

Reducing the amount of linen and towels laundered:

- saves water, energy and laundry chemicals
- reduces the amount of water in the laundry process

ACTIVITY

Considering the above stock levels, how much linen would be required for a 200-bedded hotel with 75 twin rooms and 125 double rooms?

ACTIVITY

Design the signage you would have in the bathroom to be effective in getting the environmentally friendly message across to the guests.

QUALITY

We have already established the necessity to ensure the items purchased withstand the use and washing processes. Quality check within a laundry process should consist of:

- Quality of the items purchased
- Number of times the items are used

■ The washing processes

■ The chemicals used for the washing processes

■ Tests to maintain whiteness

If an external contractor provides your establishment with a linen service, your service specification should include audits of the premises. These can either be carried out by a third party with technical knowledge or by the establishment carrying out their own audits. The audits should include:

■ The cleanliness of the laundry

■ Staff training

■ Temperature checks of the water used in the washing process

■ The segregation of clean and dirty linen

■ Maintenance records of the laundry equipment

■ Technical reports on the whiteness achieved for sheets, towels and pillowcases

■ Technical reports on the softness of items

■ The sorting process of each organizations' linen

■ The process for dealing with damaged/condemned linen

Further reading and research

Colin Dix and Chris Baird (1998) *Front Office Operations*, 4th edn. Longman.

Jeremy Huyton and Sue Baker (2001) *Principles of Front Office Operations*, 2nd revised edn. Thomson Learning.

Denney G. Rutherford and Michael J. O. Fallon (2006) *Hotel Management and Operations*, 4th edn. John Wiley and Sons.

Peter Jones and Andrew Lockwood (2002) *Management of Hotel Operations*, 3rd revised edn. Thomson Learning.

For the best practice in laundry processes refer to the hospital laundry arrangements for used and infected linen, NHS Guidelines HSG 95 (18).

Assessment of knowledge and understanding

You have now learnt about supervising the linen service to ensure that it has all the necessary staff, equipment and supplies. You know how to ensure that procedures are in place for the running of the service and that staff conduct themselves appropriately.

To test your level of knowledge and understanding, answer the following short questions. These will help to prepare you for your summative (final) assessment.

1 What are the advantages of purchasing bed linen made of cotton/polyester blends?

2 How would you ensure that new staff were trained to understand the correct tablecloth sizes?

3   List the advantages of an on-site laundry.

4   What are the advantages of an off-site laundry?

5   What are the key points when auditing an external laundry company?

6   How would you ensure items of linen maintain a high standard?

Research task

Visit an establishment with an on-site laundry, and a site with a commercial laundry off-site.

Write a service specification for a commercial laundry to supply your establishment's linen requirements.

Design an audit check sheet that you would like to use to ensure your linen is of the quality and standard you require.

22

Monitor and solve customer service problems

LEARNING OBJECTIVES

This unit is about the part of your job that involves solving immediate customer service problems. It is also about changing systems to avoid repeated customer service problems.

After reading this chapter you will be able to:

- Solve immediate customer service problems.
- Respond positively to customer service problems following organisational guidelines.
- Solve customer service problems when you have sufficient authority.
- Work with others to solve customer service problems.
- Keep customers informed of the actions being taken.
- Check with customers that they are comfortable with the actions being taken.
- Solve problems with service systems and procedures that might affect customers before they become aware of them.
- Inform managers and colleagues of the steps taken to solve specific problems.
- Identify repeated customer service problems.
- Identify the options for dealing with a repeated customer service problem and consider the advantages and disadvantages of each option.
- Work with others to select the best option for solving a repeated customer service problem, balancing customer expectations with the needs of your organisation.

■ Obtain the approval of somebody with sufficient authority to change organisational guidelines in order to reduce the chance of a problem being repeated.

■ Action your agreed solution.

■ Keep your customers informed in a positive and clear manner of steps being taken to solve any service problems.

■ Monitor the changes you have made and adjust them if appropriate.

KEY WORDS

Incentives
Payment or concession to stimulate greater output by workers.

Inputs
The resources needed to carry out a process or provide a service.

Mystery shoppers
Mystery dining is about giving restaurants genuine and objective customer feedback. To be a successful mystery diner, you'll need to demonstrate your commitment and interest in giving detailed, fair and objective feedback.

Outputs
Products, services or information supplied to meet customer's needs.

Policy
A plan or course of action, especially one of an organisation or government; a course of action thought to be prudent or advantageous.

Procedure
A particular course of action intended to achieve a result.

Service quality framework
A conceptual framework for understanding quality of service.

SERVQUAL
Or RATER is a service quality framework. It allows service providers to assess the quality of their service offerings by asking customers to react to a series of statements in five areas of performance: reliability, responsiveness, assurance, empathy and tangibles.

Total quality management
Total quality management (TQM) is a comprehensive and structured approach to organisational management that seeks to improve the quality of products and services through ongoing refinements in response to continuous feedback.

INTRODUCTION

Customer service is the single most important aspect of your business. Why? Because if the customer is not happy or satisfied with the service and product that they received they will not return. It is also likely that they will tell friends, colleagues and acquaintances about their experience too. It is a well-known fact that an unsatisfied customer will tell more people about their experience than a satisfied customer.

A satisfied customer will return to your business and bring their friends the next time.

This chapter will consider what customer service is as well as illustrate how to manage and deal with customer service problems effectively. It will help you to find ways to monitor customer service and to train your team to embrace customer service.

WHAT IS CUSTOMER SERVICE?

Customer service is a series of activities designed to enhance the level of customer satisfaction – that is, the feeling that a product or service has met the customer expectation.

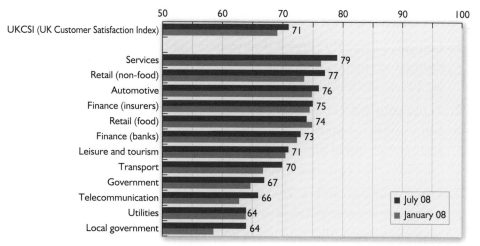

A government statistical analysis of customer satisfaction for two months in 2008

Common mistakes made in customer service

■ **Untrained staff.** It does not matter whether you have 2 or 200 employees, you *must* train everyone in the art of customer service. Customers and clients will not tolerate rudeness, incorrect information, or apathy on the part of your staff

■ **Trying to win the argument.** It is worth remembering that it takes five times more effort and cost to gain one new customer than it takes to maintain one current customer. Therefore, to win an argument and lose a steady customer, you are punishing your business

■ **Inaccessibility.** If you want to see repeat business, you need to be accessible to your customers. If it is difficult to contact the customer service department or speak to a manager, customers may not return

■ **Standing by your policy.** While the person who is scared that they may lose their job can say 'That's our policy', customer service representatives and managers should be able to find ways to bend policies to build customer relationships. The phrase 'If I do that for you, I'll have do to it for everyone', is one of the fastest way to lose customers

■ **Unfulfilled promises.** If you promise a customer that something would be ready by Thursday, then it should be there by Thursday. When you cannot make this happen, do not make excuses; the only words you need to remember are 'We're sorry', backed up by an extra effort to make the customer happy

■ **The runaround.** People do not like being passed from one person to another or sent from one person or department to another

■ **Failure to listen.** Staff routinely do not listen closely to customers. Typically they respond with an answer that does not match the problem because they were not paying attention

■ **Forgetting the basics.** 'Please', 'thank you', 'we're sorry about the inconvenience', and so on are simple phrases that cost nothing, take little effort and win big points

Ten rules for great customer service

1 **Commit to quality service.** Everyone in the company needs to be devoted to creating a positive experience for the customer. Always try to go above and beyond customer expectations.

2 **Know your menus.** Convey a clear and in-depth knowledge of products and services to win customer trust and confidence. Know your products and services inside and out. Where possible, foresee the types of questions that customers will ask.

3 **Know your customers.** Try to learn everything you can about your customers in order to tailor your service approach to their needs. Talk to customers about their experience with your company, and listen to their complaints.

4 **Treat people with courtesy and respect.** Remember that every time that you, your employees and your colleagues make contact with a customer the interaction leaves an impression with that customer.

5 **Never argue with a customer.** You know very well that the customer isn't always right. However, it is important that you do not focus on the missteps of a particular situation; instead, concentrate on how to fix it.

6 **Don't leave customers in limbo.** Call-backs, and emails need to be handled with a sense of urgency. Customers want immediate resolution, and if you can give it to them, you will probably win their repeat business.

7 **Always provide what you promise.** Fail to do this and you'll lose both credibility and customers.

TIP

Research shows that the instance of repeat business goes up to 95 per cent when complaints are resolved on the spot.

8 **Assume that your customers tell the truth.** Even though it may appear that customers lie to manipulate a situation to their advantage, it is to your advantage to give them the benefit of the doubt.

9 **Focus on making customers — not on sales.** Staff who get paid on commission sometimes focus on the volume of sales instead of on the quality of the sale.

10 **Make it easy to buy.** The buying experience should be as easy as possible. Eliminate unnecessary paperwork and forms, help people to find what they need, explain how products work, and do whatever else you can to make a transaction easy.

WHAT IS SO IMPORTANT ABOUT CUSTOMER SERVICE ANYWAY?

> **! REMEMBER**
>
> Research shows that it costs six times more to attract a new customer than it does to keep an existing one.

TASK

1 Describe a time when you received excellent customer service.

2 Describe a time when you received terrible customer service.

3 Describe a time when you received average customer service.

In carrying out this task try to recollect:

- The place
- Time of day
- Occasion
- Describe the member of staff in terms of their personality, mannerisms, etc.

4 In recollecting the average or terrible customer service experience, did you complain? If you did.

- How was it handled?
- Did you leave content?
- How many people (friends, colleagues, etc.) did you tell?

5 In your role as a supervisor, what changes would you make to your own staff and their service provision in order to give excellent service and make amends for poor service?

6 Finally, which of the instances above was more easy to remember and which one of the instances above were you able to provide more information for?

Consumer protection

The United Kingdom has several Acts of Parliament that protect the customer/consumer. These include:

- Misrepresentations Act 1967
- Unfair Contract Terms Act 1977
- Sale of Goods Act 1979
- Consumer Protection Act 1987

- Unfair Terms in Consumer Contracts Regulations 1999
- Consumer Protection (Distance Selling) Regulations 2000
- Electronic Commerce Regulations 2002
- General Product Safety Regulations 2005

The most important of these is the **Consumer Protection Act 1987**. Key elements to this Act include:

- Part 1 implemented European Community (EC) Directive 85/374/EEC, the product liability directive, by introducing a regime of strict liability for damage arising from defective products
- Part 2 created government powers to regulate the safety of consumer products through Statutory Instruments
- Part 3 defined a criminal offence of giving a misleading price indication

Customer service policy and procedures

In changing the way you operate internally to improve customer service you will want to refer to or create a customer service policy.

Here are some basic policies you should establish and enforce:

1 **Courtesy is the most important aspect of customer service.** All customers should be treated in a courteous manner at all times. This may sound obvious, but how many times have you experienced the rude sales-person who snaps or loses their patience quickly or is not interested in you?

2 **Be professional when on the sales floor.** All employee breaks and personal business should be conducted out of the view of customers.

3 **Go the extra mile for a customer.** A conscious effort should be made to assist a customer in finding what they need and/or in resolving a problem. If there is a policy, it should be stated politely. There is no room in customer service for 'attitude'.

4 **Dress appropriately.** Employees dealing with customers are expected to present themselves in a professional manner and dress accordingly.

5 **Develop a connection with the regulars.** Encourage your staff to get to know regular customers, greet them when they come in, and make them feel comfortable.

6 **Have resources readily available.** There's no better way to kill a sale then being unable to find what you need. Make sure you maintain your stock.

7 **Train and retrain.** It is very important that you train your staff in the manner that you want them to interact with customers and conduct themselves while at work. Since it is human nature to slip and revert to bad habits, to retrain occasionally allows for new ideas and reinforces positive conduct. Work with your employees, use role play and seek out their input.

8 **Don't let your staff become slaves to your computers.** Streamline your process to the best of your ability.

TASK

Does your company have a policy for customer service?

If it does can you describe the key elements of it?

How does the company reinforce the message about their customer service policy?

How do they encourage staff to engage with the policy and exel in providing customer service?

TIP

The more involved your team feel in creating the policy, the more pride they will take in providing quality customer service.

Organisational procedures for dealing with customer service problems

What happens in your workplace when a customer complains?

■ Do you all run around in a blind panic?

■ Does the waiter automatically get the supervisor?

■ Do you ignore the customer and hope they go away?

■ Or do you have a procedure....? For example **'The 6 R's'**

1 Remove – the offending item – meal, drink, bug, unclean linen, etc.

2 Replace – the removed item with a new menu item, drink, towels, sheets, room.

3 Refund – the offending item off the guest's bill.

4 Report – the incident to the supervisor/manager – write it in a book that reports complaints.

5 Rectify – return to the customer to ensure they are now happy. In addition add something complimentary – desserts or coffees for the party, a fruit bowl through room service or a chilled bottle of wine.

6 Review – the complaints each day/week and summarise the key areas of concern/complaint from customers. How can these be avoided in future?

Organisational procedures and systems for identifying repeated customer service problems

Do you have a method by which you record customer complaints in your place of work?

For example:

■ A log book in each department

■ A central log book – it might even be electronic

■ The duty manager's diary

■ Or?

How often is this log reviewed? How often do you think it should be reviewed?

■ Daily

■ Weekly

■ Monthly

■ Never

Example of a customer complaint form found on the Internet

Hotel Complaint Form

Name: [   ]

Email Address
(not a psaairlines.net address): [   ]

Room Number: [   ]

Date of Stay: [   ]

Hotel Issue: ☐ Rooms ☐ Food ☐ Security/Safety ☐ Transportation

Hotel Issue: [   ]

Did you address this issue with
the hotel's management? [Yes ▾]

What was the hotel's response? [   ]

Evidence: Please attach up to three files supporting your case.

Please be patient after hitting the submit button as large file uploads may take a few moments.

[Submit Complaint] [Reset Form]

Note how the complaint form also gives an opportunity for the customer to submit photos as part of the evidence.

What should happen when the records are reviewed and it appears there are a number of complaints about the same thing?

TASK

These could be considered through a role play activity where you work in threes – one is the customer, one is the member of staff and one is the observer who can reflect on how the complaint was handled.

Whoever plays the customer – be as difficult as possible with **some** of these in order to challenge the member of staff in how they deal with a complaint.

What would you recommend as a solution for the following complaints?

1 'The steak is too tough.'

2 'The towels are not clean.'

3 'My room has not been thoroughly vacuumed.'

4 'There is lipstick still on the glass from the last user.'

5 'This doesn't taste fresh.'

6 'There is a caterpillar in my salad.'

7 'There was too much noise rising from the function room below last night – I couldn't sleep.'

8 'I had to wait over an hour from ordering my room service to it being delivered.'

9 'The staff in the brasserie look miserable.'

10 'My complaint was ignored.'

GROUP PROBLEM-SOLVING

TECH SKILLS ✓

It is useful to look at complaints as a group or team so that you are all focused on the same goal and all have the opportunity to be innovative and creative in considering how you handle complaints and problems.

ADVANTAGES TO SOLVING A PROBLEM AS A GROUP	DISADVANTAGES TO SOLVING A PROBLEM AS A GROUP
■ No matter how much knowledge a single person brings to the task, the total information possessed by all members of the group is bound to be greater	■ Groups tend to make decisions prematurely. If members suggest several solutions, the first solution to gain a majority support may be adopted even though the winning of the support may be due to the skill of the presenter rather than the quality of the suggestion
■ Groups can suggest more approaches to a problem. There is no way of knowing beforehand which approach will achieve the best or desired results. The more approaches considered the greater the chance of finding the best solution	■ Group discussions can be dominated by a designated or undesignated leader
■ Group problem-solving increases the chance that decisions or solutions will be accepted.	■ Members of the group eventually become committed to a plan as a way of solving a situation and alternative solutions may not always be heard
■ People are more likely to know and understand a decision and its outcome when they have helped to make it	■ Some group members may already be committed to a particular solution and argue strongly for it without considering the merits of later ideas

DO	DON'T
Listen and pay attention to what others have to say	Vote – this divides people into winners and losers
Try and get underlying assumptions out into the open	Make early, quick, easy agreements and compromises
Encourage others, particularly the quieter ones, to offer ideas	Foster internal competition
Treat differences of opinion as a way to gather additional information, clarify issues and force the group to seek better information	Railroad the group into agreeing with your thoughts and ideas

Negotiating and reassuring customers while problems are being solved

Handling the complaint

1 Do not interrupt the customer – let them have their say and make their point.

2 Apologise – but only for the specific problem or complaint.

3 Restate the complaint briefly back to the customer to show you have listened and understood.

4 Agree by thanking the customer for bringing this matter to our attention. This shows you are looking at the problem from the customer's perspective.

5 Act quickly, quietly and professionally.

Never:

■ Lose your temper

■ Take it personally

■ Argue

■ Blame another member of staff or another department

While the complaint is being dealt with assure the customer of the following:

■ Explain how you are going to redress the problem

■ Explain to the customer how they should then feel

■ Check that the customer is happy with the solution and whether they require anything further in order to improve the situation

■ Explain to the customer how long this is going to take

- If this is going to take a period of time, say more than an hour, check back with them every so often to update them on how far along you are in solving the problem
- Reassure them of the final deadline by which the problem will be solved

TIPS FOR EFFECTIVE NEGOTIATION

PREPARE FOR NEGOTIATION	USE COMMUNICATION SKILLS TO OPTIMISE OUTCOMES, INCLUDING:
■ Clarify interests of guests and the organisation	■ Appropriate non-verbal communication
■ Gather essential information including evidence and logs	■ Appropriate language
■ Prioritise goals	■ Questioning
■ Select appropriate style and strategy – calm and friendly or aggressive and rigid	■ Clarifying
	■ Summarising
■ Assess bargaining power – who has the upper hand and what do you have to offer the person you are negotiating with?	■ Conflict resolution
	■ Reach a mutually satisfying agreement
	■ Confirm the areas of agreement
■ Consider influencing factors including time, personalities and cost precedents	■ Record the agreement

How can effective dealing of customer service contribute to loyalty from external customers and improve working relationships with internal customers?

Much of this chapter so far has dealt with our external customers. They bring in the business and the success of their experience in our workplace leads to the profitability of the organisation. However, there is also the internal customer – yes, that is you and your team. It is just as imperative that you are well looked after and have few complaints in your workplace. A happy member of staff generally means a happy customer.

So how can we monitor happy customers and happy staff? Well, there are two quality systems – SERVQUAL for the external customer and TQM (total quality management) for the internal customer.

SERVQUAL

SERVQUAL is a process of checking that the operation has performed to the plan – first that the process has been carried out correctly and then that the outputs or outcomes of the operation can be checked.

This generally involves periodic inspection and checks whether procedures are being followed as opposed to controlling the process when it happens.

The method used is a walk-through-audit for each department/operation. The key aspects of service interaction are then recorded and a detailed checklist prepared to cover all those aspects. Each heading can have a series of items to be checked.

By monitoring the process, the quality of service delivery can be checked to ensure it is performing to the required standards.

This is often monitored in operations through the use of mystery shoppers or mystery diners who visit the unit as a normal customer but prepare a report on their experiences against established criteria. Companies then often use this to prepare league tables of top performing outlets and use incentives to motivate.

TQM

Total quality management is a combination of quality control and quality assurance – it looks at approaches to inspecting the quality of the finished product or service.

Quality inspection finds defects in a product or service before it reaches the customer by introducing an inspection stage. There needs to be a specification of what the product should be like for comparison with the product that has been produced and is being checked. The checking of the product is generally carried out by staff and where problems are found the product will be rejected.

REFLECTION

SERVQUAL was developed by Parasuraman, Zeithaml and Berry in 1986.

It was originally measured on 10 aspects of service quality: reliability, responsiveness, competence, access, courtesy, communication, credibility, security, understanding or knowing the customer and tangibles.

It measures the gap between customer expectations and experience.

By the early nineties the authors had refined the model to the useful acronym RATER:

- Reliability
- Assurance
- Tangibles
- Empathy and
- Responsiveness

TIP

Blueprinting service quality

Focus mainly on the 'touch points' at which the customer interfaces with the service providers.

Enhance the blueprint by looking at the sensory side of the customer experience. At each stage of the experience what does the customer see, hear, smell, touch or taste?

Look at the process. Look at the customer chain and understand how customers relate to the process.

Quality control centres on inspection but recognises the need for a detailed specification and that quality checks should be made throughout the production process, not just at the end. The emphasis is still on finding the problems and fixing them, but it will not improve the product or service if it has gone wrong – it will just highlight that there is a problem.

Quality assurance recognises the inefficiencies of waiting for mistakes to happen and strives to design quality into the process so that things cannot go wrong or if they do they are identified and corrected as they happen. The emphasis is now on prevention rather than inspection and sees the introduction of a number of tools and techniques to support this.

Total quality management focuses on the customer and the scale and nature of internal and external involvement. The driving force behind TQM is the satisfaction of customer needs. Anything that gets in the way of delivering customer satisfaction should be removed: this can include suppliers as well as the whole organisation. TQM places emphasis:

- On the people in the organisation and their roles
- Through a broadening of their outlook and skills
- Through encouraging creativity, training and empowerment
- Measuring performance and finding ways to improve it

ISO 9000

ISO 9000 is a group of standards used for quality management systems. ISO 9000 is maintained by ISO, the International Organisation for Standardization, and is administered by accreditation and certification bodies. A company or organisation that has been independently audited and certified to be in conformance with ISO 9001 may publicly state that it is 'ISO 9001 certified' or 'ISO 9001 registered'. Certification to an ISO 9000 standard does not guarantee any quality of end products and services; rather, it certifies that formalised business processes are being applied.

There are five key areas:

1. Quality management system.
2. Management responsibility.
3. Resource management.
4. Product realisation.
5. Measurement analysis and improvement.

ISO 9000 includes standards:

- *ISO 9000: 2000, Quality management systems – fundamentals and vocabulary.* Covers the basics of what quality management systems are and also contains the core language of the ISO 9000 series of standards. This is a guidance document, not used for certification purposes, but an important reference document to understand terms and vocabulary related to quality management systems. In the year 2005, revised ISO 9000: 2005 standard was published, so it is now advised to refer to ISO 9000: 2005

- **ISO 9001: 2000 Quality management systems – requirements** is intended for use in any organisation which designs, develops, manufactures, installs and/or services any product or provides any form of service. It provides a number of requirements which an organisation needs to fulfil if it is to achieve customer satisfaction through consistent products and services which meet customer expectations

- **ISO 9004: 2000 Quality management systems – guidelines for performance improvements** covers continual improvement. This gives you advice on what you could do to enhance a mature system. This standard very specifically states that it is not intended as a guide to implementation

To gain the maximum benefit from ISO 9000: 2000 there are a number of steps to take:

1 Define why your organisation is in business.

2 Determine the key processes that state what you do.

3 Establish how these processes work within your business.

4 Determine who owns these processes.

5 Agree these processes throughout the organisation.

Investors in People

Developed in 1990 by a partnership of leading businesses and national organisations, the Standard helps organisations to improve performance and realise objectives through the management and development of their people. Since it was developed, the Standard has been reviewed every three years to ensure that it remains relevant, accessible and attractive to all.

The Investors in People Standard is based on three key principles:

- **Plan** – Developing strategies to improve the performance of the organisation

- **Do** – Taking action to improve the performance of the organisation

- **Review** – Evaluating the impact on the performance of the organisation

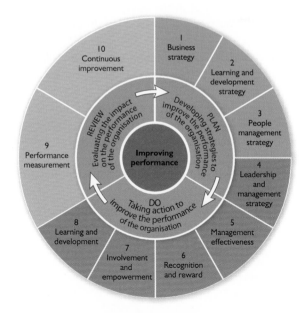

Developing strategies to improve the performance of the organisation

1 **Business strategy** – a strategy for improving the performance of the organisation is clearly defined and understood.

2 **Learning and development strategy** – learning and development is planned to help achieve the organisation's objectives.

3 **People management strategy** – strategies for managing people are designed to promote quality of opportunity in the development of the organisation's people.

4 **Leadership and management strategy** – the capabilities managers need to lead, manage and develop people effectively are cleary defined and understood.

Taking action to improve the performance of the organisation

5. **Management effectiveness** – managers are effective in leading, managing and developing people.

6. **Recognintion and reward** – people's contributions to the organisation are recognised and valued.

7. **Involvement and empowerment** – people are encouraged to take ownership and responsibility by being involved in decision-making.

8. **Learning and development** – people learn and develop effectively.

Evaluating the impact of the performance of the organisation

9. **Performance measurement** – investment in people improves the performance of the organisation.

10. **Continuous improvement** – improvements are continually made to the way people are managed and developed.

AND FINALLY...

✔ **TIP**

Six Tips for Great Customer Service

1 **Hire 'customer friendly'**   You can train, teach and coach a lot of things but being friendly is not one of them. And beyond just friendly, you should look for employees who make a habit of focusing on the customer, who go out of their way to take care of customer's needs.

2 **Know what your customers want**   There are two effective ways to discover what your customers want. First, just ask. If you have good rapport with them, then ask them directly. If that's not comfortable, use a short survey. No more than three questions.

3 **Post reminders**   This sounds basic but it works. Make posters of the top things your customers want from you. Include your 'Customer service standards' so everyone knows what the expectations are. Place them around your business so everyone can see them. Also, use post-it notes, emails, 'customer service calendars' and any other fun ways you can think of to refresh your employees' memories.

4 **Celebrate good news**   When customers give you and your staff good feedback, publish it. Have a party! Let all your staff know about it. Show your employees how important it is.

5 **Learn from negative feedback**   Avoid criticising specific employees but make sure everyone knows when there is bad news. Use it as a learning opportunity. Discuss what went wrong and how you might prevent it in the future.

6 **Get customers involved**   Make it easy for your customers to be a part of your customer service efforts. Find ways to help them communicate with you. Invite them to 'customer service coffees' or other events (make sure there's food!) to get their input. People want to be helpful but you need to make it easy. Use email, websites, blogs, and whatever else you can think of to connect with them.

CASE STUDY

Travelodge Customer Service Case Study

Travelodge currently has 26,500 rooms in 384 hotels in the UK, with expansion plans for the UK that have seen a new hotel opening every 6 days on average throughout 2008 and into 2009. In addition, Travelodge are focusing on overseas expansion in a number of locations. The main focus is Spain, where the company has committed to opening 100 hotels by 2020 with further development work already underway.

'Making hotels available to everyone'

Customer service is essential to what Travelodge does. Travelodge is not a typical 'full service' hotel company and therefore has to adapt the customer service strategy accordingly, while focusing on the basics – **'a clean room and good value'**.

Customer service is a high focus at every level of the business and Travelodge focusses on service delivery. Travelodge's key aspects of their customer service policy include:

■ Making hotels accessible to everyone

■ Providing a clean fit for purpose room

■ Being simple, efficient, friendly and fair

When dealing with customer service problems Travelodge has categorised customer contact into two areas:

BRAND COMPLAINTS

■ These relate to brand level complaints/policies or general enquiries

■ They are reviewed and resolved by the Quality Management and Customer Service Team centrally

■ This is because they relate to something central to the organisation that isn't the responsibility of the front of house employee, but is the responsibility of someone who has set standards centrally

OPERATIONAL COMPLAINTS

■ These relate to any operational failing. For example cleanliness, staff attitude or food. They include any operational failing at hotel level

■ They are received centrally by the Customer Service Team and sent to the Hotel Managers/District Managers/Regional Directors for resolution

■ The level of issues resolved by managment will depend upon the central assessment of the complaint

Travelodge has a mix between 50% low risk complaints and 50% high risk complaints. High risk complaints include failure complaints where low risk complaints include issues classed as outside of the brand (operational).

In reporting complaints centrally at the first stage of the complaint the Operations Team can receive first hand feedback and ensure that action is taken to resolve and fix the future problems.

A monthly review meeting is then held with the Operations Team and Heads of Department from across the brand, chaired by the Quality Manager in order to review volume and issues and agree actions that need to be addressed. They also review future changes and activity to understand the risks to the customer and contact volume. They consider this a very proactive method of responding to and forecasting customer contact volumes and trends, as well as preventing potential complaint topics.

In order to measure customer complaints throughout the country, Travelodge measure each hotel with a **complaint ratio** showing a comparable performance across the brand. Operational Managers can seek bonuses based on their ranks in terms of their comparable performance. In addition, Travelodge have a Brand Audit which is a 2 day audit for each hotel and reviews brand standard compliance, i.e. a hotel's compliance to the brand standards set. Travelodge sees these as working effectively at this time

Good Customer service is rewarded through recognition. This process enables Travelodge to identify exceptional performance through central customer contact and hotel complaint ratio. This then prompts a letter from the Chief Executive, Grant Hearn, to thank the individual/s for their contribution. This will often include a bottle of champagne or equivalent recompense. Poor Customer service is also noted through letters that are issued to the individual noting poor performance. To date Travelodge have seen a very positive reaction to this process and it has added value to have recognition from a senior level.

Internal Customer service (Total Quality Management) is also encouraged at Travelodge and this includes:

■ A Quality Management (QM) team based at the Head Office for Travelodge that acts as a support function to the business

■ A large volume of the employees within Travelodge interact with the team for guidance, help and support when dealing with customers

■ Service Level Agreements are set for the way the QM team interacts with internal customers – these are considered key to the success of the customer service strategy

Travelodge has identified that although **SERVQUAL and TQM** have been considered in the past, neither has not been fully integrated or measured through their customer service policies. With this in mind Travelodge is currently reviewing its customer service strategy, to focus and re-launch some time in 2009... Watch this space...

Courtesy of Travelodge

Assessment of knowledge and understanding

You have now learnt about monitoring and solving customer service problems including solving immediate customer service problems, identifying repaired customer service problems and options for solving them and taking action to avoid the repetition of customer service problems.

To test your level of knowledge and understanding, answer the following short questions. These will help to prepare you for your summative (final) assessment.

1 How can you lead your team in effectively responding to customer service problems?

2 What methods are best for ensuring that complaints are reported and monitored?

3 Can you recognise an environment in which customer complaints are monitored, evaluated and solutions found to ensure they aren't repeated? If you can, explain the following (if you can't go to question 4):

   (a) What is the process by which the complaints are recorded?

   (b) What is the process by which the complaints are monitored?

   (c) Who is involved with monitoring the complaints?

   (d) How are solutions found?

   (e) How are solutions introduced to the staff?

   (f) Do you think this is done effectively or could it be improved?

4 If you can't recognise an environment in which customers' complaints are monitored, then prepare a plan for how they could be monitored, who would be involved and how feedback from that monitoring process would be introduced to the rest of the team effectively.

Research task

Continue to research TQM and SERVQUAL, particularly in relation to hospitality, then describe how you might introduce a mechanism into your workplace that monitors one of the processes to improve the internal/external customers' experience of your operation. Also consider:

- How would you put the concept into practice in your workplace?

- Who would be involved?

- How would you implement it?

- Who would monitor the outcomes?

- How would the outcomes be monitored?

- How would you monitor its success?

- What would be your expected outcomes from using such a concept and why would that be important to your business?

23

Improve relationships with customers

HS23 Improve relationships with customers

LEARNING OBJECTIVES

This unit is about building and improving relationships with customers. These may be internal customers or members of the public. It is about making customers feel that you genuinely want to give them high levels of service and that you will make every possible effort to meet or exceed their expectations. This encourages loyalty from external customers or good working relationships with internal customers.

After reading this chapter you will be able to:

- Select and use the best method of communication to meet your customers' expectations.
- Take the initiative to contact your customers to update them when things are not going to plan or when you require further information.
- Adapt your communication to respond to individual customer's feelings.
- Meet your customers' expectations within your organisation's service offer.
- Explain the reasons to your customers sensitively and positively when their expectations cannot be met.
- Identify alternative solutions for your customers either within or outside the organisation.
- Identify the costs and benefits of these solutions to your organisation and to your customers.
- Negotiate and agree solutions with your customers which satisfy them and are acceptable to your organisation.

■ Take action to satisfy your customers with the agreed solution.

■ Make extra efforts to improve your relationship with your customers.

■ Recognise opportunities to exceed your customers' expectations.

■ Take action to exceed your customers' expectations within the limits of your own authority.

■ Gain the help and support of others to exceed your customers' expectations.

KEY WORDS

Auditory
To do with the sense of hearing.

Communication
This term refers to the transfer of information, verbally, physically or via another means such as email.

Empathetic
Showing understanding of another person's situation.

Exceed
Going above and beyond.

Expectation
An individual's belief of how something should be.

Eye accessing cues
Movements of the eyes in certain directions which indicate visual, auditory or kinaesthetic thinking.

Internal representation
Patterns of information we create and store in our minds in combinations of images, sounds, feelings, smells and tastes.

Kinaesthetic
The feeling sense, tactile sensations and internal feelings such as remembered sensations and emotions.

Leading
Changing your own behaviour with enough rapport for the other person to follow.

Loyalty
Gaining a customer's commitment to come back again providing repeat business.

Matching
Adopting parts of another person's behaviour for the purpose of enhancing rapport.

Mirroring

Precisely matching aspects of another person's behaviour.

NLP

Neurolinguistic programming – a way of communicating effectively, using all your senses to achieve outstanding results.

Pacing

Gaining and maintaining rapport with another person over a period of time by subtly mirroring and matching their behaviour.

Perception

What an individual believes they see, from their point of view.

Physiology

To do with the physical part of a person.

Rapport

The process of establishing and maintaining a relationship of mutual trust and understanding between two or more people.

Visual

To do with the sense of sight.

INTRODUCTION

The relationship we have with our customers, whether they be internal or external to the organisation, is extremely important. The way we communicate with them, understanding their expectations, finding ways to go above and beyond what they expect and being able to wow them will help to keep our customers loyal to us.

This chapter will look at the art of communication and demonstrate some methods to enhance the customer relationship. Looking at what is meant by empathy and perception and seeing that the way we act as an individual will have an impact on the outcome when dealing with our customers. It will show you how to solve problems by looking at alternative solutions with your customers. It will help you to identify your different customer needs and look at how to negotiate and agree solutions which can be actioned, thereby satisfying both your customers and your organisation.

© ISTOCKPHOTO.COM/CHRIS SCHMIDT

HOW DO WE COMMUNICATE?

TECH SKILLS ✔

Communication is about being able to convey a message clearly to another person, and for that other person to be able to make sense of that message. All too often the message we think we are communicating is interpreted and received in a totally different way, which then leads to mistakes and misunderstandings.

ACTIVITY

Conveying a message

Everyone sit round a table or stand in a line. The first person in the group is to whisper a message to the next person – ensure nobody else in the group hears this. The second person whispers this message to the third person and so on until the message has been passed from one person to another. The last person in the group is to say out loud the message they received. The first person can then reveal what the intended message was. No doubt there will be a difference in the message given, and the message received.

Why do you think that is?

To find out how we communicate we first need to examine our own state of mind. Communication starts with our thoughts, and we use words, tonality and body language to convey them to the other person. What happens is something will occur in the environment around us from which we need to make meaning out of it. So for example if you hear shouting, this could be caused by several different things – an angry customer, an excited salesman, or maybe spectators at a sporting event. We won't be able to make meaning until we have some more information, so we will gather visual, auditory and kinaesthetic clues to work out what happened. From absorbing this information this will form our state of mind. So if with the sound of the shouting, we also saw a man slamming his fist on the reception desk we would probably assume we have an angry customer to deal with. When we first hear the shouting we may feel concerned as to why there are raised voices, then when we see our customer we might let out a heavy sigh and drop our shoulders. This would be our physiology reacting to the situation which would also create our state of mind, from which we would then behave in a certain way, depending on what experiences we have of dealing with customer complaints.

It is from these past experiences that we have built up our own database of information which we have picked up and 'recorded' and this is what will influence the way we behave. So let's look at our angry customer. In the first example, we let out a heavy sigh and drop our shoulders as in our past experience an angry customer means having to deal with a customer complaint and we've had so many to deal with it feels like 'here we go again!' However, for a less experienced person the sight of an angry customer might fill them with anxiety, and they might start sweating as they may be very nervous about having to approach the customer and deal with this situation.

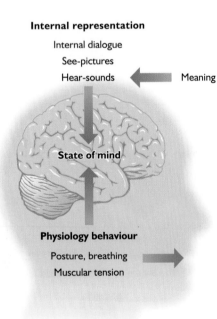

Internal representation

Internal dialogue
See-pictures
Hear-sounds ← Meaning

State of mind

Physiology behaviour

Posture, breathing
Muscular tension

The model left shows a diagrammatic representation of how this occurs. It is based on the NLP work of Richard Bandler and John Grindler. NLP stands for neurolinguistic programming and is a way of communicating effectively, using all your senses to achieve outstanding results.

THE NLP MODEL OF BEHAVIOUR

So the way you handle a situation will all depend on your state of mind. The way you are feeling will show through your body language and the way you react to someone. If you are in a bad mood and you have to handle a customer complaint you will probably not handle it as well as you could have done, as your bad mood will reflect on the guest and both of you will end up feeling as bad as each other. The reason for this is that when we communicate with another person we unconsciously imitate them – their physiology, their tone of voice and movement. So whenever we have to communicate with our customers we need to ensure that we are in a much more positive frame of mind. How do we do this? By simply changing our physiology. So stand up tall, take a deep breath in and out, look up, roll your shoulders and smile. Now try feeling tired. Not so easy, because now your brain is getting a message to be alert and resourceful, so that is what you have become.

READING BODY LANGUAGE

TECH SKILLS ✓

There are three main ways in which we pick up signals from other people:

1 Visual
©ISTOCKPHOTO.COM/SEB CHANDLER

2 Auditory
© ISTOCKPHOTO.COM/MORE PIXELS

3 Kinaesthetic
© ISTOCKPHOTO.COM/SCHMEL

As individuals we will also use these signals. So you may be predominantly a visual person who makes pictures in their mind, be someone who is very attuned to listening, or be someone who has a gut feeling for things.

For a supervisor to communicate clearly with your customers you need to use all three:

1 You need to make eye contact with your customer
2 You need to listen to them
3 You need to show empathy.

To find out more about your customer, you need to find out if they are predominantly visual, auditory or kinaesthetic. You can match your body language and tone of voice to them, and in this way it will be easier to solve any issues. Your customer will also be feeling very comfortable with you as you would have built rapport with them.

There is a very easy technique to find out if someone you are looking at is visual, auditory or kinaesthetic. Some people will show you this through the words they use, their body movements as well as their eyes:

'Let me see' (move head up to the left) – visual.

'That sounds okay to me' (move body to left/right) – auditory.

'I feel downright depressed' (move body down right) – kinaesthetic.

ACTIVITY

Eye accessing cue questions

In pairs, take it in turns to ask each other the following questions. As you do this, the person asking the question is to make a note of where their partner's eyes go when they answer. After each question and answer discuss what happened:

Person A What colour is your favourite shirt?

Person B When was the last time you saw your signature?

Person A How did the last piece of music you heard sound?

Person B What does your car look like?

Person A How does laughing feel?

Person B Describe the contents of a room you would like to create.

Person A Imagine yourself ten years from now, describe this.

Person B How does it feel to slip on ice?

Visual people tend to look upwards – eyes to the right means they are remembering, eyes to the left mean they are constructing.

Auditory people tend to look side to side.

Kinaesthetic people tend to look down. They go inside themselves and their internal dialogue starts talking to them.

EYE ACCESSING CUES

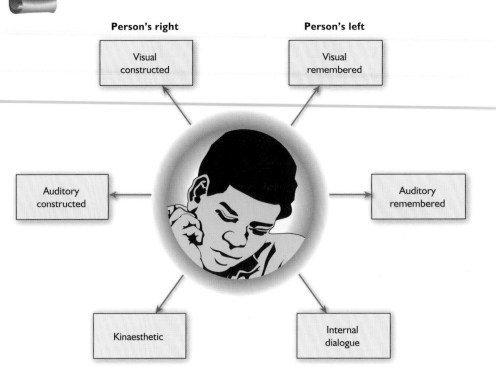

As you can see it is easy to work out if a person is thinking in pictures, sounds or feelings as there are visible changes in our bodies when we think in different ways.

Why is it important to know this? Well, if we can work out how a person thinks, it can help us to build rapport with them by subtly matching and mirroring them.

MATCHING AND MIRRORING

Once we have worked out the preferred way our customer likes to communicate we can communicate back in the same way.

If someone is visual, communicate in a visual way by showing them things, describing things so they can picture it in their mind. Visual people like you to get to the point, so they may talk fast and their breathing tends to be shallow.

Someone who is auditory likes to speak clearly and slowly and you will notice that their breathing is even and deep. So slow your speech down.

If your customer is predominantly kinaesthetic they will speak even slower with long pauses between words. In this case then respond to them in a very empathetic way.

By subtly matching and mirroring you can build rapport with your guest. You do this by pacing them, for example slowing down your own breathing, and they will start to relax and feel comfortable with you. You can then lead them and they will start to mirror you unconsciously and be open to your suggestions and actions.

REPRESENTING INFORMATION

We need to be clear in our communication and often confusion can cause mistakes to be made as we assume we know what the other person means. The way we present or rather 're-present' information can be different from one person to another. So for example what do you think when you hear the phrase

'The cat sat on the mat'

- It could be you see a black cat sitting on a brown mat
- It could be you see an image of a cartoon cat scratching at the door to get out
- It could be you imagine you hear the sound of a cat meowing sitting on a mat, calling for its owner to feed it
- It could be you get a sense of warmth as you recall the feeling of stroking a cat sitting on a mat
- It could be you see the words in clear handwriting written on a blackboard as it reminds you of when you were at school learning to read and write

There are many interpretation of what that one sentence means, and it will be different for each individual, depending on their experiences, which is why communication must be crystal clear.

ACTIVITY

Perception

Have a look at this picture – What can you see?

PERCEPTION

At first glance at the picture in the activity to the right, you may see a pretty young lady with a bonnet on her head, her hair swept behind her ear flowing down her back. You can see the profile of her face, she has a small nose and on her neck she is wearing a choker.

Now look away and look at the picture again. Can you still see the pretty young lady or in her place can you see an old woman with a large beady eye, big crooked nose with a wart on it, tightly pierced lips and a large chin?

There are in fact two pictures within this picture and depending on your perception you will either see the young lady or the old lady first. You can change your perception to see the other picture.

Likewise when we communicate there can be two sides to the story, so in order to be an emphatic listener we need to be able to see both sides and understand where the other person is coming from.

NEGOTIATING WITH CUSTOMERS

TECH SKILLS ✓

We will need to negotiate with our customers for different reasons, to put together a business deal or it could be if a customer complains, they may not be happy with something that has happened or something they have experienced and they are looking for an immediate solution to the problem they have given to you. For a negotiation to be 'win-win', both parties should feel positive about the negotiation once it's over. This helps people keep good working relationships afterwards.

© ISTOCKPHOTO.COM/NIKADA

CONSIDER

The key questions to consider for building good customer relations through negotiation

Goals: What do you want to get out of the negotiation? What do you think the other person wants?

Trades: What do you and the other person have that you can trade? What do you each have that the other wants? What are you each comfortable giving away?

Alternatives: If you don't reach agreement with the other person, what alternatives do you have? Are these good or bad? How much does it matter if you do not reach agreement? Does failure to reach an agreement cut you out of future opportunities? And what alternatives might the other person have?

Relationships: What is the history of the relationship? Could or should this history impact the negotiation? Will there be any hidden issues that may influence the negotiation? How will you handle these?

Expected outcomes: What outcome will people be expecting from this negotiation? What has the outcome been in the past, and what precedents have been set?

The consequences: What are the consequences for you of winning or losing this negotiation? What are the consequences for the other person?

Power: Who has what power in the relationship? Who controls resources? Who stands to lose the most if agreement isn't reached? What power does the other person have to deliver what you hope for?

Possible solutions: based on all of the considerations, what possible compromises might there be?

ACTIVITY

Dealing with customer complaints through negotiation

Keeping in mind the key questions in the Consider box, use these to work out how you would deal with the following scenario. Person A is the hotel guest, and Person B is the receptionist.

After a busy day Mr Brown returns to his hotel where he has been staying whilst away on business. He goes straight to his hotel room at 6.00 p.m. which he enters, only to find it has not been serviced. The towels are still where he left them, the bed has not been made up, and the remains of his room service breakfast are still on the table. He phones reception and finds the number engaged, so he decides to go downstairs to speak to someone. He approaches reception where a young man asks if he can be of help. Mr Brown explains that he has just returned to his room to find that it has not been made up.

BUILDING BRIDGES

Imagine if you were on one side of the road and your customer was standing on the other side of the road: it would make it very difficult to communicate clearly. You would need to build a bridge so that you could go over to their side of the road and then bring them back to your side. This metaphor is the same as when you negotiate.

When looking for solutions you need to find something that will be of benefit to both the customer and your organisation. One way to do this is to think about the language we use. How many times have you heard people say 'I hear what you say but…'. When we hear the word but it disconnects the sentence. When we replace it with the word 'and' we can retain it.

Imagine you have two customers that approach you as they want you to organise a party and decide on a theme for their company.

If with the first customer whenever a suggestion is put forward, a response comes back 'yes but…' How far do you think you would get in organising that party? On the other hand with the second customer when a suggestion came up and there was not full agreement on it, rather than saying 'yes but', you could say 'and'. For example 'I like the idea of having a theme and I would also suggest we consider the cost implications'.

The negotiation itself is a careful exploration of your position and the other person's position, with the goal of finding a mutually acceptable compromise that gives you both as much of what you want as possible. In an ideal situation, you will find that the other person wants what you are prepared to trade, and that you are prepared to give what the other person wants. If this is not the case and one person must give way, then it is fair for this person to try to negotiate some form of compensation for doing so. Ultimately, both sides should feel comfortable with the final solution if the agreement is to be considered win-win.

COSTS AND BENEFITS TO THE CUSTOMER AND THE ORGANISATION

Whenever you come to an agreement with your customer with regards to what they want and what your organisation can provide for them you need to work out the costs and benefits to the both of you. So what value will this add? Let's look at our example of a customer approaching your organisation and wanting you to organise a themed party for their company. Having spoken to the customer we have discovered that they are are a large corporate chain who are looking to throw a lavish awards dinner party for their key employees. Your organisation is a small catering company that normally caters for private parties on a much smaller scale.

	COST	BENEFIT
Customer	Investing money in the party	Make their team feel valued and looked after
Organisation	Taking a risk with a new venture, company reputation could be on the line	Gained a new client, could create repeat business

For any activity you undertake there will be a cost and a benefit which has to weighed up.

ACTIVITY

Cost and benefit to your customer and your organisation

Think of a situation at work where you have had to negotiate with your customer. Use the key questions above to work out how the negotiation went.

Put together a grid showing the cost and benefit to both of you from the agreement made.

TAKING THE INITIATIVE

When working with customers, whether it be on a project or organising an event as in the example above, it is important as a supervisor that you take the initiative and keep your customers updated when things are not going to plan, or when you require further information. This could be a simple phone call, or a follow-up email. So for example if we look at our themed party for the employee awards, the problem could be that the company has asked for a specific table decoration which you cannot source within the budget given. Rather than saying you can't supply the table decoration they have requested, you should offer an alternative. This shows that you have seen foreseen a potential problem, and come up with a possible solution for your client.

! REMEMBER

You can take the initiative and apply this to any everyday occurrence.

ACTIVITY

Taking the intiative

Look at the following scenarios and discuss three different actions you could take to avoid a possible complaint situation.

Scenario 1
You are on your way to the weekly head of department's meeting and you are rushing as you are a little late. You see a dirty room service tray left in the corridor – what would you do?

Scenario 2
Restaurant breakfast is extremely busy and as the front office supervisor you are standing behind the reception desk with three other receptionists. The desk is very quiet, you see the situation in the restaurant – what would you do?

Scenario 3
As you walk through the hotel lobby you see a courier trying to deliver an urgent package for a guest at your hotel. The reception is busy checking in a group, the concierge porters are all busy unloading the luggage from the coach – what would you do?

MEETING CUSTOMER EXPECTATIONS

Nearly all large organisations will have a mission statement and company values which they use to demonstrate how they work with their customers – for example see White's of Wexford's company website (http://www.whitesofwexford.ie/hotel-policy.html).

In order to put this in to practice and to be able to meet our customer's expectations we need to know what the customer wants. Below is a list of what customers have said they want when getting a service from an organisation. As you read through the list you will notice that all focus on the human elements, so we need to remember if we carry this through in a consistent manner then our customers who appreciate the way they've been treated uncomplainingly accept occasional delays and glitches, which can occur due to human error. It is in our nature after all!

Claridges, London

1 To be taken seriously.
2 Competent, efficient service.
3 Anticipation of my needs.
4 Explanations in my terms.
5 Basic courtesies.
6 To be informed of the options.
7 Not to be passed around.
8 To be listened to (and heard).
9 Dedicated attention.
10 Knowledgeable help.
11 Friendliness.
12 To be kept informed.
13 Follow-through.
14 Honesty.
15 Feedback.
16 Professional service.
17 Empathy.
18 Respect.

SERVICE STANDARDS

Many companies these days have service standards so their employees as well as their guests both know what to expect. Service standards are expectations-managing statements used to minimise uncertainty about when some specified event will occur. The 'when' may be a specific date or time, or more often, a time frame within which the event will take place. For example if you stay in a hotel as a guest you will be informed of what time you can check in, what time you are expected to check out, the times the restaurant is open for meals and that there is 24-hour room service. Usually within the service industry there will be more specific standards too:

- Answering the telephone within three rings
- Room service order will be delivered within 20 minutes

As long as we deliver on these service standards you normally have a satisfied guest. Although do we really just want our guest to be satisfied? Will a satisfied person come back again to give us repeat business? Perhaps, although there is no guarantee.

EXCEEDING CUSTOMER EXPECTATIONS: THE WOW FACTOR

What do we mean by the wow factor? Think about receiving a service that gives you goose-bumps and makes you say wow – I didn't expect that! That's what we mean. In order to deliver that kind of service we need to go above and beyond what our guest is expecting. Although we don't need to have grand gestures to demonstrate this, in fact it is the small things that can create a wow, the things that delight and surprise us, and are unexpected... like being recognised and remembered.

From the organisation's point of view

You discover it's a customer's birthday and you send them a birthday card. Some companies have this information on their database anyway, so use it to let the guest know they are being thought about. (It's also another way of reminding the guest that your company exists!)

From the customer's point of view

You arrive at the hotel early and have dropped your luggage off as you know your room is not ready yet. The receptionist tells you they will inform you when your room is ready. You spend the day shopping and later that afternoon receive a text from the hotel letting you know your room is ready, and that your luggage has been taken to your room for you. You will be able to collect the key from reception. This makes the customer feel that the hotel have not forgotten them.

> **! REMEMBER**
>
> **Creating wow moments is about doing things differently**
>
> How to create wow moments:
>
> - Think about an everyday scenario that could happen at work
> - Now think of what you can add to this to make the service more personal with simple gestures

Whenever you can get a customer to say, 'That was nice' you have struck a chord. You have shown the person respect and consideration. You have made them feel better about their decision to deal with you.

The element of surprise is tremendously important in creating positive feelings toward your business. Customers are far more likely to appreciate the customised little gestures that involve you singling them out for attention. The kind of small surprises that work best are those that are unscripted, it happens because some very observant employee spots an opportunity to do something for a customer that will truly impress them. What is most needed is a group of observant, empathetic and empowered employees who know how to bring a smile to the customer's face. It's all about seizing an opportunity to turn the expected into the unexpected.

GAIN HELP AND SUPPORT FROM OTHERS TO EXCEED YOUR CUSTOMER'S EXPECTATIONS

Learning to wow the customers is one way of improving the customer relationship, although at times you can't do this on your own. When working in hospitality it's very much about working as a team and you need to remember that as a supervisor you are not only working with your own department, but also with other departments from which you would not be able to do your job if they weren't there to support you.

Let's look at our birthday example. As the front desk supervisor you notice that you have a guest who is arriving and that it is their birthday the next day. You could organise with the housekeeping team to have a complementary bowl of fruit and birthday card placed in their room, or maybe at dinner when delivering your guest their dessert you get the restaurant supervisor to put a candle in it and get his waiters to sing happy birthday to him. All of these are wow moments, although you need to communicate with other departments to ensure they happen smoothly.

The other area you need to be aware of is that you are not an expert in everything and at times your guest may ask something of you that you do not know how to do. Again this is where the support of your colleagues can come in. If you don't know the answer to something, there will be someone in the building that does, so rather then say 'I don't know', or telling them to go and talk to another department, tell them you will find out for them and get back to them with an answer.

SINGING WAITERS ON CRUISESHIPS

Did you know that on many cruise ships, when it is a customer's birthday the waiters will bring the birthday cake to the table and sing 'Happy Birthday' to their guest?

CUSTOMER LOYALTY

Once we have met and exceeded our customer expectations, more than likely our customers will use our services over and over again, and also tell others about us. Customer loyalty is key to any business. The cost of attracting new customers is significantly more than it is to maintain your relationship with existing ones.

■ **Customer service.** Go the extra distance and meet customer needs. Train the staff to do the same. Customers remember being treated well

■ **Employee loyalty.** Loyalty works from the top down. If you are loyal to your employees, they will feel positively about their jobs and pass that loyalty along to your customers

■ **Employee training.** Train employees in the manner that you want them to interact with customers. Empower employees to make decisions that benefit the customer

■ **Customer incentives.** Give customers a reason to return to your business

■ **Product knowledge.** Know what your regular customers purchase and keep these items in stock. Add other products and/or services that accompany or complement the products that your regular customers buy regularly. And make sure that your staff understands everything they can about your products

■ **Reliability.** If you say a purchase will arrive on Wednesday, deliver it on Wednesday. Be reliable. If something goes wrong, let customers know immediately and compensate them for their inconvenience

■ **Be flexible.** Solve customer problems or complaints to the best of your ability. Excuses, such as 'That's our policy', will lose customers fast

■ **People over technology.** The harder it is for a customer to speak to a human being when he or she has a problem, the less likely it is that you will see that customer again

■ **Know their names.** Get to know the names of regular customers or at least recognise their faces

Assessment of knowledge and understanding

You have now identified how to communicate effectively, by working out another person's preferred method of communication, building rapport with them, pacing and leading them to negotiate in to a win-win agreement. You have seen the costs and benefits associated with agreements you make for the customer and the organisation and seen what customers expect, how to exceed those expectations and how to look after your loyal customers.

To test your level of knowledge and understanding, answer the following short questions. These will help to prepare you for your summative (final) assessment.

1 What are the three main ways that people pick up signals about the way we communicate?

2 Explain the NLP model of behaviour.

3 How do eye accessing cues work?

4 How can you build rapport with someone?

5 Why is the way we 're-present' information important?

6 How can you negotiate with your customers?

7 Give an example of how to wow your customer.

8 Why is customer loyalty so important to an organisation?

Research task

What would you do if you had an irate customer shouting at you demanding a refund? Think about how you could match and mirror your customer's body language to build rapport and build a bridge with them to bring them over to your way of thinking to end up with a win-win situation. Explain the methods of communication you could use to lead and pace this customer in order to calm them down and come to a rational solution.

Research task

Research a hospitality organisation of your choice (this could be one that you work in) and find out their mission statement, core values and customer service standards. Use this information to put together two detailed examples of how given the opportunity, you could wow their customer first by yourself, and second with assistance from other colleagues.

24

Provide learning opportunities for colleagues

HS24 Provide learning opportunities for colleagues

LEARNING OBJECTIVES

This unit is about helping colleagues and staff to develop their skills through a variety of learning opportunities.

After reading this chapter you will be able to:

■ Promote the benefits of learning to staff members and make sure that their willingness and efforts to learn are recognised.

■ Give staff members fair, regular and useful feedback on their work performance, discussing and agreeing how they can improve.

■ Work with staff members to identify and prioritise learning needs based on any gaps between the requirements of their work-roles and their current knowledge, understanding and skills.

■ Help staff members to identify the learning style(s) or combination of styles which works best for them and ensure that these are taken into account in identifying and undertaking learning activities.

■ Work with colleagues to identify and obtain information on a range of possible learning activities to address identified learning needs.

■ Discuss and agree with staff members a plan for development which includes learning activities to be undertaken, the learning objectives to be achieved, the required resources and timescales.

- Work with staff members to recognise and make use of unplanned learning opportunities.
- Seek and make use of specialist expertise in relation to identifying and providing learning for staff members.
- Support staff members in undertaking learning activities making sure any required resources are made available and making efforts to remove any obstacles to learning.
- Evaluate, in discussion with each staff member, whether the learning activities they have undertaken have achieved the desired outcomes and provide positive feedback on the learning experience.
- Work with staff members to update their development plan in the light of performance, any learning activities undertaken and any wider changes.
- Encourage staff members to take responsibility for their own learning, including practising and reflecting on what they have learned.

KEY WORDS

Coach

This is a person who will use skilled questioning technique to tease out information from an individual, in order to help them work out how to do something or solve a problem. The coach never gives the answer, the answer always comes from the individual.

Competence

The level at which an individual is able to carry out a skill effectively without supervision.

CPD

Continual professional development.

Development

This relates to acquiring a broad range of soft skills through planned activities and experience.

Evaluation

This is a process to establish the value of something through personal opinion.

Feedback

The process of sharing observations, concerns and suggestions between persons or divisions of the organisation with the intention of improving both personal and organisational performance.

Learning

This is the way individuals acquire information and knowledge.

Learning style

An individual's preferred approach to learning.

Mentor
This is an individual with expert knowledge and experience in a certain area and will guide a less experienced individual through a process.

Objectives
This is an achievable and realistic plan of what an individual wants to achieve in a specific time frame with measurable outcomes.

PDP
Personal development plan.

Training
A planned process through which individuals are helped to learn a new skill or technique.

Training needs analysis
A process to establish current performance in relation to required performance. The gap in the middle will indicate the training opportunities required to bring standards up to the required performance.

INTRODUCTION

The training of new skills for staff is the starting point for building a competent team of people. It is their ongoing development of these skills, through a variety of different learning opportunities, that will release their full potential. Staff should be made aware of how they can update their knowledge and be encouraged to have their own development plan. They should continually update and review this, thereby taking responsibility for their own learning.

This chapter will look at the benefits of learning for staff, and identify their preferred learning style, from which a variety of learning opportunities can be put in place. It will demonstrate the art of giving feedback and also show how to write development plans, and the importance of evaluating any learning that has taken place.

HOW DO WE LEARN?

The word 'learning' means being able to acquire information and knowledge. It is gained through being taught new skills and by having a different experience. Many people assume learning is about having your head in a book and reading, or being shown how to do something, which can be true, but learning can also occur through experiences and by reflecting on what we do.

Think about what you do at work: you will have some sort of daily routine that is familiar to you. Now imagine what could happen if you changed that routine.

Maria is a new receptionist working in a busy hotel. Maria loved her job although she dreaded working a Monday late shift, as that's when all the corporate guests would be checking in and she found them very demanding. It was also the hotel's policy to overbook, which meant she would end up having to book guests out to another hotel, which is something she has not had to deal with before. Maria's way of coping with this was to hope that guests wouldn't show for their bookings or they would arrive late after her shift had finished and she wouldn't have to deal with them – not a very productive way of working. One day she spoke to her manager about this, and together they came up with a procedure of what to do in an overbooking situation. Maria is now a lot happier and less stressed. So from Maria's experience of not knowing what to do rather than avoiding a situation, she has learnt that she can approach her manager and is doing so has learnt a new procedure to make her job more satisfying.

We can all have new experiences, although we can only learn from them if we take the time to think back and reflect on what happened. We can improve the way we perform when we review what went well and what we could do better.

THE BENEFITS OF LEARNING

It is important that as a supervisor you are aware of the benefits of learning to both the individual and the organisation:

BENEFITS TO THE INDIVIDUAL	BENEFITS TO THE ORGANISATION
It helps employees reflect on their own performance	Builds a highly skilled workforce
Employees can find better ways of doing things	Leads to greater volume of work, and a more productive workforce
Better relationships between managers and employees	Frees management time, less time spent rectifying errors, and reduces wastage
Employees feel more committed to the organisation as they are learning and developing through their job	Reduces labour turnover among new and established staff
Employees are more empowered and are able to use their initiative	Better processes and procedures are implemented
Creates a positive attitude	Creates innovation and creativity

TIP

Everyone is able to learn using all four of these styles – although we tend to have a preferred learning style which we use the most.

Learning styles

Research carried out shows that we learn in different ways, and from those ways we will have a preferred style of learning.

Activist – want to learn by trial and error, has a go and takes risks

Reflector – listens and watches what is said and done

Theorist – questions, analyses information, enjoys reading and like structure

Pragmatist – debates the practicalities, questions others, very realistic.

Let's look at this in practice. All these people are asked to cook a dish for a new menu:

- Sian watches a cookery programme that shows how to make the dish, before she has a go (reflector)
- Nick finds a recipe and follows it step by step (theorist)
- Sam opens her kitchen cupboards, pulls out a load of ingredients and gets stuck in (activist)
- Tammy checks she has enough ingredients, works out how she plans to cook the dish and asks for advice from her lecturer (pragmatist)

What would you do in this situation? What do you think your preferred learning style is? What do you think is the preferred learning style of your staff?

TRAINING NEEDS ANALYSIS

We have looked at how we learn and the benefits we gain from learning, but in the workplace how do we know what we and our staff need to learn in order to do our jobs more effectively?

In order to work this out we need to look at the current performance of our employee and compare this to the required performance of our employee. The gap in between will let us know what training and learning needs to take place.

Actual performance	**Required performance**
When a customer complains our employee calls their manager to deal with it	When a customer complains our employee should be able to deal with the complaint

Performance gap

In the above example our employee would need some training in customer service complaint handling, so they can learn what they would need to do in order to resolve a customer complaint.

GIVING FEEDBACK

Imagine if the above scenario applied to a member of your staff, and they needed training in customer service complaint handling – how would you let your member of staff know this?

It is very important that staff know how they are performing and what the expectations and standards of performance required are. How often do you give this sort of feedback to your staff? At times if we have a situation where we feel it might be awkward or uncomfortable to address an issue we tend to let it go, but this is not going to improve your staff performance if they don't know what they are doing wrong. As their supervisor it is your job to inform them and help them to come up with strategies on how to improve.

THE PRAISE SANDWICH

- Good (bottom of the sandwich)
- Bad (middle of the sandwich)
- Good (top of the sandwich)

When you are making a sandwich, you start with the bread at the bottom of the sandwich, your filling is in the middle and then bread on the top. When you give feedback your aim is to give some good feedback first (bottom of the sandwich) then give the bad part although in a positive manner (the filling) and then some good praise at the end (the top of the sandwich). In this way it will make it easier for your staff member to see what they need to do to improve and will be more motivated to do better next time.

For example:

Sarah you've had a very busy shift this morning and you had quite a few complaints to handle, and it's great to see that you're still smiling. (Good)

Although what would you do if I wasn't around to help out with the customer complaints? Can you give me some suggestions of what you would do next time if there is a bill query? (Bad point being highlighted in a positive way)

(Sarah answers)

That's fantastic Sarah, so next time you are in a situation when a customer complains, see if you can deal with it first before coming to find me. In fact I believe there is a customer complaint handling workshop coming up shortly, I think attending that would boost your confidence no end. (Good)

IMAGE COURTESY OF WWW.SXC.HU

 **ACTIVITY**

The praise sandwich

Think of a situation at work where you have had to give feedback to a colleague. Use the praise sandwich technique to work out how you could give that feedback in a more positive and constructive manner.

THE TRAINING CYCLE

The training cycle is a model that can be used to carry the process through:

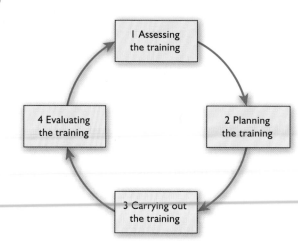

Assessing the training – this is looking at the actual performance and comparing it to the required performance to find the performance gap.

Planning the training – at this stage you would work out what training needs to be carried out, so in our example above it would be a customer service complaint handling course. However, you would also need to work out the methods of training you want to use, which will depend on a variety of factors, such as the number of people on the course, their level of knowledge and what you want them to learn at the end of the course.

Carrying out the training – at this point you will be delivering the training. This might be for a group or maybe on a 1:1 basis.

Evaluating the training – you need to get feedback on the training session at the end so that you can review it and adapt it for next time if needed.

© ISTOCKPHOTO.COM

Ways training can be carried out

There are a variety of ways in which training can be carried out. You need to consider the advantage and disadvantages of how they are carried out in relation to time, cost and resources for an organisation.

TRAINING	ADVANTAGES	DISADVANTAGES
One-to-one training	The employee is shown what to do, can practice the skill and ask questions	It can be time-consuming as the supervisor or manager will be training only one member of staff at a time
Group training	Trainees can meet other employees and learn from each other's experiences	An employee is taken out of the business to attend the training session. The supervisor or manager will have to find cover for them

TRAINING	ADVANTAGES	DISADVANTAGES
On the job training	The employee can learn how to do their job whilst carrying out their job	Mistakes may be made which could be costly
Off the job training	Employees attend a training session away from their workplace	The supervisor or manager will have to find cover for them at work
In-house training	Training is carried out in the workplace – although maybe away from the department	As employees are in the workplace they may be called back to sort a problem out in their department during the course
External training	Employee does a course outside work, such as a day release programme at a college. The employee can gain fresh ideas from others on the course from different organisation.	Will have to take time out of work to complete the course
	An external trainer is brought in to the organisation to train their staff – training can be tailored to exactly what the organisation wants	This can be very expensive
Sitting next to Nelly	A new employee will shadow an existing employee to see how to do a job	Can be very time-consuming
Self-study	Employee studies at their pace and in their own time	Employee needs to be very motivated and will be using their own time to study
Coaching	An employee is guided through a series of questions to find the outcome they need for a situation. It is a good developmental tool	The coach has to be skilled in questioning technique and must not give any answers to the employee. May take several sessions

LEARNING ACTIVITIES

Once it has been decided which is the most cost-effective way to carry out the training, and most beneficial to suit the employee, it has to be decided how to carry out the training itself. There are a variety of different training methods or learning activities that could be used to help our employees develop their knowledge, skills and attitude. Some of them are trainer-centred and some are learner-centred, and some can be a mixture of both.

Trainer-centred

This gives the trainer control over the pace and content of the learning. The trainer will decide which exercises to use, structures the session and draws out key learning points, for example through a lecture or presentation.

ACTIVITY

Commonly used training methods

The table lists the most commonly used training methods. Make a note in the last column if you think it is trainer-centred, learner-centred or both are involved.

Learner-centred

Gives the learner more or less complete control. So the learner might use self-study texts, questionnaires, learning logs or e-learning.

Trainer- and learner-centred

Coaching is an example of this. It is a process which will involve both the trainer and the learner. Through excellent questioning technique the trainer will draw out the answers and raise the awareness of the learner.

METHOD	DESCRIPTION	USUAL OUTCOME	TRAINER-, LEARNER-CENTRED OR BOTH?
Lectures and presentations	Trainer delivers prepared exposition, preferably using visual aids	Knowledge – fact and opinions	
Briefing groups	Short exposition by trainer, followed by questions and discussion	Knowledge – fact and opinions	
Discussion groups	Participative discussion led by one of the learners on a specified topic	Some knowledge – facts and opinions, attitudes and interpersonal skills	
Plenary discussion	Session following practical or other activity, usually led by the trainer to pull out key learning points and/or relate theory to practice	Reinforcement and reflection – depending on task under review	
Demonstrations	Trainer shows learners how to do a task e.g. operate a machine	Knowledge – how to, preparation for skills training	
Practicals	Learners operate under trainer's supervision and receive feedback	Psychomotor or interpersonal skills	
Role-play	Learners put themselves in someone else's shoes for the purpose of practical exercise	Changing attitudes, interpersonal skills	
Video/DVD	Sound and vision	Knowledge	
Case studies	Write up of an incident or situation with questions for analysis and/or discussion	Analytical and decision-making skills	
Business games/ computer simulations	Board or computer games or evolving case studies which allow participants to see the consequences of their decisions	Analytical and decision-making skills	

METHOD	DESCRIPTION	USUAL OUTCOME	TRAINER-, LEARNER-CENTRED OR BOTH?
Incident method	Learners are given last item in a sequence of events and asked to reconstruct circumstances through questioning trainer	Analytical and questioning skills	
In-tray exercises	Learners are given a series of memos, and other papers or electronic communications to be prioritised and dealt with	Prioritising, planning, organising, delegating and other managerial skills	
Group/individual projects	Investigation and report, usually with recommendations on issues or concern	Knowledge – facts and opinions, investigative, analytical and problem-solving skills	
Books, manuals and self-study texts	Written descriptions, analyses or instructions, sometimes with checklist and self-test questions	Knowledge – facts and opinions	
E-learning	Electronic, Internet-based media which present learner with information and/or situations and questions and provide feedback on responses	Knowledge – facts and opinions; investigative, analytical and problem-solving skills	
Embedded e-learning	Computer 'trains' operator step by step as tasks are carried out	Knowledge and skills but varying extent of actual learning	
Learning log	Diary or journal used by learner to reflect on work or learning events and draw out and record learning points	All types	
Team tasks	Practical indoor or outdoor exercises or simulations	Planning, organising, team and interpersonal skills	
Coaching	Learner takes responsibility for own learning and uses trainer as coach to raise awareness	All types	

From the activity above you would have realised that lecture and presentations through to in-tray exercises are all trainer-centred. Group/individual projects through to learning logs are learner-centred, and team tasks and coaching are both.

WWW.ISTOCKPHOTO.COM/
S KASHKIN

However, sending an employee on a training course is only the start of their learning and development journey. We need to ensure that our employee is continually updating their skills and knowledge. It would be very difficult for a manager to do this for all their employees as they will not necessary know of their individual aspirations and career intentions. It is therefore important that our employees realise that they are in charge of their own development and the easiest way to keep on top of this is to have a development plan.

THE DEVELOPMENT PLAN

A development plan looks at the personal and professional development of an individual – the main aim is to ensure that an individual is improving their learning and performance by forward planning and setting specific goals which can be measured, are realistic and achievable in a timely manner.

At college you will be required to have a PDP – a personal development plan – which will look at your personal, professional and academic goals. In the workplace you will be required to have a CPD record to show continual professional development and evidence of the updating of your professional skills and knowledge.

Benefits of your staff having a development plan

■ Gain strategies for improving personal performance

■ Gain a much better sense of their career aspirations

■ Develops confidence in the skills and qualities and attributes needed in their job

■ Able to discuss training needs and further development with their manager

■ Develops a positive attitude, creative thinking and problem-solving approach required to empower staff

Putting together a development plan

In order to put together a development plan you need to be clear about what your aims and objectives are for each goal you want to set yourself.

■ **Aim** A general statement of what you want to do

■ **Objective** A breakdown of specific points of how you are going to achieve it

Below is a typical development plan that a graduate college leaver might put together for themselves.

AIM	OBJECTIVE	DEADLINE DATE
To work in the hospitality industry	To research specific companies to contact and apply for jobs	In the next month
To develop my leadership skills	To research leadership skills that need developing	Ongoing
To run my own restaurant	To buy a franchise	2010
	To lead my own team	

At first glance this may seem reasonable, they have some career aspirations in there and they have identified an area they need to work on to improve their skills. However, this plan is much too vague.

SMART OBJECTIVES

In order to write your objectives in a much more structured way they need to be SMART:

Specific – a clear detailed description of what is to be accomplished

Measurable – the goals states clearly what is to be achieved in terms of quantity, quality, time or cost

Achievable – you have a belief the goal is within your grasp

Realistic – the goal is congruent with your organisational or personal values

Timebound – there is a clear date by when the goal is to be achieved.

> **✔ TIP**
>
> People that write down their goals in a SMART format are more likely to achieve them.
>
> Just imagine what you could achieve if you put your mind to it!

Let's look at how the first objective could be reworded to make it much more specific.

Reword the aim

From: To work in the hospitality industry

To: To spend the next 5 years working in 5-star hotels as a head chef

(Now we know which area of the hospitality industry they want to work in, how long they want to work there for and in which position.)

Rewording the objective

From: To research specific companies to contact and apply for jobs

To: To use my contacts from the Institute of Hospitality Association to find out job opportunities

To contact 10 hotels a week with speculative CV application

To apply for at least two jobs a week via the *Caterer and Hotelkeeper* magazine, and job websites such as Reed Hospitality and HCareers.

(Now we can clearly see exactly how they intend to get the job they want, with clear measurable criteria.)

Tying in to a deadline

From: In the next month

To: 1 June 2009.

(We now have a specific date by which this is to be achieved.)

So when we put that all together a much SMARTer first objective for our college graduate would be:

AIM	OBJECTIVE	DEADLINE DATE
To spend the next 5 years working in 5-star hotels as a head chef	To use my contacts from the Institute of Hospitality Association to find out job opportunities To contact 10 hotels a week with speculative CV applications To apply for at least two jobs a week via the *Caterer and Hotelkeeper* magazine, and job websites such as Reed Hospitality and HCareers	1 June 2009

Supporting colleagues

As a supervisor your role in supporting your colleagues involves helping them put together their development plan, and also ensuring that they are aware of the different learning opportunities available to them to help develop themselves further. It is also important that any learning activity undertaken is constantly reviewed and monitored to check your staff member's progress.

EVALUATION

At the end of a training course it is common practice for the trainer to give the trainees an evaluation sheet. This gives the trainer feedback on how the session went. In a similar vein your employees should be able to evaluate their own learning.

In order to do this as a supervisor you should have **regular review meetings** with your employee and ask them to **reflect** on how they are achieving the goals in their development plan. Not only will this update you, but it will also give your colleague a chance to **review** what they have done and look at their **progress** so far.

A good way of doing this is to ask the following questions:

- Which goals have been achieved?
- How were they achieved?
- How have they overcome any challenges or obstacles?
- How would they adapt their goals in light of their current situation?

If your staff member has just been on a specific training course you could ask them to write down three things they have learnt from the course and to explain how they will use these new skills in the workplace – remember learning should benefit both the individual and the organisation.

THE LEGISLATION

In implementing all of the above one key aspect that supervisors and managers need to be aware of is the equal opportunities legislation that applies to training and development. Regardless of the level of knowledge and skill that your employees have, all of them should be treated equally and be given the same opportunities to develop themselves further.

Further reading

Peter Honey and Alan Mumford (1992) *The Manual of Learning Styles*, 3rd revised edn. Peter Honey Publications.

Assessment of knowledge and understanding

You have now identified what learning means to the individual and the organisation, the ways in which people can learn and the different learning activities available in organisations. The importance of development planning for your staff and how progress should be constantly reviewed and evaluated.

To test your level of knowledge and understanding, answer the following short questions. These will help to prepare you for your summative (final) assessment.

1 How can we learn from experience?

2 What are the four main learning styles?

3 What technique can you use to give feedback?

4 What are the different ways training can be carried out?

5 What is the difference between trainer-centred and learner-centred activities?

6   Why is it important for your staff members to write a development plan?

7   How can you make objectives SMART?

8   Why is reflection an important skill?

Research task

The benefits of learning and creating development plans have been outlined in this chapter. Your task is to research an organisation in the hospitality industry (this could be your workplace), to find out what learning opportunities they have available to their staff and look in to the different ways they are utilised to assist with their staff development.

25

Supervise the use of technological equipment in hospitality services

HS6 Supervise the use of technological equipment in hospitality services

LEARNING OBJECTIVES

This unit is about how computers and technology can and could support services in hospitality. It is geared towards those in supervisory roles who are responsible for improving efficiency and accuracy of services.

After reading this chapter you will be able to:

- Understand the type of technology used in hospitality.
- Use common applications.
- Use word processing programs.
- Use a spreadsheet application program.
- Use other general purpose application programs.
- Use operating systems software.
- Understand management information systems.
- Understand communication.
- Understand supervision and control.

KEY WORDS

CRM
Customer relation management.

CRS
Central reservation system.

DBMS
Database management system.

DSS
Distribution service system.

EPOS
Electronic point of sale, could be a shop, checkout counter or location where a transaction takes place. It is also data recorded at a checkout and used for forecasting and stock control.

Hardware
The physical parts of a computer or device.

Input devices
Devices used to enter information.

Output devices
Devices used to retrieve and report information.

Peripherals
Ancillary equipment to aid computer use.

POS
Point of sale.

Software
Applications or programs to support specific functions or operations.

Storage devices
To collect and maintain data.

INTRODUCTION

This goal of this chapter is to introduce you to the various tools and applications available which are critical in ensuring effective and efficient use of time and resources.

Understanding and mastering information technology and using the various applications to one's benefit will help increase efficiency in everyday tasks facing today's supervisors. This chapter will introduce the basic technology used in hospitality. A fundamental knowledge of the terminology will be described as well as common benefits including issues faced by hospitality professionals.

This chapter will help you stay abreast of the latest applications and trends used in the industry. The move from traditional methods of handling day-to-day work has revolutionised since the adoption of modern electronic systems and the benefits include time and money saved.

INFORMATION TECHNOLOGY USED IN HOSPITALITY

Computer hardware classifications

1 Mainframe computers

- The largest computers used for data storage, critical applications and bulk data processing or financial transaction processing

2 Midrange computers-workstations

- Usually act as servers to some network (including the Internet)
- Can operate as workstation to perform specific function such as:
  - CAM computer-aided manufacturing
  - CAD computer-aided design
- Highly specialised for performing high-power functions

3 Microcomputers

- Personal computer's CPU (central processing unit)
- Laptops
- PDA personal digital assistant
- POS point of sale

! REMEMBER

Keeping up to date with modern technology will help:

- Increase efficiency
- Increase effectiveness
- Minimise mistakes and waste
- Instant access to information
- Faster communication
- Increased profits

© ISTOCKPHOTO.COM/MURAT KOC

Input devices

There are many input formats which enable us to collect information and enter data and instructions into the computer. Input devices can be manual or automatic.

Manual input devices
Keyboard, including concept keyboard

A keyboard is the most common method of manual input and mostly consists of a flat board with buttons which are assigned an alphanumeric code. The standard laptop or stand-alone computer has the traditional configuration of letters and numbers generally known by those able to touch type. The keyboard can be programmed to accommodate many different codes and instructions. To do so, an overlay sheet is placed on the keyboard with the different code, instruction or explanation for each keystroke. You see this used in fast food restaurants and supermarkets have similar overlays with either a description or picture depicting the item being purchased or ordered.

Digital cameras

Digital cameras are similar to traditional film cameras except the image is converted and compressed into a digital picture and stored in a file format which can be transferred and read by a computer. The most common file formats are GIF and JPEG.

Microphones

Microphones are used to convert sound and voice into an electronic format which is converted and compressed into a file which can be transferred and read by a computer allowing for playback. Microphones have evolved to enable the use of voice recognition technology as well as converting audio files into text to be converted by word processing programs.

Touch screen

A touch screen or visual display unit is basically a concept keyboard which is programmed onto a screen. The buttons on the keyboard are programmed with different codes, information or instructions. The person inputting touches the screen and similar to the keyboard, the computer senses which code is to be executed. The screen is simply the interface in the same way as the keyboard.

Video digitiser

A video digitiser is an application which takes traditional analogue video and converts and compresses the information in a digital format which can be transferred, stored, read and played back by a computer.

Graphics tablets

These consist of a flat pad (the tablet) and special pen which the user draws with. As the user draws on the pad the image is created on the screen. Using a graphics tablet a designer can produce very accurate on-screen drawings.

Scanners

A common way of converting images into files formats which can be stored and ready by computers. They can also be used with **OCR** (optical character recognition) software to scan in text.

Other manual input devices

Light pen

Tracker ball

Mouse

Joystick

Automatic input devices

1 Sensors.

2 Barcode reader.

Barcodes

Information is coded and stored into different groups of vertical bars that can be read by a barcode reader. Barcodes are printed on nearly every product that you buy. Shops use barcodes because they enable easy maintenance of their stock control system. The barcode contains the product details such as product name, size, manufacturer, country of origin. The price is accessed up from the shop's database. When the bar code is scanned, the shop's stock is automatically reduced by one.

© ISTOCKPHOTO.COM/ WENDELL FRANKS

MICR (magnetic ink character reader)

Magnetic ink characters are the strange-looking numbers that appear at the bottom of cheques. Banks use MICR to read the numbers from the bottom of cheques to obtain data such as account numbers and bank sort codes. This particular font is used because it is easy for a machine to discriminate between characters. The ink is magnetised because it makes it immune to creases or dirty marks.

Magnetic strip (or stripe) reader

Magnetic stripes are built into many plastic cards such as credit and debit cards, cashpoint cards and personal identity cards. The magnetic strip on the back of the card can hold the personal details of the card owner and, with the necessary PIN, will allow access to secure information e.g. bank account details. Data stored on the strip is scanned and input into a computer system by a magnetic stripe reader.

© ISTOCKPHOTO.COM/ANDREW JOHNSON

OMR (optical mark reader)

This reads marks made by pencil on a printed form into the computer. OMR systems are suited to reading pre-printed forms and check-boxes such as National Lottery number selection sheets and multiple-choice exam papers.

Output devices

Common output formats are:

- Printed paper
- Saved disk file
- Sound
- Video
- On-screen documents

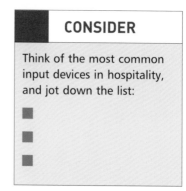

CONSIDER

Think of the most common input devices in hospitality, and jot down the list:

-
-
-

These output formats allow the computer to transfer information to the user in a format that is useable and understandable. The devices used to facilitate this transfer of information include the following:

Monitors (visual display units)

These are the most common output device and include:

- **Desktop monitors** or cathode ray tube (CRT)
- **Liquid crystal displays (LCD)** or thin film transistors (TFT)

Printers

- **Dot-matrix printers** are not so common today. They are noisy and low quality, however they are available at a low cost. They are commonly used when carbon copies or duplicates need to be made, such as for wage slips. Also, they are useful in harsher environments such as a garages and warehouses as they are sturdier than the other two types of printer
- **Ink-jet printers** offer black and white or colour printing with reduced levels of quality and speed
- **Laser printers** produce a very high-quality output, are quiet and very fast. Laser colour printers are more costly than the other printers

Plotters

A plotter can be used to produce high-quality, accurate drawings. They are usually used for computer-aided design (CAD) and computer-aided manufacture (CAM) applications such as printing out floor plans for houses and design specifications for car parts.

Other devices

- Speakers
- LCD projectors

Output can also be in the form of instructions to a device such as a robot arm.

STORAGE DEVICES

Primary storage memory

1 ROM (**read-only memory**) cannot be changed by program or user. ROM retains its memory even after the computer is turned off. For example, ROM stores the instructions for the computer to start up when it is turned on again. The operating system is loaded from the hard disk and stored in RAM whilst the machine is being used.

2 RAM (**random access memory**) is a fast *temporary* type of memory in which programs and data is stored whilst the computer is switched on. For example, when you load a word processing program it is loaded into RAM. The contents of the computer's screen are also held in RAM. If the computer loses power, data stored in RAM is lost.

Secondary storage devices

1 Hard disk. These are disks which spin at very high speeds (around 7,200 revolutions per minute – rpm) within a sealed unit inside the computer. Hard disks can usually store very large amounts of data – 250 gigabytes is common in desktop computers. The data stored here will stay where it is until deleted, but needs to be loaded into main store RAM before it can be used.

Characteristics of hard disk:

- It has space not memory
- Magnetic storage
- Space is measured with bytes
- All applications, operating system reside on hard drive
- Modern hard drives have at least 40 Gb of space
- Save the operating system
- Save software applications or programs
- Save the majority of your data files

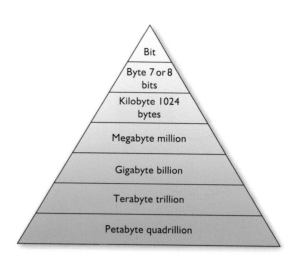

Hierarchy of storage categories

THE EVOLUTION OF INFORMATION TECHNOLOGY

COMPONENTS	EARLY 1990s	MID 1990s	MILLENNIUM	RECENT
HARDWARE	8600 series	Pentium I&II	Pentium III	Pentium IV&V
	40Mb disk	1 Gb disk	10 Gb disk	250 Gb disk
	16Mb/RAM	32Mb/RAM	128Mb/RAM	356Mb/RAM

2 Floppy disk. The commonest type of magnetic disk is the 3.5 inch floppy disk. You can read data from and write data on to a floppy disk and they can be moved between computers and usually store up to 1.44 Mb. They have three main uses:

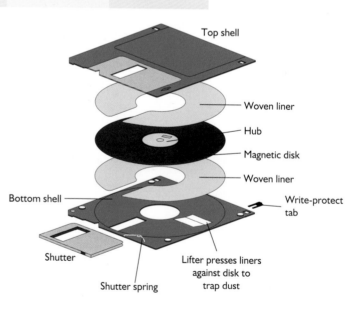

- to transfer small files of data from one machine to another
- to back up important small files that are stored on your hard disk
- to store restricted files that you don't want all other users of your computer seeing. Floppy disks are less popular nowadays as typical file sizes tend to be too large for them. With newer storage devices such as CD-RW and flash memory sticks, floppy disks are being surpassed. In fact, many machines now don't come with an A drive as standard

Zip disks are like large floppy disks, but can store 250 megabytes or more of data. They need their own drive. As with floppy disks, they are not used as frequently now as zip disk technology has been superseded

3 External backing stores: optical disks.

There are several different types of optical disk, although they all look pretty much the same.

- **CD-ROM**
  - **CD-ROM** stands for compact disk – read-only memory. They are optical disks that use the same technology as musical compact disks. They store up to 700 Mb of data and a laser beam is used to read the data off the disk
  - Data is written onto the CD-ROM disk before it is sold and cannot be changed by the user. As CD-ROMs can store large amounts of data, they can be used for multimedia applications such as encyclopaedias, and can store pictures, sounds and video clips

- **CD-R and CD-RW**
  - CD-Rs are blank optical disks onto which you can write data with a piece of hardware called a CD writer. They have a similar capacity to CD-ROMs and can be set up as multi-session disks and so you can write to them many times. Eventually of course, you will run out of disk space as you never go over the same area twice
  - CD-RWs are blank optical disks which can be written and re-written to

- **DVD**
  - DVD stands for digital versatile disk. There are several formats on the market, the more expensive ones being recordable like CDs. They are the same size as CDs, but hold much more data – a single-sided, single-layer disc can hold up to 4.7 gigabytes with a dual layer disc holding 8.4 gigabytes. Now DVDs are commonly used for video recordings, so you will often see them measured in minutes e.g. 4.7Gb = 120 minutes
  - DVD drives are often found on computers as combined DVD and CD-RW drives, so the computer can read and show DVD films, as well as read and write CDs

  - **Advantages:**
  - they can hold a lot more data
  - they can hold more multimedia material

4 **External backing stores: other types**
- **External hard drives**
  - These can store very large amounts of data – up to a terabyte – and can be plugged in to your computer via a USB or firewire port to provide extra storage

- **Memory sticks**
  - A memory stick is a small pen-top-sized device that holds a large amount of memory – from 512Mb to upwards depending on the price paid. This is a USB device and can be used in a similar way to

floppy disk, but is inserted into the USB port – it is then seen by the computer as a removable drive

- **Advantages:**
  - Both portable hard drives and memory sticks hold large quantities of data
  - They are extremely portable, so the user can take them wherever they go

MAIN GENERAL PURPOSE USED APPLICATIONS

APPLICATION	MAIN FUNCTIONS
Word processing application	Enter, edit, manipulate, store and print text
Spreadsheets	Numerical models and functions can be set up and modified
Database	Process large amounts of data and producing several reports
Web browsers	Display pages on screen and finds information published on World Wide Web
Email	Sending and receiving data from one work unit to another
Utilities	Antivirus programs and other security operations

COMPUTER SOFTWARE CLASSFICATIONS

The main types of software used in hospitality are the operating systems Widows XP, Windows Vista and Windows Millennium.

Operating systems control the backing store and peripherals such as disk drives and printers, they also control the loading and running of applications. The operating system also organises the use of memory between programs and regulates processing time between programs and users. The operating system is also responsible for categorising priorities between programs and users.

One of the main tasks of the operating systems is to maintain security and access rights of users and to deals with errors and user instructions.

Word processing program (e.g. Microsoft Word)

A basic feature of word processing programs is to enter and edit text. They are popular processing program used for creating documents such as letters,

 TIP

You can create your own template or you can download them from numerous websites.

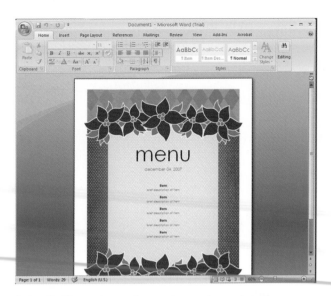

http://office.microsoft.com/en-us/templates)

brochures, menus, signs, job descriptions and many other publications used in hospitality.

The most widespread use of this application is to produce menus. Almost all versions of Word offers users numerous features which enables to produce high-quality publications. One of the most efficient is the use of templates which can be set by managers or supervisors and then be used by other colleagues and staff members.

Spreadsheet program (e.g. Microsoft Excel)

This program was developed to deal with processing large amount of data and to perform different mathematical functions. Using spreadsheets can help you with many of control tasks such as:

- Costing
- Pricing
- Calculating ratios
- Stock taking
- Labour control – timetables
- Ratios

This application can help you create charts to present different result calculated such as type of sale, trend of stock use, density of sale.

The basic spreadsheet design

The best way to design efficient spreadsheet is to design it first on paper. Good practice is to first answer on few questions:

- What is its purpose?
- Who will use it?
- How often should it be amended?
- Do you need charts?
- How many reports will be produced from one lot of data?
- And any other questions

Once you have more clear idea you can start to make a design by roughly sketching out what will be on the spreadsheet and where. The best way is to use columns starting from top left corner down rather across.

ACTIVITY

Create your own template of the menu or beverage list for daily specials

1 Open word processing application.

2 Insert borders, shades and pictures of your choice to create simple menu template.

3 Insert the general information and outline items which will change regularly.

4 Save the document as option Template.

Creating a stocktake sheet in Excel

Nowadays many businesses already have very modern systems to automatically control their stock list. However, there are many businesses who don't or who control their stock by using manual back-up.

After you have sketched your basic spreadsheet you will start creating one in Excel application:

- Open a new work book
- In cell B1 type in the spreadsheet
- Merge cells E1 and F1
- Type in Date
- In cell B2 type in Commodity
- In cell C2 type in Unit size
- In cell D2 type in Price
- In cell E2 type in Quantity
- In cell F2 type in Value
- Click and drag highlight 10 rows
- Insert table grid
- Format column B on text
- Format column C on text
- Format column D on currency with 2 decimals
- Format column E on number with 2 decimals
- Format column F on currency with 2 decimals
- In cell E13 type in Total
- Format cell F13 on currency with 2 decimals
- Create formula in cell F13 as seen on the figure below

TASK

Now choose one of your daily tasks discussed in previous chapters (e.g. supervising stock-taking) and sketch your own spreadsheet.

What data is required for a stocktake sheet? How are you going to organise it?

■ By formatting text, size and colours you can create very professional-looking stock-taking sheets

Wine Cellar	DATE				
	30.11.2007				
COMMODITY	UNIT	PRICE	QUANTITY	VALUE	COMMENTS
RED WINE					
Les Charmeuses Savigny 2001	BOT	£10.34	12.00	£124.08	
Chiant 'Fortebraccio' 2003	BOT	£7.62	11.00	£83.82	
Croze Hemitage Mieysonniers Chapoutier 2001	BOT	£7.38	8.00	£59.04	
Valserrano Reserva Rioja 1998	BOT	£10.21	13.00	£132.73	
Chateau Paveil de Luze 2001	BOT	£11.06	23.00	£254.38	offer on menu as wine of the month
Catena Cabernet Sauvignon 2002	BOT	£6.98	5.00	£34.90	
Morgan Vineyards Tweleve Clones 2004	BOT	£10.82	6.00	£64.92	
Tourelles de Longville 2002 Pauillac Boudeaux	BOT	£14.59	1.00	£14.59	reorder only 6 botles
			TOTAL	£768.46	

You can use separate worksheets for each area of the business

■ Kitchen

■ Bar

■ Stores

■ Restaurant

SNAKS								
DATE:								
COMMODITY	UNIT	COST PER UNIT	SOUTH PANTRY	NORTH PANTRY	KITCHEN PANTRY	16th FLOOR	CLOSING STOCK	VALUE
ASSORTED SHORTB BISCUITS 6 X 1kg	BOX	£4.73					0	£0.00
WLAKERS SENSATIONS 32 x 40g	CASE	£7.78					0	£0.00
MATTHEW ALGIE 54 X 4PT	pk	£0.90					0	£0.00
T & L.CUBE BROWN SUGAR X 1kg	BOX	£2.50					0	£0.00
T & L. CUBE WHITE SUGAR X 1kg	BOX	£2.50					0	£0.00
RITAZZA COFFEE 90 x 90g Bag	EACH	£1.10					0	£0.00
NESCAFE DECAF COFFEE X 750g	TIN	£6.21					0	£0.00
TEA BAGS 1100 X 1 CUP	BAG	£8.60					0	£0.00
TRADITIONAL TEA -TWINNINGS X 50	BOX	£3.20					0	£0.00
EARL GREY-TWINNINGS X 50	BOX	£3.20					0	£0.00
BLACKCURRANT & VANILLA X 20	BOX	£2.40					0	£0.00
						TOTAL		£0.00

Or if you would like to separate commodities your spreadsheet could look like this one.

Summary sheets

Summary sheets are used to control high-value items such as wine, beer, non-alcoholic drinks

Summary Sheet for April 2007							
Comodity	Opening stock	Plus purchase	Total	Transfer	Closing stock	Cost	Value of stock used
Red wine	12	24	36	30	6	£7.00	£210.00
White wine	34	44	78	16	62	£6.90	£110.40
Apple Juice	12	0	12	5	7	£2.00	£10.00

The value of the stock can be compared with the sales achieved to see whether there are any losses or more sinister activities.

HOSPITALITY-SPECIFIC APPLICATIONS

PMS (property management system)	Stores data about guest activities, their portfolios and compose several reports essential for all departments in hospitality unit. Mostly used in the hotel industry or larger restaurant chains where many departments are involved in operation.
Reservation system	An operations systems of reservation enquiries, tracks availability and rates and provides management and supervisors with essential reports.
Stock-control system	Controls and manages level of stock and use of stock, provides supervisors and management with report such as using rates, sale, stock ratios.
Recipe costing system	In relation with stock control system or independently, provides management with accurate costing for individual dishes.
Conferences and banqueting system	Similar to the reservation system although it is specialised in the booking of conferences facilities. It provides management with several essential reports.

There are three main areas in hospitality and usage of technology and applications as support.

Front of house

Front of house operations require fast, efficient and flexible technology to ensure the customer experience is enhanced. The front of house has a pivotal role in that it communicates with the customer directly as well as being the liaison to the back office and kitchen. The processes involved include:

■ Sales – records the sales information such as food and beverage ordered, timing of order and food delivery, turnover per table/per person and other key performance indicators (customer per hour, average spend, most popular items sold etc.)

■ Reservations and customer database – provides accurate information on seating plans and availability, as well as customer information such as allergies, personal preferences (favourite table, special occasions, preferred dishes and servers)

VIEW ALL AVAILABLE OFFERS

Your Restaurant
STANDARD À LA CARTE MENU

Select your preferred seating area:

Restaurant

Select your preferred session and party size (max 8):

Dinner | 2

FEBRUARY 2009						▶▶
MON	TUE	WED	THU	FRI	SAT	SUN
26	27	28	29	30	31	1
2	3	4	5	6	7	8
9	10	11	12	13	14	15
16	17	18	19	20	21	22
23	24	25	26	27	28	1
2	3	4	5	6	7	8

BOOK A TABLE ▶▶

Automated, real-time reservations facility that allows restaurant customers to make bookings online, 24 hours a day, 7 days a week

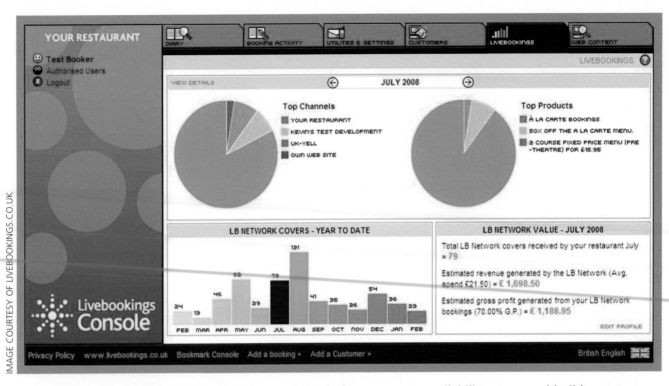

Co-ordinate on and offline reservations in one central place, manage availability, store and build a customer database, monitor booking levels and produce reports

---

! REMEMBER

The main control points in front of house processes include:

- Monitoring of key performance indicators
- Cash reconciliations
- Labour control and management
- Prevent, detect and correct mistakes and human error
- Prevent, detect and correct fraud and collusion

- Credit card processing – to enable customers to pay by debit or credit card
- End of day/shift reconciliations – involve the daily counting and reconciliation of cash, stock and banking which is vital for cash management and control and ensure fraud or collusion is prevented, detected and corrected
- Labor process – controlling shifts and hours worked ensuring the appropriate number of staff to support the customer volume

Technology available to support the front of house processes includes POS, PDA and PCs.

- POS – the main interface used to input customers food and beverage orders. POS also liaises with the kitchen and back office to ensure the orders is prepared as well as storing information for reporting and analysis. Activities such as special offers and discounts are also recorded for monitoring of effectiveness of marketing programmes
- PDA – also known as Waiter Mate, is used to input customer orders quickly and efficiently to the the bar or kitchen without losing time. PDAs control the inputted information by user (thus preventing tampering of users' orders and information whilst able to identify errors by user) and helps improve the service to customers. Up to date information is made available

to the waiter in terms of availability of dishes, offers and other changes to the menu

■ PC – collects data from POS and PDAs and stores, compiles and reports the information to enable the monitoring of individual performance, statistics and labour costs. The PC is used to disseminate and communicate the information to the back office and kitchen as well as management and updates information such as stock, customer database, supplier information etc.

The applications used in the front of house include Microsoft basic applications (Word, Excel etc.) as well as custom made applications such as Maitre D' and other similar applications to collect and distribute data.

Kitchen

As in front of house, kitchen operations have complex and time-sensitive processes which are supported by vital technology. More and more kitchens make use of technology to manage data to increase efficiency. The processes involved include:

■ Stock taking – counting and valuing the stock on hand to ensure accurate calculations of costs. This process also ensures sufficient stock is on hand to handle the sales volumes for a given period and information is analysed such as turnover, stock levels and delivery lead times to determine economic order quantity and reorder points

■ Menu costing – accurate and relevant calculations based on the underlying cost of food, labour and overhead to ensure the cost is up to date and complete. Menu costing drives decisions around portion control and creates standards the kitchen needs to adhere to

■ Menu pricing – calculating the price of food and beverage to the customer to ensure the required profit margin is achieved. The menu pricing is directly related to the cost of goods and services calculated in the menu costing process and helps drive profitability

■ Labour controls – include work hours needed for various shifts in the day as well as costing the labour and developing an appropriate manpower plan

■ Hygiene controls – of vital importance in the kitchen to ensure safe and fresh food and beverages. Automatic temperature controls as well as recording and monitoring of temperatures to ensure HACCP standards are met

Technology available to support the front of house processes includes PCs and temperature control systems.

> **! REMEMBER**
>
> The main control points in the kitchen processes include:
>
> ■ Counting and valuing stock on hand
>
> ■ Determining economic order quantity and reorder points
>
> ■ Accurate costing of food, labour and overhead
>
> ■ Accurate pricing to customers to achieve required profit
>
> ■ Managing labour work hours and manpower plan
>
> ■ Ensuring HACCP standards are met and temperature controls are monitored and maintained

The applications used in the kitchen include Microsoft basic applications (Word, Excel etc.) as well as custom-made applications such as Maitre D' and other similar applications to collect, report and distribute data.

Back office

Back office operations support both the front of house and kitchen operations as well as other departments and functions such as accounting, human resources, marketing and general and administration functions. The back office is the main hub for receiving information and communicating it back out to management and other users for reporting and analysis. The main processes include:

- Marketing – collecting customer information and profiles as well as internal stock, costing and pricing information, marketing campaigns can be developed and launched to increase awareness and brand
- Human resources – based on information obtained in the front of house and kitchen operations, individuals can be objectively measured allowing the appropriate recognition and reward
- Payroll – accurate salary to employees based on hours and shifts worked
- Accounting – the timely and accurate recording of financial information
- Financial reporting and analysis – the reporting of key financial statements such as profit and loss statements, balance sheets and stock inventory reports allows management and relevant users to assess the success of the business
- Forecasting – with the proper financial information, revenue and cost forecasting and trending can be performed to predict volumes and profits
- Purchasing – required information is needed to ensure proper decisions are made when vendors and products are selected

The technology used to support the back office processes includes PCs and database servers.

The applications used in the back office include Microsoft basic applications (Word, Excel etc.) as well as custom made applications such as Opera, Fidelio, Maitre D', Simply Accounting, Accpac, Access database or SAP and other similar applications to collect, report and distribute data.

Assessment of knowledge and understanding

You have now learnt about some key elements involved in the use of technological equipment in the hospitality industry.

As you have worked through the chapter you have already discussed some elements of technology, but to test your level of knowledge and understanding further, answer the following short questions. These will help to prepare you for your summative (final) assessment.

1   What are peripherals?

2   Name at least three input devices used in hospitality.

3   What are the main operations of spreadsheet application?

4   What is difference between POS and EPOS?

5   What operations and tasks can be supported with computer technology in the front of house?

6   What are the main characteristics of reservation systems?

26

Supervise practices for handling payments

HS26 **Supervise practices for handling payments**

LEARNING OBJECTIVES

This unit is about monitoring and controlling the handling of payments, collecting takings and processing payment information. It also requires maintaining security and dealing with difficulties that may arise in connection with payments and takings.

After reading this chapter you will be able to:

■ Make sure staff have sufficient resources to carry out the service.

■ Make sure staff have the information and skills in order to carry out their work effectively.

■ Make sure that staff communicate with customers in a way that is likely to promote goodwill and understanding.

■ Make sure staff handle payments according to your organisation's procedures and that payments and refunds are correctly authorised.

■ Make sure that staff follow payment point safety and security procedures.

■ Deal effectively with any problems which occur at payment points.

■ Collect payment point contents following your organisation's procedures.

■ Reconcile actual takings against recorded takings and follow your organisation's procedures and legal requirements to deal with any discrepancies.

■ Complete all documents relating to takings and process in line with your organisation's procedures.

KEY WORDS

Cheques
These are carried by the customer and filled in to pay for goods, they are usually backed up with a guarantee card issued by the bank.

Chip and PIN
The system used by the customer to input a PIN code when paying for goods or services.

EPOS
Electronic point of sale, could be a shop, checkout counter or location where a transaction takes place. It is also data recorded at a checkout and used for forecasting and stock control.

Financial transactions
The exchange of payments for services or products.

Float
The amount of money carried; usually small denominations in the cash till. This is used to give change to customers.

Invoice
An itemised account of what has been purchased and the payment method used.

Legal requirements
Any other law or regulation that governs health, safety and hygiene in the workplace.

Micros
A computerised system which allows kitchens, restaurants and other areas to communicate and collect billing information quickly and efficiently.

Organisation's procedures
The procedures that your organisation has developed to cover fraud, security and accountability in your area of responsibility.

Responsible person
The person or persons at work to whom you should report to regarding cash or credit discrepancies or queries; this could be your line manager or employer.

Security procedures
This may include making sure that unauthorised persons do not enter your area of responsibility, making sure that items are protected from theft, following the correct procedures when items go missing. This is especially important when dealing with payments and cash handling.

Working environment
The working area or areas for which you are responsible.

X-reading
Readings taken throughout the day from the till to monitor ongoing transactions.

Z-reading
The reading taken from the till at the end of shift to check transactions taken.

> **! REMEMBER**
>
> Always ensure the customer's bill is accurate and has been correctly processed. A business relies on its staff's professionalism and attention to detail.

© ISTOCKPHOTO.COM/DNY59

Paying the bill

INTRODUCTION
Supervising practices for handling payments

Payment handling of any kind is one of the most important parts of supervisor's responsibilities whether this involves hands on work, training or supervision.

Financial transactions are completed for the exchange of goods or services, large or small. This process is essential within the hospitality industry. The recording of sales and purchases correctly will have a direct impact on staffing levels, turnover and profit.

A supervisor is responsible for the customer's satisfaction from the time or booking/ordering to their departure from the operation. A happy customer will usually spend more and help to improve the business's standing.

An effective supervisor will ensure their staff are fully aware of their roles and responsibilities including ensuring that all customers have paid prior to leaving the establishment.

A supervisor will ensure the staff is confident collecting and processing the float, taking payments from customers, using the tills and computer systems, and conducting the end of shift reports.

There are numerous ways for customers to settle the bill including:

■ Cash

■ Cheques

■ Credit or debit cards

■ Vouchers

■ Traveller's cheques

Each type of payment requires its own way of processing from the use of serial numbers to chip and pin. Correct charging and payments will ensure a smooth operation; undercharging or overcharging will cause problems for either the customer or the business. There is also the legal aspect to consider;

incorrect charging or payment can be a criminal offence and in some cases the punishment is imprisonment.

A supervisor's responsibility will be determined by the size of the operation, for example a multi-million pound business will use touch screen technology which links into a centralised processing unit, a smaller unit may use a simple till/cash register with a paper printout.

Stock-taking may be linked into the advanced system which a supervisor will be able to access and direct the purchase of products. These systems all rely on the supervisor's ability to control the flow of money and to ensure its accountability.

DAILY RESPONSIBILITIES

The supervisor will have arranged for the float to be made accessible to staff; this will be counted, checked and accounted for.

Depending on the size of the establishment a security guard may be present and escort the supervisor during this process; it is usually best practice for two staff members to collect and distribute the money to ensure no fraudulent activities take place.

Any discrepancy in the cash totals issued must be reported to the supervisor immediately so they can be checked, investigated and amended as required.

The correct procedure for the bill is as follows:

The start of trading: a supervisor's responsibility

The supervisor has a myriad of responsibilities during this time; they must ensure that all staff are prepared for the day whether this is front of house, reception, kitchen, bar or restaurant.

Whether you are working in the restaurant, bar or reception the key to a successful day and in fact career is attention to detail and exceeding customer expectations.

TAKING ORDERS RESULTING IN PAYMENTS

Key stages are as follows:

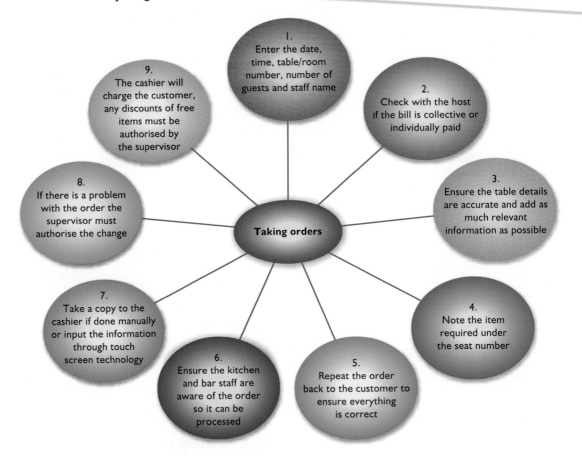

Taking orders

1. Enter the date, time, table/room number, number of guests and staff name

2. Check with the host if the bill is collective or individually paid

3. Ensure the table details are accurate and add as much relevant information as possible

4. Note the item required under the seat number

5. Repeat the order back to the customer to ensure everything is correct

6. Ensure the kitchen and bar staff are aware of the order so it can be processed

7. Take a copy to the cashier if done manually or input the information through touch screen technology

8. If there is a problem with the order the supervisor must authorise the change

9. The cashier will charge the customer, any discounts of free items must be authorised by the supervisor

The modern approach

Handheld computers are used extensively to take orders which are passed to the kitchen, bar and cashier electronically.

This system is faster, more efficient, less time-consuming and can give an air of professionalism to the customer. As with the paper version all discrepancies, problems and free items must be authorised by a supervisor and signed off.

Automated handheld computers work with the stores to maintain a balanced stock level, this can be set to order items automatically or require a supervisor's authorisation. This can save money and time which is a very beneficial factor in the hospitality industry.

Invoices

The cashier will produce detailed invoices for the customer; these should state all details of the guest's visit:

■ Food

■ Drink

■ Accommodation

■ Sundries

Ensuring the invoice is correct is essential, if there are numerous customers waiting to pay ask for help and inform the supervisor. A customer will prefer to wait a few minutes and receive the correct bill rather than spend time changing it to the correct amount.

An invoice can be produced manually or electronically; the two methods require different staff levels, training and minimise lost time.

The manual method is:

■ Collect the order dockets

■ Enter the items listed into the cash register (ensuring a copy of the food or bar list is available for perusal)

■ Ensure the bill shows the company name, address and VAT number

■ Print the invoice and pass to the waiting staff to issue

■ The waiting staff should take a moment to check the invoice before presenting it to the customer

■ The bill should be presented to the customer

■ The waiting staff should retire from the table until the customer is ready to pay

■ The payment may be in numerous forms

■ The waiting staff should return the invoice with the payment to the cashier for completion, or return to the customer if a pin or signature is required

■ A receipt should then be issued with a compliment slip

The electronic systems:

■ The bill is created automatically from the pre-inputted order

■ The system will show the date, time, server, table, guests present and a detailed invoice

■ The payment method will be the same as above

TAKING PAYMENTS FROM GUESTS

The correct steps for taking payment:

- ■ As soon as a credit card, debit card or cash is placed in the folder the waiting staff should take it to the cashier immediately
- ■ If the payment is by cash the cashier will tender the cash and provide change as appropriate
- ■ The change should be returned to the customer with the invoice and presented
- ■ If the payment is by card the cashier will process the card using available technology
- ■ Handheld machines which allow customers to stay at the table and enter their pin numbers are now readily available
- ■ For audit purposes you must record the method of payment received from each customer
- ■ Staple the credit or debit card receipt to the invoice and file them securely
- ■ If cash is paid note this on the invoice
- ■ At the end of the supervisor's shift all monies, receipts and invoices should be collated

Using handheld technology

Manual card payments

Originally the cards were processed manually by copying an imprint of the card onto carbonised paper; this then had the amount entered and a signature from the card holder completed the transaction.

This was open to fraud as cards could be copied and signatures illegally copied.

Cheque payments

Most establishments will not accept cheques unless pre-authorised or backed up with a guarantee card.

A cheque is simply an instruction to the bank to provide funds to the company. Cheques are printed by the bank featuring the account holder's name, account number, sort code and signature box.

In order for a cheque to be honoured, the account holder must have the funds available in the account. If they do not enough money in their account the bank will refuse the cheque, which is called 'bouncing'. Initially the bank will pay the money into the bank account then remove it and charge a fee. The account holder will also be charged for exceeding their limit.

This is why cheques are seen as risky forms of payment, as the customer can leave and the business will be unaware of the problem for several days.

The cheque guarantee card is used as authorisation for the payment, the details are recorded on the back of the cheque and would include the card number, start and expire date and issue number if applicable.

Cash payments

Cash is the most common form of payment and the simplest. When the payment is provided by the customer ensure you repeat the amount they hand over. This will prevent the customer accusing you of short-changing them; in the event that a customer dispute arises ensure the supervisor is informed immediately. The supervisor should then conduct the following:

■ Print the till receipts

■ Count the till float

■ Count the cheques and vouchers

■ Ensure the total amount in the till corresponds with the till receipt

This procedure will highlight any monetary discrepancies and will allow the supervisor to make an informed decision regarding the complaint.

If the customer is correct follow the establishment's policy on the correct way to handle the situation.

It is important that you refrain from getting bullied into giving more change than is required, offering more as an apology is not recommended and is classed as bad practice.

Never borrow money from the cash register, this is breaking the law and may involve the police being called.

Whether you intend to return the money at a later date, time is irrelevant as you do not have the authority to do so. Auditors are used during the year to verify receipts and cash, cheque transactions; discrepancies are highlighted and are investigated. In the majority of instances taking money or products is classed as gross misconduct: termination of employment and perhaps a police investigation will follow.

WWW.CANSTOCKPHOTO.COM

Complementary items

Any food, drink or service offered to a customer is never free of charge, if the supervisor has authorised a free meal, drink or service then this must be entered into the computer/till and then assigned an internal account number.

This account must be signed by the supervisor and then verified during auditing to ensure no misuse has occurred.

The staff food and drink policy will vary from establishment to establishment. Sometimes the service will be free for staff, at other times there is a discounted rate. Both will need to be entered through the system using discount buttons or using the internal codes.

Refunds

Refunds are given for numerous reasons:

- An incorrect bill
- Poor service or food
- A problem with the credit cards
- Too much money being taken

Incomplete transactions

- Overs – when the till has been incorrectly rung through with no additional funds being added
- Voids – when a transaction is made but no funds are available or the customer changes their mind, so the transaction must be voided
- No sales – this is a function on the till which allows the change tray to be accessed without a sale, modern day tills record this function to ensure no fraudulent activity takes place

WWW.CANSTOCKPHOTO.COM

Refunds must be authorised by the supervisor and they normally hold a key which allows this process to take place.

Recording a refund requires the computer or tills to produce what is known as a 'negative' invoice which shows a minus figure.

Producing a negative invoice and keeping the copy in the tills ensures the figures will balance. An audit trail is essential and needs to be checked after every shift as mistakes or problems are easier to rectify as soon as they occur.

Paying bills from the tills

There maybe times when a supervisor is required to pay an invoice from the till, this occasionally happens when working with small privately owned businesses.

The term 'petty cash' is used when essentials such as milk or other items are required at short notice. The policy of each establishment is different and they may not authorise this process; any cash removed must be replaced with an invoice to ensure the till balances.

If you are required to pay an invoice from the tills try to ensure the amount is not so large as to empty the float and leave the shift short of funds. If you are unsure it is always advisable to contact your supervisor for assistance.

Account holders

Some customers may hold an account with the establishment and will ask for their bill to be added to this.

This may also refer to guests who charge items and services to their room when staying in a hotel; they will then settle the bill on their departure.

The process requires the guest to show his or her room card or key, quote their room number and sign the bill. It is the supervisor's responsibility to ensure the information the guest gives matches the reservation.

Checking the information can be done by calling reception or looking at the computer system, depending on what type of establishment you work in.

There are cases of professionals who attempt to obtain free items by charging other rooms and guests for services acquired.

A customer charging services to his room

No customer should be allowed to leave without settling their bill as mistakes are difficult to rectify once the customer has left. If the name does not match the room number you should contact the supervisor immediately; follow the establishment's policy. It maybe the guest has made a simple mistake or alternatively there could be an attempted theft occurring.

THE SUPERVISOR AT THE END OF THE SHIFT

There are numerous procedures that a supervisor must follow at the end of the shift:

- Count the float
- Collate the takings so far
- Collect all invoices, receipts and vouchers and ensure they all tally
- Transfer excess funds to the safe, with security assistance if required
- If the till is incorrect, i.e. too much money taken or too little, then investigation should take place. Excess funds stored in the safe and recorded. Too little requires a supervisor's attention as fraudulent activity may have taken place or simple human error

© ISTOCKPHOTO.COM/JACOM STEPHENS

The end of shift pattern is as follows:

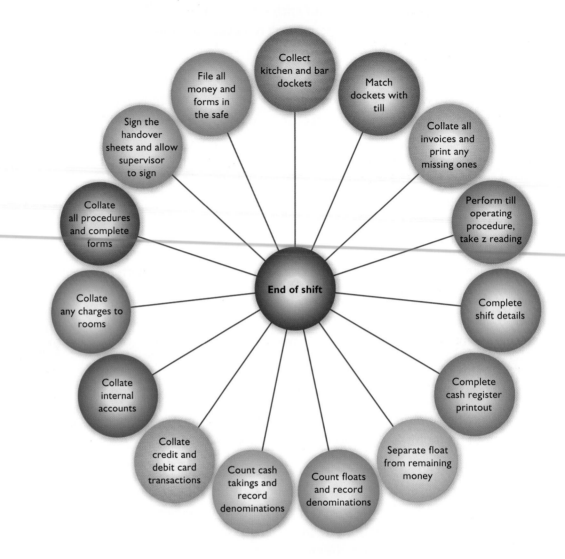

Assessment of knowledge and understanding

You have now learned about monitoring and controlling the handling of payments, collecting takings and processing payment information.

To test your level of knowledge and understanding, answer the following short questions. These will help to prepare you for your summative (final) assessment.

Invoices, cheques and cards

1 There are numerous responsibilities of a supervisor when dealing with cards and invoices; list four of them.

2 Give three examples of the implications if invoices are not correctly completed.

3 Explain why it is a good idea to keep accurate records of card transactions and the importance of keeping receipts.

4 Explain why cheques are not used or accepted in many establishments these days and the potential problems associated with them.

Cash payments

1 Detail the procedure you should adopt and follow if (i) you are aware of a colleague that is not carrying out their job correctly when dealing with cash transactions (ii) the float does not balance at the end of the shift.

2 Describe the procedure for dealing with refunds.

3 Explain and discuss the correct way of dealing with complimentary items.

4 Give two examples of why payments are sometimes made from the tills; also explain what precautions should be taken.

Accounts and end of shift

1 Give three examples of how accounts are used in the business; comment on how there may be a security risk using this type of payment.

2 Describe why operating an end of shift policy is beneficial to the business; then explain:

- Why are dockets collated and stored?
- Why is the float counted so many times?
- Why is security sometimes required?
- What does a z-reading produce?

27

Contribute to the development of a wine list

HS27 **Contribute to the development of a wine list**

LEARNING OBJECTIVES

This unit is about helping to develop new wine lists. It covers the research, analysis and introduction of wines to develop or complement a wine list.

After reading this chapter you will be able to:

■ Gather and evaluate information that will help to develop the wine list.

■ Support your suggestions for the wine list with all the information and feedback you have gathered and evaluated.

■ Assist decision makers to agree the final wine list.

■ Record the decisions taken according to your organisation's procedures.

■ Collect the information needed to introduce the new wines.

■ Make sure staff have the information, skills and resources required to support the introduction of the new wines, according to the individual jobs that they do.

KEY WORDS

Appellation

A geographical indication used to identify where the grapes for a wine were grown. The rules that govern appellations are dependent on the country in which the wine was produced. The AOC seal, or Appellation d'Origine Contrôlée, was created and mandated by French law.

New World Wines

Refers primarily to wines from New World wine regions such as the United States, Australia, South America and South Africa.

Oenology

The science and study of all aspects of wine and winemaking except vine growing and grape harvesting, which are a subfield called viticulture.

Old World Wines

Refers primarily to wine made in Europe but can also include other regions of the Mediterranean basin with long histories of winemaking. The two most guiding influence of Old World style winemaking is that of tradition and *terroir*. The former refers to the long history of a wine region while the later refers to geography and the unique characteristics of a place.

Sommelier

The trained and knowledgeable wine professional, commonly working in fine restaurants, who specialises in all aspects of wine service. The principal work of a sommelier is in the area of wine procurement, storage, wine cellar rotation, and to provide expert advice to customers.

Terroir

Originally a French term in wine, used to denote the special characteristics that geography bestowed upon them. It is a group of agricultural sites in same region which share the same soil, weather conditions and farming techniques, which each contribute to the unique qualities of the crop. It can be very loosely translated as 'a sense of place' which is embodied in certain qualities, and the sum of the effects that the local environment has had on the manufacture of the product.

Vintage

The process of picking grapes and creating the finished product. A **vintage wine** is one made from grapes that were all, or primarily, grown and harvested in a single specified year.

Viticulture
From the Latin word for *vine,* is the science, production and study of grapes which deals with the series of events that occur in the vineyard. When the grapes are used for winemaking, it is also known as viniculture. It is one branch of the science of horticulture.

Wine co-operatives
Agricultural co-operative which are involved in winemaking, and which in similarity to other co-operatives are owned by their members. The members in a winemaking co-operative are usually vineyard owners, who deliver grapes to the co-operative, which is involved in production of wine from the grapes and the subsequent marketing activities.

INTRODUCTION

Grapes in a traditional vineyard

A wine list primarily should be well matched to the cuisine it accompanies. Beyond this, however, good wine lists can vary widely in their quality. For some restaurants, a concise, well-chosen selection will suffice; for others, a professional sommelier has been employed to explore the globe for outstanding wines that fall in line with the restaurant's aim, style and cuisine. The best wine lists are comprised of careful and interesting selections with regard to the producer, vintage and origin, resulting in a list that spans a wide range of styles, price points and producers. Beyond the selection itself, the best wine lists are helpful: well organised and accessible, accurate and up to date, and offering comprehensive information about each wine, including vintages and appellations.

Evaluating and tasting wine

There are three elements to consider in evaluating a wine's quality: appearance, aroma and taste.

Colour and clarity

Observing the colour of the wine against a white background

For the evaluation of the appearance of wine, hold a half-full glass against a white background, such as a tablecloth, and observe the wine's colour and clarity. It should be radiant, rather than murky, and its colour should be appropriate for its type and age. Young white wines range in hue from a pale straw-yellow to a rich amber. The colour depends on the grape variety, the ripeness of the grapes at harvest, the way the wine was fermented and aged (white wines fermented and/or aged in barrel will have a more golden hue than those fermented and aged entirely in stainless steel tanks), and how much oxygen the wine was exposed to during vinification and bottling. As they age, white wines darken, assuming a deeper golden colour. Browning suggests either an extremely old white wine or, if found in a younger white, a wine that has been prematurely oxidised and should probably not be consumed.

Red wines, on the contrary, grow paler as they age. Young reds range in colour from a semi-transparent cherry for lighter wines such as Beaujolais or pinot noir to a deep ruby, sometimes with purplish tints, for a zinfandel or syrah. Older red wines may display a rusty tinge around the edges. This should not be present in a younger red wine.

Aroma/bouquet

The most important and revealing aspect of a wine's personality and quality is its smell. Indeed, most of what we take to a wine's taste is actually its aroma. Think of how the taste of food changes when you have a bad cold and can't smell. Swirl the wine gently to aerate the wine. When you smell the wine after swirling, your nasal receptors will pick up more bouncing esters and molecules than if you sniff a resting wine.

WWW.CANSTOCKPHOTO.COM

Swirling the wine in a glass helps to release the aromas

The volatile essences of the wine are carried by thousands of nerve endings in your nasal cavity to the olfactory bulb in your brain. The same thing happens, via the retronatal passage in the back of the mouth, when you sip and swallow wine. In effect, flavours are odours in your mouth. Swirling releases the wine's aromas and sniffing draws them into the olfactory bulb, which 'interprets' them (i.e., compares them to other familiar smells from memory).

 TIP

Cork taint
The most common fault that can be discovered during the smelling of wine is the aroma of cork taint. At low levels this can strip the wine of its fresh, fruity aromas. At its worst, it adds a pungent, wet-cardboard, earthy and musty smell to the wine.

This is a complex process, because a wine consists of over 300 different chemical compounds, many of which are identical or similar to those found in fruits, vegetables, spices, herbs and other substances. This is the reason why wine enthusiasts describe a wine's aromas in terms of various fruits, vegetables, flora, herbs and spices (e.g., apple, melon, citrus, cherry, berry, honey, peach, mint, pepper, grass, olive, clove, liquorice, cedar, etc.). This not a fanciful idea; there are actually chemical correlations underlying the comparisons, which explains the rich metaphorical language used to describe a wine's sensory characteristics.

The primary grape smells of a wine, distinct by variety, make up its aroma, while secondary characteristics, caused by factors such as fermentation and oak and bottle ageing, blend with its fruit smells to form the wine's bouquet.

PHOTOGRAPHY: LUCY MILLS

The aroma should be clean and fresh, with the characteristic scents associated with the variety (e.g., apple with chardonnay, melon and citrus with sauvignon blanc, cherry and blackcurrant with cabernet sauvignon, blackberry and

Different wine varieties

black pepper with zinfandel), perhaps accented by the toasty, vanilla, or spicy scents imparted by the barrels it was aged in. If the wine is older, it may have a less fresh and fruity aroma, but one with more complexity.

Taste

Although taste, as described above, is essentially a function of smell, tasting reveals aspects of a wine's personality that smelling cannot. It is thought that humans can perceive combinations of only five tastes: sweet, sour, bitter, umami and salty. These sensations are contained in taste buds on different parts of the tongue.

You may notice the tartness of a young dry white wine, for instance, or the astringency of a full-bodied young red. Some varieties, like riesling, chenin blanc, and gewürztraminer, are especially fruity, if not literally sweet, while a young cabernet sauvignon may taste very dry and even slightly bitter.

The 'body' of a wine – the sense of its weight on your palate – is a function primarily of its alcohol content (the higher the alcohol, the weightier the wine). A wine too high in alcohol may taste hot or harsh, while a wine low in alcohol may seem thin or watery. In red wines, the tannin acids contained in the grape skins, which are absorbed into the wine through fermentation (whites do not ferment on their skins and thus have little tannin) can promote a drying sensation, while a wine low in acidity may have an overly soft impression.

Whatever tastes a wine imparts, the key to its quality is balance, a harmony of all its elements: fruit, alcohol, acidity, wood (if any). By tasting a wine – especially by sloshing it about in your mouth before swallowing – you can gain a quick impression of its most salient elements (is it fruity, tart, soft, bitter?) and to what degree those elements are in harmony. Combined with assessing its appearance and aroma, this will complete your evaluation of the wine's quality and, most important, whether you find it pleasing or not.

Tasting the wine in a wine tasting session

The evaluation sheet

To prepare for a wine tasting ensure that each wine is served at the correct temperature. Serve each individual wine in a clean, dry glass and always use a new glass for a new wine. Always hold the glass by the stem to prevent your hands from warming the wine. You may wish to have some bread or an unflavoured cracker to cleanse your palate between each wine and maybe some cold tap water available. Usually spittoons are provided to deposit the mouthful of wine.

An evaluation sheet similar to the one here should be given out to each member of the panel and the notes made should be entirely their own thoughts.

An example of an evaluation sheet for wine tasting

VARIETAL AND VINTAGE: _____	WINERY:_____
	Visual (0–4 points) Fill the glass halfway, hold it up against a white surface in bright light. Is the colour clear or obscure? What is the intensity of the colour? Look for clarity, brilliance and appropriateness of colour.
	Aroma (0–6 points) Swirl the wine around in the glass to release the odours, then close your eyes and smell. Is it pleasant or bland? Can you identify a particular aroma? Berries? Tropical fruit? Leather? Tobacco? Floral? Fresh-mown grass? Is the aroma intense or delicate? Look for complexity and intensity.
	Texture (0–4 points) Take a small amount of wine in your mouth and briefly hold it on your tongue. How does the wine feel? Is it soft or heavy? Does it have a refreshing zing around the edges of your tongue? Is it flat and limp? You may notice that red wine feels prickly – this is the feel of tannins, which are used in these wines to keep them from spoiling. Younger red wines are usually more tannic. Look for smoothness, a velvety feeling in your mouth.
	Taste (0–10 points) Lightly swirl it around in your mouth so all your taste buds are exposed, then keep it there for a brief period. Is the taste consistent with the aroma? Is it sweet, acidic, crisp, sour? Is it light or full-bodied? Look for balance and intensity of fruit.
	Finish (0–6 points) Swallow the wine (or use a 'spit' cup). Is there an aftertaste? Can you identify the flavours? Are they the same or slightly different from the mouth taste? Does it linger? How long? Does it make you want another sip?
	Overall impression (Total of points)
25–30 marks	Excellent – a great wine
20–24 marks	Outstanding – superior character
15–19 marks	Good to very good – special qualities
10–14 marks	Average

TASK

Select up to six wines from different regions and grape varieties of the same colour (red, white or rosé).

With your team, using the guide for tasting and the evaluation sheet, taste each wine and then compare notes.

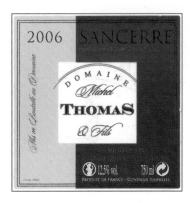

An example of an Italian wine label

THE ANATOMY OF A WINE LIST

The organisation of a wine list varies greatly from restaurant to restaurant, however the overriding principle of most wine lists is to present the wine to the customer in a logical, easily accessible manner. Wines are usually divided into at least two sections, most commonly by portion size (such as wines by the glass and wines by the bottle), or grape category (such as sparkling, red, rose and white). Larger wine lists often employ even further classification, such as by grape type (chardonnay, sauvignon blanc, merlot, cabernet sauvignon), location (Bordeaux, Burgundy, Chianti, California), or even wine styles ('crisp whites', 'bold reds'). Often several classification methods are combined to create more specific categories on a wine list ('French reds', 'New World whites', 'Australian shiraz'), especially if the wine list is extensive. Within categories, wines are often listed from lightest to heaviest, both in terms of flavour and body.

No matter how they are classified, it is important that wines will be clearly identified. Most wine lists include the producer, the region, the grape type, the year and of course the price of the wine. Some will even go as far as to offer a brief description, or occasionally, a suggested food pairing.

Wine mark-up

It is common for restaurants to price wines at two to three times the retail price, and sometimes more. If your main concern is wine mark-up, you may choose to consider wines from unfamiliar regions, made from unusual grape varieties, or from different vintages. These are often included on a wine list because a sommelier recognises their merit, but they may not be marked up as much as a popular cabernet or chardonnay, which your restaurant operation knows will be accepted. Consider wines from regions such as Alsace in France, or countries such as Spain or South Africa, or consider different varietals such as zinfandel, or chenin blanc and sparkling wines such as prosecco and cava. If you are adventurous, this can be an excellent way to discover and try new wines.

Label design on wine bottles

Some wineries place great importance on the label design. There are wineries that have not changed their label design in over 60 years, as in the case of Château Petrus, while others hire designers every year to change it. Labels may include images of works by artists such as Picasso and these may be collector's pieces. The elegance of the label will not determine the wine's quality. It is the information contained within the label that can provide your customers with such knowledge. The information contained in labels is important to determine the quality of the wine. For example, great importance needs to be attached to vintage dates when there are differences in climate. The taste and quality of the wine can change from year to year depending on the climate. Knowing the vintage is especially important when

An example of a French wine label

purchasing fine wines because the quality of the wine can vary from year to year due to climatic differences. The quickest way to determine the quality of the year is to use a wine chart.

Most New World consumers and increasingly, European consumers, prefer to purchase wine with varietal labels or with brand name labels. Producers often attempt to make selecting and purchasing wine easy and non-intimidating by making their labels inviting. The financial success of New World wine attributed to striking label designs have lead European producers to follow suit, as in the case of the redesign of the well-known French estate of Mouton Cadet.

Differences by country Wine classification systems differ by country. Wines may be classified by region and area only, which can be confusing to consumers. For example, there are 151 châteaux in Bordeaux with 'Figeac' and 22 estates in Burgundy with 'Corton' on their labels. In Burgundy, there are 110 appellations in an area only one-fifth the size of Bordeaux. Complicating the system is the fact that it is common for villages to append the name of their most famous vineyard to that of the village. This promotes sales but confuses consumers. In Spain and Portugal, the authenticity of the wine is guaranteed by a seal on the label or a band over the cork under the capsule. This is promulgated by the grower's association in each area. German wine labels are particularly noted for the detail that they can provide in determining quality and style of the wine.

WWW.CANSTOCKPHOTO.COM

Wine bottles and casks in a cellar

Almost every New World wine is labelled by grape variety and geographic origin. Semi-generic designations were once quite common in countries such as Australia and the USA, but the wine authorities in areas such as Champagne have not been afraid to bring lawsuits against the use of their names outside their region, and semi-generic names are falling out of use.

A wine label may include the producer, the bottler and the merchant's names. The bottler's name must always be included in the label. The importer's name must be included in the label only for countries outside the Common Market. While it is not necessary for a wine to be bottled at its place of origin, it is obligatory for classed growth claret and vintage port to be bottled in Bordeaux and Oporto. Also, bottling of Alsace must be done within the appellation. Thus, it is important to look for terms such as *mis en bouteille au château* or *mis au domaine* because they tell you the wine is estate bottled.

Misleading information Labels may include fancy terms that are often misleading. Blanc de blanc is a French phrase which means 'white wine made from white grapes'. The term originated in France's Champagne region (where most champagnes are made from a combination of the white chardonnay grape and the red pinot noir grape) to describe champagne made entirely from chardonnay. Blanc de blancs are usually light and delicate. The term also refers to still whites. Although the word *château* is most associated with Bordeaux, it does not mean that the wine comes from Bordeaux, and there may not be any kind of building – let alone a château – associated with the vineyard. The name château can even be included in wines from Australia or California.

Labelling regulations There are different reasons for wine laws. Labelling regulations can be intended to prevent wine from sounding better than it is. Also, it is illegal to say that a wine is made from one grape when it is actually from another. The label must also include the name and address of the bottler of the wine. If the producer is not the bottler, the bottle will say that the wine was bottled by a specific bottler for a particular producer. Table wines may carry the name of the bottler and the postal code. The label must also include the country of origin.

Alcohol content must be included in the label. In Australia and the United States a wine label must also mention that it has sulphites in certain circumstances.

Regulations may permit table wines to be labelled with only the colour and flavour, and no indication of quality. The use of words such as cuveé and grand vin in labels is controlled. A vin de pays must never be from a château, but from a domaine. New Zealand and Australian labelling regulations require an allergen warning to appear on wine labels since 2002 due to the use of egg whites, milk and isinglass in the fining and clarifying of the wine.

On a wine label the European Common Agricultural Policy (Wine) Regulations state that specific mandatory information must be shown, in one field of vision. These include nominal volume (e.g. 75cl), alcoholic strength (e.g. 11.5 per cent vol), bottler's details, country of origin, type of wine. In addition a statement about the sulphur dioxide content will be required on any label when this exceeds 10mg/litre. Specified optional items may also be shown on certain types of wine, e.g. vine variety, vintage. Further information may be shown, providing it does not conflict with mandatory or specified details and that there is no risk of confusion.

MATCHING WINES TO FOOD

One of wine's greatest pleasures is its ability to enhance the dining experience, to join its solid counterpart at the table and to transform a meal from simple nourishment to sensual pleasure. At its best, a well-matched wine will enhance the tastes and textures of a dish. There is no single rule that can apply to wine pairing in general. Both wine and food can be quite complex, and the possibilities in pairing the two even more so. (The

decades-old adage 'red wine with red meat; white wine with white meat,' hardly applies to the full spectrum of foods and wines.)

The overall goal in selecting a wine to accompany a meal is to have the wine and food balance – you don't want the wine to overpower the food or vice versa. There are two reliable approaches you can use to achieve this: you can select wines whose features complement those of the food, or wines whose features contrast those of the dish. Several things factor into pairings.

Body

The body is the actual weight or thickness of a wine, or how a wine feels (not tastes) in the mouth. Light-bodied wines are comparable to the feel of water in your mouth; full-bodied wines feel more like double cream. In terms of body, it is usually advisable to look for complementary features – to pair light-bodied wines with lighter food, and full-bodied wines with heartier fare. For this reason, full-bodied whites, such as chardonnay, often do not pair well with delicate seafood, and lighter reds, such as Beaujolais, don't do justice to a hearty steak but will pair well with chicken or pork.

CLASSIC PAIRINGS

Full-bodied chardonnay with cream or butter-based sauces, medium-bodied pinot noir with salmon, light-bodied sauvignon blanc with delicate fish dishes.

Tannins

Tannins are a chemical compound present in grape skins, seeds and stems, as well as in wood barrels. They are especially prominent in red wines, as grape skins are left on for a portion of the wine-making process, but are also present in some oak-aged white wines. Tannins are a natural preservative and are most prominent in young wines; as wines age they become less tannic. Tannins taste dry (astringent) and bitter, and have a very particular effect when paired with certain foods. For example, salty foods bring out the bitterness in tannins, and cream-based foods make tannins seem more astringent. Tannic wines pair well with low-salt and high-fat food, like well-marbled meat. When enjoyed together, fat lessens the astringency of tannins, and conversely tannins prevent fat from seeming too rich.

CLASSIC PAIRINGS

Cabernet sauvignon, which has high tannins, with red meat such as sirloin steak.

Acidity

Acidity in wine comes from both the grapes and the fermentation process. There is some degree of acidity in all wines, although it can be overshadowed, or masked, by tannins. Acidity is most noticeable in wines where tannins are not very prominent. White wines, such as sauvignon blanc and pinot grigio, often have prominent acidity, which gives them their crispness. Low-tannin red wines also present acidity, such as Beaujolais and Chianti. As a general rule, acidic wines are very food-friendly. Acidic wines pair well with acidic foods, including citrus fruits, tomatoes, and tomato sauces, as well as rich, creamy foods, as the acidity 'cuts through' the richness. They pair particularly well with fish as well as fried foods – the acid in the wine serves the same role as the acid in fresh lemon so often squeezed on these dishes. Acidic wines also often pair well with salty foods, helping to

CLASSIC PAIRINGS

Sauvignon blanc which has an acidity can be successfully paired with fish and a Chianti with a fresh tomato sauce-based dish.

cut the salty taste on the palate. Conversely, low-acid wines often clash with acidic foods – the pairing of the two should be avoided.

Sweetness

Sweetness in wine is a result of sugar in the grapes that is not converted to alcohol (called residual sugar). In an excellent example of contrast, sweet wines are a natural match for very spicy or salty foods. However, the sweet flavour of semi-sweet or off-dry wines also pairs well with naturally sweet dishes, such as honey-glazed ham, or pork with a port wine reduction sauce. Sweet wines are also often served alongside desserts. The general rule with sweet and semi-sweet wines is to pair them with foods that are less sweet than the wine itself.

CLASSIC PAIRINGS

A sweet Sauternes is paired with foie gras, riesling with some spicy Asian dishes and a sweet monbazilac with crème brûlée.

Alcohol

The percentage of alcohol in a wine can influence a wine's ability to pair with certain foods. Cream-based, spicy, or salty foods particularly clash with high-alcohol wines – cream makes alcohol seem stronger; alcohol makes spicy foods seem spicier; and alcohol together with salt can taste bitter. High-alcohol wines often pair well with high-fat dishes, such as steaks, as the fat can lessen the intensity of the alcohol.

CLASSIC PAIRINGS

Chardonnay with lobster and a butter-based sauce, a zinfandel wine with grilled red meat.

Other considerations

Balance/intensity. The intensity of a wine should match the intensity of a dish. If you are going to sample rare, mature Bordeaux wine, you be looking for the delicate complexity of the wine to be heightened, not overshadowed, by the intricate complexities of the food it accompanies; similarly if you are going to drink simple Beaujolais wine, you do not wish for a complex, intricately flavoured dish that will make the wine seem thin or lacklustre.

Progression. If you are going to be matching wines against a tasting menu over the course of the dinner, you should also consider the intensity of the wine. The flavours of wines should become more intense as the menu progresses. In general, aim to enjoy light, fresh wines before luxurious, rich ones; steel-fermented before oak-aged, simple before complex, dry before sweet, and less tannic before more tannic.

Location. Thousands of years ago, before wine became an international commodity; wines made in a region were enjoyed with traditional foods of that region. Based on the theory that grapes from a climate will pair with foods native to the same climate, it is safe to assume that regional foods will pair well with wines from the same region, such as pinot grigio with prosciutto or riesling with wiener schnitzel.

Wine in food. If a dish is prepared with wine, such as coq au vin or bœuf bourgignon, consider matching the wine you drink to the wine in the dish.

SUMMARY

We have seen in this chapter that wine menus have a significant impact on attracting diners to match a wine choice with their food and that a well-balanced, constructive and easy to follow menu can make this a less intimidating experience. A clear and correctly laid out wine list can ensure that the full profitable potential of your wine offering is realised. While there are many ways of presenting wines – by country; by region; by price; by style – the wine list is an ideal opportunity to engage your customer at the beginning of their dining experience and keep them coming back for more.

Checklist

◼ A wine list must be created with the both customer and business needs in mind – building lasting relationships with your customers and suppliers is critical

◼ Make sure the wines selected complement the style, price structure and menu of your business

◼ Selling wine by the glass can encourage interest, curiosity and trading-up

◼ Nominate one person to undertake ordering – this will avoid any confusion among staff and suppliers

◼ Do not buy wines that require protracted cellaring prior to serving – cellaring wine ties up funds and clogs up cash flow

◼ The average price of wine sold on your list is the most crucial price point you have – when buying new wines, add an interesting selection either side of this price

◼ Profitability of the wine list will depend on the margins you achieve on your house wines and fast movers

◼ Convey as much relevant information as possible on a wine list – vintage, title name, producer, region and country

◼ Order little and often to help manage deliveries, storage, accounting and cash flow

Choosing from the wine list

The menu is the key selling tool together with the service staff and sommelier who will help to promote profitable wines. The wine menu will also aid the creation of a theme for a particular operation or restaurant.

It is of the highest importance that the menu reflects accurately and honestly the wines and spirits being sold so that customer expectation and restaurant delivery match. Provided that the meal experience meets customer expectations the menu can become a talking point long after the customer has left the restaurant.

Further reading

Franson, P. (2006) Labels gone wild. *Wine Enthusiast,* 19(3), 28–33.

George, R. (1989) *The Simon & Schuster Pocket Wine Label Decoder*, Simon and Schuster.

Morrison, P. (1996) Menu engineering in upscale restaurants. *International Journal of Contemporary Hospitality Management*, 8(4), 17–24.

Johnson, H. and Robinson, J. (2007) *The World Atlas of Wine*, 6th revised ed. Mitchell Beazley.

Vinopolis Wine Information Centre http://www.vinopolis.co.uk/ask.php

The Wine Anorak online wine magazine http://www.wineanorak.com/

Wine Labels of the World http://users.skynet.be/winelabelsworld/Engels/HomeEng. htm

Personalised Wine Labels www.personalisedwinelabels.co.uk/

Assessment of knowledge and understanding

You have now learnt about some key elements involved in planning a wine menu.

As you have gone through the chapter you have already tried out some tastings and discussed some elements of writing the menu, but now to test your level of knowledge and understanding further, answer the following short questions. These will help to prepare you for your summative (final) assessment.

Legislation

1   What are the consequences if you should choose to deviate from any of the aspects of wine label legislation laid out earlier in the chapter?

2   What policies and procedures does your organisation have in relation to the purchase of wines?

3   List a series of references – websites, books and journals – where you could find more information in relation to legislation relevant to the service of alcohol and wines in the hospitality industry and useful to you as a supervisor.

The wine menu

1   What are the main requirements of the wine menu?

2   What are the main objectives in relation to the matching of food and wine?

3   What systems and procedures does your organisation have in relation to the changing and updating of the wine menu?

4   Recognise and list the areas where there is a potential to add wines in your most recent menu.

Communicating the wine menu

1   List the changes to your new wine menu. Now consider how you would go about communicating the changes to your team? What policies and procedures do you need to follow?

2   What policies and procedures are in place or could be in place to monitor the effective sales of individual wines on a regular basis?

Research task

As the restaurant supervisor of a four-star hotel restaurant you have been asked to produce a new wine menu. Using various sections of this chapter design the process you would adopt to complete this task and the rationale for your choice.

28

Manage the environmental impact of your work

HS28 Manage the environmental impact of your work

LEARNING OBJECTIVES

This unit is about managing work activities and resources in your area of responsibility in order to minimise the negative impact and maximise the positive impact they may have on the environment.

After reading this chapter you will be able to:

■ Use different ways of communicating effectively with members of a team.

■ Organise work activities and the use of resources in your area of responsibility so that they are efficient and effective.

■ Explain the importance of organising work activities and the use of resources so that they minimise their negative and maximise their positive environmental impact, and how to do so.

■ Be aware of the importance of identifying the environmental impact of work activities and the use of resources in your area of responsibility, and how to do so.

■ Understand the importance of reporting promptly any identified risks to the environment which you do not have the ability to control, and how to do so.

■ Encourage people to make contributions.

■ Identify and implement changes to work activities and the use of resources that will reduce their negative and increase their positive environmental impact.

■ Use the principles of effective communication.

KEY WORDS

Brainstorming
A group creativity technique designed to generate a large number of ideas for the solution to a problem. The method was first popularised in the late 1930s by Alex Faickney Osborn in a book called *Applied Imagination.*

Carbon footprint
A 'measure of the impact that human activities have on the environment in terms of the amount of greenhouse gases produced, measured in units of carbon dioxide'. These gases are produced by the burning of fossil fuels for our everyday living. For example, heating and electricity: its purpose is for individuals, nations and organisations to conceptualise their personal (or organisational) carbon dioxide contribution.

Demographics
Refers to selected population characteristics including race, age, income, disabilities, educational attainment, home ownership, employment status and even location.

Economy
The social system of a country's revenue based on their ability to produce, exchange, distribute and consume goods and services. An economy is the result of a process that involves the uses of the country's technology, history, geography and natural resources among other factors.

Social responsibility
An ethical or ideological theory that a government, corporation, organisation or individual has a responsibility to behave appropriately towards the rest of society.

Sociology
The scientific study of individual behaviour in society.

Sustainable
The ability to maintain a certain process or state, i.e. to sustain the existing environment.

INTRODUCTION

In order to run any successful business all employees need to be aware of their environment and how to react within it. This can include a range of different impacts affecting business or alternatively can be national and sometimes international. We will examine all of this in this chapter alongside your responsibility to accommodate these changes and how you and your team can be prepared for them and react to them effectively.

The environmental impact

It is thought that the UK will be affected by most of the expected global impacts of climate change.

Green issues are increasingly important for all of us. With growing public concern about climate change, we need to improve the sustainability of the tourism and hospitality industries. The UK must position itself as a premier sustainable destination, promote good practice and encourage visitors to enjoy a visit or a stay offered by sustainable businesses.

WWW.SXC.HU

Some green facts and figures

■ The Carbon Trust reckons the UK restaurant and hotel industry could cut its £1b-plus annual energy bill by 20 per cent – or more than £200m

■ The Hospitable Climates Programme (run by the Institute of Hospitality on behalf of the Carbon Trust) believes its 5,000 participants save £13m a year in energy costs

■ Simple and inexpensive water-efficiency measures could save businesses between 20 and 50 per cent

■ A recent YouGov poll found that about 70 per cent of workers in London wanted their employers to have sound environmental policies

■ The Soil Association claims that the food system accounts for 40 per cent of all UK road freight – and road and air food miles generated nearly 18 million tonnes of CO_2 in 2004

■ A leaky tap producing one drip per second wastes about four litres of water a day, and 90 litres if the drips break into a stream

Transport

■ Taking one short car journey a week fewer could reduce pollution

■ Car traffic is forecast to increase by 22 per cent by 2010 from the current levels of 321 billion vehicle kilometres (per year) if no action is taken (source: Department of the Environment, Transport and the Regions transport report for 2010: *The 10 Year Plan*)

■ Seven out of 10 journeys to work are by car.

■ At the peak school travel time of 8.50a.m., nearly one in five cars on urban roads are taking children to school

CONSIDERATE HOTELIERS

Mission statement:

To encourage the adoption of economically, socially and environmentally sustainable policies and practices among Hoteliers in a way which enhances the viability of their businesses, the environment and the quality of the experience on offer to their guests, staff and visiting tourists.

WWW.CONSIDERATEHOTELIERS.COM

- A double-decker bus carries the same number of people as 20 fully occupied cars but takes up a seventh of the road space (source: Environmental Transport Association www.eta.co.uk)

- A 10 per cent increase in the number of people cycling regularly would lead to a 4 per cent reduction in the number of people with heart disease, saving the NHS £200 million a year (source: Going for Green www.goingforgreen.co.uk)

- Over the last 20 years, the average distances cycled and walked have both fallen by a quarter

Energy (sources: Digest of UK Energy Statistics www.berr.gov.uk/energy/statistics, DTI www.dti.gov.ph/ and ETSU www.etsu.co.uk)

- The energy consumed each year by UK commerce and industry releases about 60 million tonnes of carbon into the atmosphere

- By turning down your thermostat by 1°C, or using one hour less heating a day, you could cut your fuel bills by 10 per cent

- Using just one energy-saving light bulb could save you £5 a year, and if every household installed one, we could power the lighting currently used in 2 million homes for a year

- If everyone boiled only the water they needed to make a hot drink, instead of filling the kettle every time, we could save enough electricity to run practically all the street lighting in the country

Water

Indoors

- One drip per second wastes around 1,200 litres of water per year

- Take a shower instead of a bath and save enough water each week for 1000 cups of tea (source: Department of the Environment, Transport and the Regions)

- 20–25 per cent of energy consumed in a hotel is used to heat water in the kitchen and bathroom

Outdoors

- In half an hour, a garden sprinkler uses as much water as a family of four in a day

- Using a hose to wash the car wastes up to 300 litres or 33 buckets of water

Waste

- The volume of waste produced in the UK in one hour would fill the Albert Hall (source: Local Government Brief Publications)

© ISTOCKPHOTO.COM/RYERSON CLARK

■ In one day there would be enough waste to fill Trafalgar Square up to the top of Nelson's Column (source: Local Government Brief Publications)

■ In just over a week, we produce enough rubbish to fill Wembley stadium. Over half can be recycled (source: Department of the Environment, Transport and the Regions)

■ In one year there would be enough waste to fill dustbins stretching from the Earth to the Moon (source: Local Government Brief Publications)

Packaging

© ISTOCKPHOTO.COM/ERNESTO SOLLA

■ Packaging is typically 25–35 per cent by weight of dustbin waste, but developments in material strength and manufacturing technologies have allowed less material to contain the same volume of goods. Compared to 50 years ago:

● food cans are 50 per cent lighter
● yoghurt pots are 60 per cent lighter
● glass milk bottles are 50 per cent lighter
● plastic carrier bags are half as thick

■ Reducing the weight of packaging saves on transport costs and emissions as well as reducing consumption of raw materials (source: INCPEN (Industry Council for Packaging and the Environment) www.incpen.org)

Metals

■ Every year in the UK we use 13 billion steel cans which, if placed end to end, would stretch to the moon three times (source: Steel Can Recycling Information Bureau www.scrib.org)

■ Producing steel from recycled materials saves 75 per cent of the energy needed to make steel from virgin materials (source: Steel Can Recycling Information Bureau)

■ About 20,000 tonnes of aluminium foil packaging, worth £8 million, is wasted each year. Only 3,000 tonnes is recycled, worth £1.2 million (source: alupro The Aluminium Packaging Recycling Organisation www. alupro.org.uk)

■ If all the aluminium cans sold in the UK were recycled, there would be 12 million fewer full dustbins each year (source: Alucan alucan.org.uk)

Paper

■ Each tonne of paper recycled saves 15 average-sized trees, as well as their surrounding habitat and wildlife (source: World Wildlife Fund http://www. wwf.org.uk/)

■ Reclaimed waste paper represents around 63 per cent of the fibre used to produce paper and board in the UK (source: The Paper and Pulp Information Centre http://www.paper.org.uk/)

© ISTOCKPHOTO.COM/GABYJALBERT

Glass The energy saving from recycling one bottle will:

■ Power a 100 watt light bulb for almost an hour

■ Power a computer for 25 minutes

■ Up to 90 per cent of new glass can be made from reclaimed scrap glass, which saves energy and raw materials (source: British Glass http://www.britglass.org.uk/index.html)

■ On average, every family in the UK uses around 330 glass bottles and jars each year. However, we only recycle 30 per cent of these containers

■ There are more than 50,000 bottle banks in the UK (source: British Glass http://www.britglass.org.uk/index.html)

Plastic

■ Of the 2.4 million tonnes of plastic waste, an estimated 1,400,000 tonnes is household plastic waste, 200,000 tonnes is 'process scrap', and 800,000 tonnes is commercial waste: 61 per cent of the total plastic waste from Western Europe is packaging, which typically has a 'life' of less than 12 months (source: AEA Technology http://www.aeat.co.uk/cms/)

To be environmentally friendly doesn't just mean recycle or switch off the gas, it can also include some of these examples below, taken from the *Caterer and Hotelkeeper's* top 25 tips to be more socially responsible:

1 Pass on or recycle your technology – i.e. work computers could be taken home to be used by the family.

2 Look after employee health.

3 Set up a charity.

4 Recycle office supplies.

5 Cycle to work.

6 Cut delivery miles.

7 Work with local producers.

8 Set your staff a challenge to reduce/recycle the waste. and incentivise the challenge.

9 Share your swimming pool.

10 Purchase from sustainable stocks.

11 Serve Fair Trade.

12 Reward greener guests.

13 Use green service suppliers.

14 Educate your clients.

15 Educate your staff.

Serving Fair Trade products, like these coffee beans, is a great way of being socially responsible.

© ISTOCKPHOTO.COM/STEVE SIMZER

Considerate Hoteliers says that hotels can reduce energy consumption by 20 per cent through regular staff training in the importance of being green. Staff can also take what they learn into their everyday lives.

CASE STUDY 1

Reduce Your Water Consumption

There's no getting around it - hotels, restaurants and catering firms use a lot of water. Bathrooms, kitchens, spas and swimming pools are all water-hungry environments.

Yet, with Envirowise, the government-funded sustainable business body, estimating that average water bills have gone up 18 per cent over the past five years, and with the trade using some 391 billion litres of water every year (enough to fill 156,400 Olympic-sized swimming pools), much of it metered and therefore coming straight off the bottom line, reducing water usage can clearly make not just environmental but commercial sense.

When the 321-bedroom Jurys Inn in Glasgow, for example, carried out a 'water audit' back in 2004, the results were startling.

Cleaning vegetables or washing pasta under the cold tap, they'd not just leave it running while they were doing it, but leave the tap on between jobs', explains financial controller Sharon McLeish.

'Or, when rooms were being cleaned, sometimes the toilet was being flushed as many as three times. It'd get flushed after the cleaning fluid was put in, when the cleaner left the room, and then the supervisor would come round and flush it a third time. So we very quickly put in a one-flush policy', she adds.

This change, along with ongoing education for staff and the installation of water-saving 'hippos' in cisterns to reduce the amount of water used with each flush, has cut the hotel's water consumption by 1.5 million litres a year and, crucially, its water bill by 14 per cent.

Source: *Caterer and Hotelkeeper*, October 2008.

CASE STUDY 2

The Price Of Power

Fuel bills have rocketed in the past year, and while you could shop around between various suppliers to find the best option, it's frequently a choice between very expensive and even more so. Until recently the industry has been held back from taking greener options by the cost of new equipment, but research shows that the sums add up to taking a different approach now.

To its guests, the Nare hotel at Veryan-in-Roseland, Cornwall, presents a staunchly traditional front, with daily cream teas and ties preferred for gentlemen in the dining room. But behind the scenes it's a pioneer, one of a handful of establishments breaking new ground to solve a very twenty-first-century problem. Only if they venture down to the seafront and squint directly back towards its beach huts will they notice 20 solar slates glinting in the sunlight, which, between them, generate enough energy to heat the Nare's water to 60°C before it even reaches the boilers.

Proprietor Toby Ashworth is one of a growing number of hospitality operators who are turning to alternative sources of energy to beat the spiralling costs of fuel. He spent about £20,000 installing the solar slates on the beach huts and on other south-facing spots on the hotel buildings when he replaced his two old boilers last winter, on the basis that they would pay for themselves within five or six years.

The volatility of oil prices has already halved that – in the past two months he's saved 1,650 litres of oil, worth £6,500.

Source: *Caterer and Hotelkeeper*, October 2008.

THE LEGISLATIVE IMPACT

From 1 July 2007, new European regulations – the EU WEEE (Waste Electrical and Electronic Equipment) Directive – came into force for the treatment of such items. Producers are now required to set up systems to provide for the collection, treatment, recovery and environmentally sound disposal of such waste. All hoteliers should be aware of this and be ready to advertise their eco-friendly electrical waste policy.

What is good for the planet is also good for business. Reminding guests about their responsibility to the environment even when they are not at home does not diminish luxury, but can easily reinforce the hotel's ethical reputation in the mind of a guest – which will only mean they will want to come back.

In the last 10 years the Labour government has enacted over 180 separate pieces of legislation that are employment-based.

The Climate Change Levy (CCL)

Essentially an 'energy tax', the CCL is designed to improve energy efficiency and reduce emissions of greenhouse gases. Starting from April 2007 the CCL, which applies to the use of common types of energy like gas and electricity by UK businesses, will increase each year in line with inflation.

Duty of Care Regulations for Waste

These regulations require that waste, including that sent for recycling, is stored and disposed of responsibly by an authorised body. Details must be recorded on Waste Transfer Notes, to be kept for two years.

Hazardous Waste Regulations (HWR)

These require that 'hazardous' waste items such as fluorescent tubes, TVs and pesticides are stored separately and disposed of by a specialist contractor. Businesses producing such waste should register with the Environment Agency (EA). Businesses in Scotland and Northern Ireland need not register but must notify the EA in advance of any hazardous waste movements (see http://www.environment-agency.gov.uk/subjects/waste).

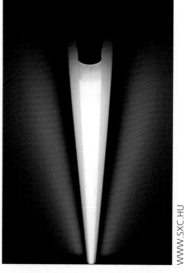

WWW.SXC.HU

Fluorescent tubes and other hazardous waste must be disposed of by a specialist.

The Landfill Directive (England and Wales) 2002, and October 2007 amendments

This limits the amount and range of products that can go to landfill. From 30 October 2007 non-hazardous waste liquids will be banned from landfill and non-hazardous solid waste must be treated before going to landfill (see http://www.environment-agency.gov.uk/subjects/waste).

Trade effluent and discharge consents

These consents cover any liquid waste discharged to a sewer by a business other than sewage and uncontaminated rain water. For any other forms of liquid waste you need to sign a trade effluent agreement, or a discharge consent if the discharge is going to controlled waters such as a ditch, stream or rivers, or a drain connecting to such.

All waste should be disposed of conscientiously

WEEE (Waste Electrical and Electronic Equipment) Regulations

The WEEE regulations, designed to reduce landfill, came into force on 2 January 2007 and place the onus for the responsible disposal of electronic or electrical items on either the owner or the producer. Businesses can get WEEE collected free if it was bought after 15 August 2005, or if you are replacing it with equivalent equipment. Otherwise they must store, collect, treat, recycle and dispose of WEEE separately from other waste and keep records to show it was responsibly disposed of using a suitable contractor.

The Companies Act (2006), changes in October 2007

The Companies Act has been amended to request all listed companies with 1,000 or more employees to provide a corporate social responsibility (CSR) statement in their annual directors' report. In other words the government feels that this is such an important aspect of good practice by companies that they have created a legal obligation for companies to consider their impact on the community and the environment.

Waste management licensing

Hospitality businesses won't normally require a waste management licence to store their own waste but you may need to get one, or at least register for an exemption with the Environment Agency, if you treat your own waste, for example using a solvent recovery still or a baler.

THE CLIMATE CHANGE BILL OF NOVEMBER 2008

The Climate Change Bill, the first of its kind in the world, sets out a framework that will put Britain on the path to become a low-carbon economy, with clear, legally binding targets to reduce carbon dioxide emissions by at least 60 per cent by 2050, and 26 to 32 per cent by 2020, against 1990 levels.

Key points in the Climate Change Bill include:

- Legally binding targets to cut CO_2 emissions by at least 60 per cent by 2050 and 26 to 32 per cent by 2020

- A new system of legally binding five year 'carbon budgets', set at least 15 years ahead, to provide clarity on the UK's optimum pathway towards its key targets

- A new statutory body, the Committee on Climate Change, to provide independent expert advice and guidance to government

- A new system of annual open and transparent reporting to parliament

- A requirement for government to report at least every five years on current and predicted impacts of climate change and on its proposals and policy for adapting to climate change

Specialist advice and a who's who in climate change

- Business in the Community – http://www.bitc.org.uk/
- The Carbon Trust – http://www.carbontrust.co.uk/
- Considerate Hoteliers Association – http://www.consideratehoteliers.com/
- DEFRA – http://www.defra.gov.uk/
- Energy Cost Advisors – http://www.eca-group.co.uk/
- Envirowise – http://www.envirowise.gov.uk/
- Hospitable Climates – http://www.hospitableclimates.org.uk/
- Sustain – http://www.sustainweb.org/
- Tourism Partnership – http://www.tourismpartnership.org/

There are other organisations that are represented on the committees of those listed above, but as a separate entity they can also offer specialist advice to organisations in regard to how they can react positively to changes in the working environment. These include:

- British Hospitality Association – http://www.bha.org.uk/
- The Institute of Hospitality – http://www.instituteofhospitality.org/
- The Tourism Society – http://www.tourismsociety.org/

CASE STUDY 3

Environmental Policy: The Royal Garden Hotel, London

The Royal Garden Hotel Limited is committed to the implementation of proactive measures to help protect and sustain the local, national and global environment for future generations. The directors recognise the impact of its operations on the environment and aim by increasing the understanding in respect of these activities to minimise any detrimental effects that may occur. By working together we can create a safe and clean environment and ensure that environmental issues are kept at the forefront of everyone's mind and given proper attention at all times.

Our aim is to:

1 Fully comply with the law, current legislation and regulations and to take a proactive approach to future legal requirements or obligations.

2 Ensure that everybody within the company has a duty of care for the environment, its habitats and biodiversity.

3 Encourage our employees to work in an environmentally responsible manner. An active Environmental Committee consisting of employees from all levels operated with the company which formalises new ideas and working methods.

4 Seek to conserve natural resources by ensuring the responsible use of energy, water and materials and still provide the quality of service expected by our guests.

5 Measure performance and set objectives that will be regularly revisited with the aim of continual improvement by reducing, re-using or recycling in areas such as:
- Water consumption
- Waste materials produced
- Energy consumption

6 Gain support from our customers and ensure they are made aware of our environmental policy.

7 Source products that have minimal environmental impact. These include items such as packaging, recyclable products, local sourcing of services and products and energy efficient electrical equipment.

8 Work with our suppliers and contractors and ensure that they are made aware of our policy and that they have compatible policies for managing their impact on the environment.

9 Regularly conduct reviews to ensure the hotel operations remain compliant with this policy and to set or revise targets to ensure continual improvement for the future.

10 Provide all of our employees with the information, instructions and training necessary to fulfil this policy.

ACTIVITY

Having read some of these key facts and figures and considered this case study, now look at your own organisation.

List 10 action points that your own workplace should incorporate into the day-to-day running of the workplace, in order to improve their impact on the environment.

TECH SKILLS

IMPLEMENTING CHANGE

As a supervisor it is your responsibility to ensure that your team is able to embrace possible changes in your work environment. This can include ensuring their compliance with new methods and activities, but it can also include getting the team to identify new methods to implement into the workplace. Ultimately your behaviour underpins effective performance, and as part of the criteria for this module, you are required to:

1 Recognise changes in circumstances promptly and adjust plans and activities accordingly.

2 Present information clearly, concisely, accurately and in ways that promote understanding.

3   Keep people informed of plans and developments.

4   Comply with, and ensure others comply with, legal requirements, industry regulations, organisational policies and professional codes.

5   Act within the limits of your authority.

6   Be vigilant for possible hazards.

7   Make appropriate information and knowledge available promptly to those who need it and have a right to it.

8   Encourage others to share information and knowledge efficiently within the constraints of confidentiality.

9   Make best use of available resources and proactively seek new sources of support when necessary.

10 Identify the implications or consequences of a situation.

COMMUNICATE THE BENEFITS OF ENVIRONMENTAL CHANGE

Here are some top tips from the experts on how to **implement change successfully**:

1   Be a good listener. Pay attention to your employee's needs and requirements.

2   Get your team involved in making decisions to implement actions for change. If you exclude them from the decision-making process and ideas, you will not have their support when you try to implement the changes.

3   Make time for your team – regular, one-on-one meetings with your team members are important, give them a chance to ask questions.

4   Put out a consistent message about your values. Knowing who you are, and what you stand for, can help your employees make better decisions on their own.

5   Give regular feedback to your team.

When giving your message to the team remember some key **language skills**:

- Keep it simple
- Use clarifying and rephrasing techniques – don't be afraid to check what you have understood. Clarifying (or rephrasing if the other person doesn't understand) saves time in the future
- Ask if you don't understand
- Prepare for meetings, presentations and negotiations.
- Write it down – follow up meetings or spoken agreements with a written note

ACTIVITY

What negative communication behaviours have you noticed in your workplace?

What impact do these behaviours have on the team and in implementing change?

And some **personal skills:**

■ Respect different cultures – different cultures have different business etiquette, customs and ethics

■ Be flexible – your ideas are not the only good ideas – listen to your team and embrace their ideas too

■ Be polite

For more information refer to Chapter 14, Contribute to promoting hospitality services and products.

Assessment of knowledge and understanding

You have now learnt about some key elements in managing the environmental impact of your work in the hospitality industry.

To test your level of knowledge and understanding, answer the following short questions. These will help to prepare you for your summative (final) assessment.

1 Think about how as a supervisor you could react to some of these factors to improve your working environment.

● How can you maintain the strengths?

● How can you overcome the weaknesses and threats?

● What could you do to turn the opportunities into a reality?

2 A scenario to consider. Your workplace would like to implement change in relation to its impact on the environment – this is for two reasons:

(a) to save money on bills, and

(b) to reduce its carbon footprint

As a supervisor, how would you go about implementing change in your particular department? In your response, consider the following:

(a) Encouraging your team to embrace this need for change

(b) Actions would you recommend are implemented

(c) Realistic implementation of recommendations within your team

(d) Legislation/hazards

(e) The limits of your authority

(f) Making best use of the resources you already have

(g) Budgetary/financial requirements

(h) Possible consequences of these changes

Research task

■ Identify a change in environmental legislation that has impacted the hospitality industry over the last 5 years.

- Describe the legislation.

- Note how the industry has been affected by this new/updated legislation.

- What has the industry done to react to this legislation positively? You may wish to use specific case studies here.

- Has this legislation had any negative impacts to the industry? If so, what?

- What could the industry be doing to embrace the impact of this legislation more positively?

29

Contribute to the selection of staff for activities

HS29 Contribute to the selection of staff for activities

LEARNING OBJECTIVES

This unit is about helping to identify suitable personnel for work. Businesses can only deliver high-quality services to their customers if they have staff with the right attitudes, experience, training and potential to grow in their jobs.

After reading this chapter you will be able to:

■ Identify staffing requirements which take account of work objectives and working constraints.

■ Make sure that the staffing requirements you identify are based on valid and reliable information.

■ Present identified staffing requirements to the relevant people at a time and in a format appropriate to your organisation.

■ Use assessment and selection methods suited to your organisation to assess and select staff.

■ Make sure your selection is based on an objective assessment of the available information against agreed selection criteria.

■ Make sure records of your contribution to the selection process are complete, accurate, clear and meet organisational requirements.

KEY WORDS

Assessment

This is when a person is given a task to carry out and a judgement will be made on how they performed. This could be an interview, a role play, or a presentation.

Attitude

This is an individual's characteristic way of responding to an object or situation. It is based on experience and leads to certain behaviour or the expression of certain opinions.

Criteria

This is the measurement by which an assessment takes place.

Job description

This is a document which explains the job role and duties that a job holder will be required to carry out.

Knowledge

This is the information that a person holds on a subject. It can be gained through education and experience.

Labour turnover

This is a calculation which gives a guide as to how much an organisation needs to recruit. If there is high labour turnover this means lots of staff are leaving, which can be a cause for concern.

Person specification

This is a document which will outline the attributes that an individual will need in order to carry out a job.

Policies

These are statements of intent about how the organisation proposes to conduct its business and achieve its strategic objectives.

Recruitment

This is the first part of the process of filling a vacancy; it includes the examination of the vacancy, the consideration of sources of suitable candidates, making contact with those candidates and attracting applications from them.

Selection

This is the stage after recruitment. At this point you assess the candidates by various means, and make a choice followed by an offer of employment.

Skills

These are the mental and/or physical activities that a person carries out. Through repeated training and other experiences they can be built upon.

Statutory

This is the legal requirement to carry something out.

Validity

This means a test has been designed to measure the characteristics that it is intended to measure. For example an intelligence test should measure intelligence.

INTRODUCTION

The recruitment and selection of staff is only part of what the human resource department of an organisation does, however it is crucial to the business that they get it right first time. In the hospitality industry this process can be more complex as it is renowned for its high labour turnover, so organisations have to work out how many staff they need in order to run effectively and efficiently.

Even before a potential employee works for an organisation there are many laws which the organisation has to adhere to, in order to ensure that their processes are fair and non-discriminatory. There are also many different ways in which organisations can attract staff, some more costly than others. So in order to select the best staff, potential recruits are usually put through various assessments.

This chapter will look in to the different processes and methods that organisations can use to recruit and select staff within the statutory framework in order to meet the organisation's requirements.

The recruitment and selection process: an overview

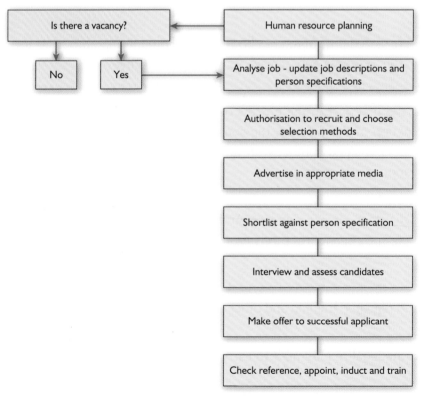

HUMAN RESOURCE PLANNING

It is extremely important for an organisation to plan how many staff they will need in order for it to run effectively and efficiently. Let's look at an example of how a hotel might be structured in terms of its staffing:

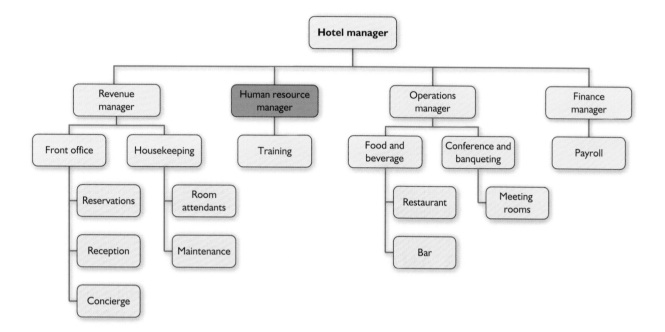

The above diagram gives you a general idea of the different departments that a hotel could have. It is the job of the human resource manager to ensure there is enough staff to run the various functions of the hotel. The difficulty for the human resource manager is that their department does not bring in any money for the hotel, unlike the other operations of the hotel, but they will spend it on recruiting and training staff. Therefore the staff that are selected have to be able to do the jobs they are recruited for in order to generate a profit for the hotel. For any additional staff required it is up to the human resource manager to make a case for why it is necessary. This is done through the process known as **human resource planning.**

Human resource planning is linked to the business strategy in order to forecast the human resources required – i.e. the numbers of staff for each department and each job role. By doing this:

- It encourages employers to develop clear links between their business strategy and human resource plans
- It allows better control over staffing and numbers employed
- Informed judgements can be made about the skills and attitude mix in the organisation
- It provides a profile of current staff which helps with the promotion of equal opportunities

> **! REMEMBER**
>
> It can cost up to 10 per cent of a salary to recruit someone in to your organisation. That could mean approximately £2,000 per person or more!

ACTIVITY

Human resource planning for a department

Think about a department that you are familiar with in a hotel. For example if we look at the front office, how many staff would you need to run this department? Consider the following:

- The hours the organisation is open – so for a hotel this would be 24 hours a day

- The different shifts people would work – remember you will also need to cover the night shift

- What are the different job roles you would have in this department – remember the front office department would include reservation staff, reception staff and concierge staff

- You would also need to consider if your staff will be working full time, or part time

As you can see, human resource planning is not that simple. Let's break it down a little more to give you an idea of the detail it involves.

JOB ANALYSIS

Human resource planning

When someone in the organisation leaves, the initial thought is that there is automatically a job vacancy, however before this can be assumed the current job holder's role should be analysed, to find out whether or not that role needs to be replaced or if it needs to be changed in any way. Therefore the aim of **job analysis** is to answer the following questions:

- What is the job holder expected to do?
- How is the job performed?
- What skills are required, and what is the level of those skills?
- Should the job be reorganised – will the hours change, what are the levels of responsibility, could it incorporate duties from other posts?

By carrying out this analysis it will help in putting forward a case for staffing. From this you would also get the information needed to put together the **job description** and **person specification**.

JOB DESCRIPTIONS

In general terms a job description simply describes the job. Organisations have their own standard template for job descriptions and although they can very enormously, they generally will include some standard elements (see the example of a basic job description).

Most organisations usually have some sort of clause at the end stating that the job holder will be required to carry out other duties not mentioned, as it would be difficult to include every single duty that has to be carried out. As mentioned previously the job may also change whilst the job holder is in the position. For example a new computer system might be introduced which may affect the way the role is carried out. Another area of good practice is for the job holder to sign and date the job description to show that they agree with what they are being asked to do. This is usually countersigned by their manager or human resources, depending on how the organisation operates.

SAMPLE JOB DESCRIPTION

Organisation: The Hospitable Hotel, Welcoming, Kent

Department: Front Office

Job title: Reservations Agent

Reports to: Front Office Manager

Responsible for: No staff

Overall aim of the job:

To make reservations for the hotel through a variety of ways including telephone bookings, email and fax ensuring rates quoted are competitive and that the hotel is running at maximum occupancy

Main duties:

1 To answer the telephone in a courteous and polite manner.
2 To maintain good customer relations when responding to reservation enquiries.
3 To quote competitive rates in accordance to the booking policy.
4 To input all reservations via the property management system.
5 To manage individual and group bookings.
6 To ensure the hotel is running at maximum occupancy where possible.
7 To liaise with the other departments to ensure all booking requirements are fulfilled.
8 To carry out any other reasonable request.

This job description is not exhaustive and the job holder will also be required to attend training and meetings when necessary.

Job holder's name:_____ Signature:_____ Date: _____

Front Office Manager:_____ Signature:_____ Date:_____

ACTIVITY

Job description

If you are currently employed and have a job description, have a look at it now and see if it covers the above elements. If you do not have a job description have a look on the Internet and see if you can find an example of a job description. Many companies will now put job descriptions on their websites, to make it easier for potential job applicants to find out what will be required of them should they apply.

PERSON SPECIFICATIONS

Whilst the job description relates to the tasks to be undertaken, a person specification outlines the human attributes seen as necessary to do the job. Its purpose is to detail the specific qualities that match the profile of the ideal person for the job. It is therefore looking at the personal qualities needed.

These days the person specification looks at four key areas:

1 The job requirements.

2 The essential requirements – the job holder must have this as a minimum in order to be considered potentially able to fulfil the job role.

3 The desirable requirements – a better job applicant will also be able to demonstrate these qualities too.

4 Method of assessment – the way in which the job holder will be assessed to show they have the qualities asked for.

So if we have several candidates applying for a position, the candidate that fulfils both the essential and the desirable elements would be the stronger person and could potentially be the right person for the job. Although the candidate will have to be able to demonstrate this, which is why the method of assessment is our way of checking this. So if we go back to our reservation agent position, a typical person specification may look like this:

SAMPLE PERSON SPECIFICATION FORM

Company name: The Hospitable Hotel
Job title: Reservations Agent
Department: Front Office

JOB REQUIREMENTS	ESSENTIAL REQUIREMENT	DESIRABLE REQUIREMENT	METHOD OF ASSESSMENT
Qualifications	English and maths GCSE	Minimum of 5 GCSEs including English and maths	Application form and certificate check
Experience	General customer service experience	Experience of working in a hotel environment in a front office department	Application form, interview, and references
Knowledge and skills	Up-to-date knowledge of the hotel industry	Studying for a qualification in hospitality management	Application form, interview, and references
	Computer literate	Experience of working with Fidelio	
Personal qualities	Good communicator – written and oral skills, good judgement, confident, persuasive, approachable, dependable, uses initiative, average numeracy		Application form, interview, group exercise, tests and references
Motivation and expectations	Desire to develop career in hotels. High expectations of self and others		Application form, interview and references

To recap, once you have carried out your job analysis, updated your job description and person specifications you will have a much clearer idea of what jobs you have available and the types of people you want to fill them. The next thing you have to work out is how many jobs you have available.

AUTHORITY TO RECRUIT

As we have seen recruiting staff is a very costly business and therefore when someone leaves the organisation, an **authority to recruit** is normally called for. This is basically where you would have to justify to your hotel manager for example why you need to recruit for a job role. So let's look at our reservation agents. How many reservation agents will you need in your hotel? This will depend on the size of your hotel, and the hours required for this job. So it may be you need two full-time reservations agents, although will this always be the case? If for example one of your reservation agents resigned, would you really need to replace them? This would all depend on how busy the hotel is, and the economic climate. So if the hotel is extremely busy and running at 95 per cent occupancy you probably would want to have another reservation agent, however if the hotel was not doing very well, you may want to save costs and not replace that job. It could be that the duties of the reservation agent would be carried out by the receptionist. This is another reason why it is important to carry out human resource planning: the numbers of staff you require and the job roles will change according to the requirements of the organisation.

THE LEGAL REQUIREMENTS

When it comes to recruiting and selecting staff there are several laws which have to be taken in to consideration in order to avoid discrimination. At the time of publication the following legislation will affect the way staff are employed namely:

- The Equal Pay Act 1970 – pay and contracts must be the same for men and women doing like work
- The Sex Discrimination Act 1975 – makes it unlawful to treat less favourably on grounds of sex, sex-reassignment or marital status
- The Race Relations Act 1976 – makes it unlawful to treat less favourably on grounds of colour, race, ethnic origin or nationality
- Trade Union and Labour Relations (Consolidation) Act 1992 – makes it unlawful to discriminate on the grounds of trade union membership
- Disability Discrimination Act 1995 – makes it unlawful to discriminate against disabled people in their terms of employment, promotion opportunities, dismissing them or by subjecting them to any other detriment

> **! REMEMBER**
>
> Before anyone is employed the discriminatory laws are still applicable. This means for example you have to be very careful with the way you word job titles to avoid them being sexist. You may have noticed you won't see 'Chambermaids' being advertised these days.

■ Part Time Workers (Prevention of Less Favourable Treatment) Regulations 2000 – provides part-time workers, who are on the same contract as full-time workers, equal treatment

■ Fixed Term Employees (Prevention of Less Favourable Treatment) Regulations 2000 – provides fixed term employees the right to treatment that is equal to that of equivalent permanent employees

■ Employment Equality (Sexual Orientation) Regulations 2003 – protects people against discrimination on grounds of sexual orientation of any kind

■ Employment Equality (Religion or Belief) Regulations 2003 – makes it unlawful to discriminate on grounds of religion or belief

■ Employment Equality (Age) Regulations 2006 – prohibits unjustified age discrimination in employment and vocational training

© ISTOCKPHOTO.COM/DNY59

As a supervisor or manager it is important that you are aware of how the above statutory requirements will impact on the way you recruit and select your staff. **It is key that the processes you use are fair and non-discriminatory**.

The human resource manager may do a lot of the background work for you by putting in place policies and procedures, but at the end of the day it is usually the supervisor or manager that recruits a new employee into the organisation.

THE LABOUR MARKET

So you have now worked out the job roles, person specifications and have gained your authority to recruit the numbers of staff you require for your hotel. Where are you going to find these potential employees?

The labour market is the pool of potential recruits available to fill vacant positions. These can be internal and external to the organisation. The internal pool of labour would consist of staff that currently work for your organisation and could be looking to change job roles. The external labour will consist of candidates that do not work for your organisation.

When looking to recruit staff there are other variables which will affect how easy or difficult it will be to fill a vacancy, such as knowledge and skill level required. So let's look at our reservations agent position. According to our person specification we would be looking for someone who has English and maths GCSEs, customer service experience, is computer literate and an interest in a career in hospitality as a minimum requirement. Internal to the organisation it may be we have an employee currently working in food and beverage who wants to get some more front office experience, so that could be a potential applicant. However, if there is no one in the organisation who is interested in our reservations agent vacancy, then we would have to look outside the organisation.

When we look outside the organisation we need to consider the level of knowledge and skills that are available. In order to do this we can look at the labour profile for the location of our organisation. So for our reservations agent we would be looking for someone who has a minimum equivalent qualification level of NVQ2. The labour profile will give us additional information such as the number of people that are employed, unemployed, actively seeking work, and pay levels which will help us to determine whether there will be enough potential candidates for our job.

Once we have established our labour markets we can decide whether or not we need to advertise the vacancy we have. Advertising can be very costly to an organisation, and it can be cheaper to fill a vacancy by looking at what resources the organisation currently has. This could be people currently working for us, or speculative applications that we may have received.

 ACTIVITY

Labour market profile
Have a look at the labour market profile of the location of where you work by going to the following website: http://www.nomisweb.co.uk

Consider how this information could be useful to you if you were looking to recruit for a vacant position. Make a note of numbers of people that are economically active and economically inactive and the skill levels available.

JOB ADVERTS

For some positions it may be necessary to advertise the job, depending on the number of jobs available and the types of people the organisation is looking for. For many of the front of house positions in the hospitality industry the focus is more on the behaviour of people. When recruiting employers look for a good attitude and are often willing to train the more technical skills.

When writing a job advert it must catch the **attention** of the target audience and hold the reader's **interest** so the whole message is read. Further it should arouse **desire** for the opportunity offered and stimulate **action** in the forms of applications. This is the typical selling formula known as AIDA – Attention, Interest, Desire and Action.

What to include in job adverts:

- ■ Job title, location and salary
- ■ Brief description of the job
- ■ Brief description of the organisation
- ■ Brief description of the 'ideal' person
- ■ Organisational benefits and facilities
- ■ Unique features (such as hours of work, accommodation)
- ■ Application procedures and closing date
- ■ Reference number (if used)
- ■ Equal opportunities statement
- ■ Reference to the organization's website

 **TIP**

Some organisations recruit actors to work in their bars and restaurants because they have a great attitude towards their customers. Smile, you're on stage ☺

ACTIVITY

Writing a job advert
Using the AIDA formula write a job advert for the position for our reservations agent, taking in to account what should be included in your job advert.

When advertising a job you need to consider the cost implications of this. If you were to advertise a job in a newspaper the cost can go up depending where you position the advert. So for example adverts on the top right-hand side of a page can be more expensive, as this tends to be where people look first when they open a newspaper, and therefore you could get a higher response rate than if you placed it in the bottom left-hand corner. There are many different ways in which you can advertise your job: what else can you think of? For your organisation it is important to use the most cost-effective method. These days a lot of organisations will advertise on their company website.

JOB APPLICATIONS

Once you have decided how to advertise your job you also need to decide on the best way for a candidate to apply:

- Application form – paper or electronically
- Curriculum vitae – paper or electronically
- Letter of application – paper or electronically
- Handwritten or typed submission
- Personal call

Any of the above methods are acceptable – although you need to consider the most cost-effective way. Using an application form will make it easier for you to shortlist who you want to assess further, as the information will be in a standard template. Some organisations will not accept curriculum vitaes for this reason. Imagine if you had received 100 applications for our reservations agent position – and this was through a mixture of CVs, application forms, letters and phone calls. How would you be able to sort through them in a fair and consistent manner to shortlist the five you want to interview?

When using application forms below is the type of information you may require from a potential candidate:

- Job post applying for
- Name and address of applicant
- Employment experience – brief summary of duties for most recent employer
- Previous employment – start with most recent first
- Education and training – start with most recent first
- Memberships of professional associations
- Additional information – applicant to state why they are the most suitable candidate for the job
- References – usually from two previous employers
- Declaration – signed and dated by job applicant
- Equal opportunities monitoring – normally a tear-off slip or separate page

SHORTLISTING

You have now received your applications for our reservations agent position. The recruitment process has ended and you are now going to select the right person for the job. It is important that the process you use to select your potential employee is fair, valid and reliable. The easiest way to do this is to shortlist your applicants against the person specification.

Let's have a go at this. For the purpose of this exercise we will look at two applications for our vacancy. One is from an internal candidate and the other from an external candidate. We will use the information in their application and compare this against the person specification.

ROBERT JENNINGS	GERALDINE WASHEY
Robert has worked at The Hospitable Hotel for the past 12 months in the restaurant, serving breakfast, lunch and dinner. He has maths and English GCSE and is currently doing an NVQ 2 in customer service at the hotel. He is not computer literate but is eager to learn more. He has been voted Employee of the Month.	Geraldine left school with 5 GCSEs including English, maths and computing. She has worked in hotels since leaving school and has two years' experience in the restaurant and bar and one year's experience in reception using Fidelio. She has been commended on her complaint-handling skills.

From the information above who do you think would be more suitable for the position? Robert is an internal candidate so has the added advantage that he knows how the hotel operates and is eager to learn. Geraldine is an external candidate who has more qualification and experience than Robert. Let's use the person specification to find out who would be the best candidate for the job:

CANDIDATES	ROBERT JENNINGS		GERALDINE WASHEY	
	ESSENTIAL	DESIRABLE	ESSENTIAL	DESIRABLE
Qualifications	Maths and English GCSE		Maths and English GCSE	5 GCSEs in total
Experience	12 months in the hotel restaurant		Two years in restaurant and bar	One year working on reception
Knowledge and skills	Knowledge of the hotel		Knowledge of the industry	Knowledge of Fidelio
			Has computing GCSE	
Personal qualities	Has been voted Employee of the Month		Can use initiative by complaint handling	
Motivation and expectations	Studying NVQ2 in customer service		Has built a career in hotels	

From the above it can be seen that both candidates fulfil the essential criteria, however Geraldine also fulfils some of the more desirable elements which means that she would at this stage appear to be the most suitable candidate.

The shortlisting process would be used for all the applications received and normally the final few would then be selected for interviewing and further assessment activities.

INTERVIEWING

© ISTOCKPHOTO.COM/ARLINDO71

Welcome
Acquire
Supply
Part

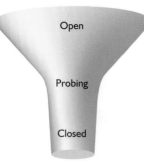

Interviewing is the most common way of selecting potential employees, as it is quick and cheap, although it is only as effective as the interviewer. Interviewing is a skill that has to be learned and requires the ability to plan, question, listen and summarise. When interviewing there has to be a clear approach so the interviewer can get the information they need from this process. A simple way to structure the interview is to use the **WASP** approach:

Welcome – introduce yourself to the candidate and explain the format of the interview

Acquire – this is about looking at the information you already have on the candidate (application form) and obtaining additional information from the candidate, through questioning

Supply – this will happen at the end of the interview when you will give the candidate any additional information they may require from you

Part – this is when you end the interview, and let the candidate know what will happen next and then they can depart

In order to structure the interview at the acquire stage it can be useful to use the application form as a guide to ensure you cover all the information you need. It is at this stage that questioning is key and a good way to do this is to use the **funnel approach** for each topic you are questioning on:

An open question is a question that is likely to receive a long answer, and the aim is for the candidate to respond to you in a sentence.

Using open questions

Open questions have the following characteristics:

■ They ask the respondent to think and reflect

■ They will give you *opinions* and *feelings*

■ They hand control of the conversation to the respondent

Once you have started with an **open question**, depending on what the candidate's response is, you can then ask another open question to **probe** for more detail. You can then end that topic of conversation with a **closed** question. This is a question which will give a limited answer or a 'yes' / 'no' answer.

For example:

Open 'I notice from your application that you have used Fidelio. How have you used Fidelio?'

(Candidate then responds)

Probing 'You mention that when on reception you have used Fidelio to check in guests. What exactly is your check-in procedure, talk me through it?'

(Candidate then responds)

© ISTOCKPHOTO.COM/JAMES TUTOR

Closed 'You said that the reservations team normally put the reservations in the system and then you would check the guest in when they arrive at reception. If you had a walk-in guest would you know how to make a reservation on Fidelio?'

(Candidate then responds)

In order to ensure that your questioning is fair you would use the same structure of questions for each of the candidates that you would be interviewing for the position. It is perfectly acceptable for you to take notes during the interview, although you must be very careful of what you write down, as under the Data Protection Act 1998, the candidate has a right to ask to see the interview notes if they so wish. You must therefore ensure that anything you write down is non-discriminatory and only relevant information to the interview is recorded.

ASSESSMENT ACTIVITIES

Other than interviews there are many other types of assessment activities that could be used to select the best person for the job. These can include psychometric tests, presentations, group activities, in-tray exercises. Whichever method or methods are used it is important that they are run fairly and any assessments made are objective. Such assessment activities usually will involve more than one person to run, and to ensure objective decisions are made, those involved need to be trained in how to assess knowledge, skills and attitude.

> **! REMEMBER**
>
> When recruiting and selecting staff it is important you select the right person for the right job. In order to do this you will have to assess their knowledge, skills and attitude.

ASSESSMENT ACTIVITY	ADVANTAGES	DISADVANTAGES
Interview	Cheap and easy to administer	Can be time-consuming, an interview can take between 30 minutes to an hour. It is only as good as the interviewer.
Psychometric tests	Easy to administer, results can be obtained quickly through specialist computer programs	Costly to run. Only those licensed can administer them and are able to interpret results accurately. Debates as to gender and ethnic bias.
Presentations	Easy to set up. Candidate can demonstrate their presentation skills	Would only be suitable for specific positions such as managerial or training where presentations would be part of the job.
Group activities – role playing, problem-solving	Candidates can demonstrate their problem-solving skills	Can be time-consuming to set up. Situation is false and you may not see the true potential of a candidate.
In-tray exercises – candidate will be given a set of typical tasks they would have to undertake in their everyday role	Candidates can demonstrate how they make decisions and solve problems	Can be time-consuming to set up.

As you can see from above, the various different types of assessment activities have advantages and disadvantages associated with them. The best way to get a more accurate prediction of who would be the best candidate for the job would be to use a combination of methods. Some organisations do this and will run what is called an assessment centre. This is normally only cost-effective if there are a large number of positions available, and could be used for example for a hotel opening.

A typical format for an assessment centre might be:

Assessment 1 – Individual psychometric test – all candidates to do this at the same time

Assessment 2 – Group problem-solving task – all candidates involved with this

Assessment 3 – Individual presentation to a panel – (candidates will have been given topic prior to the assessment day and would have had time to prepare for this)

Assessment 4 – Individual interview to a panel.

ACTIVITY

Assessment centre task

Imagine if you have been asked to put together an assessment centre task for our reservations agent position. Consider which method you think would be suitable in order to assess the organisational skills of our potential employee.

MAKING THE OFFER

Once the selection process is over the organisation should give feedback to both the successful and the unsuccessful candidates as soon as possible. This feedback should be specific and constructive and leave the candidates with a positive image of the organisation.

The successful candidate is usually sent an offer letter although this is normally subject to receiving satisfactory references first. References are not usually checked until the offer stage, as this can be time-consuming, and could cause bias in the selection process if received earlier on. Once the new employee is appointed, it is important that they are properly inducted in to the organisation, given any training required and their performance monitored. Recruiting and selecting an individual in to the organisation is just the start, the next step is to retain and develop them further.

Further reading

Alec Rodger (1952) *The Seven Point Plan*. National Institute of Industrial Psychology.

Assessment of knowledge and understanding

You have now learnt about some of the methods and processes used when recruiting and selecting staff within the hospitality industry. This should give you some thoughts and ideas on how you could make a case for additional staffing, and what processes to use to select the right candidate for the job.

To test your level of knowledge and understanding, answer the following short questions. These will help to prepare you for your summative (final) assessment.

1 What is the purpose of human resource planning?

2 Why is it important to carry out job analysis?

3 What is the difference between a job description and a person specification?

4 Which laws do you need to be aware of in order to avoid any discriminatory practices when recruiting and selecting?

5 Why is it useful to have an understanding of the labour market?

6 What should be included when writing a job advert?

7 What documentation would you need to short list a candidate?

8 What are the different types of ways you could assess a candidate?

Research task

Human resource planning is the key element to identifying your staffing requirements. You are to put together a case which you would present to your general manager identifying where you may need additional staffing in your organisation. In doing this you should produce a job description, person specification and suggest appropriate selection methods for this position ensuring that your process is fair and non-discriminatory.

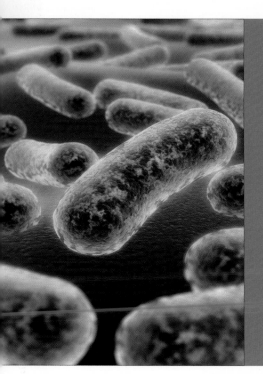

30

Ensure food safety practices are followed in the preparation and serving of food and drink

HS30 Ensure food safety practices are followed in the preparation and serving of food and drink

LEARNING OBJECTIVES

This unit refers to the competence required in ensuring that all food and drink that is prepared, cooked and served is carried out following the appropriate food safety practices and procedures. It is designed for anyone who supervises the preparation and delivery of food and/or drink to consumers.

After reading this chapter you will be able to:

■ Understand and implement relevant information and recognising your responsibilities regarding food safety procedures.

■ Ensure that good hygiene practices are in place.

■ Carry out your responsibilities for the implementation of food safety procedures.

■ Provide feedback to the person responsible for the organisation's food safety procedures on their effectiveness.

■ Monitor and be constantly alert to the possibility of food safety hazards in your area of responsibility.

■ Identify indicators of potential sources of food safety hazards.

■ Identify food safety hazards and appropriate control methods.

■ Report any new potential food safety hazards for review and evaluation of food safety procedures to the person responsible.

KEY WORDS

Cleaning schedule
A permanent list of all the cleaning task to be completed and the frequency of those cleans.

Control points
In reference to the HACCP system these are the steps at which food safety could be compromised and therefore action need to be taken.

Cross-contamination
The transfer of pathogens from a contaminated food or surface to another food either directly or indirectly.

Detergent
A chemical that removes soils but does not sterilise equipment.

Due diligence
A collection of procedures designed to prove that at every step along the production and service route care and safety is maintained.

Food allergy
A physiological reaction caused when the immune system mistakenly identifies a normally harmless food as damaging to the body.

Food intolerances
A condition whereby a person is unable to tolerate certain parts of foods. This is different from a food allergy because the immune system is not involved.

Food poisoning
An acute illness resulting from eating contaminated or poisonous food.

Food-borne illness
A general term often used to describe any disease or illness caused by eating contaminated food or drink.

FIFO
Fist in first out – a principle referring to the rotation of foodstuffs.

HACCP (hazard analysis critical control point)
A food safety and self-inspection system that highlights potentially hazardous foods and how they are handled in the food service environment.

Hazard
This refers to anything that has the potential to cause harm.

Hygiene
To keep clean and safe in order to prevent diseases and maintain health.

Pests

Unwelcome visitors to the food preparation areas in the form of rodents, insects and birds.

Risk

The likelihood of a hazards potential being realised.

Sanitiser

An agent which yields a significant reduction in the level of harmful bacteria.

Training need

Required when there is a gap between the knowledge and skills required for an employee to be able to do their job.

Training programme

A broad outline of training that indicates the stages of the training and the time allowed for each part.

INTRODUCTION

Ensuring food safety hygiene practice in the preparation and serving of food and drink

As a food and drink service provider you have an enormous responsibility to provide food and drink that is not only high in quality but also safe for the consumer. It is essential that the legislation that surrounds this area is followed closely at all times. As a supervisor you will also be responsible for knowing and understanding all the current legislation and also training to ensure that members of staff follow the procedures in place.

LEGAL REQUIREMENTS OF HEALTH AND SAFETY AT WORK

Over the years many new health and safety regulations have been implemented and it is ensured that existing laws/Acts are regularly updated to cater for ever-expanding technology, changing working methods and increased numbers of employees within the workplace.

The main regulations that need to be addressed, implemented and adhered to by an employer in an establishment, by law, are as follows:

The Health and Safety at Work Act (1974)

This Act is in place to cover employees, employers, the self-employed, customers and visitors. It lays down the minimum standards of health, safety and welfare required within each area of the workplace. As with all health and safety provisions, it is an employer's legal responsibility to ensure that the Act is fully implemented and that as far as reasonably practicable the health and safety of all those they are responsible for is correctly managed. The reason this Act was enforced is to reiterate, establish and enforce the ongoing maintenance of a safe and healthy working environment within a kitchen at all times.

The Health and Safety (Information for Employees) Regulations (1989)

Current regulations require that an employer must provide employees with health and safety information in the form of notices, leaflets and posters: all are available through the Health and Safety Executive.

Where an employer has in excess of five employees, a written health and safety policy must be in place for the establishment. This should be issued to every employee, clearly outlining their personal health and safety responsibilities to the employer, other staff and/or customers, visitors, the public.

Food Safety Act (1990)

This Act makes it clear that businesses must not cause food to be dangerous to health, present or describe food in a way that can mislead, sell or keep food that is unfit for consumption and sell food that is not what the customer is entitled to expect with regards to quality or content

THE FOOD SAFETY PROCEDURES

Within the production and service areas of food and drink there are numerous procedures set in place that are designed to ensure that due diligence is upheld. Organisation is a vital skill to acquire in order to produce a successful, professional and motivated workforce. Some tasks are daily and others are weekly. These food safety procedures are vital to the business and more importantly the consumers who use them.

Daily activities that need to be completed are:

- Monitoring of temperatures of fridges and freezers
- Receipt of food temperature monitoring
- Cold and hot hold temperature monitoring
- Core temperature monitoring
- All contact areas to be disinfected

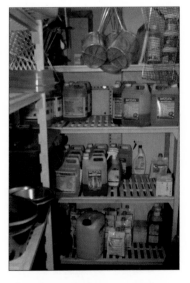

Cleaning products must be used to disinfect contact areas.

Weekly activities that need to be completed are:

■ Deep cleaning of the kitchen

■ All records to be checked, signed and collated

■ Record files to be updated and kept for a minimum of 3 months

Types of food safety hazards

Factors that can cause food poisoning include various types of contaminants:

■ Bacterial contaminants

■ Physical contaminants

■ Chemical contaminants

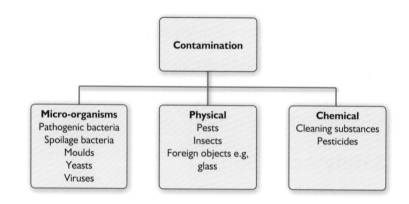

Contamination factors

Bacterial contamination is caused when ideal conditions are afforded to bacteria such as warmth, food, moisture and time.

Poor personal hygiene practices, cross-contamination, storage, chilling and cooking can all lead to food poisoning. Food poisoning is caused when pathogenic bacteria (harmful) are present in sufficient amounts to make the body ill.

Bacteria affect the body in different ways and the end result can be diarrhoea, vomiting, dehydration or even death.

Types of bacteria and the food they contaminate

Bacteria are a single-celled organism which can only be seen through microscope. Bacteria that cause disease are called 'pathogens'. When certain pathogens enter the food supply, they can cause food-borne illness. Only a few types cause millions of cases of food-borne illness each year.

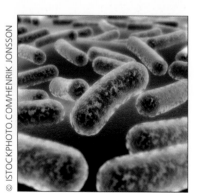

BACTERIA TYPE	FOUND IN	TRANSPORTED BY	SYMPTOMS
Campylobacter jejuni	Intestinal tracts of animals and birds, raw milk (unpasteurised), untreated water, and sewage.	Contaminated water, raw milk, and raw or under-cooked meat, poultry, or shellfish.	Fever, headache, and muscle pain followed by diarrhoea (sometimes bloody), abdominal pain and nausea that appear 2 to 5 days after eating; may last 7 to 10 days.
Clostridium botulinum	Widely distributed in nature: in soil and water, on plants, and in intestinal tracts of animals and fish. Grows only with little or no oxygen present.	Bacteria produce a toxin that causes illness. Improperly canned foods, garlic in oil, and vacuum-packaged and tightly wrapped food.	Toxin affects the nervous system. Symptoms usually appear within 18 to 36 hours, but can sometimes appear within as few as 4 hours or as many as 8 days after eating; double vision, droopy eyelids, trouble speaking and swallowing, and difficulty breathing. Fatal in 3 to 10 days if not treated.
Clostridium perfringens	Soil, dust, sewage, and intestinal tracts of animals and humans. Grows only in little or no oxygen.	Many outbreaks result from food left for long periods at room temperature. Bacteria destroyed by cooking, but some toxin-producing spores may survive.	Diarrhoea and gas pains may appear 8 to 24 hours after eating; usually last about 1 day, but less severe symptoms may persist for 1 to 2 weeks.
Escherichia coli O157:H7	Intestinal tracts of some mammals, raw milk, unchlorinated water; one of several strains of *E. coli* that can cause human illness.	Contaminated water, raw milk, raw or rare ground beef, unpasteurized apple juice, uncooked fruits and vegetables, person-to-person.	Diarrhoea or bloody diarrhoea, abdominal cramps, nausea, and malaise; can begin 2 to 5 days after food is eaten, lasting about 8 days.
Staphylococcus aureus	On humans (skin, infected cuts, noses, and throats).	People-to-food through improper handling. Multiply rapidly at room temperature to produce a toxin that causes illness.	Severe nausea, abdominal cramps, vomiting, and diarrhoea occur 1 to 6 hours after eating; recovery within 2 to 3 days – longer if severe dehydration occurs.
Salmonella	Intestinal tract and faeces of animals; and in raw eggs.	Raw or under-cooked eggs, poultry and meat, raw milk and dairy products, seafood.	Stomach pain, diarrhoea, nausea, chills, fever, and headache usually appear 6 to 48 hours after eating; may last 1 to 2 days.

Moisture

Warmth

Time

Food

Factors affecting bacteria growth

Physical contamination is caused when an objectionable substance is present in food, e.g. an earring in a bowl of soup, a fragment of machinery, loose fixture or fitting, stones, pips and bones. This can occur anywhere along the food chain. Most manufacturers protect against this type of contamination by using metal detectors on their production lines. Good handling practices include not wearing jewellery and use of blue-coloured dressings. Physical contamination can produce symptoms in the same way as bacterial poisoning.

Chemical contamination occurs when a chemical such as sanitiser, bleach or furniture polish comes into contact with food and is ingested by a person. The usual reaction is vomiting but it can also cause burning while vomiting.

Allergies and intolerances

Where vegetarian or allergen-free food is prepared alongside other food, a risk assessment to identify, segregate or manage any allergens or ingredients that could cause harm or dissatisfaction to customers is important. Although it possible to be intolerant to any food, the most common are wheat, gluten and lactose.

Wheat allergies or **coeliac disease** is when some people with have an immune reaction that is triggered by gluten, a collective name for a type of protein found in the cereals wheat, rye and barley. By eating gluten it causes the lining of the gut (small bowel) to become damaged and may affect other parts of the body. A few people are also sensitive to oats.

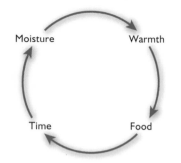

Nuts can trigger allergic reactions

Nut allergies can be found in both peanuts and tree nuts (e.g. walnuts, pecans, almonds, etc.) The reaction occurs when the body's immune system battles against something your body is allergic to (an allergen). This can be triggered by very small quantities and symptoms can include tightness of the throat, rashes or hives, swelling of the face as well as increased heart rate and a drop in blood pressure.

Milk allergies are a reaction to the proteins found in milk. This is different to lactose intolerance where the sufferer has an inability or problem producing the enzyme lactase required to break down the lactose.

To control these allergies it recommended that the following procedures are put into place:

- Limit use of potential allergens on menus
- Segregation of allergens in stores to prevent cross-contamination
- Include markers on menus to show customers what is in their food
- Train staff on allergies and brief staff on food with potential allergens included

FOOD SAFETY CONTROLS

Food safety needs to be addressed by ensuring there are controls in place. These controls vary from those which require regular adjustment to those such as design and building of premises which cannot be altered.

All control measures should be built into the organisation's framework and continually monitored by senior personnel who are responsible for the implementation of them.

Controls come in many forms such as spot checks of staff uniform or advanced training and HACCP.

Staff should be regularly tested on their knowledge and effectiveness of the monitoring systems used in the organisation. A kitchen is only as effective as its weakest member of staff; if a chef is unable to take temperatures, cook correctly or follow standard hygienic practices then an incident is likely to occur.

When food safety is compromised there are always causes. Some of these causes would include lack of supervision, lack of labelling information, poor supplier quality, cross-contamination, bad premises and waste management, poor personal health, handling issues and pests.

In order to maintain food and drink safety it is vital that the hazards are recognised step by step.

Spot checks of staff uniform can be a good monitor of hygiene

HACCP (hazard analysis, critical control points)

The food hygiene laws mean that all food businesses need to have an HACCP system. The system means that producers need to understand how, why and where food could become contaminated and then set out to prevent it from happening.

These records show that the system is working and can support a defence of due diligence should a complaint be made against the business.

Due diligence is the main legal defence endorsed by the Food Safety Act 1990. It provides the best protection to companies that need to demonstrate in court that all reasonable precautions have been taken to avoid the sale of unsafe food.

The first step for food handling businesses in developing an HACCP system is to set up a team who need to be adequately trained in HACCP principles and their application. This team will also decide who should be responsible for implementing it.

The next stage is to carefully identify each step in the preparation of each dish, starting with the purchase of the ingredients and ending with sale to the customer, and to formulate these steps into a flow chart.

HACCP involves the following seven steps:

1 Identify what could go wrong (the hazards).

2 Identify the most important points where things can go wrong (the critical control points – CCPs).

3 Set critical limits at each CCP (e.g. cooking temperature/time).

4 Set up checks at CCPs to prevent problems occurring (monitoring).

5 Decide what to do if something goes wrong (corrective action).

6 Prove that your HACCP Plan is working (verification).

7 Keep records of all of the above (documentation).

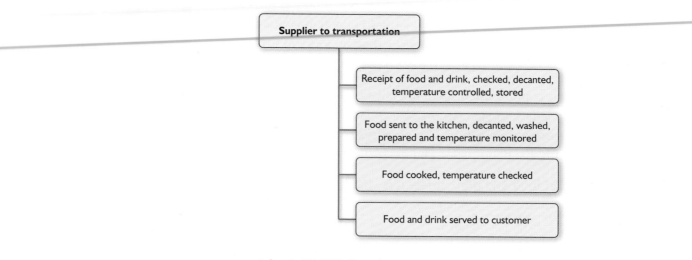

A basic HACCP flowchart

Each step then needs to be carefully analysed to identify what could go wrong to result in a safety hazard to the customer. Such hazards include bacteria, foreign bodies and chemical contaminants.

Identifying what can be done to control potential hazards is the next step. Controls may include separation of raw and cooked foods to avoid cross-contamination, personal hygiene rules to avoid contamination by bacteria and correct cooking times and temperatures to avoid the survival of harmful bacteria.

The company will be required to consider whether or not the customer will be harmed if nothing is done at the step where you have identified a potential hazard, and that will dictate which steps are critical control points.

The next stage is to set standards, or critical limits, for the controls. These will specify the conditions which must be met to ensure that the food and drink will be safe. Checks should be carried out at predetermined times and records kept to show that the controls are working.

A usual list of CCPs would include: receipt, storage, preparation, cooking, hot holding, serving, chilling, reheating and freezing. The flow will not always be one way and some points may be visited more than once.

If monitoring shows that critical limits are not being met, a designated person must take and record and act using corrective action.

Whenever there is a recipe change, an addition to the menu, a new activity is introduced or the structure of the kitchen and/or restaurant changes, the HACCP system must be reviewed. Even if no changes take place, a review of the HACCP system should take place at least once a year.

The HACCP checklist

- Decide who will develop your HACCP system
- Draw a flow chart of your food preparation processes
- Identify where food safety hazards can occur
- Identify what can be done to control hazards
- Identify corrective action when monitoring shows that controls aren't working
- Review the HACCP system after a year
- Keep all documentation and records

SAFE FOOD STORAGE

An HACCP food management system will also examine the point of food storage. It should cover the receiving of goods where the core temperatures and condition of the delivery is thoroughly checked. Fresh meat that has been delivered should have a core temperature of a maximum of 8°C. All fresh produce should be delivered in unbroken, clean packaging and in clean delivery vehicles that are refrigerated. If you suspect a delivery has not met the requirements of your HACCP it should not be accepted but returned immediately to the supplier. A goods inwards sheet showing the company, invoice number, core temperature, any problems and how they were dealt with, allows received goods to be monitored.

Food temperatures

It is important to learn and remember the legal temperatures associated with receipt, storage, cooking and hot holding of foodstuffs.

- Delivery – below 8°C
- Storage – 0–5°C
- Cooked foods – above 75°C for 2 minutes
- Chilled food – must be chilled down to below 8°C in 90 minutes or under
- Hot holding of food – held at 64°C or above

> **! REMEMBER**
>
> You are legally responsible for adhering to food temperature taking and recording.

Staff training

Training is the development of the workforce and is designed to meet various objectives.

Health and safety should be discussed with all employees upon appointment and further detailed in any contract of employment, either giving full details of procedures, advising of any staff handbook that may be available or giving contact details of a relevant health and safety officer to contact for further information.

It is the responsibility of an employer to ensure that all new staff are fully trained in accordance with health and safety as well as maintaining ongoing training for existing members of staff so that everyone is up to date with procedure and the correct operation, maintenance or plan to follow in line with current legislation.

Given the enhanced vulnerability of those that work within a food preparation and service area, there are four main areas that require particular attention when assessing health and safety:

1　The safe and hygienic handling, storage and usage of food.

2　The personal hygiene, cleanliness and appearance and of employees.

3　The provision of safe premises and the correct training for use of and safe storage of equipment.

4　The correct labelling, notification, training, handling and storage of hazardous substances.

PRINCIPLES IN GOOD WORKPLACE DESIGN AND LAYOUT

In order to maintain the safety of food and drink within an establishment it is important to consider the numerous points that will affect how your business flows. Below is a list of points that require thought when design an establishment that will not only be practical, but also safe:

1　Workflow.
2　Deliveries.
3　Storage.
4　Preparation.
5　Cooking.
6　Final preparation.
7　Serving.
8　Lighting.
9　Ventilation.
10　Plumbing.
11　Equipment.
12　Surfaces.
13　Staff facilities.
14　Cleaning.
15　Refuse.
16　Pest control.

© ISTOCKPHOTO.COM/DRAGAN TRIFUNOVIC

A professional and clean kitchen

A well-designed kitchen will have delivery points separate from the kitchen, close to storage facilities and well away from refuse areas. When food and drink enter the establishment raw food should not come in to cooked food areas or cross over their route.

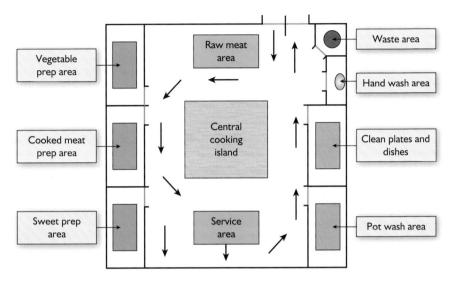

A simple design of workplace flow

Dangers of pest infestation

There are three kinds of pests commonly found in food areas:

1 **Rodents** – such as mice and rats.
2 **Insects** – such as flies, cockroaches, ants and other insects associated with food.
3 **Birds** – such as pigeons, magpies and sparrows.

These pests eat and spoil the food. They also carry food poisoning bacteria that can be transferred to the food from their bodies and their excreta.

Pests seek out food, warmth and shelter; therefore, steps should be taken to keep them out.

■ Keep doors and windows closed
■ Use of fly screens on windows
■ Checking of delivery for signs of pests
■ Find the ways that pests may gain access
■ Do not do anything that may attract pests to the premises, for example, leave outside waste disposal areas uncovered

Other effective control measures are included in good working practices. Examples of good practice would include:

■ Prompt removal of food spillages and particles from both floors and work surfaces

- High standards of general cleanliness
- Food is covered and not left out overnight
- Equipment and utensils are kept clean
- Dried foods are stored in containers with tight-fitting lids and not on the ground
- Regular checks on all food storage areas
- Bins are emptied regularly throughout the day and last thing at night

Signs of pest infestation can be found, particularly in the morning, as many pests work at night.

- Droppings
- Marks on foods
- Small mounds of food debris
- Unusual smells
- Damage to woodwork and cables
- Grease marks along walls and edges
- Holes in containers

It is essential that food and drink that is suspected of contamination by pests is removed immediately.

Advice on pest control can be obtained from the local health authority and it is advisable that pest control companies assist with the prevention and cure of pests.

WWW.SXC.HU

Waste disposal

Disposal of waste is another HACCP matter, as bacteria and pathogens can multiply at an alarming rate in waste disposal areas. In ideal circumstances the areas for cleaning crockery and pots should be separate from each other and from the food preparation area.

Waste bins in the kitchen should be emptied at regular and short intervals and be kept clean. Food waste can be safely disposed of in a waste disposal unit. Oil can only be disposed of by a specialist oil disposal company and must not be placed in a sink or waste disposal unit.

EFFECTIVE CLEANING METHODS

Cleaning is designed to achieve two tasks:

1 The removal or grease, food debris and dirt.
2 The destruction of bacteria (disinfection).

There are commonly two ways of ensuring your workplace is kept clean. The first is instilling a mentality of 'clean as you go' in the workforce. This is the immediate cleaning between jobs and is designed to prevent cross-contamination as well as keep areas clean and tidy. The other is the 'scheduled cleaning' as previously explained.

Dry cleaning

Dry cleaning is any cleaning process for textiles using an organic solvent rather than water. Dry cleaning is necessary for cleaning items which would otherwise be damaged by water and soap or detergent.

Wet cleaning

In the cleaning of equipment and work areas there are commonly six stages involved in the cleaning process:

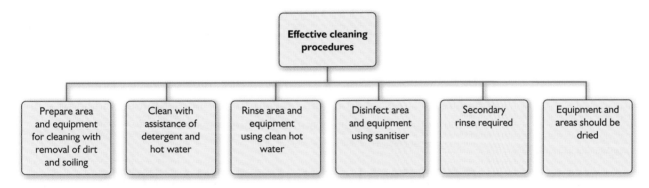

The 6 stage cleaning process

The use of dishwashers for the cleaning of small equipment is particularly useful. Service items are cleaned to a high specification with high-temperature water which kills bacteria and also dry rapidly.

Food temperature control

Bacteria will grow rapidly in foods, particularly those considered high risk, that have been left with the danger zone −8°C to 63°C

Below 8°C bacteria do not grow, or grow only very slowly. They do not grow at temperatures exceeding 63°C. Therefore, in order to maintain food safety, food should either be kept hold or cold and out of the danger zone. Correct temperature control is one of the most powerful weapons against infection of food by food poisoning bacteria.

It is important to remember that some bacteria can be **spore forming** (e.g. *Clostridium perfrigens* and bacillus) and therefore are not killed by extremes of temperature but instead hibernate in the form of a spore. When the conditions become favourable again the bacteria will resume their ability to multiply.

STORAGE METHODS

Freezers should be maintained at a maximum temperature of −18°C. All food should be covered to prevent freezer burn and labelled with the date of production and a use-by date.

Fridges should operate between 1°C and 5°C. Ideally separate fridges are used for raw and cooked products as well as dairy. If this is not possible should be kept on separate shelves. Again all food must be clearly labelled with production dates and use-by dates.

Ambient stores should be clean and well ventilated, with mesh over windows and doors to help with pest control. All foodstuffs must be stored away from the floor and be rotated on a first in and first out basis.

Chilling food not for immediate use should ideally be achieved in blast chillers where the core temperature is brought down from 70°C to 8°C in 90 minutes or less. With these temperature ranges both pathogenic and bacterial growth is inhibited although not completely stopped.

If food that has been cooked is not for immediate consumption, or is to be frozen, it should be well-covered with cling film or ideally vacuum packed to create an airtight barrier and prevent freezer burn. Storage should be within manufacturer's guidelines and the foods must be clearly labelled.

PERSONAL HYGIENE PRACTICES

Good hygiene systems are required to be followed by all food handlers.

Regular hand washing is a requirement of the chef, and in all aspects of a chef's working day. The following procedures should apply:

1 An approved hand washing detergent should be provided by the employer, preferably in liquid form and from a dispenser.
2 Hot water and an approved drying system should be in place.
3 The application of an alcohol-based hand disinfectant allows for maximum disinfection.

> **! REMEMBER**
>
> You are the biggest vehicle for bacterial movement – keep yourself clean at all times.

Hand washing must be undertaken:

■ Before commencing work (to wash away general bacteria)
■ After using the toilet or in contact with faeces
■ After breaks
■ Between touching raw food and cooked food
■ Before handling raw food
■ After disposing of waste
■ After cleaning the work space

Hand washing

■ After any first aid or dressing changes.

■ After touching face, nose, mouth or blowing your nose.

■ **Hand washing and sanitation should take place at every possible opportunity**.

Cuts, boils and septic wounds

Food handlers should always cover cuts, grazes, boils and septic wounds with the appropriate dressing or with brightly coloured (blue) waterproof plasters. Cuts on fingers may need extra protection with waterproof fingerstalls or latex disposable gloves.

Jewellery and cosmetics

Food handlers and chefs should not wear earrings, watches, rings or other piercing because they can harbour dirt and bacteria. Plain wedding bands are permitted, but these can still harbour significant levels of bacteria. Strong-smelling perfume may cause food to be tainted and make-up should be used minimally.

Protective clothing

Every person handling food must wear protective clothing. It should be lightweight, washable and strong. White clothing has the advantage of showing up dirt more easily. Food service providers should not travel to work in their uniform and it should be kept clean and smart in the same manner as the food preparation staff.

© ISTOCKPHOTO.COM/DAMIR KARAN

Cross-contamination

Cross-contamination occurs when bacteria are transferred either directly, e.g. raw and cooked food come into direct contact, sneezing or coughing over food or indirectly with the assistance of a vehicle such as hands, pests and dirty utensils.

Storage of foods

All foods should be kept covered when in storage and pests and animals must be prevented from entering these areas.

Worktops and chopping boards

It is very important to keep all worktops and chopping boards clean because they touch the food your customers are going to eat. If they are not properly clean, bacteria could spread to food and make your customers ill.

■ Always wash worktops before you start preparing food

■ Wipe up any spilt food straight away

- Always wash worktops thoroughly after they have been touched by raw meat, including poultry, or raw eggs
- Never put ready-to-eat food, such as tomatoes or fruit, on a worktop or chopping board that has been touched by raw meat, unless you have washed it thoroughly first

Ideally, it is standard practice to have separate chopping boards for raw meat and for other foods. A standardised system of coloured boards and knife handles help to minimise cross-contamination are widely available. They should be as follows:

Red	Raw meat and poultry
Yellow	Cooked meat and poultry
Blue	Raw fish
Brown	Vegetables
Green	Fruit and salads
White	Dairy and pastry items

> **! REMEMBER**
>
> All staff should be aware of the colour coding for this practice to be effective – staff need to be trained regularly.

With regards to the service of food it is equally important for service trays, plates and utensils to be clean and sanitised.

Supervisory role

As a food preparation and service supervisor your role will not only be those of a normal employee but also the checking and reporting on company procedures. You will be required to delegate jobs, ensure the proper application of control measures, monitor the control measures and ensure corrective action is taken should the control measures fail. It is vital that you a vigilant to the possibility of food safety hazards and how to look out for them.

Assessment of knowledge and understanding

The following projects, activities and assessments are directly linked to the essential knowledge and understanding for unit HS30.

Make sure that you keep this for easier referencing and along with your work for future inclusion in your portfolio.

To test your level of knowledge and understanding, answer the following short questions. These will help to prepare you for your summative (final) assessment.

Health and safety

1   List the three types of contamination in food areas and give four examples for each type.

2   What are the factors that are required for bacteria to grow? What practices could you implement to restrict any of these factors?

3   What are the temperatures for hot holding, final cooking and storage of foods?

4   What are the three most common types of pests and the signs that there may be infestation?

5   Research the possible penalties incurred from not adhering to the Health and Safety at Work Act (1974).

6   Produce a cleaning schedule suitable for a workplace. Inclusion of equipment and areas to be cleaned and their frequency of clean are essential. A signature box to ensure this is carried out and inspected should also be included.

Research task

Design and draw your own restaurant service area based upon a medium-sized premise with approximately 12 waiting staff. Include ideas of flow of movement around this area. You will then need to work on a detailed training programme for the staff and a necessary health and safety action plan to implement.

It should be ensured that the premises, equipment and storage of, chemicals storage, room size and space and number of staff are all taken into consideration.

31
Lead meetings

HS31 Lead meetings

LEARNING OBJECTIVES

This unit is about passing on information and knowledge to staff. It involves using a variety of techniques to communicate information. It is relevant to the important role that hospitality supervisors have in keeping staff informed and briefing them for their work.

After reading this chapter you will be able to:

■ Establish the purpose and objectives of the meeting and confirm that a meeting is the best way to achieve these objectives.

■ Prepare carefully how you will lead the meeting and identify who needs to participate.

■ Invite participants, giving them sufficient notice to enable them to attend and stating:

   I the importance of the meeting

   II the role they will be expected to play, and

   III the preparation they need to do.

■ Circulate relevant information in advance and, if required, brief participants individually on the content and purpose of the meeting and their roles.

■ Set a fixed time for the meeting to begin and end and allocate time appropriately for each agenda item.

- State the purpose of the meeting at the start and check that all participants understand why they are present.
- Clarify specific objectives at the beginning of each agenda item.
- Encourage all participants to make clear, concise and constructive contributions from their perspectives, whilst acknowledging and building on the contributions of other participants.
- Discourage unhelpful comments and digressions, refocusing attention on the objectives of the meeting.
- Manage time flexibly, giving more time to particular agenda items, if necessary, whilst ensuring key objectives are met and participants are kept informed of changes in the agenda.
- Summarise the discussion at appropriate times and allocate action points to participants at the end of each agenda item.
- Take decisions within the meeting's authority, remit or terms of reference.
- Observe any formal procedures or standing orders that apply to the meeting.
- Check that decisions and action points are accurately recorded and promptly communicated to those who need to know.

KEY WORDS

Consensus
General agreement, characterised by the absence of sustained opposition to substantial issues by members of the meeting group and by a process that involves seeking to take into account the views of all parties concerned and to reconcile any conflicting arguments.

Feedback
The process of sharing observations, concerns and suggestions between persons or divisions of the organisation with the intention of improving both personal and organisational performance.

Information
Knowledge acquired through study or experience or instruction.

Knowledge
This is the information that a person holds on a subject. It can be gained through education and experience.

Mediate
Occupy an intermediate or middle position or form a connecting link or stage between two others.

ACTIVITY

Imagine what would happen at work if no one held meetings with you for a whole week. Think about:

- ■ the people who communicate with you
- ■ the messages they give you
- ■ how these messages enable you to do your work and have a life outside work

Objectives

This is an achievable and realistic plan of what an individual wants to achieve in a specific time frame with measurable outcomes.

INTRODUCTION

Knowledge is gained through information and information is gained through communication. Communication takes a variety of forms in the workplace. Without communication the workplace would become chaotic and unproductive. An essential element to communication and problem-solving is the supervisor's use of meetings. This chapter looks at effective communication strategies during meetings and also more practical elements such as setting and planning for successful meetings. As part of the introduction to this chapter have a look at the activity and consider the issue it raises.

TECH SKILLS ✓

TYPES OF COMMUNICATION

There are three key types of communication:

1 **Interpersonal communication skills.** This is direct, face-to-face communication that occurs between two persons. It is essentially a dialogue or a conversation between two or more people. It is personal, direct, as well as intimate and permits maximum interaction through words and gestures. Interpersonal communications maybe:

 i **Focused interactions.** This primarily results from an actual encounter between two persons. This implies that the two persons involved are completely aware of the communication happening between them

 ii **Unfocused interactions.** This occurs when one simply observes or listens to persons with whom one is not conversing. This usually occurs at stations and bus stops, as well as on the street, at restaurants, etc.

2 **Non-verbal communication skills.** This includes aspects such as body language, gestures, facial expressions, eye contact, etc., which also become a part of the communicating process; as well as the written and typed modes of communications.

3 **Mass communication.** This is generally identified with tools of modern mass media, which includes books, the press, cinema, television, radio, etc. It is a means of conveying messages to an entire populace.

It is also sometimes classified into the following categories:

■ Verbal and non-verbal

■ Technological and non-technological

■ Mediated and non-mediated

■ Participatory and non-participatory

1 **Oral communication.** Effective oral communication is not learned from reading: it takes practice, practice, and more practice. It requires understanding the fundamentals of good grammar. It involves developing a vocabulary that allows you to express your opinions, to state your position during a dialogue relative to reaching a decision, to phrase your questions clearly and concisely, and to make your wishes known on any number of matters.

2 **Written communication.** We learn to write by writing and not by reading about writing. Written communication takes on many different forms. It includes general correspondence, reports of different types, project proposals, procedures, record keeping, operating instructions, spreadsheet data, announcements, documentation and presentations.

3 **Graphic and pictorial communication.** Graphics and pictures can often communicate ideas and concepts more effectively than the use of a lot of words. However, graphics and pictures must be presented clearly just like any other form of communication.

4 **Listening as communication.** Managers need to develop their listening skills. That involves hearing the message and not jumping to conclusions without a full understanding of the message. There are times when we get impatient when listening to the views of others, and perhaps with justification.

5 **Reading as communication.** Reading is an important part of your responsibility as a supervisor or manager. Reading stimulates creative thought – the kind of thinking required to move the organisation forward. You can learn from those news accounts about organisations and their activities. You can learn what others have done and are doing. You can how the actions of others can impact your own operations.

Reading can help in your role as supervisor or manager

Some of the types of communication used in business include:

Email	Interviews
Face-to-face	Listening
One-to-one	Staff parties
Team meetings	Pre-shift meetings

1 Are there any further methods of communication that can be added to this list?

2 How are each of these methods used for communication with both customers and staff?

3 Which of these are the most effective methods for communicating with staff?

4 Which of these are the most effective methods for communicating with customers?

5 Provide examples of how you have seen any of these methods used ineffectively.

Appraisals	Training sessions
Text message	Internet
Posters	Fax machine
Memorandums	Telephone
Orders taken from customers	Complaints

Email as an effective form of communication

Email is an extremely popular form of communication, but it can often lead to major problems if the underlying tone of the email message is misinterpreted at one end. If the people involved are in different emotional states of mind, the slightest disagreement via email can quickly spiral out of control leading to a full-blown argument. This breakdown in communication occurs because the average email communicator's intended written emotion gets lost in translation.

Sometimes when email writers start using text phrases to characterise emotion that would normally be delivered via physical body language, the intended message can be misunderstood by the reader due to a misinterpretation of the writer's emotional tone. So it is important to decide whether emails is always the most appropriate form of communication. There isn't a single correct answer, but here are four helpful tips to help you out:

1 **Be clear. Be brief.** Write short email messages with a crystal clear point. Do not write long-winded confusing paragraphs that leave room for misinterpretation.

2 **Proofread.** Proofread your message multiple times. If the email deals with touchy subject matter, have a third party read it over as well. This can give you added perspective on how well it will be received by the intended recipient.

3 **Wait.** Write the email, proofread it, and then sit on it for a little while. If your emotions were flaring when you wrote the email, a little time can allow these emotions to settle, allowing you to evaluate the message in a different light.

4 **Pick up the phone!** While email can be a convenient communication channel, certain discussions need to be handled over the phone, or if possible, in person. If you notice that the situation is starting to deteriorate, don't send another email, it's time to pick up the phone or arrange a face-to-face meeting.

COMMUNICATION AND THE ORGANISATIONAL STRUCTURE

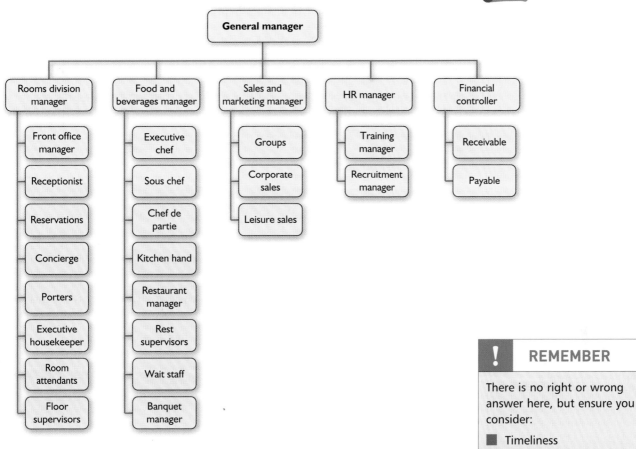

An example of an organisational chart in hospitality

Using the organisational chart above, prepare answers to the following activity:

1 How would the rooms division manager communicate with the whole team?

2 How would the front office manager communicate new policies to the receptionists?

3 How would the food and beverages manager communicate the new menu to the waiting staff?

4 How would the HR manager communicate new legislation and its impact to the whole hotel's staff?

5 How would the general manager communicate target sales and profits to the whole hotel?

Did you consider?

■ The HR manager could use posters

■ The general manager could set up an 'all hotel' meeting or could relay the message to the next line of managers below him, who would then relay to their team, and so, on, until the message reached the workers at the bottom of the organisational chart

■ The food and beverages manager could do a tasting session for all the staff so they could try out dishes from the new menu

■ The front office manager could do a team meeting, followed up with a memo and a feedback session some days later to see how the team is getting on with the new policies and their implementation

■ The rooms division manager could organise a whole team meeting or relay the message to their managers, to relay to their teams

---

✔ TIP

As a supervisor, it is important that you consider the following when relaying a message to your team:

■ The accuracy

■ The reason

■ The importance

ACTIVITY

The importance of accuracy in communication
Have you ever played Chinese whispers? Why don't you have a go now?

■ Get yourselves into a circle and choose one person to make up a sentence

■ Whisper that sentence to the person on your left and get them to pass it on to the person on their left

■ Keep doing this until you have gone round the whole circle and the message has got to the last person in the circle

■ The last person should say out loud what the message was

■ Now compare it with the original message

■ Has it changed at all?

© ISTOCKPHOTO.COM/CHARITY MYERS

The Chinese whispers exercise illustrates how a message can become distorted or incorrect as it passes through different people. This can also include the interpretation of the original message too.

YOUR RESPONSIBILITY AS THE CHAIRPERSON WHEN LEADING MEETINGS

✔ TIP

Meeting aims or objectives should be at the top of every agenda. These are key decisions that must be made or actions that must occur at the meeting. If you are not clear on aims and purposes, don't hold your meeting!

What to do before the meeting

A large part of what makes a meeting successful occurs in the preparation stage. Although it may vary by committee or department, there are seven significant responsibilities expected of chairs or supervisors before a meeting is held. Each is explained in detail below.

Clarify objectives and aims A clearly stated objective or aim describes the key decisions that must be made or actions that must occur at the meeting. The purpose of a meeting should be stated at the top of the meeting agenda.

Some example objective statements may possibly look something like these:

- Share best practices in graduate recruitment and identify opportunities to recruit collaboratively across departments
- Identify primary goals for next year's budget
- Examine and update department policy on healthy eating
- Decide how to get feedback from customers, staff and suppliers

Create an agenda Everything else on the agenda including topics, times and presenters are the activities that, taken together, will accomplish the aims. An agenda is a framework that guides and supports the meeting. Agendas are similar to road maps or recipes. It should help to focus the group's work toward achieving desired outcomes. Good agenda items provide focus and structure for a meeting.

Some example agenda items might look something like these:

- Report on customer trends
- Identify members for a health and safety committee
- Generate list of possible solutions for the customer service problem with pros and cons of each

Schedule a meeting Scheduling a meeting involves much more than just making a list of attendees. It requires identifying key people who must attend and either finding times that work for them or notifying them of the time of the meeting and its location. Once the best possible date and time are agreed upon, a meeting location can be selected. Remember that the choice of meeting locations can sometimes dictate meeting dates because of potential attendee's ability to reach that location.

Other scheduling activities might include some of the following issues;

- Create a scheduling grid for invited attendees to complete
- Create an electronic mailing list for the committee or meeting attendees
- Draft the final meeting notification early on, with date, time and location added later

Send an agenda An agenda should be sent to participants ahead of time to help them prepare to contribute. There are certain requirements for posting meeting notices.

For departmental and standing committee meetings you should do the following:

1 Provide at least 24-hour advance notice of a meeting via a central bulletin board, memo or email. In limited cases, 2 hours' advance notice should be allowed.

TIP

Each item on the agenda should begin with an action word (verb). These items should support the expectations of attendees.

Decide – *decide* the best method for a customer survey.

Discuss – *discuss* the use of terminology on a menu.

Review – *review* recommendations from a health and safety report.

Finish – *finish* reviewing job specifications for the bar and cellar area.

TIP

One of the more successful ways to contact individuals is through email. Since you will be corresponding with a particular meeting group more than once, you can create a special email group just of those individuals.

By doing this, you do not have to rekey the individual email addresses every time you contact this group, and more importantly, you eliminate the chance of forgetting someone's name.

2 Allow for attendees to add to the agenda in good time provided the additions meet the meeting objective.

Circulate any supporting information You should always circulate supporting materials to participants in advance of the meeting. However, deciding how much information to send in advance can present a dilemma. Some people will not read anything prior to the meeting and some will conscientiously read all the supporting information they can. Here are some things to consider when deciding what and how much to send out ahead of time:

Do:

■ Provide enough information before the meeting so attendees arrive with a general familiarity and framework of the issues to be discussed

■ Provide website URLs instead of paper documents where possible

■ Extract information in a summary wherever possible to make it unnecessary for attendees to read long documents

Don't:

■ Assume that everyone wants their own copy of very large reports in the meeting. Two people can often share a copy during the actual meeting. This can save paper and staff time resources

■ Send documents without an explanation of how they relate to the agenda

■ Send anything this is too complex or technical that it requires someone to interpret it. Hand it out at the meeting and then explain what it means

Make room arrangements Ensure that room arrangements (including refreshments) are made. Room arrangements can make a big difference in how well a meeting performs. Most important is that attendees can see and hear each other.

Although a U-shape arrangement or open square is ideal for smaller groups of 20 or less, it is not usually a good choice for larger groups. The yawning hole in the middle makes communication difficult. A herring bone arrangement of tables is usually better for these larger groups.

Arrange for a minute keeper The recorder or minute keeper takes notes on paper, laptop or on flip charts. Meeting notes should be distributed as soon as possible after the meeting. The longer the gap, the less confidence the members have that their investment in time will result in action.

For groups that meet regularly, the recorder is responsible for keeping previous meeting notes and agendas in one place where they can be referenced later, such as from a notebook or shared network drive.

✔ **TIP**

For groups over 20, consider a herringbone arrangement of tables and chairs with four or five people at each. These arrangements enable people to easily see and interact with others, not only at their own table, but at the tables around them as well. Have as many tables as are required so that no one must sit at an uncomfortable angle to see what is happening at the front.

What to do during the meeting

The meeting leader or supervisor can make an enormous difference in a group's productivity. The following meeting leader actions can maximise the group's time and productivity.

■ Start the meeting promptly on schedule and do not wait for others to arrive. A large amount of professional time is wasted by meeting leaders who wait for more people to arrive before starting a meeting. It may require a change in the culture, but once people know that you start your meetings on time, they will arrive on time

■ Always briefly review the agenda including the aims and objectives as the meeting begins. This helps participants focus their attention and understand what will be required of them. In reviewing the agenda, the chair should make it clear what decisions must be made or actions must be taken

© ISTOCKPHOTO.COM/ JACOB WACKERHAUSEN

An active meeting

■ Focus on agenda items. Even if these items are clearly listed and emphasised, resourceful, intelligent and committed attendees may stray from the topic. To get a runaway meeting back on track, the chair person can state, 'Although this is quite important, we are moving off topic and need to consider…' Then the chairperson repeats the topic, issues or question again. Some meeting groups maintain a 'parked agenda' on a separate piece of paper for important issues that raised but are not directly related to the discussion. The 'parked agenda' can be consulted for future agenda planning for ensuing meetings

■ Effective meetings are participatory and good leaders try to get everyone involved. Some ways to encourage full participation include:

(a) Begin the meeting with a question that everyone can answer and go round the table asking the same question to everyone in attendance. The question should be stated on the agenda and an example might be, 'What are your hopes for the outcome of this meeting?'

(b) When asking for solutions or ideas, go round the table at least once so everyone has a chance to offer an opinion

(c) On a flip chart or projected from a laptop, maintain a list of ideas and opinions being generated so people can see their ideas in front of the group

■ When *brainstorming*, ensure that ideas/suggestions are not critiqued as they are offered. Get all the ideas on the table before critiquing. Waiting to critique will generally increase the amount of participation

■ A group reaches consensus when it finally agrees on a choice or a plan of action. Be clear before the discussion begins how the final decision will be made; if votes will be taken or if the decision will be made by consensus. When a group seems to have come to a consensus or decision, restate and summarise what the final decision is. This helps to ensure that all members hear the same thing and everything is clarified. Clarification at this point can prevent problems later

 TIP

Brainstorming is a method used to develop ideas or solutions. Essentially a brainstorming session is meant to be very open and non-critical. A 'bad' or 'impractical' idea may lead to an initiative that is very helpful, so suggestions are left unjudged at first. It is best to set a rough deadline for this free-for-all part of the session, after which the ideas and solutions are evaluated for whatever usefulness they may have.

Again, it is very important that the ideas are not criticised when first presented. To brainstorm effectively, you cannot stifle the creative process. If your group has a difficult time with this aspect of the exercise, you could try having them write their ideas down and submit them anonymously. When nobody knows who suggested which ideas, everyone will feel free to say what they want.

■ An action plan outlines the specifics that must be done. Not every goal needs an action plan, but for goals that involve more than one person, it is usually helpful to be specific about who will do what by when (see the sample action plan)

Action Plan

Goal: _____

Measure of success: _____

Goal point person (ensures the goal moves forward):_____

Check Date(s): _____

Objectives/activities	Person(s) involved	Dates	Cost	Products/ results	Measure(s) of success

An example of an action plan

■ Every goal should have a point person, which is an individual charged with ensuring that the goal is moving forward. The point person is not expected to complete the goal personally but to connect the people involved, make progress reports and seek assistance or resources needed to keep the goal moving forward

■ Ask for agenda items for the next meeting from the floor or ask a small group of two or three members to work on creating agendas. People are more likely to participate in a meeting if they have had some input into building the agenda

■ Even if every item suggested cannot be dealt with in a meeting, look for ways to provide information via handouts, email, or creating connections with other members of the meeting group

What to do after the meeting

Do not assume that ideas discussed during a meeting will be put into action or even remembered. To ensure follow-through and accountability a meeting leader needs to do three key tasks after the meeting ends. These are discussed below.

Distribute the minutes Ensure that minutes are produced and promptly distributed to all attendees including guests. Meeting minutes do not need to include everything everyone said. Most word processing software includes templates for agendas and minutes. However, they do need to include following:

■ Date, time and location

■ Attendees names

■ Key points raised and decisions made

■ Motions and voting results if votes taken

■ Who is responsible for what follow-up action and by when

■ Name of the recorder/minute keeper

Archive meeting documents All meeting documents including the agenda, minutes and supporting documents should be kept together and archived. These records can be checked when questions arise about past decisions or actions. It is discouraging to committee or group members to rehash prior discussions or decisions because of poor record keeping.

Check on the action points Often people need a gentle push to remind them about completing action items. Supervisors need to check to ensure that action is taking place as agreed. The check can be an email or phone call to the point person or a meeting devoted to checking on progress. Not checking may send a message that not much action is really expected.

✔	TIP

Every goal and action item needs a 'point person'. This person is responsible for reminding everyone of action items connecting people to their work and following up with colleagues to make sure the work has been completed. The point person also reports on results.

TECHNIQUES TO GAIN AND MAINTAIN ATTENTION AND INTEREST IN A MEETING

1   Before communicating, be clear what you are trying to **achieve**.

   (a)   Break down your message into a series of points that you want to get across. The fewer, the better

2   Find out about your **attendees**.

   (a)   Are they interested in what you have to say?
   (b)   Are they already well informed?
   (c)   Are they likely to be receptive or hostile to the information you are communicating?

3   **Structure** your message carefully.

   (a)   Start by explaining the purpose of the meeting
   (b)   Present your ideas in order of importance
   (c)   Organise written information by using clear numbering and headings
   (d)   In a meeting, end by summing up all the important points again

4   Use **language** your audience understands.

   (a)   Use simple, direct words and short sentences
   (b)   Avoid vagueness
   (c)   Avoid jargon and use technical terms sparingly. Specialist vocabulary can confuse teams

© ISTOCKPHOTO.COM/JACOB WACKERHAUSEN

Personal communication skills

Ask questions that draw out ideas, as well as information. This is partly a question of using the right techniques.

■ Ask positive, open-ended questions to involve people in solving problems

■ Open questions are phrased so that the answers are not just 'Yes' or 'No'

■ You can then follow up with more specific, closed, 'yes or no' questions

■ Avoid letting the way you phrase a question imply that there are no other options or alternatives you can choose

A key element in good communication is the ability to **listen** and **understand**.

■ Paraphrase to check what you think you have heard. Ask 'Am I right in thinking that you think…?' or 'So, just to be clear, are you saying…?'

■ Show you are listening by responding to what is being said, without interrupting

■ Do not answer on someone else's behalf or finish off what is being said

■ Do not show impatience

Your **body** is also a powerful element in communicating with people.

■ Maintain eye contact

■ Avoid negative postures such as folding your arms tightly in front of you or pointing at people

---

 TIP

Non-verbal communication (body language)

Pay attention to other people's non-verbal signals
People can communicate information in numerous ways, so pay attention to things like eye contact, gestures, posture, body movements, and tone of voice.

Concentrate on your tone of voice when speaking
Your tone of voice can convey a wealth of information, ranging from enthusiasm to disinterest to anger.

Use good eye contact
When people fail to look others in the eye, it comes across as though they are evading or trying to hide something. Equally, too much eye contact can seem confrontational or intimidating. Some communication experts recommend intervals of eye contact lasting four to five seconds.

Use signals to make communication more effective and meaningful
Remember that verbal and non-verbal communication work together to convey a message. You can improve your spoken communication by using non-verbal signals and gestures that reinforce and support what you are saying.

Practice, practice, practice
By noticing non-verbal behaviour and practising your own skills, you can dramatically improve your communication abilities.

Presentation skills in meetings

Whether you are talking to one individual or a room full of people, presentation skills help you get your message across.

1   Involve your meeting attendees.

2   Summarise what you are going say, say it, and then repeat what you have said in a different way to underline the facts.

3   Use prompts such as OHP slides, cards or PowerPoint presentations with a few key words typed in large print.

4   Do not read your speech from a typed-out sheet. Your audience will become disconnected.

5   Speak a little louder and more slowly than you normally would.

6   Use visual aids like PowerPoint presentation, flip charts and whiteboards carefully to present or gather ideas. Be careful to be accurate in representing the feedback from the group of people in the room.

COMMUNICATION IN MEETINGS AND BEHAVIOUR THAT UNDERPINS EFFECTIVE PERFORMANCE

1   Recognise the opportunities presented by the diversity of people.

2   Identify people's information needs.

3   Listen actively, ask questions, clarify points and rephrase others' statements to check mutual understanding.

4   Identify people's preferred communication media and styles and adopt media and styles appropriate to different people and situations.

5   Present information clearly, concisely, accurately and in ways that promote understanding.

6   Comply with, and ensure others comply with, legal requirements, industry regulations, organisational policies and professional codes.

7   Check the validity and reliability of information.

8   Make appropriate information and knowledge available promptly to those who need it and have a right to it.

9   Seek to understand people's needs and motivations.

10 Take timely decisions that are realistic for the situation.

PREPARING FOR ONLINE MEETINGS AND VIDEO CONFERENCING

The ability to hold meetings across geographic areas and time zones has revolutionised the way people conduct business. An online meeting, or Web conference, saves time and money, and is only a mouse-click away – as long as you are all connected to the World Wide Web. Contract catering businesses that have many different outlets across the country find this a cost- and time-effective way of meeting. These meetings should be organised using the same rules as previously described, however there is an additional checklist that needs to be followed to set up these types of meetings;

© ISTOCKPHOTO.COM/JEFFREY SMITH

1 Review the programme software being used to support the meeting. Identify an IT administrator who can support you by setting up and managing user access and permissions to ensure the meeting flows without any technical hitches.

2 Ensure your computer meets the minimum system requirements for leading the online meetings. Work with your IT administrator to do this.

3 Before the meeting begins, create a meeting room and arrange the meeting room layout and computers. Once you have a meeting layout that meets your needs, you can reuse the same meeting room for a series of similar online meetings.

4 Upload all content to the meeting room before the meeting begins. You can load content from your personal computer, memory stick, CD or a laptop.

5 Test your Internet connection prior to the start of every online meeting.

6 Perform a practice run-through of your meeting presentation before the scheduled meeting. If possible, set up two personal computers. Present content from one computer (as the host) and monitor content on the other (as a participant). This way, you see what your audience will see – which helps you pace your presentation and prevent technical issues.

7 Correspond with participants before the scheduled meeting to check that their computers meet the system requirements for participating in the meeting.

8 If you plan to use conference calling during an online meeting, make sure participants have dial-in numbers and access codes ahead of time.

9 Have participants prepare discussion questions or statements ahead of time.

10 Mute all phones and put a sign on the door to indicate a group or you are participating in a live broadcast.

Assessment of knowledge and understanding

You have now learnt about passing on information and holding effective meetings. It involves a variety of techniques and is relevant to your important role as a supervisor, in order to keep your team informed and brief them for their work.

To test your level of knowledge and understanding, answer the following short questions. These will help to prepare you for your summative (final) assessment.

1 Identify the daily pieces of information that you need to communicate to your team.

2 Identify the pieces of information that are communicated one-to-one with individual team members throughout the day.

3 What methods do you use on a day-to-day basis to communicate with your team?

4 Why is it so important to e accurate about the information you give to people?

5 How can you ensure meetings are recorded efficiently?

6 How can you ensure you are confident when giving a message to the attendees in your meeting?

7 Why shouldn't you use jargon?

8 What method can you use to ensure that people participate in meetings?

Research task

A well-known high street bank recently created a series of adverts to illustrate their global presence in the world of banking and how they know and understand different cultures in relation to doing business. This research task requires you to consider the different cultures in your workplace and how you need to communicate differently.

1 Identify the cultures in your organisation in relation to nationality and background.

2 Identify the cultures in your organisation that develop based on job roles.

3 Think about and make notes on how these different cultures impact on your communication style when you hold meetings.

4 Identify different methods of communication that you need to develop in order to communicate effectively in meetings with all of the cultures you have identified in 1 and 2.

5 Do these different cultures impact on the media you use, the language, style, timing and pace, in order to communicate effectively? If so how?

6 Are there any reasons why you may need to change the media, language, style and pace when you communicate to teams in meetings, other than cultural?

Name: ANNELIESE K.J. HAINZ

Position: Reservations Director

Establishment: Gordon Ramsay Holdings

Current job role and main responsibilities: Responsible for a large team of reservationists who handle up to 3500 calls and 700 email enquiries per day, ensuring that all enquiries are politely and efficiently handled as per targets set to the department. In charge of ensuring all restaurants are filled to their maximum possible capacity and setting targets and procedures for new openings.

What factors influence the setting of targets for your reservations team?

Season: for example, in August it is quieter, so the team needs to ensure that enquiries are handled much more quickly in order not to lose covers.

Type of restaurant/cuisine/service: a pub requires a much less formal approach than a three Michelin-starred dining experience.

Demand for the restaurant: guests who enquire for a restaurant that is fully booked should be offered another restaurant within the company that has availability.

When did you realise that you wanted to pursue a career in the hospitality industry?

When I worked as a receptionist in a fine dining restaurant. Having studied performing arts, I loved the drama of the dining room and how a good restaurant team can make a dinner as much of an experience as a trip to the theatre.

Experience: (brief focus on the establishments you have worked)

- Busy 200 cover restaurant in Kensington which taught me how to stay calm under immense pressure
- Customer services advisor for The London Eye
- Spent some time at The Greenhouse in Mayfair and then became reception manager at The Admiralty in Somerset House
- From there moved to Gordon Ramsay at Claridge's as Assistant Reservations Manager before becoming Reservations Director for Gordon Ramsay Holdings where I have been part of the expansion of the company since 2002

What do you find rewarding about your job?

When I can promote staff members I feel a real sense of achievement. I am also always extremely excited when guests write to us and tell us what a wonderful and memorable experience they had in one of our restaurants. Winning an Acorn Award (an award that recognises the top 30 managers under the age of 30 in the hospitality industry) was one of the highlights of my career so far.

What do you find most challenging about the job?

Working with a large number of very different people and ensuring that I always work in their best interests. Whilst a company director will always be happy when the restaurant is very busy, this may create a very challenging service for the restaurant team. Trying to co-ordinate all the different requirements can be difficult at times.

What advice would you give to students just beginning their career?

Be punctual: persistent lateness will hinder you in your future career.

What traits do you consider essential for anyone entering a career in the hospitality sector?

Honesty – never try to cover up a mistake. Admit what you have done and find a way to resolve it.

Dedication – you may not always feel like going to work, but show up anyway and don't let your colleagues down.

Diplomacy – you need to be able to work with a number of different characters.

Can you give one essential management tip or piece of industry advice?

Be realistic and don't expect the impossible. In any industry in which you deal with human beings, mistakes will be made and these need to be addressed appropriately. Investigate: why was the mistake made? What can be done to avoid it in the future and how should it be dealt with? Then explain this to your whole team so everyone can learn from the situation and ensure it doesn't happen again.

Name: BEN PURTON

Position: Executive Chef and Director of Food and Beverage

Establishment: Hyatt Regency London – The Churchill

Current job role and responsibilities: As Executive Chef and Director of Food and Beverage I am responsible for all food and beverage items that are served within the hotels operation. I oversee a culinary team of 32 and a front of house team of 70.

Within the hotel we have the Montagu restaurant which seats 130, the Churchill Bar which serves some of the best whiskies and champagnes in London, room service for 444 rooms, and 9 other function rooms

What emphasis would you place on interaction and knowledge of other departments within The Churchill?

It is very important to know the people that you work with, what they do and how what you do affects them and their ability to do their jobs well. Teamwork is the key to all successful operations. The times have gone when a chef only needs to know how to cook, a waiter how to serve and a receptionist how to check guests in. You will be expected to know a little of all of your surrounding departments and you will find that by knowing this and understanding them a little better, it will make your job easier to do. Hopefully everyone else will know a bit about your role too and what they can do to help you.

When did you realise that you wanted to pursue a career in the hospitality industry?

If I'm honest – I fell into it and I'm so glad that I did … I went into my local hotel and asked for a job – they needed a kitchen porter at weekends and I started that Saturday. The place amazed me and I was attracted to the kitchen immediately but it looked so intense that I didn't think that I could do that …. After about 4 months the chef came up and asked if I fancied being a chef as he needed one, and that was that! I never looked back. This industry is astonishing and you get out what you put in. You meet the most amazing people and visit some of the most amazing places; I cannot think of any other industry quite like it.

Training and experience: (detailing any college training/apprenticeship and where you started out)

- Apprenticeship at the Woodford Moat House in Woodford Green for 3 years and during this time I attended Waltham Forest College for my City & Guilds and NVQ qualifications
- Hyatt Carlton Tower in December 1994 as a Commis Chef and went to TVU in Slough for a further 2 years doing an Advanced Diploma in Culinary Arts and NVQ 3
- In my 10 years at TVU, I worked in all departments including the Lowndes Hotel which is just around the corner and moved from Commis to Chef de Cuisine within the time I was there
- April 2004: Moved to run the food and catering outlets in Selfridges where I oversaw 17 food and beverage outlets
- July 2005: Went back to the Hyatt Regency London as Executive Chef and Food Beverage Director

What do you find rewarding about your job?

The most rewarding part about my job now is to bring through the new generation of chefs and pass on as much knowledge and advice as possible to help them in their long careers ahead. To see how much your team can develop with the right direction and guidance, and to see them moving forward as individuals and as a team is what it's all about.

What advice would you give to students just beginning their career?

Turn up on time: 9a.m. means 8.30. Turn up every day wanting to learn and wanting to develop. Listen to everything that you are told and remember as much as you can – a pen and a notepad should be your best friend for the first 3 months.

What traits do you consider essential for anyone entering a career in the hospitality sector?

Hard working, dedicated, team player, flexible, open-minded, willing to learn and develop.

Can you give one essential management tip or piece of industry advice?

Take your time. Don't be afraid to ask for help and learn as much about your industry as possible – you never know when you're going to need it.

Name: SIRIEIX FRED

Position: General Manager

Establishment: Galvin at Windows

Current job role and main responsibilities: My role is to ensure the highest quality throughout, the training and development of the team and the profitability of the business.

What is the main inspiration behind the idea for the Galvin Cup Competition?
The idea is to bring together the schools and their students with the professionals to build the necessary bridges and to motivate, train and develop tomorrow's generation.

When did you realise that you wanted to pursue a career in the hospitality industry?
When I was 15 I wanted to become a pastry chef and worked as a chef in various restaurants. However after one year at catering college, my preference changed to front of house.

Training: (detailing any college training/apprenticeship and where you started out)

- Cap/Bep service at Souillac catering college 1998–1990
- Bac professional at Souillac catering college 1990–1992

Experience: (brief focus on the establishments you have worked)
I started my career in Michelin-starred restaurants such as Gavroche and Tante Claire. These gave me the product knowledge, discipline, attention to detail and the focus I needed to start with. Then I moved on to the Conran group where speed, personality and IT were very important. I then opened several restaurants from the Glasshouse in Kew, Brasserie Roux and Galvin at Windows. For a while I also ran a few of Soren Jessen's night clubs.

What do you find rewarding about your job?
The balance between seeing the business flourish and the development of the people I work with.

What do you find most challenging about the job?
By far it is about being consistent with all our targets and quality objectives.

What advice would you give to students just beginning their career?
Work hard and learn, but ensure you have fun.

Who is your mentor or main inspiration?
Throughout my career I had several mentors and inspirations: Silvano Giraldin and Chris Galvin are amongst those who have helped me (and still do) along the way. More recently however my daughter Andrea has been the force and the drive behind everything I do.

What traits do you consider essential for anyone entering a career in the hospitality sector?
Balance, honesty, integrity and ambition.

A brief personal profile: (explain your interests and achievements to date)
My most recent achievements to date were to open successfully Galvin at Windows and to be awarded the Front of House Award at the Tatler Awards 2006 and the Best Team Award at the Hotel and Cateys Award 2007.

The Galvin Cup 2007 and 2008 were also great achievements and I very much look forward to the 2009 Cup at the Dorchester.

At home I spend my time with my daughter Andrea and my partner Alex. I am a keen sportsman and like to compete in races such as the London Triathlon. André Garrett and I competed as a team in the 2008 event and we finished 21st out of 200.

Can you give one essential management tip or piece of industry advice?
There are so many to give. I have however noticed recently that it pays to believe in one's dream and goals. To make it happen just ask, don't take no for an answer and keep going.

INDUSTRY PROFILE

Name: GERRY CLINTON

Position: Borough Catering and Schools Traded Services Manager

Establishment: London Borough of Havering

Current job role and main responsibilities: I am responsible for the direct provision of services to schools such as catering, H&S support, cleaning and grounds maintenance, relief school keepers, as well as the daily delivery of 400 meals on wheels to the elderly and vulnerable clients of the borough.

How do you maintain a tight control over resources in a multi-unit business such as school catering?

We only have two main areas of expenditure: food and labour accounts for 90 per cent of our expenditure and by controlling these costs we can keep within budget.

Each unit has a staffing profile which lists the staff allocated to that unit and the number of hours that they work each day. The hours allocated to each unit is dependant on the budgeted income. If income targets are not met then hours are adjusted to meet targets that is either up or down. All staff have an element of "flexible hours" in their contract which can be removed/added depending on the level of business.

All food contracts are tendered and best prices are obtained by collaborative purchasing with neighbouring authorities.

When did you realise that you wanted to pursue a career in the hospitality industry?

I started in the restaurant of the local Littlewoods high-street store in Ilford. I chose the restaurant because at the time it paid 10p an hour more that the shop floor! I found working in the restaurant was a real buzz and I loved the atmosphere and working with food and the general public. When I left school I pursued a career with Littlewoods' management training program and became their youngest restaurant manager in the country at that time.

Experience: (brief focus on the establishments you have worked)

- Spent 10 years with Littlewoods running both restaurants on Oxford Street, London for over 18 months and opened their Flagship Restaurant at Oxford Circus
- Regional manager post with RHM retail for two years
- Monitoring officer in the London Borough of Barking and Dagenham for 11 years. This was at the time compulsive competitive tendering (CCT) was introduced and local authorities were seeking people with a commercial background to oversee catering contracts.
- L.B.Havering Catering and Facilities manager: a position I have held for over 4 years.

What do you find rewarding about your job?

I love the daily challenges. No day is the same, being responsible for over 400 staff ensures that. I love working with people and getting out to meet with our customers.

What do you find most challenging about the job?

We are constantly prevented from doing our jobs effectively by all the forms and targets that we are given by central and local government, most of which have little or no impact on the real job.

What advice would you give to students just beginning their careers?

Don't get involved in catering unless you love hard work; there are many easier jobs out there but none as rewarding as serving a great meal and the customer really appreciating it.

What traits do you consider essential for anyone entering a career in the hospitality sector?

Hardworking, a good communicator both with public and staff, able and willing to work the hours required.

Can you give one essential management tip or piece of industry advice?

Try to be firm and fair in your dealings with staff and colleagues so that people know exactly where they stand.

Name: JOHN WILLIAMS

Position: Executive Chef

Establishment: The Ritz

Current job role and main responsibilities: Overseeing and directing Food Operation of all The Ritz outlets and services.

What are the main aspects of menu planning in your kitchens and restaurant areas at The Ritz?
Seasonality, haute cuisine, speciality products.

When did you realise that you wanted to pursue a career in the hospitality industry?
When I was 13 years old, after being stimulated by Graham Kerr and the Galloping Gourmet.

Training: (detailing any college training/apprenticeship and where you started out)

- South Sheilds Marine and Tech College
- Westminster College

Experience: (brief focus on the establishments you have worked)
The Ritz, Claridge's, The Berkeley, The Royal Garden, Restaurant 'MA Cuisine' – all these were cooking haute cuisine.

What do you find rewarding about your job?
Making people happy with the food we serve.

What do you find most challenging about the job?
Staffing the kitchens with highly skilled chefs.

What advice would you give to students just beginning their career?
Always use good common sense, work hard, communicate well and use all senses of the body to cook. Enjoy seasonsal products and this will stimulate you.

Who is your mentor or main inspiration?
Michel Bourdin.

What traits do you consider essential for anyone entering a career in the hospitality sector?
Human touch, good people skills, organisation, common sense, hardworking, a deep desire and a flair for cooking.

A brief personal profile: (explain your interests and achievements to date)
Chairman of the Academy of Culinary Arts, MBE, Ordre du Merit d'Agricole, Honory Fellow of TVU, Citizen & Cook of London. Outside of work, I also play golf.

Can you give one essential management tip or piece of industry advice?
Treat people fairly and give the correct direction and information.

INDUSTRY PROFILE

Name: PHIL BROAD

Position: Managing Director UK and Ireland

Establishment: Starbucks Coffee Company

Current job role and main responsibilities: Overall responsibility for 700 retail stores, food service and licenced stores. We employ circa 10,000 and serve over two million customers a week.

How is customer service monitored in such a huge, international company as Starbucks and how do you respond to customer feedback? We have an external company that measures the level of service our partners are providing on a daily basis to our customers. We always recognise colleagues who are going the extra mile to provide the uplifting experience and individually handcrafted beverages. If we get feedback into our customer care team, we always provide a very prompt reply and I personally speak to customers every week.

When did you realise that you wanted to pursue a career in the hospitality industry?
When I was about 14 I realized that hospitality was for me. I enjoyed food, beverage and conversation. I always say if you find a job you love then you'll never work a day in your life.

Training: (detailing any college training/apprenticeship and where you started out)
I was really lucky that I went to Westminster College in Vincent Square and had an absolutely fantastic time. It really was a brilliant place to learn.

Experience: (brief focus on the establishments you have worked)
I worked in the House of Commons refreshment department, Quadrant Catering, Allied in the Muswells Café bar chain, Grandmet Retailing, Pizza Hut, Tescos, ran my own business for 6 years and now I'm with Starbucks.

What do you find rewarding about your job?
I really enjoy seeing all the people that work for me develop.

What do you find most challenging about the job?
When someone asks for your time, you have to find a way to give it, thats a challenge.

What advice would you give to students just beginning their careers?
It's a long journey and you'll travel down roads you never thought about but its worth it in the end. Treat people as human beings.

Who is your mentor or main inspiration?
I currently have a mentor/coach called Carissa Bub who is a brilliant, intellectual coach who helps to make the impossible possible. You need someone to bounce off even when you get to the top. You are never as good as you think you are and can always improve. Life and work are two great journeys intertwined and a coach helps you to absorb and learn.

What traits do you consider essential for anyone entering a career in the hospitality sector?
The love of people and an eye for detail, they have helped me throughout.

A brief personal profile: (explain your interests and achievements to date)
I have three wonderful children that I try and spend time with, although with a 24/7 business it can be a challenge. Thankfully they all play sport so watching them play is relaxing! I have been managing director of three well-known brands in the UK and I'm only 45 so I'm really pleased to be able to give back to the industry I love.

Can you give any essential management tips?
Avoid mediocrity and everything matters!
An uncompromising commitment to the little things … the customers and staff will notice.
Smile from the heart, you're in a great industry.
Ultimately our business is about the people, all of them!

Name: ROBYN JONES

Position: Co-founder and Chief Executive

Establishment: Charlton House Catering Services Ltd

Current job role and main responsibilities: I am responsible for the strategic growth of the company and for driving innovations to ensure that our food and service standards remain at the cutting edge of the contract catering sector.

Can you describe how you present a strong leadership example for your team at Charlton House?
I work tirelessly to get things right. In this business you are only as good as your last meal so I feel very passionate about keeping standards high. There is a great sense of pride within Charlton House, which in turn leads to a motivated, passionate team and a happy customer base.

When did you realise that you wanted to pursue a career in the hospitality industry?
From a very early age. I have always loved cooking and knew that I wanted to work in hospitality on leaving school.

Training: (detailing any college training/apprenticeship and where you started out)
I completed an OND in Hotel Catering and Institutional Management at High Peak College in Buxton, Derbyshire, followed by a HCIMA in Hotel Catering and Institutional Management at Norwich City College.

What do you find rewarding about your job?
I get a great buzz when clients are delighted with what we provide and when someone in the company comes to me with a new idea or innovation. The business is evolving all of the time and it's great when other people share our passion and interest. We are known for our cutting edge approach to food in the workplace so it's important that we seek out new ways of exciting and satisfying our customers.

What advice would you give to students just beginning their career?
Follow your dreams and never give up. If you really feel that you want to do something, then just do it. Put all of your efforts into making it successful. If you work hard now, you can play hard in years to come.

Who is your mentor or main inspiration?
I have a quote on my wall by Sir Winston Churchill: 'Never, never, never give up'. That says it all.

What traits do you consider essential for anyone entering a career in the hospitality sector?
Attention to detail and a sense of pride. Food and service standards have to be impeccable. People are so discerning these days and second best will never be acceptable. I think it's important to give it your all, whether you work back of house or front of house.

A brief personal profile: (explain your interests and achievements to date)
I am a trustee of the PM Trust and a patron of the Association of Catering Excellence. I am also a guardian member of Hospitality In Action, a benevolent organisation for people within the hospitality industry. I was named the Credit Suisse Outstanding Woman in Business at the National Business Awards 2006 and appeared in 29th place in the CatererSearch 100 league table of the UK's 100 most influential people in hospitality.

Charlton House now has a current annual turnover of £75 million and we employ 1,900 people nationwide. One of our recent highlights was to win a Cateys award, the hospitality industry's equivalent to an Oscar. In 2006 we were named Cost Sector Caterer of the Year and last year we were listed fourth in an industry poll of Britain's top 50 companies within the hospitality sector. We won our second Cost Sector Catering Award this year for a company-wide marketing initiative.

Juggling work with the needs of our two young children keeps me busy, but in my spare time I love to cook, swim and travel.

Can you give one essential management tip or piece of industry advice?
Always deliver your promises.

Name: **PHILIP E. CORRICK**

Position: Group Executive Chef

Establishment: The Royal Automobile Club

Current job role and main responsibilities: Oversee 2 clubhouses, multi-catering outlets, 80 chefs, menus, budgets and organising promotions with restaurants in Europe.

When did you realise that you wanted to pursue a career in the hospitality industry?
At 15 years old, working in the school holidays in a small hotel. The owner was also the chef, and he greatly encouraged me.

Training: (detailing any college training/apprenticeship and where you started out)
A two-year full-time course at college, followed by work at Claridge's, the Sheraton Park Tower and Sheraton Heathrow.

What do you find rewarding about your job?
Developing young chefs and creating opportunities. Also, filling restaurants!

What do you find the most challenging about the job?
The increase in food prices and recruitment in today's climate, and also demand outstripping supply.

What advice would you give to students just beginning their career?
Listen, work hard, and at some point you will be rewarded.

Who is your mentor or main inspiration?
Michel Bourdin – the chef at the Connaught Hotel.

What traits do you consider essential for anyone entering a career in the hospitality sector?
Enthusiasm, motivation, willingness to work hard and above all, enjoyment!

A brief personal profile: (explain your interests and achievements to date)
I am a member of The Academy of Culinary Arts, The Association Culinaire Française and holder of the Cordon Culinaire and the Maitrise Escoffier Diploma. I have also been listed in Debrett's People of Today.

Can you give one essential management tip or piece of industry advice?
Never forget the word 'team' – being a team player is essential.

Glossary

24-hour service Round the clock continual service for consumers.

Accommodation services Can also be referred to as 'room division'. This refers to individual departments who are responsible for the upkeep and selling of rooms within the establishment.

Active documentation This term is used to describe the paperwork or files being used at the present time in relation to a function, e.g. the booking sheets, menus.

Advanced deposit This term refers to a set amount of money paid to secure the event. This will ensure the room is not double-booked.

Allergy An acquired, abnormal immune response to a substance that can cause a broad range of inflammatory reactions.

Ambience The mix of background noise and other reflected sounds that make up a room's character.

Appellation A geographical indication used to identify where the grapes for a wine were grown.

Appraisal A judgment or assessment of the professional performance of someone, especially a subordinate.

Assessment This is when a person is given a task to carry out and a judgement will be made on how they performed.

Audit A review, check or inspection of something, such as a process or goods.

Auditory To do with the sense of hearing.

Bill of fare Menu: a list of dishes available at a restaurant.

Blacklisted This term refers to guests who have been systematically barred from the establishment for non-payment of the bill or unacceptable behaviour.

Bulk checkout This refers to groups of guests whose accommodation and any other authorised services are charged back to the tour operator.

Carbon footprint A measure of the impact that human activities have on the environment in terms of the amount of emitted carbon dioxide.

Cask-conditioned beer The cask is a barrel made of aluminium, stainless steel or oak, used to store beer.

Cellar A room used to store beer and drinks, sometimes found in the basement, underground.

Cheques These are carried by the customer and filled in to pay for goods, they are usually backed up with a guarantee card issued by the bank.

Chip and PIN The system used by the customer to input a PIN code when paying for goods or services.

Cleaning frequencies The amount of time an area or item needs cleaning and how often.

Cleaning schedule A permanent list of all the cleaning task to be completed and the frequency of those cleans.

Colleagues An associate that one works with – a workplace team member.

Communication This term refers to the transfer of information, verbally, physically or via another means such as email.

Communication barrier Poor communication skills such as poor language, listening, noise, prejudice or verbal skills.

Competence The level at which an individual is able to carry out a skill effectively without supervision.

Concierge This name refers to the person or persons who are in charge of the portering.

Conference groups This refers to groups of guests who are attending a conference, this can be internal or external.

Confidential information Information that you should only share with certain people, for example your manager or personnel officer

Consensus General agreement.

Contingency plans Plans that allow you to identify and plan for things that may go wrong. Back-up plans.

Control points In reference to the HACCP system these are the steps at which food safety could be compromised and therefore action need to be taken.

Controlling This refers to the information made available to the management team for decision-making purposes.

CPD Continuing professional development.

Credit check This check is occasionally used to ensure the organiser has sufficient funds to pay for the event.

Criteria This is the measurement by which an assessment takes place.

CRM Customer relation management.

Cross-contamination The transfer of pathogens from a contaminated food or surface to another food either directly or indirectly.

CRS Central reservation system.

Customer requirements Understanding and determining what the customer expectations and needs are on an individual basis.

Customers These include individual clients, plus other departments within your organisation and external organisations to whom you may provide a service.

Daily running sheet A schedule of events that must occur prior to the event, the list will involve the day's work and checks are made to ensure all tasks are carried out efficiently.

Database A collection of data which has been organised so that a computer program can quickly select desired items.

DBMS Database management system.

Deep cleaning A thorough clean, that would normally create disruption to an area, requiring the removal of furniture.

Demographics Refers to selected population characteristics including race, age, income, disabilities, educational attainment, home ownership, employment status and even location.

Detergent A chemical that removes soils but does not sterilise equipment.

Development This relates to acquiring a broad range of skills through planned activities and experience.

Diet A regulated daily food allowance.

Disclaimer This limits the liability amount which is payable to the guests, including theft, loss, damage whether in the car park, restaurant, suites or function rooms.

Dispense counter The bar area where staff will order and prepare drinks to serve to customers.

Diversity When there are people you work with who belong to different races, cultures, religions or who have specific needs.

Drive To compel or force or urge relentlessly. Exert coercive pressure on, or motivate strongly.

DSS Distribution service system.

Due diligence A collection of procedures designed to prove that at every step along the production and service route care and safety is maintained.

Durable Tough, hardwearing and long-lasting.

Economy The social system of a country's revenue based on their ability to produce, exchange, distribute and consume goods and services.

Effectiveness Ensuring that all tasks are executed with optimum efficiency to ensure the targets are met and if possible exceeded.

Efficiency When a task is completed to its optimum level by using the minimum amount of resources.

Empathetic Showing understanding and experience of another person's situation.

Environment The surroundings that you are working in, which includes the atmosphere and location.

Environmental conditions The temperature, lighting and humidity under which wines should be stored.

EPOS Electronic point of sale, could be a shop, checkout counter or location where a transaction takes place. It is also data recorded at a checkout and used for forecasting and stock control.

Ergonomics Applied science concerned with the human characteristics.

Establishment Another word for a business, organisation or group.

Evaluation This is a process to establish the value of something through personal opinion.

Exceed Going above and beyond.

Expectation An individual's belief of how something should be.

Extras and Extras account This refers to additional services offered which are purchased on top of the base products. These are then invoiced to the extras account – this is sometimes referred to as cross-selling.

Feedback The process of sharing observations, concerns and suggestions between persons or divisions of the organisation with the intention of improving both personal and organisational performance.

FIFO First in first out – a principle referring to the rotation of foodstuffs.

Financial transactions The exchange of payments for services or products.

First impressions The first thing someone experiences in an establishment which makes up their mind or influences them and can produce a positive or negative opinion.

Float The amount of money carried; usually small denominations in the cash till. This is used to give change to customers.

Food allergy A physiological reaction caused when the immune system mistakenly identifies a normally harmless food as damaging to the body.

Food hazards A hazard is anything that could cause harm to the consumer.

Food intolerance A condition whereby a person is unable to tolerate certain parts of foods.

Food poisoning An acute illness resulting from eating contaminated or poisonous food.

Food service Places, institutions, and companies responsible for any meal prepared outside the home.

Food-borne illness A term often used to describe any disease or illness caused by eating contaminated food or drink.

Function catering This term is used to describe the service of a particular event, for a set number of guests, with a set menu with predetermined drinks.

Gross profit The profits before overhead (fixed operating expenses) have been deducted.

Gueridon A style of service which food items are prepared in the dining environment.

HACCP (Hazard Analysis Critical Control Point) A food safety and self-inspection system that highlights potentially hazardous foods and how they are handled in the food service environment.

Handover This important function is carried out by two or more staff members who share information regarding the days work, functions etc. to ensure a smooth transition.

Hardware The physical parts of a computer or device.

Hazard This refers to anything that has the potential to cause harm.

Hired On loan, not belonging to the organisation.

Honesty Honesty is the human quality of communicating and acting truthfully related to truth as a value. This includes listening, and any action in the human repertoire — as well as speaking.

Hygiene To keep clean and safe in order to prevent diseases and maintain health.

Inanimate loads A lifeless load, often heavy.

Incentives Payment or concession to stimulate greater output by workers.

Induction A formal introduction to the company which includes instruction, training and orientation.

Industry codes of practice Guidelines which show how businesses should follow the law and deliver high standards to the customer.

Information Knowledge acquired through study, experience or instruction.

Information management Presenting information clearly, accurately and in ways that promote understanding

Initiative Being the first to take action without being prompted by others.

Inputs The resources needed to carry out a process or provide a service.

Input devices Devices used to enter information.

Interconnecting rooms Most commonly found in function rooms, these fold away doors increase or decrease capacity as required.

Internal representation Patterns of information we create and store in our minds in combinations of images, sounds, feelings, smells and tastes.

Inventory A record, list or account.

Invoice An itemised account of what has been purchased and the payment method used.

Job description This is a document which explains the job role and duties that a job holder will be required to carry out.

Keg The word used for a barrel, cask or drum to store beer or lager.

Knowledge This is the information that a person holds on a subject. It can be gained through education and experience.

Labour The workers or employed body of staff of a company.

Labour turnover This is a calculation which gives a guide as to how much an organisation needs to recruit. If there is high labour turnover this means lots of staff are leaving, which can be a cause for concern.

Leadership This refers to a person who influences another person; using positive reinforcement to motivate and train.

Learning This is the way individuals acquire information and knowledge.

Learning style An individual's preferred approach to learning.

Legal requirements Any law or regulation that governs health, safety and hygiene in the workplace.

Legislation Term may refer to a single law, or the collective body of enacted law. Legislation can have many purposes: to regulate, to authorise, to grant, to declare or to restrict.

Logo Badge or symbol of the organisation.

Loyalty Gaining a customer's commitment to come back again providing repeat business.

Loyalty cards This is a programme that rewards guests who use the establishment's facilities frequently, offering free items, discounts and additional services.

Maintenance Regular servicing and upkeep of machinery, utensils and systems.

Management The process associated with organising work, people and events to run in a controlled efficient manner.

Market segmentation A subgroup of people or organisations sharing one or more characteristics that cause them to have similar product needs.

Meal plans Detailed lists showing what meals the guests require, whether breakfast, lunch or dinner, and any special requirements.

Mediate To occupy an intermediate or middle position or form a connecting link or stage between two others.

Memorandum (memo) This is an internal document used to communicate between staff or departments.

Mentor This is an individual with expert knowledge and experience in a certain area and will guide a less experienced individual through a process.

Merchandising This refers to the methods, practices and operations carried out to promote and sell certain products.

Micros A computerised system which allows kitchens, restaurants and other areas to communicate and collect billing information quickly and efficiently.

Minutes Function minutes are extremely important as they convey the exact requirements of the organiser. They should be typed and sent to the organiser for their approval prior to the function taking place.

Mirroring Precisely matching aspects of another person's behaviour.

Mnemonic A mnemonic device is a memory aid.

Monitor To check, track or observe processes and procedures.

Motivate Helping staff to feel enthusiastic about their jobs and keen to achieve high standards

Mystery shoppers Mystery dining is about giving restaurants genuine and objective customer feedback. To be a successful mystery diner, you'll need to demonstrate your commitment and interest in giving detailed, fair and objective feedback.

Net profit The profits remaining in a business after all expenses have been taken out, but before tax.

New World Wines Refers primarily to wines from the United States, Australia, South America and South Africa.

NLP Neurolinguistic programming – a way of communicating effectively, using all your senses to achieve outstanding results.

Nutrition A source of materials to nourish the body.

Objectives This is an achievable and realistic plan of what an individual wants to achieve in a specific time frame with measurable outcomes.

Occupancy level This refers to the number of rooms occupied within the establishment; the figures are usually represented as a percentage.

Oenology The science and study of all aspects of wine and winemaking except vine growing and grape harvesting, which are a subfield called viticulture.

Old World Wines Refers primarily to wine made in Europe but can also include other regions of the Mediterranean basin with long histories of winemaking.

On-the-job training Takes place in a normal working situation, using the actual tools, equipment, documents or materials that trainees will use when fully trained.

Operation Business operations are the repeated activities involved in the running of a business.

Ordering The action of requesting a tradesman to supply goods or services under certain terms of delivery.

Organisation A business or group.

Organisational procedures A set of procedures that relate to health and safety in the workplace.

Output devices Devices used to retrieve and report information.

Outputs Products, services or information supplied to meet customers' needs.

Over-booking Too many reservations for the number of rooms available.

Overheads Operating expense: the expense of maintaining property.

Pacing Gaining and maintaining rapport with another person over a period of time by subtly mirroring and matching their behaviour.

Package A package designed to encourage occupancy, sometimes offered when large bookings are made.

Paging Discreet way to contact staff members who are not located in one particular area.

PDP Personal development plan.

Perception What an individual believes they see, from their point of view.

Periodic cleaning Cleaning that is carried out on a cycle or regular basis.

Peripherals Ancillary equipment to aid computer use.

Persistence Continue firmly, ignoring obstacles; enduring.

Person specification Document outlining the attributes that an individual will need in order to carry out a job.

PEST analysis 'Political, economic, social, and technological analysis'.

Pests Unwelcome visitors to the food preparation areas in the form of rodents, insects and birds.

Physiology To do with the physical part of a person.

Policies Statements of intent about how the organisation proposes to conduct its business.

Porterage The charged service or storing and delivering luggage to and from a guest's room.

Porters Staff members who form part of the concierge team responsible for luggage delivery.

POS Point of sale.

Presentation rooms The high standards expected when setting up rooms for an event.

Preventative maintenance Maintenance carried out to prevent a breakdown, or the piece of equipment failing.

Procedure A particular course of action intended to achieve a result.

Processing food orders Taking and recording the food order and passing it on to the appropriate person.

Promotional activities Activity that take place to increase sales and profit for a business.

Purchase order A commercial document issued by a buyer to a seller, indicating the type, quantities and agreed prices for products or services the seller will provide to the buyer.

Purchase requisition An authorisation for a purchasing department to procure goods or services.

Purchase specification Detailed description of the measurable characteristics desired in an item to be purchased.

Purchasing A function concerned with the search, selection and final use of a commodity.

Quality Character with respect to fineness, or grade of excellence. Offering a product or service at their best.

Rack rate Standard rate assigned to rooms; they are usually the top end rate which is then negotiable at the supervisor's discretion.

Receipt A copy of a transaction of goods or services.

Reservation Booking of a room or service within an organisation.

Resources The machines, workers, money, land, raw materials and other things that a business uses to produce goods and services and to make its economy grow.

Responsible person The person or persons at work to whom you should report to regarding cash or credit discrepancies or queries; this could be your line manager or employer.

Risk The likelihood of a hazards potential being realised.

Rotation of stock Ensuring that old stock be used before new.

Safety measures and procedures Activities and precautions taken to improve safety.

Sales mix The proportions of sales coming from different products or services.

Sanitiser An agent which yields a significant reduction in the level of harmful bacteria.

Seasonality Products that are available for a limited or seasonal period.

Service equipment Specific items required to aid in the service of food to the customer.

Service quality framework A conceptual framework for understanding quality of service.

SERVQUAL or RATER A service quality framework.

Silver service The method used to deliver food to the table on a platter held by the waiter and served to the customer's plate using a fork and spoon.

Social responsibility An ethical or ideological theory that a government, corporation, organisation or individual has a responsibility to behave appropriately towards the rest of society.

Sociology The scientific study of individual behaviour in society.

Sommelier A trained and knowledgeable wine professional.

Sous vide A method of cooking involving heating ingredients for an extended period of time at relatively low temperatures.

Statutory This is the legal requirement to carry something out.

Supplies The materials, goods, food or provisions required to perform the task, job or role.

Sustainable The ability to maintain a certain process or state, i.e. to sustain the existing environment.

SWOT analysis A strategic planning method used to evaluate the strengths, weaknesses, opportunities and threats involved in a project or in a business venture.

Synthetic Man-made fibre.

Target market The market segment to which a particular good or service is marketed.

Terroir A group of agricultural sites in same region which share the same soil, weather conditions and farming techniques, which each contribute to the unique qualities of the crop.

Total quality management (TQM) An approach to organisational management that seeks to improve the quality of products and services through ongoing refinements in response to continuous feedback.

Training A planned process through which individuals are helped to learn a new skill or technique.

Transaction An operation that takes place, sometimes classed a business deal.

USP The unique selling point.

Ventilation Ventilation can be simply described as air circulation.

Vintage The process of picking grapes and creating the finished product.

Viticulture The science, production and study of grapes which deals with the series of events that occur in the vineyard.

Wine cellar A room used to store wines, spirits and drinks.

Wine co-operatives Agricultural cooperatives which are involved in winemaking.

Working environment The working area or areas for which you are responsible.

Working practices Any activities, procedures, use of materials or equipment and working techniques used to carry out a particular job.

X-reading Readings taken throughout the day from the till to monitor ongoing transactions.

Z-reading The reading taken from the till at the end of shift to check transactions taken.

Index